SPECIAL EDUCATION

ADVANCES IN SPECIAL EDUCATION

Series editors: Festus E. Obiakor and Jeffrey P. Bakken

Previous Volumes:

ADVANCES IN SPECIAL EDUCATION   VOLUME 38

SPECIAL EDUCATION: ADVANCING VALUES

EDITED BY

FESTUS E. OBIAKOR

Sunny Educational Consulting, USA

AND

JEFFREY P. BAKKEN

Bradley University, USA

United Kingdom – North America – Japan
India – Malaysia – China

Emerald Publishing Limited
Emerald Publishing, Floor 5, Northspring, 21-23 Wellington Street, Leeds LS1 4DL

First edition 2024

Reprints and permissions service
Contact: www.copyright.com

British Library Cataloguing in Publication Data
A catalogue record for this book is available from the British Library

ISBN: 978-1-83753-467-8 (Print)
ISBN: 978-1-83753-466-1 (Online)
ISBN: 978-1-83753-468-5 (Epub)

ISSN: 0270-4013 (Series)

Printed and bound by CPI Group (UK) Ltd, Croydon, CR0 4YY

INVESTOR IN PEOPLE

CONTENTS

ABOUT THE CONTRIBUTORS

Innocent J. Aluka is a Professor in the College of Arts and Sciences at Prairie View A & M University, Prairie View, Texas. He is a well-known professional who mentors at-risk and vulnerable students and faculty on college campuses. His research interests are in Geological sciences, equity in science education, and recruitment and retention of minority students and faculty. His interest in STEM programs has inspired him to work with college students with special needs.

Nkechi Amadife is a Professor and Head of the Department of Public Services and Coordinator of Library Instruction at Kentucky State University. She earned her PhD degree in Educational Policy Studies with specialty in Higher Education from the University of Kentucky. Dr Amadife has over 20 years of experience working in higher education, and her research interests include information literacy, special education, biculturalism, and inclusion.

Jeffrey P. Bakken is a Professor of Special Education at Bradley University. He has a Bachelor's Degree in Elementary Education from the University of Wisconsin-LaCrosse and graduate degrees in the area of Special Education-Learning Disabilities from Purdue University. Dr Bakken has received the College of Education and the University Research Initiative Award, the College of Education Outstanding College Researcher Award, the College of Education Outstanding College Teacher Award, and the Outstanding University Teacher Award from Illinois State University. He also just recently received the College of Education and Health Sciences Faculty Achievement Award for Research at Bradley University. His specific areas of interest include: learning disabilities, emotional and behavioral disorders, reading comprehension, response to intervention, collaboration, transition, teacher effectiveness, assessment, learning strategies, assistive technology, smart classrooms and smart universities. He has published over 215 works that include books, chapters, journal articles, proceedings at international conferences, audio tapes, encyclopedia articles, newsletter articles, book reviews, a monograph, a manual, and one publisher website. He has also made over 275 presentations at International/National and Regional/State conferences. Lastly, he has authored or co-authored numerous grants totaling over $1,000,000.00.

David F. Bateman, PhD, is a Principal Researcher at the American Institutes for Research. He is a former professor at Shippensburg University in the Department of Educational Leadership and Special Education where he taught courses on special education law, assessment, and facilitating inclusion. He is a former due process hearing officer for Pennsylvania for hundreds of hearings. He uses his knowledge of litigation relating to special education to assist school districts in providing appropriate supports for students with disabilities and to prevent and to recover from due process hearings. He has been a classroom teacher of students with learning disabilities, behavior disorders, intellectual disability, and hearing impairments. Dr Bateman earned a PhD in special education from the University of Kansas. He has recently co-authored the following books: *A Principal's Guide to Special Education, A Teacher's Guide to Special Education, Charting the Course: Special Education in Charter Schools, Special Education Leadership: Building Effective Programming in Schools, Current Trends and Legal Issues in Special Education,* and *A School Board Members Guide to Special Education.*

Floyd D. Beachum is the Bennett Professor of Urban School Leadership at Lehigh University. Before becoming a faculty member, he worked as a substitute teacher, social studies teacher, and lead teacher for social studies. His research interests are leadership in urban education, moral and ethical leadership, and social justice issues in K-12 schools.

Emily Bouck is a Professor in the Special Education Program and Interim Associate Dean for Research in the College of Education at Michigan State University. Her research agenda focuses on mathematical interventions for students with disabilities and those at risk.

Frederick J. Brigham is a Professor at George Mason University. He earned his PhD at Purdue University. His current research interests include informal assessment procedures for classroom learning, content instruction for students with disabilities, as well as spatial learning and cognition.

Chris Claude is an OSEP-funded third year Doctoral Student and graduate research assistant at George Mason University's College of Education and Human Development studying special education research and policy. His research focuses on special education students who access the general education curriculum in the secondary setting.

Phillip Clay Jr is an Associate Professor and Chair of the School of Education at Kentucky State University. He recently led the School of Education successfully through both EPSB and CAEP Accreditations. Additionally, he serves as the Director of Disability Services at Kentucky State University.

Jason Chow is an Associate Professor of Special Education at Vanderbilt University. His research focuses on language, social, and behavioral development, adaptive interventions to support children with disabilities and their families, and supporting the uptake, implementation, and sustainability of adoptable and effective practices and programs in educational and community settings.

Yalitza Corcino-Davis is a Doctoral Student in the Educational Leadership Department at Lehigh University. Her dissertation focuses on how access to dual enrollment programs influences Latinx students' postsecondary aspirations. Her research interests include dual enrollment, college math performance, college readiness, and Latinx P-16 education outcomes.

Julie Cox, CCC-SLP, is an Assistant Professor and Graduate Coordinator in the Department of Speech Pathology & Audiology at Western Illinois University. Dr Cox teaches a variety of courses and conducts pedagogical research. She holds the Certificate of Clinical Competence from ASHA and the Illinois professional license.

Lucinda Dollman is an independent consultant, providing professional learning and coaching services to PK-12th school districts. Lucinda has worked at classroom, school, district and regional levels of education in and around the central Illinois area. Lucinda specializes in school improvement initiatives striving to promote application from research into everyday practices.

Colleen Lloyd Eddy, PhD, is a Visiting Assistant Professor in the Applied Developmental Psychology program at the University of Pittsburgh School of Education. She is a counseling psychologist, and her research focuses on improving teachers' well-being and reducing burnout and youth mental health in schools.

Asola Eugene is a Professor of Teacher Education, at Dewar College of Education and Human Services, Valdosta State University. He is a *Carnegie African Diaspora Fellow-Alumni*, Managing Editor for the Multicultural Learning and Teaching Journal, and a reviewer for the National Association for Kinesiology in Higher Education Journal (NAKHE).

Michael Faggella-Luby is a Professor in special education at Texas Christian University in the Department of Teaching & Learning Sciences. He is a Past-President of the Division for Learning Disabilities of the Council for Exceptional Children. Dr Faggella-Luby's research and teaching address learning disabilities, literacy, secondary education, and cognitive learning strategies.

Nicholas A. Gage is a Senior Researcher in Special Education at WestEd. His research is focused on advancing rigorous research in special education. Specific expertise includes research design, multi-tiered system of supports (MTSS), universal behavioral management, positive behavioral interventions and supports (PBIS), and evaluation of special education programs.

Lenwood Gibson Jr is an Associate Professor of Graduate Programs in Special Education at Queens College. His current research focus includes: (a) improving academic achievement for students from marginalized communities; (b) the use of Culturally Responsive strategies to improve treatment outcomes for children and families from Culturally and Linguistically Diverse (CLD) communities.

Lisa Goran, PhD, CCC-SLP, is an Associate Teaching Professor at the University of Missouri. She is president-elect of the Division for Learning Disabilities of the Council for Exceptional Children. Dr Goran's professional work focuses on teacher preparation, related services in special education, and the language-literacy connections for students with disabilities.

Larissa Jakubow is a Doctoral Student at Michigan State University in the Educational Psychology and Educational Technology program. She also holds a Bachelor's degree and Master of Teaching degree from the University of Virginia. Her research interests include students with high-incidence disabilities, US history curriculum, and accessibility of primary source documents.

Stacy Kelly is a Professor in the Visual Disabilities Program at Northern Illinois University in DeKalb, Illinois where she specializes in the preparation of personnel who are licensed and/or certified to provide instruction to people who are visually impaired.

Jennifer Kurth is an Associate Professor of Special Education at the University of Kansas and Chair of the Department of Special Education. Her research centers on inclusive education for students with extensive and pervasive support needs. This includes (a) teacher preparation, (b) supports and services for students in inclusive settings, and (c) instructional planning.

Paul Luelmo is an Assistant Professor in the Department of Special Education in the area of Mild/Moderate disabilities at San Diego State University. His research focuses on addressing inequities in special education by working with families, teachers, and under-resourced racial and ethnic minority communities.

Angi Martin, CCC-SLP/A, is a dual-certified speech-language pathologist and audiologist. Her area of interest is young children with communication disorders. Her primary area of interest is parent coaching and parent involvement in the early intervention process, specifically intervention for children with hearing loss.

Emmanuel Mbagwu is a Doctoral Candidate in the Department of Education at Liberty University, Lynchburg, Virginia. He is an educator in the State of Georgia and works with K-12 public school leaders in Behavioral Disabilities. And, he continues to serve as an advocate for parents and their children with exceptionalities. His research interests are in multicultural special education, comparative/international special education, and parental advocacy.

John William McKenna is an Associate Professor of Special Education at the University of Massachusetts Lowell and is an affiliate of the Center for Autism Research and Education (CARE). His research interests include evidence-based academic and behavioral interventions for students with emotional and behavioral disabilities, responsible inclusion, and school–family partnerships. His service interests center on improving student access to empirically based instruction and intervention.

Christie Nelson holds an MA in Mental Health Counseling from Gardner-Webb University and a PhD in Counselor Education and Supervision from the University of North Carolina at Charlotte. Christies' clinical experience includes providing counseling, supervision, and case management in mental health, addictions, and developmental disabilities in outpatient, residential, and community settings.

Stephanie L. Obi is an Adjunct Professor at Kentucky State University and Achievement and Compliance Coach at Fayette County Public Schools. She coordinates and assists administrators and teachers in the implementation of policies and procedures related to special education services and adherence to federal regulations. Dr Obi earned her Ed D in Leadership Education with distinction from Spalding University, Kentucky. She has over 10 years of clinical, classroom, and administrative experiences in working with individuals with disabilities. Her research interests include response to intervention, early childhood special education, and positive behavior intervention.

Sunday Obi is a Professor and Program Director at Kentucky State University. Prior to coming to KSU, he was a faculty member at both Murray State University and Morehead State University. At Morehead State University, he played a major role in revamping the Special Education Program – the Moderate and Severe Certification and Learning and Behavior Disorder Certification. Dr Obi has over 20 years of classroom and clinical experience working with individuals with disabilities. Dr Obi is the Initiator and Founder of the Master's degree in Special Education at KSU. He is a teacher, researcher, and scholar. He is the author or coauthor of more than 80 publications, including books, book chapters, and articles, and has presented papers at many national and international conferences.

Festus E. Obiakor is the Chief Executive Manager, Sunny Educational Consulting, Shorewood, Wisconsin. He earned his Master's degree in Special Education (Educational diagnostician) at Texas Christian University, Master's degree in Psychology (Instructional Psychology) at New Mexico State University, and PhD degree in Special Education (and minor in Educational Administration and Leadership) at New Mexico State University. He has taught at Rust College, The University of Tennessee-Chattanooga, Henderson State University, Emporia State University, University of Wisconsin-Milwaukee, The City College of New York, and Valdosta State University. He served as Department Chair/Head at both The City College of New York and Valdosta State University, respectively. Dr Obiakor's honors include the 1990 and 1991 School of Education Outstanding Research and Scholarship Award, the University of Tennessee-Chattanooga; the 1992 Horace J. Traylor Minority Leadership Award, the University of Tennessee-Chattanooga; the 1993 and 2001 Distinguished Service to Diversity Award, the National Black Caucus of Special Educators, Council for Exceptional Children (CEC); the 1995 Presidential Award for Distinguished Service to Diversity, Emporia State University; the 2007 Outstanding Service Award as Co-Editor of *Multiple Voices*, the Division of Culturally and Linguistically Diverse Learners (DDEL), CEC. As a teacher, scholar, leader, and consultant, he has served as a Distinguished Visiting Professor at a variety of universities. He is the author of more than 200 publications, including books, chapters, articles, and commentaries, and he has presented 250 papers at national and international conferences. He serves on the editorial boards of reputable nationally and internationally refereed journals, including *Multicultural Learning and Teaching* (*MLT*) in which he serves as Founding/Executive Editor. Dr Obiakor is a leader involved in many landmark scholarly works in the fields of general and special education, with particular focus on African American and other culturally and linguistically diverse (CLD) learners. He continues to prescribe multidimensional methods of assessment, teaching, and intervention for these individuals. Based on this premise, Dr Obiakor created the Comprehensive Support Model (CSM), an intervention model that values the collaborative, consultative, and cooperative energies of students, families, teachers/service providers, communities, and government agencies.

Gina C. Obiakor earned her Doctorate degree in Public Health from Loma Linda University, Loma Linda, California. She is the Owner and Founder of Unify-Public, a Los Angeles-based, public health consulting and communications firm that focuses on various public health topics, such as health equity and vulnerability, and maternal healthcare. Currently, she is an Adjunct Professor of Public Health Policy at Tennessee State University, Nashville, Tennessee where she earned her Master's degree in Public Health. She serves on the editorial board of *Multicultural Learning and Teaching* (*MLT*), and her Podcast, "*Because We Care*" focuses on health issues of at-risk and vulnerable populations.

Molly Pasley is an Assistant Professor in the Visual Disabilities Program at Northern Illinois University in DeKalb, Illinois where she teaches courses to prepare future teachers of students with visual impairments, and orientation and mobility specialists in the field of visual impairments.

Sarah Reilly is a Doctoral Student at Michigan State University in the Educational Psychology and Educational Technology program. Her research interests involve literacy for students with disabilities who are emergent bilinguals.

Kristina Rios is an Assistant Professor of Special Education in the Department of Literacy, Early, Bilingual, and Special Education at California State University of Fresno. Her research interests include parent advocacy for Latinx families of children with intellectual and developmental disabilities.

Sarah Urbanc is an Assistant Professor in the education department at Bradley University in Peoria, Illinois. Prior to teaching at the collegiate level, she was the ESL coordinator and language specialist for a local school district. Her research interests include linguistic identity, positioning theory, and student motivation.

Margaret P. Weiss is an Associate Professor in special education at George Mason University. She is the past president of the Teacher Education Division of the Council for Exceptional Children. Dr Weiss is a former special educator at the elementary, secondary, and postsecondary level. Her research and scholarship center on coteaching, eCoaching, and special education teacher preparation.

Quentin M. Wherfel is an Assistant Professor and Program Director for Teacher Education in the Department of Education, Counseling, and Leadership at Bradley University in Peoria, Illinois. His current research focuses on access to the general education curriculum, assessment and decision-making practices, collaboration, and interventions, and supports for students with disabilities.

Alison Zagona is an Assistant Professor of Special Education at the University of Kansas. Her research is focused on inclusive education for students with extensive support needs, including general and special education teacher preparation for inclusive education and academic instruction and supports, particularly in the area of literacy.

PREFACE

In all works and professions of life, change is an inevitable consequence; however, it can have a good or bad consequence. When it is good, it can lead to progressive actions; but, when it is bad, it can lead to retrogressive actions. *Special Education: Advancing Values* is a change-oriented book that values the creation and advantages of special education while also doing an evaluative exploration of special education. It is a book that cumulatively reaffirms the authenticity of special education as an important educational phenomenon that is now intertwined with our changing society, and to a large measure reiterates that any society that fails to value people with special needs fails itself in our progressive and civilized world.

Historically, individuals with disabilities were unvalued, undervalued, disadvantaged, and demeaned by their homes, schools, communities, and governments. Visibly, their experiences were loaded with all kinds of vulnerabilities at all levels. However, as people got more enlightened, educated, focused, and dedicated, the society advanced; and as it advanced, rooms began to be created for advocacies, litigations, and protective laws that remediated the plights of persons with disabilities. *Special Education: Advancing Values* authenticates these facts and presents real ideas, real problems, real solutions, and real future perspectives that could help transform the field of special education in good and multiple ways.

This book reiterates the fact that special education is blessed with authentic hard-fought advocacies, litigations, and laws that are inextricably tied to fundamental human rights and human valuing (e.g., *Brown vs the School Board of Topeka*, Kansas Case of 1954 and Public Law 94-142 of 1975 that has been reauthorized and amended several times for good). For example, the fundamental ingredients of Public Law 94-142 have continued to be the major pillars of special education, and they include (a) free and appropriate public education (FAPE), (b) referral and identification of student, (c) parental involvement, (d) multidisciplinary team, (e) nondiscriminatory assessment, (f) due process rights, (g) procedural safeguards, and (h) Individualized Education Program (IEP). While these pillars do not necessarily reflect the concrete order of services provided to learners with special needs, they at least, reveal the multidimensionality of services that they are obligated to receive despite their assigned categories of exceptionality (e.g., learning disability, emotional and behavioral disability, intellectual disabilities, deaf/hard of hearing, visual impairments, students with extensive support needs, traumatic brain injury, and physical and other health impairments). Interestingly, these categories are the central foci of the chapters in this book. And, for the functionality of special education to be futuristically entrenched, parental voices, voices of people from culturally and linguistically diverse (CLD) backgrounds, and futuristic voices must be heard and considered – fortunately, chapters on these topics are included in this book. Clearly, to a large measure, this transformational book brings to the forefront, "what was," "what is," and "what will be" in special education.

Special Education: Advancing Values is a book that is aimed at helping us as researchers, scholars, and educators in the field of special education to positively and intentionally engage in professional reflections. In more ways than one, this book has exposed what special is all about, the values and benefits of special education, the pitfalls that have hampered special education, and what we can do to advance the values of special education. As authors, we believe such reflections have value-added benefits that could develop our students, transform our schools and communities, and advance our future in general and special education and other related fields.

Finally, *Special Education: Advancing Values* is a worth-while book that has historical implications. For sure, it would not have been successful without the supports of our colleagues and well-wishers. In addition, we thank the staff of Emerald Publishing for their commitment throughout this book project. To our families, we especially thank you for lovingly hanging in there with us during this venture.

Festus E. Obiakor
Jeffrey P. Bakken
Series Editors

CHAPTER 1

SPECIAL EDUCATION: ADVANCING VALUES

Jeffrey P. Bakken and Christie Nelson

Bradley University, USA

ABSTRACT

Intrinsic values to the field of special education include advocacy, inclusivity, individuality, and empiricism. From early days of providing custodial care in segregated settings, special education has evolved into a program that seeks to educate students with a wide range of learning needs in inclusive settings and identify a robust research base that informs its policies and practices. Important concepts such as inclusion and continuum of services have not only been valuable in conceptualizing and in providing intervention for students with disabilities but have also been valuable in advancing the field. Research in special education and students with disabilities has been instrumental in moving the field forward. In the future, special education will continue to be valuable in supporting students whose learning and survival needs deviate from the norm in meaningful ways by delivering responsive evidence-based instruction.

Keywords: Special education; advancing values; appropriate individualized services; critical values; least restrictive environment

HISTORICAL FOUNDATIONS OF SPECIAL EDUCATION

For thousands of years, individuals with unique physical and mental needs have been targets of discrimination across cultures on virtually every continent. These individuals experienced isolation, exclusion, and even death. In the United States, the history of special education has been influenced by changing societal and philosophical beliefs about the extent to which individuals with differing abilities and exceptional needs should be feared, segregated, categorized, and educated

Special Education
Advances in Special Education, Volume 38, 1–9
Copyright © 2024 Jeffrey P. Bakken and Christie Nelson
Published under exclusive licence by Emerald Publishing Limited
ISSN: 0270-4013/doi:10.1108/S0270-401320240000038001

(Salend & Duhaney, 2011). This history has also involved a discourse of a progressive attitude not acknowledging the equality of all persons evolving from early negative preconceptions (Conrad, 2020).

Beginning in the 13th century, individuals with exceptionalities were categorized as subhuman, totally and permanently unable to engage in rational thought and as a result, could be treated charitably but not equitably (Conrad, 2020; Rossa, 2017). Continuing through the 1700s, these individuals were ignored, isolated, subjected to inhumane treatments, and at times put to death (Rossa, 2017; Salend & Duhaney, 2011). In the late 1700s, asylums were built, and although some institutions viewed their purpose as providing vocational and educational programs, many just provided medical and custodial care and served as a vehicle to control individuals who were perceived as deviants who should be removed from public spaces (Conrad, 2020; Salend & Duhaney, 2011). A turning point came in 1801 when Jean Marc Gaspard Itard's work with Victor, the Wild Boy of Aveyron, was published. Itard developed a system for educating children with severe intellectual disabilities that (a) believed every child should be educated to the greatest extent possible and (b) consisted of carefully sequenced individualized instruction within a structured environment, immediate reward for correct performance, and tutoring in functional skills (Conrad, 2020; Cook & Schirmer, 2003; Salend & Duhaney, 2011). As it appears, Itard's work is commonly viewed as the genesis of modern special education.

The term special education seems to have been first used by Alexander Graham Bell in 1884 at an International Education Association meeting (Salend & Duhaney, 2011), and the first record of a class for students with exceptionalities occurred in New York City public schools in 1899 (Wehmeyer, 2022). Hundreds of school districts across the United States had created public school special education programs in the 1920s; however, almost all the students were housed in separate classrooms or buildings (Wehmeyer, 2022). By the late 1950s and early 1960s, laws were passed to provide financial support to colleges and universities for training teachers and researchers to provide educational services to children with special needs. Despite these laws and funds, many children remained unserved or underserved because most states gave school districts free reign to deny enrollment to students they deemed uneducable (Martin et al., 1996; Salend & Duhaney, 2011).

Between the early 1970s and 1990s, several important pieces of legislation were passed (e.g., the Vocational Rehabilitation Act of 1973, Education for All Handicapped Children Act, Individuals with Disabilities Education Act [IDEA], and Americans with Disabilities Act [ADA]), giving parents equal protection and due process rights related to their children's education. The Vocational Rehabilitation Act of 1973 established the provision of grants for services at the state level and put more responsibility upon the federal government to conduct research and provide training to support individuals with disabilities. In 1975, the Education for All Handicapped Children Act set forth a mandate for any public school accepting federal funding to (a) provide equal access to education, (b) evaluate students with special needs, and (c) provide an equitable educational plan including parental involvement. Signed into law in 1990, IDEA revamped the previous law and provided students with exceptionalities a Free Appropriate Public Education comparable to their nonexceptional peers. The ADA was also signed into law in 1990 to extend the protection of civil rights and prohibit discrimination based on disability. In 2004, a major reauthorization and revision of IDEA was enacted to align more closely with the No Child Left Behind Act to include early intervention, enhanced training for special education teachers, and required schools to use research based interventions. Noteworthy outcomes of these laws were that (a) schools could no longer discriminate on the basis of disability, (b) students were afforded individualized education programs (IEPs), (c) parents had the ability to discuss changes in the education plans before they occurred, (d) parents had the right to appeal decisions made by the school district, and (e) children would be served in the least restrictive environment (LRE), meaning that specific services and programs were to be provided in a general education classroom to the greatest extent possible (Cook & Schirmer, 2003; Martin et al., 1996; Salend & Duhaney, 2011). Also, during this time, special education moved from being a separate system to being integrated within general education (Salend & Duhaney, 2011), and new questions arose regarding the technical aspects of instruction in the areas of assessment, curriculum development, and classroom management (Cook & Schirmer, 2003).

In practical terms, education reform laws marked the beginning of a new era in which individuals with exceptionalities were not simply placed out of sight but legislated for in ways that honored their status as bearers of human rights (Conrad, 2020). This afforded them the opportunity to receive meaningful and beneficial educational services. From 1976–1977 through 2021–2022, the number of students aged 3–21 years old served in federally supported special education programs rose from 3,694,000 to 7,259,000 across all disabilities in the US. In other words, the number of children served as a percent of total enrollment went from 8.3% to 14.7% from 1976 to 2022 (National Center for Education Statistics, 2022). In recent years, there has been an uptick in the number of students receiving special education services. For example, students who are diagnosed on the autism spectrum or with an attention deficit disorder and those with socially constructed disabilities (i.e., emotionally disturbed and learning disabled) make up the majority of students being served in special education (Salend & Duhaney, 2011).

From early days of providing custodial care in segregated settings, special education has evolved into a program that seeks to educate students with a wide range of needs (Salend & Duhaney, 2011). According to Conrad (2020), if the field is to progress ethically through the 21st century, educators and researchers must identify and address deeply entrenched prejudicial attitudes inherited from history that are still present in public policy. In other words, the current over-representation of certain ethnic groups in special education settings has been problematic. Because it is likely that there will always be individuals with exceptionalities whose learning needs deviate from the norm in meaningful ways, special education has become very valuable in meeting these needs by delivering appropriate instruction (Cook & Schirmer, 2003). To a large measure, these are valuable plans to educate and maximize the potential of all learners who belong to all categories of exceptionalities as required by IDEA, namely: autism spectrum disorder, deaf-blindness, deafness, emotional disturbance, hearing impairment, intellectual disability, multiple disabilities, orthopedic impairment, other health impairment, specific learning disability, speech or language impairment, traumatic brain injury, and visual impairment, including blindness.

IMPORTANT CONCEPTS OF SPECIAL EDUCATION

Some important concepts have been instrumental in conceptualizing and in providing services for students with disabilities. These concepts are a continuum of services, inclusion, and supportive environments. They all have been important in advancing the field.

Continuum of Services

The continuum of services identifies different service delivery models which provide specially designed instruction to students with disabilities (Rix et al., 2013). Federal law requires that (a) students be placed in the LRE that meets their needs and (b) that school districts provide a continuum, or range, of placement options that ensures appropriate exposure to the curriculum as well as maximum interaction with nondisabled peers. Services range from self-contained classrooms to the general education classroom as well as services such as consultant teachers and integrated co-teaching services which are directly designed to support the student in his/her general education class. As per IDEA, school districts must offer a continuum of options, called the continuum of alternative placements (e.g., instruction in the general education classroom, self-contained classroom, and instruction in hospitals; IDEA, 2004, Regulations 34 CFR § 300.115) to support a student's unique academic and functional needs. These include the provision of supplementary aids and services (e.g., professional development for general education teachers, use of paraeducators, providing assistive technology, instruction in a resource room) provided in conformity with the general or regular class placement (Yell et al., 2020). Inclusion is one of the placement options in the continuum of services that has received a great deal of attention when considering the best possible educational environment for students with disabilities. On the whole, providing the continuum of services demonstrates professional and legal values of special education.

Inclusion

In their National Study of Inclusive Education, the National Center in Educational Restructuring and Inclusion (NCERI, 1995) defined inclusion as providing to all students, regardless of disability, equitable opportunities to receive effective educational services, with supplementary aids and support services as needed, in age-appropriate general education classes in their neighborhood schools (Francisco et al., 2020). The goal of inclusion is to prepare all students for productive lives as full members of society (National Center on Restructuring and

Inclusion, 1995). The term "inclusion" was used globally in special education for the first time in the Salamanca Statement in 1994, where it was specifically stated that the integration of children with disabilities could be possible through inclusive schools (Rodriguez & Gil, 2014). Earlier, Lipsky and Gartner (1999) argued that inclusion is not just another reform but instead a response to the need to educate a diverse group of learners and provide them with similar opportunities and quality education with their mainstream peers. The problem is that training is needed in order to allow this environment to be effective for teachers and students. Inclusion requires collaboration and openness to new ideas. And it is not something that can be implemented hastily since as many people need to be involved for successful implementation. See Table 1.1 for components of inclusion. To a large extent, they show the benefits and values of special education and its fundamental ingredients.

Table 1.1. Components of Inclusion.

- Knowledge of curriculum, differential instruction, and ongoing planning in order to be effective.
- Equitable co-teaching (i.e., shared teaching and planning responsibilities).
- Curricular adaptations, differential instruction strategies, and innovative approaches to learning in order for all students to benefit from instruction.
- Students benefitting from this mutual respect.
- Fosters an "us" mentality (i.e., we are all in this together – general and special education teachers and students).
- Students having the same opportunities in the classroom.
- Teachers and parents being on the same team and working together to educate the child with and without disabilities.
- Families being valued for their expertise on their children.

Source: The Cascade Counselor. (n.d.). Advocating for students with amplified needs. https://www.thecascadecounselor.com/special-education-services. Accessed on 10 August 2023.

Supportive Environments

One of the key constructs in special education and supportive laws is supportive environments (i.e., the LRE; McGovern, 2015). There are many educational environments for students with and without disabilities (see Fig. 1.1). In all environments, students need supports. Supportive environments include school supports (e.g., general and special education teachers, parental supports, community supports, and government supports).

RESEARCH IN SPECIAL EDUCATION

Whatever we do in special education is research and evidence-based. Over the years, research in special education has been very important in advancing the field. Research involves the willingness to know and the willingness to put into practice what we know. Research has helped to document strengths and

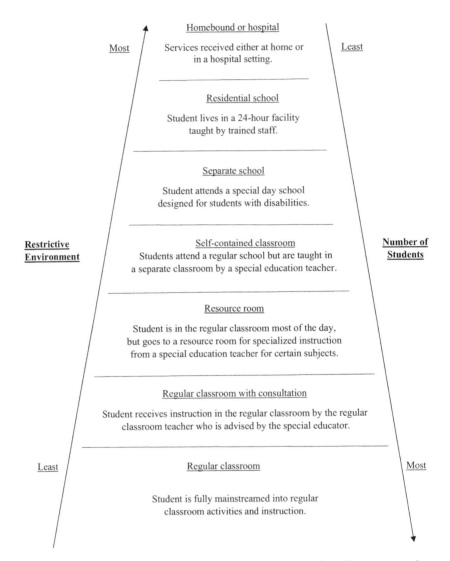

Fig. 1.1. Least Restrictive Environment. *Source:* Michigan Department of Education Office of Special Education. (2022, October). Least restrictive environment (LRE) continuum. https://www.michigan.gov/mde/-/media/Project/Websites/mde/specialeducation/iep/LRE_Continuum.pdf.

deficiencies of students with disabilities. With research, we investigate the impact and effectiveness of strategies for those in controlled settings. Below are discussions about characteristic and intervention research.

Characteristics Research

Characteristics research was used to investigate students with disabilities to document deficiencies of this specific population. The goal was to document and differentiate the learning behavior of students with disabilities as compared to their peers who did not have a disability. For example, Bos and Filip (1984) investigated the comprehension monitoring skills of students with learning disabilities compared to average seventh-grade students. Students were required to read expository passages with text inconsistencies under a standard condition and a cued condition (i.e., where students were cued to look for text inconsistencies). Results indicated that the students without the disabilities spontaneously activated comprehension monitoring strategies in which they figured out there were text inconsistencies regardless of the condition. Students with learning disabilities, however, only activated these strategies when they were cued to do so. This study supported the fact that students with learning disabilities were inactive learners. This study was very important to the field as it showed that this population would not activate strategies to be successful. This means that they need different strategies in different areas to be successful. This study and others like it paved the way for the need and the importance of research on interventions for students with disabilities. Clearly, using results to teach and learn has been important in special education.

Intervention Research

Intervention research was used to focus on teaching students with disabilities interventions with the understanding that students do not implement them on their own when needed. This research tried to answer the question: what would be the outcome if interventions were implemented with students with disabilities? Scruggs and Laufenberg (1986) investigated the use of mnemonic strategies with students who had mental retardation. They wanted to know if mnemonic strategies could be implemented with this population to help them learn. They reviewed several applications of mnemonic strategies with students with mental retardation by using mnemonic pictures (pictures and words) to teach native language vocabulary, numbered or ordered information, and digit series. Results indicated that mnemonic strategies have a great potential in enhancing the learning of individuals with disabilities. This research was important because it showed that students with disabilities could be taught interventions to improve their learning on academic material. This research and other intervention research paved the way for other researchers to investigate the use and implementation of other strategies with other students with disabilities (see Bakken et al., 1997; Mastropieri et al., 1992). Clearly, intervention research has critical value for learners with disabilities.

FUTURE PERSPECTIVES

Based on the aforementioned details, special education has values that deserve to be advanced. Some important concepts have been instrumental in conceptualizing and in providing services for students with disabilities. These concepts are a continuum of services, inclusion, and supportive environments. They all have been important in advancing the field. Whatever we do in special education is research and evidence-based. Over the years, research in special education has been very important in advancing the field. Research involves the willingness to know and the willingness to put into practice what we know. Research has helped to document strengths and deficiencies of students with disabilities. With research, we investigate the impact and effectiveness of strategies for those in controlled settings.

CONCLUSION

This chapter reiterates that special education is an important educational phenomenon that has fundamental values. While historically people with special needs have been unfairly treated, they now have protective values. In this modern era, parents, teachers, and policymakers have made valuable efforts. Special education has uplifted human rights and afforded individuals the opportunity to receive meaningful and beneficial educational services. Special education has enhanced inclusivity. Through inclusion, all students, regardless of disability, are provided equitable opportunities to receive effective educational services, supplementary aids, and ancillary support in age-appropriate general education classes in their own neighborhood schools to prepare them for productive lives as integral members of society. Special education also values individuality. IDEA law requires a full range of placement options to be available to meet a student's needs. By recognizing individual needs and strengths and providing students with a continuum of placements, inclusion is safeguarded through the IEP and by considering the LRE. Lastly, as evidenced by the progression of research over time, we see that special education values empiricism. Special education has done so much good; however, it has been viewed as a negative label. Special education has led to misassessment, miscategorization, disproportionate placement, and misinstruction. In other words, it has been misused by poorly trained teachers and professionals. Special education deserves to be valued.

REFERENCES

Bakken, J. P., Mastropieri, M. A., & Scruggs, T. E. (1997). Reading comprehension of expository science material and students with learning disabilities: A comparison of strategies. *The Journal of Special Education, 31*(3), 300–324.

Bos, C. S., & Filip, D. (1984). Comprehension monitoring in learning disabled and average students. *Journal of Learning Disabilities, 17*(4), 229–233. https://doi.org/10.1177/002221948401700409

Conrad, J. (2020). On intellectual and developmental disabilities in the United States: A historical perspective. *Journal of Intellectual Disabilities, 24*(1), 85–101. https://doi.org/10.1177/1744629518767001

Cook, B. G., & Schirmer, B. R. (2003). What is special about special education? Overview and analysis. *The Journal of Special Education, 37*(3), 200–205.

Francisco, M. P. B., Hartman, M., & Wang, Y. (2020). Inclusion and special education. *Education Sciences, 10*(9), 238. MDPI AG. https://doi.org/10.3390/educsci10090238

Individuals With Disabilities Education Act, 20 U.S.C. § 1400 et seq (2004).

Lipsky, D. K., & Gartner, A. (1999). Inclusive education: A requirement of a democratic society. In H. Daniels, P. Garner, & C. Jones (Eds.), *Inclusive education* (pp. 11–62). Taylor & Francis.

Martin, E. W., Martin, R., & Terman, D. L. (1996). The legislative and litigation history of special education. *The Future of Children*, 25–39.

Mastropieri, M. A., Scruggs, T. E., Bakken, J. P., & Brigham, F. J. (1992). A complex mnemonic strategy for teaching states and their capitals. *Learning Disabilities Research & Practice, 7*(2), 96–103.

McGovern, M. (2015). Least restrictive environment: Fulfilling the promises of IDEA. *Widener Law Review, 21*, 117–137.

National Center on Educational Restructuring and Inclusion. (1995). *National study of inclusive education*. The City University of New York.

National Center for Education Statistics. (2022). Digest of education statistics. Table 204.30. Children 3–21 years old served under Individuals with Disabilities Education Act (IDEA), part B, by type of disability: Selected school years, 1976–1977 through 2021–2022. https://nces.ed.gov/programs/digest/d22/tables/dt22_204.30.asp

Rix, J., Sheehy, K., Fletcher-Campbell, F., & Crisp, M. (2013). *Continuum of education provision for children with special educational needs: Review of international policies and practices*. National Council for Special Education.

Rodriguez, C. C., & Gil, N. G. (2014). Inclusion and integration on special education. *Procedia Social and Behavioral Sciences, 191*, 1323–1327.

Rossa, C. (2017). The history of special education. *Journal for Perspectives of Economic Political and Social Integration, 23*(1–2), 209–227.

Salend, S. J., & Duhaney, L. M. G. (2011). Historical and philosophical changes in the education of students with exceptionalities. In A. F. Rotatori, F. E. Obiakor, & J. P. Bakken (Eds.), *History of special education*. Emerald Publishing Limited.

Scruggs, T. E., & Laufenberg, R. (1986). Transformational mnemonic strategies for retarded learners. *Education and Training of the Mentally Retarded, 21*(3), 165–173. http://www.jstor.org/stable/23876548

Wehmeyer, M. L. (2022). From segregation to strengths: A personal history of special education. *Phi Delta Kappan, 103*(6), 8–13.

Yell, M. L., Katsiyannis, A., Ennis, R. P., Losinski, M., & Batman, D. (2020). Making legally sound placement decisions. *Teaching Exceptional Children, 52*(5), 291–303. https://doi.org/10.1177/00400599209065

CHAPTER 2

SPECIAL EDUCATION OF STUDENTS WITH SPECIFIC LEARNING DISABILITIES: ADVANCING VALUES IN SPECIALLY DESIGNED INSTRUCTION

Margaret P. Weiss[a], Lisa Goran[b], Michael Faggella-Luby[c] and David F. Bateman[d]

[a]George Mason University, USA
[b]University of Missouri, USA
[c]Texas Christian University, USA
[d]American Institutes for Research, USA

ABSTRACT

In this chapter, we focus on specially designed instruction (SDI) as a core value for the field of specific learning disabilities (SLD). SDI is at the heart of special education, and the field of LD has been built on the core value that effective instruction improves student outcomes. We describe a two-step test and an extended example of what is and is not SDI for Matt, a student with an SLD. Finally, we discuss some of the confusion surrounding SDI and the need for the field to return to its core value of individualized, intentional, targeted, evidence- or high leverage practice–based, and systematic instruction for students with SLD.

Keywords: Learning disabilities; students with LD; specially designed instruction; effective instruction for students with LD; core values

Special Education
Advances in Special Education, Volume 38, 11–28
Copyright © 2024 Margaret P. Weiss, Lisa Goran, Michael Faggella-Luby and David F. Bateman
Published under exclusive licence by Emerald Publishing Limited
ISSN: 0270-4013/doi:10.1108/S0270-401320240000038002

INTRODUCTION

In 2022, students with specific learning disabilities (SLD) made up approximately 35% of students identified for special education in the nation's schools (U. S. Department of Education, 2023). The term "learning disability" grew out of a need to identify and provide support for students unexpected underachievement; unexpected in that there was no previously recognized evidence or indication of learning difficulties such as a genetic disorder, intellectual disability, or emotional disorder. Rather, the critical feature of an SLD is the intraindividual differences in achievement that make it both hard to define and often difficult to diagnose (Hallahan et al., 2005; Kavale & Forness, 1997). Yet, throughout the history of SLD, a core value of the field is that instruction is paramount for improving student outcomes. Instruction that is evidence-based, systematic, targeted, intentional, individualized, and strategic is critical to meet student need and build on student strengths to improve areas of achievement deficit (e.g., Hallahan et al., 2005).

According to Patrick Lencioni in The Harvard Business Review (2002), "*core values* are the deeply ingrained principles that guide all of a company's actions; they serve as its cultural cornerstones." The field of SLD has had instruction at its core since the beginning. This core value is evidenced in the historical development of the field and codified in the Individuals with Disabilities Education Act (IDEA, 2006) as specially designed instruction or SDI. However, given that almost 75% of students with SLD are served in the general education classroom for more than 80% of their day (U. S. Department of Education, 2023), and that general educators are not responsible for providing all of the SDI necessary for students with disabilities, there appears to be confusion or lack of clarity around the core value of SDI for students with SLD (Rodgers et al., 2021). In this chapter, we provide an overview of the legal and historical development of the core value of instruction, describe what is meant by effective instruction and SDI, and then give specific, evidence-based, and pragmatic examples of effective instruction and SDI in order to clarify this core value.

DEVELOPING THE CORE VALUE OF INSTRUCTION

The field of LD grew out of the need to address students who did not have intellectual disabilities but who were not learning in ways similar to their peers and/or achieving commensurate with their abilities (Hallahan et al., 2005). Samuel Kirk and Barbara Bateman named this group of students in the early 1960s, and parents and other stakeholders have been advocating for services ever since. Soon after, researchers began to explore the characteristics of these students and identified difficulties in the information processing system, including auditory and visual processing, working memory, and executive function deficits (Hallahan et al., 2005). Though there were varying definitions, the foundational thinking was that the brain systems were intact; however, students were not learning with standard instruction and typical opportunities to practice. A variety of ineffective methods, some related to instruction, some related to a learning-physical movement connection, were developed and subsequently abandoned (Hallahan et al., 2005).

With the growing number of students identified with SLD in the late 1970s and early 1980s, the U.S. Office of Education funded five research institutes to pursue an evidence-based approach to instruction (Hallahan & Mercer, 2002). Each center had a specific target and they were all housed at major research universities (see Table 2.1). The teams at these universities created sustained lines of research across grade levels that tested instructional interventions and assessment for students with SLD through multiple studies and replications. Scholarship across the institutes laid the foundation for thinking about SLD and solidified the core value that effective instruction to meet individual student need is critical to their success.

In an article about the institutes, Barbara Keogh (1983), a leader in the field of LD at the time, stated that the institutes were productive, the research of high quality, and the major contribution "is the systematic study of learner and instructional variables" (p. 120). These institutes also clearly reported that students with SLD have functional issues, not structural issues, which can be addressed with instruction and targeted attention on teaching strategic approaches to tasks. According to Keogh (1983), the complexity of an SLD cannot be minimized, and instructional interventions must address these complexities. Outcomes of the research from the institutes laid the foundation for the evidence-based and high-leverage practices that are a critical part of the field today. Fundamentally, the results of these early studies, and those that continue today, show students with SLD can learn if their needs are targeted and effective instruction is implemented with corresponding fidelity and intensity. For students with SLD, instruction that targets their unique needs is guaranteed through IDEA as SDI.

Table 2.1. Learning Disabilities Research Institutes.

Institute	Focus	Director
Columbia University	Memory and study skills, arithmetic, basic reading and spelling, reading comprehension	Dale Bryant
University of Illinois at Chicago	Attributions and social skills	Tanis Bryant
University of Kansas	Strategy instruction (Adolescents)	Don Deshler
University of Minnesota	Identification, curriculum-based assessment	James Ysseldyke
University of Virginia	Attention issues, cognitive behavior modification	Dan Hallahan

Source: Adapted from Hallahan and Mercer (2002).

GUARANTEEING INSTRUCTION IN SDI

As the main legal framework for special education law, IDEA is the basis for all state and federal laws related to special education. The foundational principle of the IDEA is to ensure all students eligible for special education and related services receive a free and appropriate public education (FAPE), and that their rights are protected (IDEA, 2006).

SLD is one of the 13 categories of disability defined in and covered by IDEA. Once identified with an SLD, IDEA provides several guarantees for services to students during their PK-12 schooling experience. To be eligible for services under the IDEA, a student must (a) have one or more of the disabilities that are covered under the IDEA, and (b) they must require special education and related services because of their disability. In other words, a student must need special education services, related services, supplementary aids or services, or a combination of those services to be determined eligible under the IDEA. Critical to our discussion is the definition of special education as:

> Special education is *specially designed instruction* [emphasis added], at no cost to the parents, to meet the unique needs of a child with a disability. These services include the following: (a) instruction in classrooms, homes, hospitals, and other settings, including instruction in physical education, (b) speech and language pathology, (c) travel training, and (d) vocational education (IDEA Regulations Sec 300.39(a) (1)).

IDEA requires that schools provide SDI to meet the individual needs of students with SLD. Specifically, SDI means adapting, as appropriate to the needs of an eligible child, the content, methodology, or delivery of instruction:

> • to address the child's unique needs resulting from the disability; and
> • ensuring the child's access to the general curriculum so that the child can meet the educational standards that apply to all children within the jurisdiction of the public agency (IDEA Regulations Sec 300.39(b) (3)).

This two-part definition of SDI creates a broad umbrella under which exist multiple important components related to instruction. SDI is described as the adaptation of content, methodology, or delivery of instruction to address a child's unique needs. This is a direct reference to using evidence-based practices to provide instruction to ameliorate, remediate, or otherwise address the areas of need related to the SLD. It also includes a clear direction for students to access the general curriculum as possible and potentially through accommodations or other modifications (Yell, 2019).

SDI Is Instruction +

SDI focuses on the student's specific strengths and weaknesses and is tailored to the student's individual learning needs and annual goals. SDI can take many forms, such as modifications to the general curriculum, specialized instruction in a particular subject, and accommodations to the learning environment (Riccomini et al., 2017; Sayeski et al., 2022). The goal of SDI is to provide the student with the necessary instructional supports and services to enable them to participate in the general curriculum and receive an appropriate education. SDI can also include a variety of assistive technology (AT), such as computer software, adapted keyboards, and augmentative communication devices. These technologies can help a student with SLD access the curriculum and participate in the educational process. IDEA also requires that schools provide appropriate evaluations and assessments to determine the educational needs of students with SLD. These evaluations and assessments are used to help determine the SDI that is necessary for a student to receive an appropriate education and to monitor progress while SDI is delivered.

A school district is to develop an individualized education program (IEP) that provides SDI to a student with SLD that meets their unique needs, regardless of whether the same instruction is provided to other children with or without disabilities in the child's classroom, grade, or building (Yell et al., 2022). For example, if a student with SLD requires a small group for reading instruction, just because it is also provided to other students does not invalidate that it is SDI for this student. However, the instruction provided in this small group must meet the specific needs of the student with SLD, as outlined in the IEP, not just be small group instruction. SDI can be provided in the general education classroom. It does not have to be provided in a separate location or outside of the general education classroom, and for many students with SLD who receive most of their education in the general education classroom, this is an important point. Special education is a service not a place, and the core value of special education is the SDI. If a student with SLD is successful in the general education classroom 100% of the time with the SDI that is provided, that does not mean the student is no longer eligible for special education. It just means the SDI provided in the general education classroom is allowing the student to make progress and should be continued and evaluated for success on a regular basis (Bateman & Cline, 2016).

SDI is not just for academic areas. SDI can also be provided for eligible students in physical education or behavioral interventions. SDI can also include travel training. "Travel training" means providing instruction, as appropriate, to children with disabilities who require this instruction to enable them to develop an awareness of the environment in which they live and learn the skills necessary to move effectively and safely from place to place within that environment (e.g., in school, in the home, at work, and in the community; IDEA, 2004). It may also address skills such as reading a schedule, buying a ticket, and learning when and where to get off a bus or train. The key idea behind SDI is that it is targeted, systematic, intentional instruction using evidence-based or high leverage practices designed to meet the needs of the student with SLD as identified in the IEP, specifically the present level of academic and functional performance and the annual goals.

CONFUSION ABOUT SDI IN GENERAL EDUCATION SETTINGS

Again, the field of SLD has focused on instruction since the beginning and has held SDI using effective practices and teaching behaviors as a core value. When instruction is delivered to students with SLD in special education settings such as self-contained classrooms or resource rooms, it is relatively easy to identify that instruction as SDI. Clearly, it is instruction that is in some way different from the general education classroom, even if it includes content from the general curriculum. However, when students with SLD spend the majority of their instructional time in general education classrooms, teachers get confused about the identification and delivery of SDI. This is compounded by the well-documented role confusion experienced by special educators who are consulting and participating in co-teaching (e.g., Scruggs et al., 2007; Solis et al., 2012). In fact, many reviews and syntheses have found that, in co-teaching, special educators are most likely to function as the one to assist in the one-teach, one-assist configuration (e.g., Scruggs et al., 2007; Solis et al., 2012; Weiss & Brigham, 2000). In this configuration, they are not providing instruction but, rather, are moving through the classroom to assist students while the general educator is providing instruction. This is not SDI as, to satisfy the IDEA definition, SDI must be designed to (a) address the student's unique needs related to the disability and (b) provide access to the general curriculum (IDEA Regulations, 2012). Providing prompts to pay attention or answering a question during instruction does not satisfy both IDEA requirements nor does only providing accommodations and modifications. This lack of providing effective instruction to meet student need violates the core value of instruction and the idea of SDI.

SDI Defined by Student Need, Not Educational Practice

Additional confusion arises from the fact that when someone asks if a particular practice is SDI, the response is generally, "It depends." Unfortunately, that is the only accurate response when addressing a practice. For example, is explicit instruction SDI? Is strategy instruction SDI? Are guided notes SDI? None of these can be considered to *always* be SDI. Rather, as the core value of the field reminds us, the way to determine SDI is to start with the individual student and ask what instruction the student requires to make appropriately ambitious growth (Endrew F. v. Douglas County, 2017). What are the unique needs of a particular student with an SLD? In order to determine the SDI for a student with SLD, one must focus on instruction and consider the following two-step test: (1) what are the *unique needs and goals* of the student? (2) what is the *instruction* necessary to target those needs and achieve those goals? See Fig. 2.1.

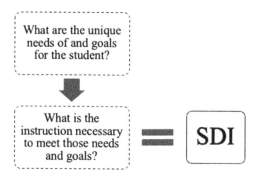

Fig. 2.1.   Two-Step Test for SDI.

THE CORE VALUE OF INSTRUCTION IN PRACTICE: MATT

To determine the unique needs of a student with SLD, one starts with examining the IEP. The needs are found in two places in the IEP: the present levels of academic achievement and functional performance (PLAAFP) and annual goals. The PLAAFP includes multiple data sources to describe the student's current performance in areas of strength and areas of need. It provides a description of the impact of these strengths and weaknesses on performance in the general curriculum and a brief statement of the student's interests and postsecondary goals. Using this present level statement, the IEP team writes annual goals that are directed toward improving relevant student knowledge and skills. Once the annual goals are written, the IEP team then determines placement, services, accommodations, and how the student with SLD will participate in the general curriculum. From this document, teachers can respond to the question: What are the unique needs and goals of the student with SLD?

The second question, what is the instruction necessary to target those needs and achieve those goals, is not written in the IEP. It exists in the day-to-day plans of the educators, specifically special educators, who provide the instruction that is implemented to get the student with SLD from where they are now (indicated in the PLAAFP) to where they are supposed to be (in the annual goals). This instruction can include accommodations but, at its core, is specially designed, evidence-based, intentional teaching practices and instruction implemented with fidelity and at an appropriate level of intensity to meet the unique needs of the student with SLD and assist in accessing the general curriculum. In the section that follows, we provide examples and nonexamples of the PLAAFP-annual goals-SDI connection to illustrate SDI for Matt, a student with an SLD. We specifically address how the examples meet or do not meet the two-step test in both annual goals and instructional planning, highlighting common mistakes or missed opportunities to provide SDI. Our goal is to emphasize the core value of effective instruction as SDI.

A SNAPSHOT OF MATT FROM THE PRESENT LEVEL OF ACADEMIC AND FUNCTIONAL PERFORMANCE

Matt is a 12-year-old, rising sixth-grade student currently at Apple Valley Elementary School. He enjoys playing soccer, drawing, and time with his family. He loves watching and talking about superhero movies with his friends, and he is fascinated by World War II, especially the Normandy Invasion on D-Day. Matt has learned to describe these strengths and interests as part of leading his IEP meeting, and he shares with his teachers and family that someday he would like to be a movie director.

At the most recent re-evaluation (02/24/2022), Matt continued to meet eligibility for an SLD in the areas of basic reading skills and reading comprehension. Matt's cognitive abilities and oral language skills were assessed to be in the average to slightly above-average range. Identified as a student struggling with basic reading skills in second-grade, Matt received reading intervention instruction and is now successfully reading most monosyllabic regular words independently. However, according to standardized assessments, he is currently reading 2.4 years below grade level due to limited fluency with decodable polysyllabic words, frequently omitting or pausing extensively when encountering prefixes and suffixes. Matt is becoming frustrated in his content area classes as the required reading includes many of these kinds of words. Standardized assessments and teacher reports also indicate that, even with ability-level texts, Matt is not able to distinguish main ideas from supporting details. Specifically, when asked about a particular passage, he frequently recounts everything he can remember without an organizing structure. While successful in remembering everything from short passages, as passages lengthen and become more content-rich, his direct recall strategy fails and he has no other strategy to organize information.

Academically, Matt's reading poses challenges in both his English/Language Arts and social studies courses as they are both reading intensive. The increased vocabulary and complicated syntax of his social studies and science texts, as well as more complicated polysyllabic vocabulary, require significant extra time for reading and note-taking. His deficits adversely impact other academic skills, such as writing and mathematics, but assessments in these areas reveal that these skills are still close to his peers. As Matt moves into 6th grade, the IEP team notes it will be important for Matt to receive instruction targeted at these unique needs as well as other supports to assist him in obtaining the content information required at grade level. The stakes are particularly high as he enters middle school because his performance in grades six to eight will determine his eligibility for classes in high school.

Clearly, Matt has literacy-related needs due to his deficits in reading skills. In order for Matt to receive the SDI to address these unique needs, the IEP team must write clear and targeted annual goals that can be translated into instruction. In this section, we provide two model goals that can guide determination of SDI as well as nonexamples of goals that fall short. Each model goal is then translated into a roadmap for instruction.

ANNUAL GOAL 1: ADDRESSING WORD RECOGNITION OF POLYSYLLABIC WORDS

Matt's PLAAFP indicates a persistent and underlying challenge with word recognition skills, specifically the grapheme–phoneme connection. Since second grade, Matt has been receiving interventions targeting decoding of monosyllabic words. While this has been helpful, as the curriculum has progressed, data indicate that he falters when using these skills to attack long, polysyllabic words, specifically skipping certain sounds in long, polysyllabic words (frequently at the end of words) during oral reading in class and 1:1 with an educator. This is likely due to spending significant short-term memory (cognitive capacity) as he sounds out each letter, trying to remember each sound separately from the beginning to end of the word. Instead of using individual sounds for these longer words, a more efficient approach to the task would be to use morphemes, the smallest part of words from which meaning can be derived across different words, to decode unknown polysyllabic words. These words are often referred to as Tier 3 words (Beck et al., 2013). Therefore, a targeted and relevant annual IEP goal for Matt might be: In 36 weeks, given a Tier 3 grade-level list of polysyllabic content vocabulary terms, Matt will accurately decode 17 out of 20 words on 4 of 5 trials. This goal directly addresses his individual need to read polysyllabic words in content areas, a skill that is necessary for his continued progress in the general curriculum. It is also broad enough to include the many subskills that will be a part of the SDI he receives.

What Is the SDI for Matt?

In order to develop Matt's skill in decoding polysyllabic words, he will require instruction in a strategy to do so, particularly a strategy focused on using morphemes or smaller components of words. For example, SDI for Matt might be instruction in an Overt Morpheme Strategy (e.g., Archer et al., 2003; Harris et al., 2008, 2011) to accomplish this goal. There are other strategies for addressing weaknesses with long words such as using vowels to find syllables, reading nonsense words, syllabification, flexibility, and intensive practice as well (for more, see Kearns et al., 2022) but, in this case, a teacher could choose explicit morpheme strategy instruction because it provides simultaneous support in meaning, spelling, and pronunciation – improving Matt's decoding skills and comprehension. Matt will benefit from explicit instruction at his ability level, with guided practice and feedback to learn to identify prefixes, suffixes, and word roots before moving to grade-level and discipline specific words. In this example, teaching an Overt Morpheme Strategy (e.g., Archer et al., 2003; Harris et al., 2008, 2011) builds on fundamental instructional principles such as strategy instruction, explicit instruction, repeated practice opportunities, and corrective feedback that are the cornerstone of effective instruction for students with SLD.

SDI in Practice for Matt

While the IEP goals and related SDI provide a big picture framework for meeting the needs of students with SLD, it is the process of translating the annual goal into a series of coordinated and well-planned lessons that is essential for meaningful student growth. Just as the PLAAFP is aligned to annual goals and related SDI, lesson plans require three aligned components: (a) the clearly articulated multi-part objective, (b) the aligned formative assessment, and (c) the SDI that supports student attainment of the objective as measured by the assessment. SDI is the bridge, enabling students with SLD to have their individual needs met, while receiving access to the general education curriculum.

Obviously, for Matt to improve his word reading abilities, his SDI will require many different lessons with a variety of learning objectives. As an example, one SDI lesson toward the end of the year after Matt has received basic instruction on the Overt Morpheme Strategy includes the instructional objective, Matt will be able to identify and segment affixes and roots on 10 out of 12 grade-level Tier 3 vocabulary words (Beck et al., 2013). Before this lesson, an educator would have taught and practiced with Matt the pronunciation and spellings of affixes and specific base words by (see Kearns et al., 2022 for more). This specific lesson begins with the educator modeling the strategy with the examples on a sheet of 20 vocabulary words with similar affixes by identifying each component, segmenting with a visual symbol (circle, box, or line), and then saying the parts fast to surface the real word. Upon completion of the model (1–2 examples), the educator and Matt will engage in guided practice over 6–7 more words with the educator first initiating the steps completed by Matt and then cueing Matt to provide and perform the strategy step sequence. Matt will then independently complete the remaining 12 words. He will use brackets (handwritten) to segment the affixes and the root word before underlining the vowel sounds in the remaining parts of the word. Finally, Matt will practice pronouncing the word and connecting it to a real word in his lexicon to check that it makes sense. The finished product will give the educator progress monitoring data on Matt's understanding and application of the strategy to guide the next lesson. If Matt does not correctly identify the morphemes, the educator can provide immediate, corrective feedback and note that he is not yet independent with specific roots or affixes. Ongoing progress monitoring like this is essential for measuring Matt's response to instruction and to guide data-based decision making for future lesson planning.

What Is Not SDI?

For Matt, participating in more sustained silent reading without explicit instruction will not meet his unique needs for learning how to segment and decode polysyllabic words effectively and efficiently. Consistent research has shown that Matt's persistent and underlying word level challenges require instruction. Similarly, teaching an overreliance on sight words by only focusing on vocabulary instruction would not develop the long-term skills Matt needs to attack unfamiliar discipline-specific vocabulary. Relying on instruction that is the same as his peers to address Matt's needs in morphological analysis will also fall short of SDI as his particular needs are not similar to his peers and the instruction provided in the general curriculum will not include the intensity necessary to ameliorate these deficits.

While it is a goal for Matt to be able to use the morpheme strategy in grade-level words, it would be inappropriate for the educator to begin instruction with the words currently being used in content area courses at grade level. These words would not have the patterns necessary to teach the strategy and could prove frustrating to Matt. Once Matt shows progress in mastering the strategy and its use in several patterned words, the educator could introduce its use in grade-level material. It is recommended that teachers start with ability-level polysyllabic words that are in the students listening comprehension vocabulary. Then the teacher can connect known words to word families to introduce new words. It is essential that educators help Matt to connect the word parts to real words that are in the student's lexicon. Without the connection to real words (as in a Word Attack task), Matt may fail to see the true purpose of the strategy as a scaffold for supporting his comprehension. Critical to this instruction is teaching Matt when to use the strategy (and when it is not necessary because he already knows the word). In this case, educators should pick rare and complicated words (Tier 3) rather than Tier 1 words that do not require the use of the strategy. A careful sequence of words with and without all three parts should be considered. This individualized approach addresses Matt's unique needs and is, therefore, considered SDI for him.

ANNUAL GOAL 2: ADDRESSING COMPREHENSION OF EXPOSITORY TEXT

Now that the word recognition and morphology challenges have been addressed in the first goal, the IEP team can turn its attention to addressing Matt's needs for SDI to improve his comprehension of expository text. In this case, a model annual goal might be, in 36 weeks, using a text-to-speech program to access grade-level nonfiction text, Matt will correctly identify the text structure and answer 5 of 6 comprehension questions on 4 out of 5 trials. This long-term goal addresses his individual need related to comprehension and is broad enough to include the many subskills that will need to be addressed to achieve it. There could be a focus on social studies, science, or other content text in this goal but we are going to leave it more broad for now, given his PLAAFP statement was not specific.

What Is the SDI for Matt?

Matt will require at least two types of SDI to accomplish this goal. First, he will need instruction in *how* and *why* to use text-to-speech programs. Specifically, an educator will need to provide explicit explanation, demonstration, modeling, and practice opportunities for Matt to use a text-to-speech program to listen to passages of different lengths. Matt may require additional practice in knowing when to use this tool to remove word recognition and fluency challenges that tax short-term memory when reading polymorphic, polysyllabic, or challenging syntactic passages. It is also important to regularly evaluate whether the text-to-speech program is working to address his needs.

Second, Matt will benefit from explicit instruction in text structures such as compare/contrast, main idea, and descriptive (Meyer et al., 1980; Williams et al., 2009). Text structure strategies "help a reader analyze a text and construct a mental representation" (Bakken et al., 1997; Hall-Mills & Marante, 2022). Student comprehension improves as they develop an organizational framework for text, increasing capacity in short-term memory, and aiding recall and inference-making (Hall-Mills & Marante, 2022). Using a mediated learning approach like the text-to-speech instruction, the educator will confirm the potential benefit of the strategy, receive a commitment from Matt to learn the strategy, demonstrate and model the strategy, provide rehearsal of strategy steps, opportunities for practice with ability-level reading passages and grade-level passages with regular assessment to guide educator feedback.

SDI in Practice for Matt

Meeting the annual goal for Matt to improve his comprehension will require many different lessons with a variety of learning objectives. As an example, one SDI lesson objective might be, Matt will be able to identify a descriptive paragraph and the topic, main idea, and three supporting details (5 elements) on a graphic organizer when reading a selection from the grade-level nonfiction text *Freedom Walkers: The Story of the Montgomery Bus Boycott.* For this lesson, SDI for Matt is both the *what* and *how* instruction can bridge from the objective to a mastery score on the lesson measure. First, in this case, Matt has already received instruction and mastered identifying descriptive text structure, topic, main idea, and supporting details separately. The purpose of this lesson is to bring those concepts together and identify all of them in real text. In order to focus on this objective, the educator will read the text aloud to Matt while conducting the lesson and the use of the text-to-speech reader will come after mastery of the lesson objective. In this specific lesson, the educator will choose several sections of text that will support the use of the text structure strategy. She will model the use of the entire strategy to identify the descriptive structure, topic, main idea, and three supporting details and record them on the graphic organizer. For the next example, Matt will help her complete the strategy and she will check for understanding. As he becomes more confident, she will then ask him to use the strategy independently.

Finally, because of Matt's SLD, it is likely he will require lots of practice, generalization instruction, and other unique elements of explicit instruction before mastering the strategy of identifying the text structure and using that for comprehension. Functionally, for this lesson, Matt will be required to identify the text structure as descriptive and complete the graphic organizer containing five blank elements from the passage, correctly labeling all but one of the elements, as formative assessment for the lesson. If Matt does not correctly identify the text structure or four of the five elements, that will be a signal to the teacher that he requires more practice in applying the cognitive strategy correctly. Ongoing progress monitoring will again guide data-based decision-making for future lesson planning.

What Is Not SDI?

First, text-to-speech programs are frequently listed as AT on an IEP and made available to students "whenever they need them." However, without explicit instruction in *how* and *why* the use of text-to-speech is appropriate, it is unlikely that students like Matt will effectively and efficiently make use of AT when they are most needed (even with teacher cueing). A second potential nonexample would be to ignore the need for cognitive strategy instruction providing explicit instruction in effective comprehension strategies such as identifying text structure. In some cases, a text structure strategy might be taught to the whole class in middle school; however, this, alone, would not be SDI for Matt as he would require the instruction to be more explicit, provide more practice opportunities, and include more intentional text both at his reading level and in a specific text structure initially.

In addition, in some whole group instruction, educators may believe it is necessary to precomplete the supporting graphic organizer for Matt, perhaps leaving one or two elements blank (as in skeleton notes). However, this denies Matt the opportunity to think deeply about the critical content. This creates inequity with classmates, blocking access to the general education curriculum. Finally, for Matt to access the general education curriculum requires careful planning to ensure that he has learned both the text-to-speech program AND had time to master the cognitive strategy. Consequently, educators must engage in thoughtful unit planning with backwards design considerations for both to-be-learned content and also how to sequence small group and individual opportunities to practice supporting skills.

IMPLICATIONS AND CONCLUSIONS

If we return to the idea that a core value is deeply ingrained in a field, Leoncini (2002) continues by saying that, "If you're not willing to accept the pain that core values incur, don't bother going to the trouble of making a values statement." The field has felt this pain and, in some cases, inflicted it upon itself. The core value of targeted, intentional, systematic, and evidence-based SDI will improve outcomes for students with SLD runs through the history of LD. IDEA supports this foundational need for instruction to meet the unique needs of each student with an SLD in its definition of special education as SDI (IDEA Regulations, 2006). SDI is determined by and individualized for the unique needs of each student with SLD (as described in the PLAAFP) and the goals set in the IEP for that student.

Though we have many more questions to answer, intervention research in the field of LD has led to better ways to meet student need, as evidenced by the rich history of the LD institutes and the continued development of interventions through careful research. But we would be remiss if we did not acknowledge that instruction occurs within the complex context of schools and classrooms. Currently, these contexts are fraught with less-than-ideal circumstances to make SDI a reality and herein lies the pain. Within this core value are multiple assumptions that, if not met, cause the pain of unintelligible goals, misaligned objectives, and confused or ineffective educators all resulting in disappointing student outcomes. However, it is critical that educators, administrators, and other school personnel recognize that a core value, such as effective, individualized instruction, is understood as so critical that they make it happen to the greatest extent possible, no matter the circumstance.

UNDERLYING ASSUMPTIONS

To be clear, effective instruction for students with SLD cannot happen without multiple contextual variables being in place. Though numerous, the critical variables include (a) a knowledgeable special educator, (b) supportive working conditions, (c) quality data (unbiased assessment), and (d) collaborative partners.

Knowledgeable Special Educator

Evidence indicates that effective teachers are the single most critical variable in student learning (e.g., Goldhaber & Anthony, 2002). Critical to effective instruction for students with SLD is an educator who can (a) interpret data, (b) develop quality student and instructional goals, (c) identify and implement effective teaching behaviors and practice, and (d) monitor student progress in that instruction. Without these skills, and the dispositions to work with and advocate for students with SLD, effective instruction is impossible. Unfortunately, the critical shortage of special educators has left the field with difficult choices as many practicing special educators are on provisional or alternative licenses (Day et al., 2023). These educators are learning on the job and often come to their position having had only an introductory course on disabilities (Day et al., 2023). It is very difficult for these new special educators to develop new knowledge and skills in instruction while also learning to write IEPs, solve behavioral issues, understand assessment data, co-teach and collaborate on professional learning teams, and collaborate with families. In fact, only a small fraction of special educators' time is spent on instruction (Vannest et al., 2011). This is a complex issue to solve but one that has a direct impact on the core value of instruction as critical to student success.

Supportive Working Conditions

Working conditions within schools and classrooms also have a significant impact on teacher instruction, engagement, and retention (Bettini et al., 2016). As described by Hirsch et al. (2022), "special educators' affective experiences of their work shape how they provide services to students" (p. 132). Working conditions are defined as the school culture, administrative and collegial support, instructional materials, instructional grouping, time for instruction, and time for planning (Bettini et al., 2016). Special educators who work with students with SLD are pulled in many directions and their working conditions are related to burnout (Brunsting et al., 2014). In addition to their responsibilities as case managers to handle IEPs and other paperwork responsibilities, they are often asked to co-teach with multiple general education partners, participate in content area professional learning teams, and oversee the work of paraprofessionals. In some cases, they do not have access to the same instructional materials that general educators do and their planning time is often used for meetings (Bettini et al., 2016). Critical to the core value of instruction is better understanding the supportive working conditions that allow special educators to provide the intentional, targeted, and individualized instruction necessary for students with SLD and research in this area will help us get there.

Quality Data

In order to build adequate PLAAFP statements and to monitor student progress toward goals, special educators require quality assessment data. These data must be free from bias and specific enough to guide instruction. Developing annual goals that will guide SDI require data that goes beyond standardized tests and a basic protocol for determining eligibility for a specific disability category (Filderman & Toste, 2017). To develop instructional goals, special educators need data that describe skills in terms of strengths and weaknesses. Saying a student "struggles with decoding" does not provide the data necessary to determine instruction. Special educators need data that indicate the specific skills a student has mastered and those that are not mastered in decoding or whatever the area may be. These data may be from evaluators, related service providers, general education teachers, parents, and other partners but the target must be data that will inform instruction (Filderman & Toste, 2017). These data are available in most cases. Special educators need to advocate for getting it and educate others on how to make it meaningful.

Collaborative Partners

Finally, providing SDI for students with SLD is a collaborative endeavor. Guided by the special educator, general educators, related service providers, paraprofessionals, parents and families, the student, and administrators must work together to build a collaborative culture that takes collective responsibility for student outcomes and believes that the pathway to positive outcomes is through effective instruction (Friend, 2022). This collaboration can take many forms, such as working with administrators to develop a master schedule that allows for common planning time for general and special educators or working with a student to determine postsecondary goals and dreams. The who and what for collaboration will shift and change over time. However, improving student outcomes is only possible if collaborative partners across disciplines believe that effective instruction delivered as SDI will build the skills necessary to get the student with SLD to reach their goals and each individual has a part to play in that instruction (Friend, 2015).

CONCLUSIONS

SDI or targeted, individualized, effective instruction to meet the unique needs of and make the general curriculum accessible to a student with an SLD is a core value of the field of LD. Research on effective practices has spanned the life of the field and many of the findings have made their way into general education classrooms (e.g., strategy instruction). However, for a variety of reasons, a confusion about what SDI is has affected its implementation in schools. This confusion has also led to a crisis of identity for some special educators as they move into general education settings (e.g., co-teaching) and are questioned about content knowledge, not instructional and learning knowledge (Weiss & Glaser, 2019; Weiss & Lloyd, 2002).

The SDI two-step test presented in this chapter is a way to build clarity around SDI and can be thoughtfully addressed in two critical places: IEP development and content delivery. IEP development involves documenting the student's unique needs and strengths, as well as the general education curriculum targets that should be addressed within the IEP cycle. From a compliance perspective, IEP documentation must address all of the legally required components. From a student-oriented perspective, the IEP is the roadmap to ensuring the student receives a FAPE. The IEP is then used to inform content planning and delivery. These aspects occur during lesson planning and lesson implementation.

First, the individual needs of the student are surfaced as part of the IEP development. As the IEP team addresses the unique needs of the student, these are connected to the skills and knowledge expected within the grade-level standards and expectations of the general education curriculum. These pieces are to be captured in the individual student PLAAFP within the IEP document. The PLAAFP drives the conversation about annual goals for the student, and the team determines how much growth is ambitious and reasonable over the next year (Endrew F. v. Douglas County, 2017). In the IEP document, SDI exists between the PLAAFP and the goals – within the services, supports, accommodations, and modifications needed for the student to access the general education curriculum.

Second, and most critical to the classroom experience of the student and educators, educators must identify what instruction and supports are needed for the student to access the general education curriculum given the unique needs identified in the IEP. This critical juncture – between the objectives and assessment – is where SDI can be found in the lesson planning and content delivery.

As we see it, it is the task of the special educator, along with the IEP team, to *articulate* the SDI that is necessary for the student with SLD (using the PLAAFP and annual goals), to *advocate* for that instruction, to *deliver* it with fidelity and adequate intensity, and to *monitor* student progress. SDI acknowledges that students with SLD have different learning needs, as evidenced by their eligibility for special education and their IEP, and therefore they require different instruction to meet their unique needs. Anything less does not fulfill the goal of FAPE and does not adhere to the core value of individualized, evidence-based instruction that will change student outcomes.

REFERENCES

Archer, A. L., Gleason, M. M., & Vachon, V. L. (2003). Decoding and fluency: Foundation skills for struggling older readers. *Learning Disability Quarterly, 26,* 89–101. https://doi.org/10.2307/1593592

Bakken, J. P., Mastropieri, M. A., & Scruggs, T. E. (1997). Reading comprehension of expository science material and students with learning disabilities: A comparison of strategies. *The Journal of Special Education, 31*(3), 300–324.

Bateman, D. F., & Cline, J. L. (2016). *A teacher's guide to special education.* The Association for Supervision and Curriculum Development and the Council for Exceptional Children.

Beck, I. L., McKeown, M. G., & Kucan, L. (2013). *Bringing words to life: Robust vocabulary instruction.* Guilford Press.

Bettini, E. A., Crockett, J. B., Brownell, M. T., & Merrill, K. L. (2016). Relationships between working conditions and special educators' instruction. *The Journal of Special Education, 50*(3), 178–190. https://doi.org/10.1177/0022466916644425

Brunsting, N. C., Sreckovic, M. A., & Lane, K. L. (2014). Special education teacher burnout: A synthesis of research from 1979 to 2013. *Education & Treatment of Children, 37*(4), 681–711.

Day, J., Nagro, S. A., & Mason-Williams, L. (2023). The nationwide trends and preparation requirements of alternative route programs in special education. *Teacher Education and Special Education,* OnlineFirst.

Endrew F. v. Douglas County School District, 137 S. Ct. 988 (2017).

Filderman, M. J., & Toste, J. R. (2017). Decisions, decisions: Using data to make instructional decisions for struggling readers. *Teaching Exceptional Children, 50*(3), 130–140. https://doi.org/10.1177/0040059917740701

Friend, M. (2015). Welcome to co-teaching 2.0. *Educational Leadership.* https://www.ascd.org/el/articles/welcome-to-co-teaching-2.0

Friend, M. (2022). *Interactions: Collaboration skills for school professionals* (9th ed.). Pearson.

Goldhaber, D., & Anthony, E. (2002). *Teacher quality and student achievement.* https://files.eric.ed.gov/fulltext/ED477271.pdf

Hall-Mills, S. S., & Marante, L. M. (2022). Explicit text structure instruction supports expository text comprehension for adolescents with learning disabilities: A systematic review. *Learning Disability Quarterly, 45*(1), 55–68. https://doi.org/10.1177/0731948720906490

Hallahan, D. P., Lloyd, J. W., Kauffman, J. M., Weiss, M. P., & Martinez, E. A. (2005). *Learning disabilities: Foundations, characteristics, and effective teaching* (3rd ed.). Pearson.

Hallahan, D. P., & Mercer, C. D. (2002). Learning disabilities: Historical perspectives. In R. Bradley, L. Danielson, & D. P. Hallahan (Eds.), *Identification of learning disabilities: Research to practice* (pp. 1–65). Erlbaum.

Harris, M. L., Schumaker, J. B., & Deshler, D. D. (2008). *The word mapping strategy.* Edge Enterprises.

Harris, M. L., Schumaker, J. B., & Deshler, D. D. (2011). The effects of strategic morphological analysis instruction on the vocabulary performance of secondary students with and without disabilities. *Learning Disability Quarterly, 34*(1), 17–33.

Hirsch, S. E., Griffith, C., Chow, J. C., Walker, A. C., & Walters, S. (2022). Professional learning and development for special educators serving students with emotional and behavioral disorders in self-contained settings. *Behavioral Disorders, 48*(1), 62–76. https://doi.org/10.1177/01987429221110838

Individuals with Disabilities Education Act. (2004). 20 U.S.C. § 1400.

Individuals with Disabilities Education Act (IDEA) Regulations. (2006). 34 C.F.R. § 300 et seq.

Individuals with Disabilities Education Act Regulations. (2012). 34 C.F.R. § 300.

Kavale, K. A., & Forness, S. R. (1997). Defining learning disabilities: Consonance and dissonance. In J. W. Lloyd, E. J. Kameenui, & D. Chard (Eds.), *Issues in educating students with disabilities* (pp. 3–26). Lawrence Erlbaum Associates.

Kearns, D., Lyon, C., & Kelley, S. (2022). Structured literacy interventions for reading long words. In L. Spear-Swerling (Ed.), *Structured literacy interventions: Teaching students with reading difficulties, Grades K-6.* The Guilford Press.

Keogh, B. K. (1983). A lesson from Gestalt psychology. *Exceptional Education Quarterly, 4,* 115–127.

Lencioni, P. M. (2002, July). Make your values mean something. *Harvard Business Review.* https://hbr.org/2002/07/make-your-values-mean-something

Meyer, B. J. F., Brandt, D. M., & Bluth, G. J. (1980). Use of top-level structure in text: Key for reading comprehension of ninth-grade students. *Reading Research Quarterly, 16*(1), 72–103. https://doi.org/10.2307/747349

Riccomini, P. J., Morano, S., & Hughes, C. A. (2017). Big ideas in special education: Specially designed instruction, high-leverage practices, explicit instruction, and intensive instruction. *Teaching Exceptional Children, 50*(1), 20–27. https://doi.org/10.1177/0040059917724412

Rodgers, W., Weiss, M. P., & Ismail, H. (2021). What is specially designed instruction? A systematic literature review. *Learning Disabilities Research & Practice, 36*(2), 96–109. https://doi.org/10.1111/ldrp.12247

Sayeski, K. L., Reno, E. A., & Thoele, J. M. (2022). Specially designed instruction: Operationalizing the delivery of special education services. *Exceptionality,* OnlineFirst. https://doi.org/10.1080/09362835.2022.2158087

Scruggs, T. E., Mastropieri, M. A., & McDuffie, K. A. (2007). Co-teaching in inclusive classrooms: A metasynthesis of qualitative research. *Exceptional Children, 73,* 392–416. https://doi.org/10.1177/001440290707300401

Solis, M., Vaughn, S., Swanson, E., & McCulley, L. (2012). Collaborative models of instruction: The empirical foundations of inclusion and co-teaching. *Psychology in the Schools, 49,* 498–510. https://doi.org/10.1002/pits.21606

U. S. Department of Education. (2023). *44th Annual Report to Congress on the implementation of the Individuals with Disabilities Education Act.* https://sites.ed.gov/idea/files/44th-arc-for-idea.pdf

Vannest, K. J., Hagan-Burke, S., Parker, R. I., & Soares, D. A. (2011). Special education teacher time use in four types of programs. *The Journal of Educational Research, 104,* 219–230. https://doi.org/10.1080/00220671003709898

Weiss, M. P., & Brigham, F. (2000). Co-teaching and the model of shared responsibility: What does the research support? In T. E. Scruggs & M. A. Mastropieri (Eds.), *Advances in learning and behavior disabilities* (pp. 217–246). JAI Press.

Weiss, M. P., & Glaser, H. (2019). *Instruction in co-teaching in the age of Endrew F. behavior modification.* Advanced Online Publication. https://doi.org/10.1177/0145445519836071

Weiss, M. P., & Lloyd, J. W. (2002). Congruence between roles and actions of secondary special educators in co-taught and special education settings. *The Journal of Special Education, 36,* 58–68.

Williams, J. P., Stafford, K. B., Lauer, K. D., Hall, K. M., & Pollini, S. (2009). Embedding reading comprehension training in content-area instruction. *Journal of Educational Psychology, 101*(1), 1–20. https://doi.org/10.1037/a0013152

Yell, M. L. (2019). *Legal issues in special education* (5th ed.). Pearson.

Yell, M. L., Bateman, D. F., & Shriner, J. (2022). *Developing educationally meaningful and legally sound IEPs.* Rowman and Littlefield Publishing Group.

CHAPTER 3

COME TOMORROW: CONSIDERING THE FUTURE NEEDS FOR STUDENTS WITH EMOTIONAL AND/ OR BEHAVIORAL DISORDERS

Frederick J. Brigham[a], Christopher Claude[a], Jason Chow[b], Colleen Lloyd Eddy[c], Nicholas Gage[d] and John William McKenna[e]

[a]*George Mason University, USA*
[b]*Vanderbilt University, USA*
[c]*University of Pittsburgh School of Education, USA*
[d]*WestEd, USA*
[e]*University of Massachusetts Lowell, USA*

ABSTRACT

Four reputed leaders for the coming years in the field of special education for individuals with emotional and behavioral disorders (EBD) each with a slightly different perspective on the field were asked to respond independently to a prompt asking what does special education mean for students with EBD and what is being done and how do we maintain tradition? The contributors' responses to the prompt are presented and then summarized across the essays. A remarkable consistency emerges across the independent essays. In addition to the tradition of providing a free and appropriate education in the least restrictive environment, the contributors identify needs to support teachers serving this population. Needs in teacher training and the expertise required to meet the needs of individuals with EBD are outlined as well as potential contributions of technology to carry out specific tasks. We conclude with a call

Special Education
Advances in Special Education, Volume 38, 29–54
Copyright © 2024 Frederick J. Brigham, Christopher Claude, Jason Chow, Colleen Lloyd Eddy, Nicholas Gage and John William McKenna
Published under exclusive licence by Emerald Publishing Limited
ISSN: 0270-4013/doi:10.1108/S0270-401320240000038003

for increased advocacy for use of the knowledge that we currently possess and that which will soon be discovered to support students with EBD as well as their teachers. We also note that the contributors' names are listed alphabetically to acknowledge the equality of each person to the final product.

Keywords: Emotional/behavioral disorders (EBD); special education; teacher preparation; technology; mental health; equity

INTRODUCTION

Chicago Tribune columnist Sydney J Harris once noted, the best thing a futurist can do is to admit that he or she has no idea what is going to happen in the future. More recently, George Will noted that "foresight. . .is a dream from which events awaken us" (2023, p. A19). We should, at this point, define one of our terms. There is a distinction between "futurism" and "futurology." Futurism is defined as an artistic movement originating in Italy in the early 1900s that rejected artistic and cultural tradition in favor of a technologically oriented future. It celebrated war as a liberating force freeing the present of the weight of the past, and admired speed, machines, youth, and violence (Buchanan, 2018a). Futurology is the study of the possible (and assumed to be likely) nature of the world in the near future based on what is known about present trends in demography, technology, and economic geography (Buchanan, 2018b). We are working from the perspective of futurology in the present text. Further, we believe that Harris was speaking of futurology when he used the term "futurist."

Despite the obvious limitations of futurology, Gorbis (2019) suggested that systematic thinking about the future is useful for helping people make better choices both as individuals and as members of an educational or government organization. Further, Gorbis asserted that thinking seriously about the future can promote consideration of a range of possibilities, allowing people to be better prepared if one of the imagined futures comes about. It is in this spirit that the present chapter was developed.

Please excuse this excursion into first person language. It seems the best way to explain how this chapter was formed. When first contacted about this chapter, I (Brigham) was enthused to have the opportunity to consider this topic. The elements of special education that need to be maintained as we move forward into a new century clearly include ensuring that each student with a disability receives a free and appropriate public education (FAPE) and that those services are delivered in the least restrictive environment (LRE). That does not mean that we, as a profession are where we want to be yet. In fact, if the profession is to remain vibrant and relevant, it is necessary that we maintain a level of "optimistic dissatisfaction" (Brigham, 2011). As we maintain an attitude of optimistic dissatisfaction (i.e., we are not happy with our current situation but believe that we can work to improve it), it is important to avoid falling into the trap described as cruel optimism (Berlant, 2011).

Berlant described cruel optimism as the condition where people hope that some future development will easily and quickly solve a given problem and make them happy. Because inflated expectations are common, the arrival of the hope for solution often leaves the recipients less rather than more happy.

One reason that this can happen is that solutions imagined for problems at a given point in time may not apply to the conditions that are present when the solution becomes available. Issues that vexed educators in one time may be replaced or superseded by issues that their ancestors could not have imagined.

Among the differences that are most notable from the 20th to the 21st century is the prominence of "culture wars" in many schools (Emba, 2023; Zimmerman, 2021). In addition to efforts to ban books in public libraries, school libraries, and classrooms, NBC News reporter Anne Fernandez noted that "The teacher is now viewed by a small, but loud contingent, not as a public servant but as a public enemy" (2021, August 23). Fernandez continued to state:

> At the most basic level, such incidents teach children that violence can and should be used in self-advocacy and to solve problems. But they also introduce damaging attitudes transmitted to children about their teachers: that they can't be trusted, don't care about them, shouldn't be listened to." The irony of our profession is "The public stigmatizes the teaching profession yet also expects teacher to solve all problems and blames them when they can't. (Robbins, 2023, p. 66)

These phenomena are related to general education programs and teachers. Services for individuals with emotional and/or behavioral disorders are, however, most often delivered in the context of the general school program; therefore, these sentiments apply to special educators as well. Professional educators appear to hold more difficult and less respected positions in society suggesting that we will encounter differing and additional needs in the coming decades than in the recent past. Therefore, the topic of the present chapter is well-justified.

The group of individuals who work to support children and youths with emotional and behavioral disorders (EBD) includes a substantial number who hold strong retrospective perceptions; however, the mission of the present chapter seemed better served by recruiting individuals who were likely to be notable leaders in this field in the coming years. To identify these individuals, I asked current and former editors of *Behavioral Disorders*, and *The Journal of Emotional and Behavioral Disorders* to identify individuals whose work was, in their opinions, substantial and forward-looking. The contributors to this chapter, Chow, Eddy, Gage, and McKenna in alphabetical order, were among those most frequently mentioned. We have chosen to list the names of contributors alphabetically to acknowledge the independence of each contribution as well as the equality of each contributor to the final product. There were many more names suggested than could possibly be used and that is a sign of hope for the profession.

Our Challenge

The topic of this chapter is "What Does Special Education Mean for Students with Emotional and Behavior Disorders? What is Being Done and How Do We Maintain Tradition?" The individual contributors to this chapter were asked to respond to this prompt in any way that they chose. The responses were limited in length to allow for the inclusion of more voices, so there is much more that each of the contributors has to say on their topics. By requesting a short response, I hoped to identify elements that were common and/or dissimilar across the contributors. Finally, the responses were received from each contributor before the names of the contributors were revealed. This was done to further support the independence of the contributions. The essays from each contributor appear in the next section. They are followed by a summary and integration section written by Chris Claude and me.

MAINTAINING THE TRADITION

Jason Chow, Section Contributor

Special education for students with EBD, at its core, should be like the special education for any student with a disability: specialized instruction that meets the individual needs for each student and allows for that student to make meaningful educational progress in the LRE. There is growing recognition that students with EBD present a multifaceted range of qualities that require preventative or intervention efforts for them to be successful in our education system. As is often the case, change and adaptation are necessary to strengthen the education and instructional environments we provide to students with EBD and their peers. The future of research to support the outcomes of students with EBD, their families, and their educators should embrace change and learn from our past by examining both the positives and the negatives. Leveraging new technologies like artificial intelligence (AI) and machine learning (ML), advances in research methodologies and designs, deeper understanding of barriers and facilitators of teacher retention, as well as contemporary assessment and measurement, while also recognizing the opportunities for reflection and change can coalesce toward a brighter future for students with EBD, their teachers, and their families.

AI and ML

It is inevitable that AI and ML models will make their way, if they haven't already, into every core aspect of education. Taking a planful approach to studying the benefits of AI-driven tools, assessments, and research technology as the opportunities to do so arise has the potential to rapidly and substantially reduce our reliance on human (and financial) resources while drastically improving reliability and, perhaps, validity of products and practitioner, administrator, and research outputs. Current work in this area includes using ML models and text-as-data methods to develop automated measures of teaching and instruction (Liu & Cohen, 2021) to reduce bias and differentiate between commonly used teaching constructions for evaluation purposes including classroom management, interactive instruction, and teacher-centered instruction. These methods are highly relevant for all teachers including those who support students with EBD given how often students with EBD are taught by general education teachers in general education settings.

Another approach that has the potential to change the landscape of EBD-focused research is building and applying AI models to improve the efficiency, reliability, and effectiveness of coaching interventions and professional development. To illustrate, developing automated tools that can precisely analyze and report out characteristics and quality of teacher talk in real time can have immediate and lasting impacts. One example relevant to research is the drastic reduction in resources needed for observation and transcription. This would take pressure off research teams (and their corresponding grants and budgets) to travel and conduct observations, and to transcribe audio data in a timely manner. This advancement can improve all types of research designs but may be uniquely advantageous for single-case design research given the need for data from observations to make phase change decisions. Research on teacher talk and teacher instructional quality overlaps well with the long history of research on teacher praise and reprimands. Current work on what teachers say and how they say it (Didion et al., 2023; Hollo et al., 2020) coupled with the power of AI models could be instrumental in understanding what works for which students with EBD given the substantial overlap between language processing and behavioral challenges (Chow, 2018).

Research Designs

Advances in research designs integrate the importance of individual differences and within-group variation to research design. These approaches include adaptive interventions, meta-analytic structural equation modeling, and network meta-analysis. Adaptive intervention designs retain the experimental rigor of randomized experiments while building in high-leverage, data- and theory-driven opportunities to allow for changes to the intervention as a function of individual participants and other units of analysis including groups, schools, characteristics, skills, or response to intervention (Chow & Hampton, 2018, 2022). They also allow researchers to isolate the effects of sequencing of components. There may also be a strategic opportunity to blend the fundamental concepts of group and single-case designs within the context of adaptive intervention frameworks. For example, in the case of sequential multiple-assignment randomized trials (SMARTs; Nahum-Shani & Almirall, 2019), researchers could design an intervention intensification strategy that uses individual single-case designs for students who are nonresponsive to initial treatment or a prior intervention strategy (Hampton & Chow, 2022). This approach aligns conceptually with multitiered systems of support frameworks, where students who are not making adequate progress in universal settings may need more intensive supports.

Network meta-analysis extends research synthesis methods by testing the value of individual study components in the context of the quantitative synthesis of intervention or program effects (see Seitidis et al., 2022). Prior to network meta-analysis and component network meta-analysis, meta-analyses were limited to synthesis of average effects of multicomponent interventions and moderators of the average treatment effects. With network meta-analytic models, syntheses have the capability to isolate the contributions of individual components within multicomponent interventions. For example, Leijten et al. (2022) reported that interventions with more behavior management content yielded the strongest effects of parent-focused interventions for reducing challenging behavior, yet the strongest combination of components for prevention-focused interventions were behavior management combined with self-management content. These methods are particularly relevant for improving outcomes for students with EBD, and understanding what works for whom, given that the multicomponent intervention approach is common for behavior-focused, school-based programming.

Well-Resourced Educational Ecosystems

To secure the future of students with EBD, we should commit to supporting teachers and the conditions in which they work with programmatic and financial investments. One way to do this is to focus on the roles administrators play in support teachers of students with EBD and to identify targets for intervention that are alterable as well as theoretically and practically malleable. To support outcomes for students with EBD and their teachers, we need to consider the broader ecosystem in which they are situated along with the constellation of inputs, demands, contextual factors, and power dynamics that are at play. There is important work being done on teacher burnout, turnover, and the working conditions of teachers of students with EBD (Bettini et al., 2019; Brunsting et al., 2023). Though much has gone into identifying problems in working conditions, future research that can have meaningful, positive impacts in the lives of students with EBD and their teachers should investigate practices that intervene not only at the teacher or classroom level, but at the administrative and system levels. Such research should measure outcomes that are proximal to the change deemed necessary to improve outcomes for students with EBD. For example, Gilmour and Sandilos (2023) provided an overview of collegial support, workload, professional development and in-service training, and areas of school safety as four high potential supports that may be particularly malleable to change by administrators.

Multidimensional Assessment

The area of assessment continues to be important in the scope of work supporting outcomes for students with EBD. There have been substantial efforts to improve screening and early identification of students who need additional behavioral supports addressing a range of challenges. One example is screening that is quick, reliable, and includes academic and social skills components for a more comprehensive picture of a student's strengths and potential challenges instead of focusing solely on behavior (see Kilgus et al., 2016). In young children, screening for key developmental domains like language simultaneously with behavior recognizes the efficiencies of supporting multiple developmental domains as well as the implications this has for policy and practice (Kaiser et al., 2022). This can help inform providers of key areas of need that can be addressed through an integrated, blended approach to early intervention and early childhood teacher professional development that supports language and social–emotional development (Cunningham et al., 2023). This is crucial for efforts in prevention, particularly given the economic costs of intensive intervention and the collateral effects of challenging behavior on teachers' emotions, instruction, self-efficacy, and overall well-being.

How Can We Maintain Tradition?

Education is not a stagnant entity, and neither is research. As we move into the future, we must maintain the tradition of responsiveness to societal change and contemporary needs of our students, their educators, and their families. We must continue to change, embracing novel ideas, to refine, build, and improve how we theorize, develop, test, interpret, and disseminate our knowledge of ways to identify and support individuals with EBD. Engaging in critical conversations that provide an avenue for multiple voices can drive a research agenda in the direction that best meets the needs of students and their communities. For example, researchers can spend the time, energy, and resources to truly grounding themselves within the community they aim to support as partners to build trust. Including community members in the development process of any intervention or program from its inception will promote interventions that best fit the community and are not simply an adaptation of a packaged intervention that was developed as a one-size-fits-all package without the specific community in mind.

We can also maintain tradition by ensuring that, at its core, special education continues to meet the individual needs of each child or student with EBD. As the field evolves and embraces new policies (e.g., inclusion), it is necessary to remember the need for specialized instruction that meets the educational needs of individual students. For example, there is evidence that the general education classroom does not support the learning outcomes as strongly as specialized, pull-out instruction (Fuchs et al., 2015). This may be particularly important for students with EBD because of common co-occurring challenges they face.

It may prove to be beneficial for us to respond to opportunities to approach EBD with more dimensionality regarding education and teacher training. For example, in the field of psychology, children who have elevated levels of anxiety are recognized for their specific needs with a designation of an anxiety disorder. Children who have elevated levels of defiance and/or aggression are recognized for their specific needs with a designation of conduct disorder or oppositional and defiant disorder. The term "disorder" and the medical model that is prevalent in psychology and psychiatry is deficit-oriented; however, the assessment and treatment children receive may be more tailored and focused based on the specific clinical label assigned to them. How does one define an evidence-based practice for individual students with EBD without taking into consideration the diverse dimensionality of "EBD"? In education, the label of EBD may be introducing some inefficiency and lack of alignment in educational and intervention decisions based on the "catch all" label for children with high anxiety as well as children who exhibit challenging and aggressive behaviors. Maintaining the tradition of specialized instruction that meets student needs and continuing to push the field to evolve and problem-solve ways to use data to ensure our systems and decisions enact positive change embraces the spirit of the origins of special education. Putting the needs of students first can be challenging in the context of a polarized, sociopolitical environment. Currently, authority figures and decision-makers appear to be more focused on what divides us and our differences than celebrating agreement and commonalities. Science needs to continue to be self-correcting, and the researchers who are responsible for scientific progress need to embrace this consequential responsibility.

SUPPORTING OUR COLLEAGUES

Colleen Eddy, Section Contributor

Teachers need to be sufficiently supported if we are to improve developmental settings in schools for youth with EBDs. When teachers are struggling to manage the demands of their roles, this can reduce their effectiveness in working with youth in many ways. Chronic stress in education has been a concern for decades (Kyriacou, 2001; Kyriacou & Sutcliffe, 1978). Yet, teaching conditions have worsened with teachers reporting higher stress along with lower abilities to cope (Herman et al., 2018, 2020a; Steiner & Woo, 2021). At the same time, mental health symptoms in youth have been increasing and exacerbated by the 2020 COVID-19 pandemic (Center for Disease Control and Prevention, 2023). This context is critical in considering ways to improve outcomes for youth with EBDs. There are effective strategies for training and supporting all teachers to reduce stress and increase well-being in the profession (von der Embse et al., 2019), and there are evidence-based interventions for working with students with EBDs. Yet in a context of too many demands and too few resources, effective interventions are not going to reach their full promise. The following section will review the problem of teacher burnout and turnover, the context of youth mental health, and recommendations for improving outcomes for students with EBDs and their teachers.

Teacher Burnout and Intentions to Leave

Teachers entering the field have intentions of making a difference for the better in the lives of students, but the many demands they face along with the limited perceived progress often leads to professional burnout (Maslach et al., 2001). Teachers balance many responsibilities simultaneously including the leading and differentiating academic instruction, managing student behaviors, and supporting the social–emotional development of every student in the classroom (Jennings & Greenberg, 2009; Kyriacou, 2001). There are many external demands including collaborating with colleagues, interacting with parents, and completing administrative tasks. The COVID-19 pandemic also increased stress by requiring a rapid shift to remote learning (Steiner & Woo, 2021). This change was especially challenging for special educators to meet individualized education plan (IEP) goals in a distance format (Mendoza et al., 2022). All of these elements can lead to a condition called "burnout."

Burnout is characterized by emotional exhaustion, depersonalization, and diminished personal accomplishment (Maslach et al., 2001). It can lead to depression, anxiety, and cardiovascular problems and can impair functioning in home and work settings (Agyapong et al., 2022; Moya-Albiol et al., 2010). Teachers who are experiencing burnout can be less effective at creating positive learning contexts for youth (Herman et al., 2018; Jennings & Greenberg, 2009). Burnout also contributes to increases in staff turnover and mobility (i.e., leaving positions) (Leung & Lee, 2006; Skaalvik & Skaalvik, 2011).

High turnover and mobility are detrimental for many reasons. Recruiting, hiring, training, and integrating new teachers into a school system require many resources (Watlington et al., 2010). Teachers who remain in positions are often left with more responsibilities and roles in assisting the teachers (likely having less experience) who are hired to replace those who have left. This cycle of high turnover and underqualified teachers can have harmful effects on the entire school climate, even reducing student achievement (Ronfeldt et al., 2013). Worse, there are higher turnover rates in districts with fewer resources and higher proportions of marginalized students based on racial identity, socioeconomic status, and students with disabilities (Watlington et al., 2010). According to a recent survey by the largest teachers' union in the United States, the National Education Association, 55% of teachers surveyed reported they were considering leaving the profession earlier than they anticipated (NEA, 2022). While initial predictions of widespread attrition after the 2020 pandemic may have been overstated (Goldhaber & Theobald, 2022), any increase in turnover is likely to have a disproportionately greater effect on special educators and students with EBDs (Espel et al., 2019; Gilmour & Wehby).

Teachers in special education are more likely to leave the profession, move to a different school, or change roles (i.e., switch from special education to general education with dual certification) in comparison to general education teachers (DeAngelis & Presley, 2011; Hopkins et al., 2019). Espel et al. (2019) reported that across multiple states, special education teachers were 72% more likely to leave their current positions in comparison to other educators. Further, having a greater percentage of students with EBDs in a classroom was associated with high odds of turnover across certification categories for teachers (Gilmour & Wehby, 2020). This is disruptive for consistent positive relationships when teachers who are working with vulnerable students are leaving their positions at higher rates.

Increases in EBDs

At the same time that teachers are experiencing high stress and may be considering leaving their positions, mental health for youth has been worsening, particularly for internalizing symptoms. Rates of depression, anxiety, suicide, and hospitalization due to nonsuicidal self-injurious behavior have been increasing since 2010 (Mercado et al., 2017; Plemmons et al., 2018; Shorey et al., 2021). Since the 2020 COVID-19 pandemic, rates of internalizing disorders have continued to rise, especially for adolescent girls and youth who identify as LGBTQ (Center for Disease Control and Prevention, 2023). Despite the increases in mental health symptoms, far fewer students are being evaluated and determined to be eligible for special education services due to an EBD (Mitchell et al.,

2019). While the increase in mental health symptoms may not be directly reflected in the prevalence of special education services, it is critical to consider because students with disabilities also likely experienced an increase in the presence and/or severity of symptoms (Mendoza et al., 2022).

Summary of Context and Recommendations

Overall, this context requires existing special educators to do more for their students with less support and fewer yet, more overburdened, teachers to share the load. Three components are recommended for teachers to effectively support youth with EBDs. First, teachers need ongoing training for using high-quality, evidence-based interventions to promote well-being of students with EBDs. Second, there needs to be a sufficient number of well-resourced special educators collaborating effectively with general educators, paraprofessionals, school psychologists, and other professionals to use these strategies. Third, teacher burnout and attrition need to be addressed through multiple levels of targeted interventions.

Training Recommendations

There are a variety of supports that can be bolstered for special educators and other professionals who work with students with EBDs. Induction into the profession is a particularly important time to prevent burnout and turnover (Gray & Taie, 2015). A mentorship model is common to assist preservice teachers as they enter the field and their first few years (Ellis et al., 2020). The effectiveness of mentorship can be improved by training mentors specifically for this role (Ellis et al., 2020) and having allocated time during the working hours to meet with mentees, instead of being added onto their existing demands (Deger et al., in press; Griffin et al., 2009). A consultation model can be beneficial and effective for ongoing professional development for teachers across their careers (DeFouw et al., 2022; Reinke et al., 2008). Since behavior management is commonly reported as a source of teacher stress (Haydon et al., 2018), ongoing performance feedback in this area is likely to benefit teachers and students with EBDs who may exhibit disruptive behaviors based on their diagnoses. Effective consultation models involve using motivational interviewing techniques to align with teachers and support their commitment to change while also supporting them with coaching and feedback in evidence-based cognitive-behavioral strategies (DeFouw et al., 2022). Finally, students with EBDs are likely to spend a great deal of the classroom day in general education setting, so they are also frequently interacting with teachers in general education (Mitchell et al., 2019); however, general education teachers report feeling ill-equipped to support students with mental health (Reinke et al., 2011; Stormont et al., 2023). This is a critical area to enhance as teacher preparation programs should ensure all teachers are better prepared to work with students with disabilities.

Evidence-Based Practices

Fortunately, evidence-based practices and systems that can benefit students with EBDs and broadly all students exist; yet, their effects depend upon fidelity of implementation. There are documented benefits to universal practices such as use of effective praise, increasing classroom engagement, clear classroom expectations, and established routines (Lewis et al., 2004). Ongoing screening efforts within multitiered systems of support may be especially beneficial in early identification of youth at risk for developing an EBD allowing for earlier intervention (Mitchell et al., 2019). Exclusionary discipline (i.e., suspension) is especially important to consider when supporting students with EBDs as they are at a greater risk of being suspended than students in general education and under other disability categories (Mitchell et al., 2019). An exacerbating factor is that when teachers are experiencing burnout, their students have greater odds of receive exclusionary discipline services, while accounting for student behavior (Eddy et al., 2020). Students with EBDs have documented disabilities, these practices should not be overused within this population.

Reducing Burnout and Turnover

Burnout and turnover in the teaching profession is a problem with many sources requiring systemic changes and intervention at multiple levels. Individual teachers in general and special education can be supported through programs aimed to reduce stress and improve coping with strategies based in psychological science (von der Embse et al., 2019). Some promising and cost-effective interventions are delivered through online or bibliotherapy formats and can reduce symptoms of depression and anxiety (Ansley et al., 2021; Eddy et al., 2022). Contextual changes are also critical to reducing demands and improving resources (Herman et al., 2020). At the administrative level, stress can be reduced by decreasing burdensome tasks that do not directly contribute to positive student outcomes and interfere with teachers' abilities to make a positive impact (Haydon et al., 2018). Given that stress and turnover are associated with high caseloads (Gilmour & Wehby, 2020), it is essential for school districts to prioritize sufficient staffing and retaining existing teachers.

Conclusion

While these contextual stressors facing special educators and students are overwhelming and there are many areas for improvement, there is hope in the profession. Even with high levels of stress, teachers report high levels of job satisfaction and fulfillment from the direct work with youth (Skaalvik & Skaalvik, 2015). There is also greater awareness and understanding of mental health symptoms and decades of research into school-based interventions that are effective in improving academic, behavioral, and social–emotional outcomes (Sanchez et al., 2018). Interventions to support teachers and students with EBDs should be given the opportunity for these promising effects to be realized.

CLARIFYING AND EMPLOYING OUR KNOWLEDGE BASE

John William McKenna, Section Contributor

Despite the provision of an IEP, students receiving special education services for EBD continue to be associated with concerning outcomes. Students with EBD have low levels of academic engagement (McKenna et al., 2021a), exhibit challenging behaviors that impact teaching and learning (Forness et al., 2012), have persistent academic difficulties (see Gage et al., 2017), and receive disciplinary exclusions at higher rates than any other student disability population (U.S Department of Education, 2022). These trends in school performance and their sequelae (e.g., transition outcomes; see Brigham et al., 2020) call into question the degree to which FAPE mandates are achieved for this student population (Yell, 2019). In the following section, areas for revitalized researcher, practitioner, consumer (e.g., students with EBD and their parents/guardians), and policymaker partnerships are made in consideration of (a) the purpose of special education, (b) misconceptions regarding its mission, and (c) the negative school and life trajectories among this student population.

Misconceptions in Special Education

Special education, particularly for students with EBD, needs significant effort at "rebranding" due to the proliferation of misconceptions and myths as well as some aspects of its historical context. In fact, special education would likely benefit from efforts to directly confront and remediate these misconceptions each and every time they are encountered. Special education may be associated with negative outcomes (e.g., segregation, warehousing, abuse, and the denial of opportunities) rather than the provision of specialized and individualized instruction and supports. But these are not the only outcomes that can be associated with receipt of special education services. Yes, there are historical examples of at best the denial of educational opportunities through the guise of special education, both in the past (Dunn, 1968; Vaughn et al., 1998) and in the present (Richards & Cohen, 2022). To improve special education for students with EBD, partnerships are needed to identify and disseminate information on model school practices. These efforts should connect characteristics of effective practice to the purpose and characteristics of a special education that is actually "special." In sum, when special education for students with EBD is observed to confer appropriate benefit in the areas of academics, behavior, and social–emotional skills, stakeholders should identify the systems, structures, resources, and educational team behaviors that contribute to this success, and disseminate this information to support replication and policy development. When practice is ineffective, efforts should be made to identify and describe the nature of these issues so that this information can be used to improve practice. In these instances, the focus should be on accountability while simultaneously employing an "all hands on deck" approach to improving the situation. Students with EBD as well as those that educate them are in need of assistance, and this assistance should be provided.

Identification of and Placement for Students With EBD

For students with EBD to receive an IEP, they must be first identified as a student with a disability associated with EBD. Our field has long attempted to obtain a more informed understanding of issues related to accurate and timely student identification (Forness et al., 2012; Kauffman & Landrum, 2009) based on the notion that improved identification methods may serve as a gateway to effective instruction and necessary support (McKenna, 2013). However, challenges with identification procedures have been noted for children who are culturally and linguistically diverse, those living in poverty, young, with internalizing disorders, and those who are at an intersectionality of these characteristics (McKenna et al., 2021b; Schoenfeld & Janney, 2008; Wiley et al., 2013). Deciding "who has it" and "who has enough" to warrant special education is likely to continue to be an issue for stakeholders to resolve. It is likely that there as yet unidentified children who are in need of services and supports that should be addressed through the development and implementation of an IEP that is appropriately individualized and addresses all areas of student need. For the tradition of special education for students with EBD to be maintained, we must improve the ability to identify those who require an IEP and then deliver on its promise.

Students with EBD require access to a full continuum of placement options that is viable (e.g., effective). Districts are mandated to consider the full continuum when determining a student's LRE, with placement decided after the other parts of the IEP are developed. To do otherwise would be predetermination, which is a FAPE violation (Yell et al., 2020). When determining LRE, it is assumed that most students with disabilities can be educated in general education classrooms with appropriate supports through inclusive models of instruction (Salend & Duhaney, 1999; Vaughn & Schumm, 1995) and tiered systems of support (McKenna et al., 2021a; Swanson et al., 2012). When IEP teams believe that students require instruction and/or support outside of general education for any amount of time, they are mandated to provide a justification (Yell et al., 2020). However, practitioners are not required to provide a justification for time spent in inclusive classrooms, which may contribute to instances in which students with EBD languish in general education classrooms in the absence of necessary supports (see Kauffman & Badar, 2016; McKenna et al., 2022a; Scruggs et al., 2007). Part of this issue may be an overreliance on general education placement and the belief that students with disabilities will benefit from improved access to the general education curriculum. However, there are misconceptions if not a stigma associated with more highly specialized school settings, which are commonly referred to as "substantially separate." This term, substantially separate, may evoke perceptions of racial segregation rather than the provision of specialized opportunities which is its true mission within the continuum. To address this issue, it may be advantageous for preservice training programs, policymakers, and in-service educators to refer to these educational environments as "dedicated school settings" (i.e., placements designed to provide highly specialized instruction and support to students who require it). These "dedicated settings" can provide opportunities for students with EBD to develop skills to better prepare them for success in less specialized educational settings and life, as well as support the transition to general education settings when they are ready to practice skill transfer and generalization (e.g., "old school" flexible resource room models of support).

Enhancing the Quality of Instruction

Researchers have expressed concerns with the quality of instruction and support that students with EBD receive across the continuum of placement options (McKenna et al., 2022b; Vaughn et al., 2002). Issues in teacher preparation and in-service training (State et al., 2019; Sutherland et al., 2005) as well as contextual factors that either impede or support teacher efforts to enact their training (Gilmour & Sandilos, 2023) and their relationship to teacher burnout and well-being (Granger et al., 2023; Scott et al., 2023) contribute to these phenomena. For preservice preparation, dual certification programs that provide minimal opportunities to develop knowledge and skill in specialized methods (example, three special education courses and a practicum within a 4-year undergraduate program) are insufficient to meet this challenge, particularly when the program has a noncategorical approach rather than a focus on students with EBD. Instead, preservice and in-service training should be based on what teachers of students with EBD need to know and be able to do in actual school settings (e.g., coherence between preparation and training and professional responsibilities). In regard to working conditions, the field is largely well-informed of factors that contribute to or prevent educator success with students with EBD. Efforts should be made to enact these lessons learned within practice so that more teachers and students with EBD teach and learn in conditions that support their mutual success. These contextual factors include, but are not limited to: administrator support, opportunities to collaborate with other professionals, access to curricular materials, clearly defined professional responsibilities, manageable workloads, and a consideration of the unique needs of educators who are culturally and/or linguistically diverse.

Maintaining a Strong Special Educator Workforce

Perhaps nothing is more critical to maintaining the tradition of providing specialized supports to students with EBD than having a sufficient pipeline of special educators. Despite its clear importance, special education teacher shortages continue and negatively affect school capacity to provide appropriate services to students with EBD. To have a viable continuum of placement options, there must be a sufficient pool of special educators with the training and professional and personal dispositions required to provide an appropriate education within each part of the continuum. It is easy to find districts and specialized schools for students with EBD that are forced to rely on persons with emergency teaching credentials and/or have positions that they are unable to fill. Thus, efforts to maintain the tradition of special education for students with EBD rely on efforts to effectively address the shortage of highly qualified special educators that better approximates the diversity of K-12 students. Increasing the quantity and quality of special educators require comprehensive initiatives focusing on recruitment, preservice and in-service training, and retention efforts. For example, mentoring can be provided to educators of students with EBD from recruitment, through preservice preparation, and into their early and later years as a professional, with the nature of mentoring activities changing and being more responsive to educator needs as they progress through the profession. Financial incentives, training coherence, working conditions, and efforts to promote educator well-being are likely to play interrelated and complementary roles to improve the pipeline of special educators ready and able to provide an appropriate education for students with EBD.

THE ROAD AHEAD AND THE WORK TO BE DONE

Nick Gage, Section Contributor

Special education is many things. It includes the tradition of specialized instruction and services designed for and delivered to students with disabilities as outlined in their IEP. It manifests the evolving tradition of legal protections afforded to students with disabilities, including the right to a free and appropriate education that is "reasonably calculated to enable a child to make progress appropriate in light of the child's circumstances" (Endrew, 2017, 137 S.Ct. at 1000). It is a funding mechanism for the resources necessary to ensure students with disabilities receive what they need. Fundamentally, it is a belief that all students, regardless of disability, can and should learn in the LRE.

Students with EBD may not benefit as much from special education and the legal protections afforded them as individuals with other kinds of disability conditions. The reasons for this are not simple or easily remedied. The purpose of this chapter is not doom and gloom, but to answer the second question. Every day, teachers and paraprofessionals as well as other school staff work tirelessly to support students with EBD and to make a lasting difference in their lives. For decades, researchers and scholars have examined, developed, and refined programs, interventions, and approaches to increase positive behavior, academic achievement, and wellness for students with EBD. Thus, there is a rich tradition of advocacy, research, scholarship, as well as field-based practice; yet, there remains much work to be done.

In 1976, Bob Marley released his song *War*, with lyrics taken almost verbatim from a 1963 speech by the Ethiopian Emperor Haile Selassie before the United Nations General Assembly. The speech, and subsequent song, is a rallying call for equality for all without regard to race, class, or nationality. In Marley's song lyrics, each verse ends with the word "war" to signify an ongoing struggle and fight to attain equality. To answer the questions posed in this chapter, I am going to use this song as inspiration. I have reworked each verse to briefly describe the factors I believe impact both access to and the success of special education, highlighting the historical and current context for each. Instead of "war", I call for more "work", because there is much work remaining to be done.

[Verse 1] *Until the belief that praising and rewarding children for appropriate behavior is manipulation and robs them of their 'creativity' is finally and permanently discredited and abandoned, everywhere is work.* In 1967, Becker et al. demonstrated that student problem behavior in classrooms could be meaningfully reduced by simply making classroom rules explicit, ignoring disruptive behaviors unless someone was getting hurt, and, critically, praising appropriate classroom behaviors. In the subsequent 50 plus years, numerous studies have demonstrated the power of contingent and specific praise for increasing appropriate behaviors and decreasing problem behaviors (Ennis et al., 2020; Royer et al., 2019). Praise creates positive classroom environments, motivates most students to learn, and is very easy to implement. Classrooms serving students with EBD should be full of praise, acknowledging and rewarding students for doing what they are supposed to be doing. Yet, for many years, research has shown that praise is rarely delivered, especially to students with EBD (Scott et al., 2017; Shores et al., 1993). One possible reason for the low rates of praise and other rewards for appropriate behavior is a belief that such "rewards" are manipulation, coercion, or bribery and do not help children develop intrinsic motivation (see Kohn, 1993). Typically, this belief is aligned with a constructivist perspective on teaching (Schunk, 2020).

Reinforcing appropriate behavior through rewards is a fundamental component of a behavioral approach to learning (Baer et al., 1968) and the foundation of positive behavior support (PBS; Carr et al., 2002). Functional behavior assessment (FBA) and subsequent behavior intervention plans (BIP), school-wide positive behavior interventions and supports (SWPBIS; Sugai & Horner, 2020), and most evidence-based classroom and behavior management approaches are based on these theories of learning. From this perspective, special education involves specialized instruction *and* ecological interventions, with an emphasis on direct and explicit teaching. To date, most evidence-based (Zaheer et al., 2019) and high-leverage practices (McLeskey et al., 2022) for students with EBD operate from a behavioral approach to learning that emphasizes PBS. Thus, general and special education teachers need to believe that positive reinforcement in the form of contingent praise and reward, when associated with the function of a behavior, can improve problem behaviors.

[Verse 2] *That until special education is no longer a place, but specialized instruction delivered in the LRE, and all effort is made to ensure students with EBD are in the general education classroom, everywhere there is work.* Special education is not a place. Special education is specialized instruction, legal protections, and a mechanism to fund the resources needed to meet an IEP. Yet, many students with disabilities are found in separate buildings and separate classrooms. Students with EBD are among the most likely to be educated in a separate or exclusionary settings of all of the different disability conditions (Williamson et al., 2020). According to the most recent IDEA Report to Congress (U.S. Department of Education, 2022), only students with deaf-blindness and multiple disabilities were more likely than students with EBD to be educated outside of their typical public school. In fact, only 50% of students with EBD spend the majority (80% or more) of their time inside a regular classroom. The data are clear, most students with EBD are not educated alongside their peers in general education settings.

It is important here to distinguish between the goal of creating environments that have the requisite behavior prevention and intervention systems in place to meet the needs of students with EBD and the full inclusion movement. Full inclusion, or radical inclusion, is the belief that students with disabilities, including those with EBD, should be educated in general education classrooms alongside their peers 100% of the time. This is not what I mean here. Lewis et al. (1994) addressed the significant problems with full inclusion and students with EBD 30 years ago. Now, the work that needs to be done is helping all teachers successfully develop behavior prevention and intervention systems. The LRE does not have to be a static thing. General and special educators can and should work together to increase the use of evidence-based classroom management skills, to enact ecological interventions, and to develop universally designed approaches for learning that increase the likelihood that students with EBD can be successfully educated alongside their peers.

[Verse 3] *That until special education services are equally guaranteed to all in need without regard for, or because of, race everywhere there is work.* Disproportionality continues to be a significant and critical challenge in education broadly and in special education specifically, especially for students with EBD. Disproportionality is the likelihood that an event, such as a suspension from school or identification for a disability, is more likely for one group than another (Gage, 2022). Statistically, Black students with disabilities are significantly more likely to be suspended from school, receive a restraint, be secluded, experience corporal punishment, or be arrested in school (Gage et al., 2022). Black students are also significantly more likely to be identified for special education services for EBD than other disability categories. At the national level, Black students are 80% more likely to be identified as having EBD than students of other races (U.S. Department of Education, 2022). Conversely, Morgan et al. (2015) found that, when the academic and behavioral profiles of students are considered, Black students may be under-identified. This suggests that Black students are being denied the specialized instruction they need. However, this research is not without controversy and disagreement (Skiba et al., 2016). Regardless, issues of race and disproportionality remain challenging and require continued study, understanding, attention, and development of solutions.

[Verse 4] *That until the day special education is integrated and interconnected with mental health services and wrap around programs, the dream of lifelong success for students with EBD will remain but a fleeting illusion to be pursued but never attained...now everywhere is work.* Special educators alone cannot fully remediate the challenges faced by students with EBD. Not only do students with EBD present myriad academic and behavioral challenges, but they also experience or have experienced significant adverse childhood experiences that exacerbate efforts to remediate academic and behavioral challenges (Bomysoad & Francis, 2020). Calls for in-school and wraparound mental health support are not new. From the innovations of Project Re-Ed in the 1960s and 1970s (Hobbs, 1983) to the wraparound programs of the 1990s and 2000s (Eber et al., 1997;

Olson et al., 2021), many different approaches have been proposed and tested. Yet, few have been successfully scaled for broad implementation and impact. There is, however, one newer approach, the interconnected systems framework (ISF), which brings together SWPBIS with school mental health services (Weist et al., 2022). ISF is designed to bring community-based mental health services into schools and for mental health teams to be integrated into SWPBIS teams. Importantly, SWPBIS is currently implemented in over 20,000 schools across the globe (Sugai & Horner, 2020); therefore, a solid base appears to be in place for bringing IFS to scale.

The special education of students with EBD has a long history of success, but much work remains. I've highlighted four major issues that I believe need to be the focus of research and practice. Tireless efforts of educators and scholars continue, but there is work to be done.

LOOKING FORWARD TOGETHER

Across four independent scholars, each with a slightly different perspective and research agenda, a remarkable consistency emerges. The essays in this chapter are united in the belief that the future of special education for students with EBD will rely on individualized and specialized adaptations, harnessing the potential of new technologies – while recognizing that technology itself is no panacea – to improve student-focused interventions and teacher preparation. Further, the field will need to continuously evolve in response to societal changes, the unique needs of students, teachers, and families, and community involvement in the development of interventions and programs.

Teacher preparation is a critical theme addressed by the contributors. The use of AI and ML may assist with automated teaching tools designed to reduce bias, enhance classroom management, improve instructional evaluation, and identify sources of variance. It should be noted that the promises of ML remain for the most part unrealized. Nevertheless, "...the digital classroom is imminent, and the computational future for teaching and learning is inescapable" (Watters, 2021, p. 11). Further, teacher preparation that dispels misconceptions about the utility of praise, investigates disproportionate rates of identification, and centers the unique experiences of students with EBD, is vital. Given the high turnover rates for teachers of students with EBD, the adequacy of the training programs for many currently working with these students is questionable.

Although teachers have reported high satisfaction in their career, teacher burnout and high levels of stress are prevalent, particularly in special education. These issues contribute to high turnover rates and reduced student achievement. The solutions suggested in this chapter included more coherent preservice and in-service training programs, and initiatives focusing on recruitment, training, and retention of special educators. Additional recommendations to tackle teacher burnout include ongoing training on high-quality interventions, increased collaboration between special educators and other education professionals, and multi-level interventions to address teacher attrition. These strategies, coupled with the potential of AI and ML, may help reshape the landscape of special education, especially in the context of EBD.

Issues of placement for students with EBD highlight the need for the development of effective behavioral prevention and intervention systems. There is also an urgent need for better integration of mental health services within special education due to the numerous challenges faced by students with EBD. This could potentially be addressed by frameworks combining school-wide positive behavior interventions with school mental health services.

The changing nature of the conditions of practice for our field is not really new. Nor are they restricted to education. In 2002, political scientist, Richard Claude wrote:

> In a dynamic society, it is impossible to draw a strict line between science and the tides of social change. They overlap, and if it is argued that science is value-free the same cannot be said of scientists. If scientific freedom is half the operative equation, responsibility is the other half. Where trouble comes is in identifying the issues on which scientists should take a stand and in defending the legitimacy of such interventions. Perhaps the only rules to go by are the well-formed conscience and the informed expression of convictions protected by free speech and robust debate. Therein lies the importance, indeed the necessity, for scientists occasionally to take on the mantle of activist. (Claude, 2002, p. 145)

Thus, just as researchers should occasionally adopt the role of activists, special education teachers, too, should be prepared to advocate for their students, especially those with EBD. Such advocacy requires a critical understanding of educational policies, practices, and the unique challenges faced by students with EBD. Additionally, school administrators bear responsibility for maintaining schools that are supportive of teachers as opposed to the environments that are associated to frequent teacher turn over.

Teachers should be equipped with the latest research-based strategies for inclusive education but should also be encouraged to question and contribute to these strategies based on their direct experiences and observations in the classroom. Additionally, researchers specializing on students with EBD need to be acutely aware of the practical implications of their research and the potential for it to either perpetuate or challenge existing inequities. They also need to be prepared to defend their research and engage in debates about its implications, relevance, and application in the real world. Parties on both sides of the research to practice gap bear responsibility in its resolution.

Education stakeholders, including special education teachers and researchers, are increasingly recognizing their roles as agents of social change. They are expected to take a stand on important issues impacting special education, such as funding, accessibility, and inclusivity, and defend the rights and opportunities of their students in both policy and practice. We believe this activism is also deeply entrenched in the future of special education, especially for students with EBD. It is the heart of optimistic dissatisfaction.

REFERENCES

Agyapong, B., Obuobi-Donkor, G., Burback, L., & Wei, Y. (2022). Stress, burnout, anxiety and depression among teachers: A scoping review. *International Journal of Environmental Research and Public Health, 19*(17), 10706. https://doi.org/10.3390/ijerph191710706

Ansley, B. M., Houchins, D. E., Varjas, K., Roach, A., Patterson, D., & Hendrick, R. (2021). The impact of an online stress intervention on burnout and teacher efficacy. *Teaching and Teacher Education, 98*, 103251. https://doi.org/10.1016/j.tate.2020.103251

Baer, D. M., Wolf, M. M., & Risley, T. R. (1968). Some current dimensions of applied behavior analysis. *Journal of Applied Behavior Analysis, 1*(1), 91. https://doi.org/10.1901/jaba.1968.1-91

Becker, W. C., Madsen, C. H., Arnold, C. R., & Thomas, D. R. (1967). The contingent use of teacher attention and praise in reducing classroom behavior problems. *Journal of Special Education, 1*, 287–307. https://doi.org/10.1177/00224669670010030

Berlant, L. G. (2011). *Cruel optimism*. Duke University Press.

Bettini, E., Wang, J., Cumming, M., Kimerling, J., & Schutz, S. (2019). Special educators' experiences of roles and responsibilities in self-contained classes for students with emotional/behavioral disorders. *Remedial and Special Education, 40*(3), 177–191. https://doi.org/10.1177/0741932518762470

Bomysoad, R. N., & Francis, L. A. (2020). Adverse childhood experiences and mental health conditions among adolescents. *Journal of Adolescent Health, 67*(6), 868–870. https://doi.org/10.1016/j.jadohealth.2020.04.013

Brigham, F. J. (2011). Optimistic dissatisfaction: A summary of group discussion on ways to better serve students with emotional disabilities. In I. Walker-Bolton, R. A. Gable, S. W. Tonelson, P. Woolard, & M. K. Gable (Eds.), *Summit on better serving students with emotional disabilities* (pp. 36–41). Virginia Department of Education.

Brigham, F., McKenna, J., & Brigham, M. (2020). Memories of the warmth: Transition for students with emotional and/or behavioral disorders. In J. Bakken & F. Obiakor (Eds.), *Special education transition services for students with disabilities. Advances in special education* (Vol. 35, pp. 35–52). Emerald Publishing Limited. https://doi.org/10.1108/S0270-401320190000035007

Brunsting, N. C., Bettini, E., Rock, M., Common, E. A., Royer, D. J., Lane, K. L., . . . Zeng, F. (2023). Working conditions and burnout of special educators of students with EBD: Longitudinal outcomes. *Teacher Education and Special Education, 46*(1), 44–64. https://doi.org/10.1177/08884064221076159

Buchanan, I. (2018a). *Futurism*. Oxford University Press. https://www.oxfordreference.com/view/10.1093/acref/9780198794790.001.0001/acref-9780198794790-e-276. https://doi.org/10.1093/acref/9780198794790.013.0276

Buchanan, I. (2018b). *Futurology*. https://www.oxfordreference.com/view/10.1093/acref/9780198794790.001.0001/acref-9780198794790-e-277. https://doi.org/10.1093/acref/9780198794790.013.0277

Carr, E. G., Dunlap, G., Horner, R. H., Koegel, R. L., Turnbull, A. P., Sailor, W., Anderson, J. L., Albin, R. W., Koegel, L. K., & Fox, L. (2002). Positive behavior support: Evolution of an applied science. *Journal of Positive Behavior Interventions, 4*(1), 4–16. https://doi.org/10.1177/109830070200400102

Center for Disease Control and Prevention. (2023). *Youth risk behavior survey 2011–2021: Data summary and trends report*. https://www.cdc.gov/healthyyouth/data/yrbs/pdf/YRBS_Data-Summary-Trends_Report2023_508.pdf

Chow, J. C. (2018). Comorbid language and behavior problems: Development, frameworks, and intervention. *School Psychology Quarterly, 33*(3), 356–360. https://doi.org/10.1037/spq0000270

Chow, J. C., & Hampton, L. H. (2018). Sequential multiple-assignment randomized trials: Developing and evaluating adaptive interventions in special education. *Remedial and Special Education, 40*(5), 267–276. https://doi.org/10.1177/0741932518759422

Chow, J. C., & Hampton, L. H. (2022). A systematic review of sequential multiple-assignment randomized trials in educational research. *Educational Psychology Review, 34*(3), 1343–1369. https://doi.org/10.1007/s10648-022-09660-x

Claude, R. P. (2002). *Science in the service of human rights*. University of Pennsylvania Press.

Cunningham, J. E., Chow, J. C., Meeker, K. A., Taylor, A., Hemmeter, M. L., & Kaiser, A. P. (2023). A conceptual model for a blended intervention approach to support early language and social-emotional development in toddler classrooms. *Infants & Young Children, 36*(1), 53–73. https://doi.org/10.1097/IYC.0000000000000232

DeAngelis, K. J., & Presley, J. B. (2011). Toward a more nuanced understanding of new teacher attrition. *Education and Urban Society, 43*(5), 598–626. https://doi.org/10.1177/0013124510380724

DeFouw, E. R., Owens, J. S., Margherio, S. M., & Evans, S. (2022). Supporting teachers' use of classroom management strategies via different school-based consultation models: Which is more cost-effective for whom? *School Psychology Review, 1–16.* Advance online publication. https://doi.org/10.1080/2372966X.2022.2087476

Deger, G. K., Moore, M., Riden, B., & Taylor, J. (in press). Behavior, paperwork, instruction, and supervision…oh my!: A review of the literature on mentorship for teachers of children with ebd. *Journal of Emotional and Behavioral Disorders.*

Didion, L., Filderman, M. J., Roberts, G., Benz, S. A., & Olmstead, C. L. (2023). Using audio recordings to reliably and efficiently observe teacher behavior related to explicit instruction. *Assessment for Effective Intervention, 48*(4). https://doi.org/10.1177/15345084221148202

Dunn, L. (1968). Special education for the mildly retarded- Is much of it justifiable? *Exceptional Children, 35*(1), 5–22. https://doi.org/10.1177/001440296803500101

Eber, L., Nelson, C. M., & Miles, P. (1997). School-based wraparound for students with emotional and behavioral challenges. *Exceptional Children, 63*(4), 539–555. https://doi.org/10.1177/001440299706300414

Eddy, C. L., Herman, K. C., Huang, F. L., & Reinke, W. M. (2022). Evaluation of a bibliotherapy-based stress intervention for teachers. *Teaching and Teacher Education, 109,* 103543. https://doi.org/10.1016/j.tate.2021.103543

Eddy, C. L., Huang, F. L., Cohen, D. R., Baker, K. M., Edwards, K. D., Herman, K. C., & Reinke, W. M. (2020). Does teacher emotional exhaustion and efficacy predict student discipline sanctions? *School Psychology Review, 49*(3), 239–255. https://doi.org/10.1080/2372966X.2020.1733340

Ellis, N. J., Alonzo, D., & Nguyen, H. T. M. (2020). Elements of a quality pre-service teacher mentor: A literature review. *Teaching and Teacher Education, 92,* 103072. https://doi.org/10.1016/j.tate.2020.103072

Emba, C. (2023, March 7). For a snapshot of the culture wars. watch a school board meeting. *The Washington Post.* https://www.washingtonpost.com/opinions/2023/03/07/loudoun-county-school-board-meeting-public-comments/

Endrew F. v. Douglas County School District, 580 U.S. ____ (2017).

Ennis, R. P., Royer, D. J., Lane, K. L., & Dunlap, K. D. (2020). Behavior-specific praise in pre-k–12 settings: Mapping the 50-year knowledge base. *Behavioral Disorders, 45*(3), 131–147. https://doi.org/10.1177/0198742919843075

Espel, E. V., Meyer, S. J., & Weston-Sementelli, J. L. (2019). *Factors related to teacher mobility and attrition in Colorado, Missouri, and South Dakota (REL-2019-008).* U.S. Department of Education, Institute of Education Sciences, National Center for Education Evaluation and Regional Assistance, Regional Educational Laboratory Central. https://ies.ed.gov/ncee/edlabs/regions/central/pdf/REL_2019008.pdf

Fernandez, A. L. (2021, August 23). School COVID mask rules have sparked parent-teacher violence. We can't ignore it. *NBC News.* https://www.nbcnews.com/think/opinion/school-covid-mask-rules-have-sparked-parent-teacher-violence-we-ncna1277415

Forness, S., Freeman, S., Paparella, T., Kauffman, J., & Walker, H. (2012). Special education implications of point and cumulative prevalence for children with emotional or behavioral disorders. *Journal of Emotional and Behavioral Disorders, 20*(1), 4–18. https://doi.org/10.1177/1063426611401624

Fuchs, L. S., Fuchs, D., Compton, D. L., Wehby, J., Schumacher, R. F., Gersten, R., & Jordan, N. C. (2015). Inclusion versus specialized intervention for very-low-performing students: What does access mean in an era of academic challenge? *Exceptional Children, 81*(2), 134–157. https://doi.org/10.1177/0014402914551743

Gage, N. A. (2022). Methodological issues and debates in the study of disproportionality in education. In N. A. Gage, L. J. Rapa, D. K. Whitford, & A. Katsiyannis (Eds.), *Disproportionality and social justice in education* (pp. 75–98). Springer.

Gage, N., Adamson, R., MacSuga-Gage, A., & Lewis, T. (2017). The relation between the academic achievement of students with emotional and behavioral disorders and teacher characteristics. *Behavioral Disorders, 43*(1), 213–222. https://doi.org/10.1177/0198742917713211

Gage, N. A., Rapa, L. J., Whitford, D. K., & Katsiyannis, A. (2022). *Disproportionality and social justice in education.* Springer.

Gilmour, A. F., & Sandilos, L. (2023). The crucial role of administrators in shaping working conditions for teachers of students with EBD. *Journal of Emotional and Behavioral Disorders, 31*(2), 109–119. https://doi.org/10.1177/10634266221149933

Gilmour, A. F., & Wehby, J. H. (2020). The association between teaching students with disabilities and teacher turnover. *Journal of Educational Psychology, 112*(5), 1042–1060. https://doi.org/10.1037/edu0000394

Goldhaber, D., & Theobald, D. R. (2022). Teacher attrition and mobility over time. *Educational Researcher, 51*(3), 235–237. https://doi.org/10.3102/0013189X211060840

Gorbis, M. (2019). *5 principles for thinking like a futurist.* https://er.educause.edu/articles/2019/3/five-principles-for-thinking-like-a-futurist

Granger, K., Sutherland, K., Conroy, M., Dear, E., & Morse, A. (2023). Teacher burnout and supporting teachers of students with emotional and behavioral disorders. *Journal of Emotional and Behavioral Disorders.* Advance online publication. https://doi.org/10.1177/10634266221149970

Gray, L., & Taie, S. (2015). *Public school teacher attrition and mobility in the first five years: Results from the first through fifth waves of the 2007–08 beginning teacher longitudinal study (NCES 2015-337).* National Center for Education Statistics, U.S. https://nces.ed.gov/pubs2015/2015337.pdf

Griffin, C. C., Kilgore, K. L., Winn, J. A., Otis-Wilborn, A., Hou, W., & Garvan, C. W. (2009). First year special educators: The influence of school and classroom context factors on their accomplishments and problems. *Teacher Education and Special Education, 32*(1), 45–63. http://doi.org/10.1177/0888406408330870

Hampton, L. H., & Chow, J. C. (2022). Deeply tailoring adaptive interventions: Enhancing knowledge generation of SMARTs in special education. *Remedial and Special Education, 43*(3), 195–205. https://doi.org/10.1177/07419325211030669

Haydon, T., Stevens, D., & Leko, M. M. (2018). Teacher stress: Sources, effects, and protective factors. *Journal of Special Education Leadership, 31*(2), 99–107. https://www.researchgate.net/profile/Todd-Haydon/publication/327703860_Teacher_Stress_Sources_Effects_and_Protective_Factors/links/5b9ff5c292851ca9ed11ae5e/Teacher-Stress-Sources-Effects-and-Protective-Factors.pdf

Herman, K. C., Hickman-Rosa, J., & Reinke, W. M. (2018). Empirically derived profiles of teacher stress, burnout, self-efficacy, and coping and associated student outcomes. *Journal of Positive Behavior Interventions, 20*(2), 90–100. https://doi.org/10.1177/1098300717732066

Herman, K. C., Prewett, S. L., Eddy, C. L., Savala, A., & Reinke, W. M. (2020). Profiles of middle school teacher stress and coping: Concurrent and prospective correlates. *Journal of School Psychology, 78,* 54–68. https://doi.org/10.1016/j.jsp.2019.11.003

Herman, K. C., Reinke, W. M., & Eddy, C. L. (2020). Advances in understanding and intervening in teacher stress and coping: The coping-competence-context theory. *Journal of School Psychology, 78,* 69–74. https://doi.org/10.1016/j.jsp.2020.01.001

Hobbs, N. (1983). Project Re-ED: From demonstration project to nationwide program. *Peabody Journal of Education, 60*(3), 8–24. https://doi.org/10.1080/01619568309538403

Hollo, A., Staubitz, J. L., & Chow, J. C. (2020). Applying generalizability theory to optimize analysis of spontaneous teacher talk in elementary classrooms. *Journal of Speech, Language, and Hearing Research, 63*(6), 1947–1957. https://doi.org/10.1044/2020_JSLHR-19-00118

Hopkins, M., Bjorklund, P., Jr., & Spillane, J. P. (2019). The social side of teacher turnover: Closeness and trust among general and special education teachers in the United States. *International Journal of Educational Research, 98,* 292–302. https://doi.org/10.1016/j.ijer.2019.08.020

Jennings, P. A., & Greenberg, M. T. (2009). The prosocial classroom: Teacher social and emotional competence in relation to student and classroom outcomes. *Review of Educational Research, 79*(1), 491–525. https://doi.org/10.3102/0034654308325693

Kaiser, A. P., Chow, J. C., & Cunningham, J. E. (2022). A case for early language and behavior screening: Implications for policy and child development. *Policy Insights from the Behavioral and Brain Sciences, 9*(1), 120–128. https://doi.org/10.1177/23727322211068886

Kauffman, J., & Badar, J. (2016). It's instruction over place- not the other way around. *Phi Delta Kappan, 98*(4), 55–59. https://doi.org/10.1177/0031721716681778

Kauffman, J., & Landrum, T. (2009). Politics, civil rights, and disproportional identification of students with emotional and behavioral disorders. *Exceptionality, 17*(4), 177–188. https://doi.org/10.1080/09362830903231903

Kilgus, S. P., Eklund, K., von der Embse, N. P., Taylor, C. N., & Sims, W. A. (2016). Psychometric defensibility of the social, academic, and emotional behavior risk screener (SAEBRS) teacher rating scale and multiple gating procedure within elementary and middle school samples. *Journal of School Psychology, 58*, 21–39. https://doi.org/10.1016/j.jsp.2016.07.001

Kohn, A. (1993). *Punished by rewards: The trouble with gold stars, incentive plans, A's, praise, and other bribes.* Houghton Milton Harcourt.

Kyriacou, C. (2001). Teacher stress: Directions for future research. *Educational Review, 53*(1), 27–35. https://doi.org/10.1080/00131910120033628

Kyriacou, C., & Sutcliffe, J. (1978). A model of teacher stress. *Educational Studies, 4*(1), 1–6. https://doi.org/10.1080/0305569780040101

Leijten, P., Melendez-Torres, G. J., & Gardner, F. (2022). Research review: The most effective parenting program content for disruptive child behavior–A network meta-analysis. *Journal of Child Psychology and Psychiatry, 63*(2), 132–142. https://doi.org/10.1111/jcpp.13483

Leung, D. Y. P., & Lee, W. W. S. (2006). Predicting intention to quit among Chinese teachers: Differential predictability of the components of burnout. *Anxiety, Stress and Coping. An International Journal, 19*(2), 129–141. https://doi.org/10.1080/10615800600565476

Lewis, T. J., Chard, D., & Scott, T. M. (1994). Full inclusion and the education of children and youth with emotional and behavioral disorders. *Behavioral Disorders, 19*(4), 277–293. https://doi.org/10.1177/019874299401900404

Lewis, T. J., Hudson, S., Richter, M., & Johnson, N. (2004). Scientifically supported practices in emotional and behavioral disorders: A proposed approach and brief review of current practices. *Behavioral Disorders, 29*(3), 247–259. https://doi.org/10.1177/019874290402900306

Liu, J., & Cohen, J. (2021). Measuring teaching practices at scale: A novel application of text-as-data methods. *Educational Evaluation and Policy Analysis, 43*(4), 587–614. https://doi.org/10.3102/0162373721009267

Maslach, C., Schaufeli, W. B., & Leiter, M. P. (2001). Job burnout. *Annual Review of Psychology, 52*, 397–422. https://doi.org/10.1146/annurev.psych.52.1.397

McKenna, J. W. (2013). The disproportionate representation of African Americans in programs for students with emotional and behavioral disorders. *Preventing School Failure, 57*(4), 206–211. https://doi.org/10.1080/1045988X.2012.687792

McKenna, J. W., Adamson, R., & Solis, M. (2021). Reading instruction for students with emotional disturbance: A mixed methods investigation. *Behavior Modification, 45*(3), 399–437. https://doi.org/10.1080/09362830903231903

McKenna, J. W., Brigham, F., Garwood, J., Zurawski, L., Koc, M., Lavin, C., & Werunga, R. (2021). A systematic review of intervention studies for young children with emotional and behavioral disorders: Identifying the research base. *Journal of Research in Special Educational Needs, 21*(2), 120–145. https://doi.org/10.1111/1471-3802.12505

McKenna, J., Garwood, J., & Solis, M. (2022). Reading instruction for students with and at risk for emotional and behavioral disorders: A synthesis of observation research. *Journal of Behavioral Education, 31*, 1–27. https://doi.org/10.1007/s10864-020-09425-y

McKenna, J. W., Newton, X., Brigham, F., & Garwood, J. (2022). Inclusive instruction for students with emotional disturbance: An investigation of classroom practice. *Journal of Emotional and Behavioral Disorders, 30*(1), 29–43. https://doi.org/10.1177/1063426620982601

McLeskey, J., Maheady, L., Billingsley, B., Brownell, M. T., & Lewis, T. J. (Eds.). (2022). *High leverage practices for inclusive classrooms*. Routledge.

Mendoza, M. E., Brewer, T. F., Smith, M. S., Stein, M. A., & Heymann, S. J. (2022). Lessons from United States school district policies and approaches to special education during the COVID-19 pandemic. *International Journal of Inclusive Education*, 1–20. Advance online publication. https://doi.org/10.1080/13603116.2022.2056643

Mercado, M. C., Holland, K., Leemis, R. W., Stone, D. M., & Wang, J. (2017). Trends in emergency department visits for nonfatal self-inflicted injuries among youth aged 10 to 24 years in the United States, 2001–2015. *JAMA: Journal of the American Medical Association, 318*(19), 1931–1933. https://doi.org/10.1001/jama.2017.13317

Mitchell, B. S., Kern, L., & Conroy, M. A. (2019). Supporting students with emotional or behavioral disorders: State of the field. *Behavioral Disorders, 44*(2), 70–84. https://doi.org/10.1177/0198742918816518

Morgan, P. L., Farkas, G., Hillemeier, M. M., Mattison, R., Maczuga, S., Li, H., & Cook, M. (2015). Minorities are disproportionately underrepresented in special education: Longitudinal evidence across five disability conditions. *Educational Researcher, 44*(5), 278–292. https://doi.org/10.3102/0013189X15591157

Moya-Albiol, L., Serrano, M. Á., & Salvador, A. (2010). Burnout as an important factor in the psychophysiological responses to a work day in teachers. *Stress and Health: Journal of the International Society for the Investigation of Stress, 26*(5), 382–393. https://doi.org/10.1002/smi.1309

Nahum-Shani, I., & Almirall, D. (2019). *An introduction to adaptive interventions and SMART designs in education (NCSER 2020-001)*. U.S. Department of Education. National Center for Special Education Research. https://ies.ed.gov/ncser/pubs/

National Center for Education Statistics. (2022). *Students with disabilities*. https://nces.ed.gov/programs/coe/indicator/cgg/students-with-disabilities

Olson, J. R., Benjamin, P. H., Azman, A. A., Kellogg, M. A., Pullmann, M. D., Suter, J. C., & Bruns, E. J. (2021). Systematic review and meta-analysis: Effectiveness of wraparound care coordination for children and adolescents. *Journal of the American Academy of Child & Adolescent Psychiatry, 60*(11), 1353–1366. https://doi.org/10.1016/j.jaac.2021.02.022

Plemmons, G., Hall, M., Doupnik, S., Gay, J., Brown, C., Browning, W., Casey, R., Freundlich, K., Johnson, D. P., Lind, C., Rehm, K., Thomas, S., & Williams, D. (2018). Hospitalization for suicide ideation or attempt: 2008–2015. *Pediatrics, 141*(6), 1–10. https://doi.org/10.1542/peds.2017-2426

Reinke, W. M., Lewis-Palmer, T., & Merrell, K. (2008). The classroom check-up: A class wide teacher consultation model for increasing praise and decreasing disruptive behavior. *School Psychology Review, 37*(3), 315–332. https://doi.org/10.1080/02796015.2008.12087879

Reinke, W. M., Stormont, M., Herman, K. C., Puri, R., & Goel, N. (2011). Supporting children's mental health in schools: Teacher perceptions of needs, roles, and barriers. *School Psychology Quarterly, 26*(1), 1–13. https://doi.org/10.1037/a0022714

Richards, J., & Cohen, J. (2022). *The school that calls the police on students every other day*. ProPublica and the Chicago Tribune. https://www.propublica.org/article/students-police-arrests-illinois-garrison-school

Robbins, A. (2023). *The teachers: A year inside America's most vulnerable, important profession* (1st ed.). Dutton.

Ronfeldt, M., Loeb, S., & Wyckoff, J. (2013). How teacher turnover harms student achievement. *American Educational Research Journal, 50*(1), 4–36. https://doi.org/10.3102/0002831212463813

Royer, D. J., Lane, K. L., Dunlap, K. D., & Ennis, R. P. (2019). A systematic review of teacher-delivered behavior-specific praise on k–12 student performance. *Remedial and Special Education, 40*(2), 112–128. https://doi.org/10.1177/0741932517751054

Salend, S., & Duhaney, L. (1999). The impact of inclusion on students with and without disabilities and their educators. *Remedial and Special Education, 20*(2), 114–126. https://doi.org/10.1177/074193259902000209

Sanchez, A. L., Cornacchio, D., Poznanski, B., Golik, A. M., Chou, T., & Comer, J. S. (2018). The effectiveness of school-based mental health services for elementary-aged children: A meta-analysis. *Journal of the American Academy of Child & Adolescent Psychiatry, 57*(3), 153–165. https://doi.org/10.1016/j.jaac.2017.11.022

Schoenfeld, N., & Janney, D. (2008). Identification and treatment of anxiety in students with emotional or behavioral disorders: A review of the literature. *Education and Treatment of Children, 31*(4), 583–610. https://doi.org/10.1353/etc.0.0034

Schunk, D. H. (2020). *Learning theories: An educational perspective.* (8th ed.). Pearson.

Scott, L., Bettini, E., & Brunsting, N. (2023). Special education teachers of color burnout, working conditions, and recommendations for research. *Journal of Emotional and Behavioral Disorders.* Advance online publication. https://doi.org/10.1177/10634266221146495

Scott, T. M., Hirn, R., & Cooper, J. (2017). *Teacher and student behaviors: Keys to success in classroom instruction.* Rowman & Littlefield.

Scruggs, T., Mastroieri, M., & McDuffie, K. (2007). Co-teaching in inclusive classrooms: A meta-synthesis of qualitative research. *Exceptional Children, 73*(4), 392–416. https://doi.org/10.1177/001440290707300401

Seitidis, G., Nikolakopoulos, S., Hennessy, E. A., Tanner-Smith, E. E., & Mavridis, D. (2022). Network meta-analysis techniques for synthesizing prevention science evidence. *Prevention Science, 23*(3), 415–424. https://doi.org/10.1007/s11121-021-01289-6

Shores, R. E., Jack, S. L., Gunter, P. L., Ellis, D. N., DeBriere, T. J., & Wehby, J. H. (1993). Classroom interactions of children with behavior disorders. *Journal of Emotional and Behavioral Disorders, 1*, 27–39. https://doi.org/10.1177/106342669300100l

Shorey, S., Ng, E. D., & Wong, C. H. (2021). Global prevalence of depression and elevated depressive symptoms among adolescents: A systematic review and meta-analysis. *The British Journal of Clinical Psychology, 61*(2), 287–305. https://doi.org/10.1111/bjc.12333

Skaalvik, E. M., & Skaalvik, S. (2011). Teacher job satisfaction and motivation to leave the teaching profession: Relations with school context, feeling of belonging, and emotional exhaustion. *Teaching and Teacher Education, 27*(6), 1029–1038. https://doi.org/10.1016/j.tate.2011.04.001

Skaalvik, E. M., & Skaalvik, S. (2015). Job satisfaction, stress and coping strategies in the teaching profession-what do teachers say? *International Education Studies, 8*(3), 181–192. http://doi.org/10.5539/ies.v8n3p181

Skiba, R. J., Artiles, A. J., Kozleski, E. B., Losen, D. J., & Harry, E. G. (2016). Risks and consequences of oversimplifying educational inequities: A response to Morgan et al. (2015). *Educational Researcher, 45*(3), 221–225. https://doi.org/10.3102/0013189X1664460

State, T., Simonsen, B., Hirn, R., & Wills, H. (2019). Bridging the research-to-practice gap through effective professional development for teachers working with students with emotional and behavioral disorders. *Behavioral Disorders, 44*(2), 107–116. https://doi.org/10.1177/0198742918816447

Steiner, E., & Woo, A. (2021). *Job-related stress threatens the teacher supply. Key findings from the 2021 State of the U.S. Teacher Survey.* RAND Corporation. https://www.rand.org/pubs/research_reports/RRA1108-1.html

Stormont, M., Herman, K. C., Eddy, C. L., Yang, W., Sebastian, J., & Reinke, W. M. (2023, February 3–8). *Teacher stress and well-being: Understanding the impact and intervening [Symposium].* NASP 2023 Convention, Denver, CO, United States.

Sugai, G., & Horner, R. H. (2020). Sustaining and scaling positive behavioral interventions and supports: Implementation drivers, outcomes, and considerations. *Exceptional Children, 86*(2), 120–136. https://doi.org/10.1177/0014402919855331

Sutherland, K., Denny, R., & Gunter, P. (2005). Teachers of students with emotional and behavioral disorders reported professional development needs: Differences between fully licensed and emergency-licensed teachers. *Preventing School Failure, 49*(2), 41–46. https://doi.org/10.3200/PSFL.49.2.41-46

Swanson, E., Solis, M., Ciullo, S., & McKenna, J. (2012). Special education teachers' perceptions and instructional practices in response to intervention implementation. *Learning Disability Quarterly, 35*(2), 115–126. https://doi.org/10.1177/0731948711432510

U.S Department of Education. (2022). Office of special education and rehabilitation services, office of special education programs. In *43rd annual report to congress on the implementation of the individuals with disabilities education act, 2021, Washington, DC.* https://sites.ed.gov/idea/files/43rd-arc-for-idea.pdf

Vaughn, S., Levy, S., Coleman, M., & Bos, C. (2002). Reading instruction for students with LD and EBD: A synthesis of observation studies. *The Journal of Special Education, 36*(1), 2–13. https://doi.org/10.1177/00224669020360010101

Vaughn, S., Moody, S., & Schumm, J. (1998). Broken promises: Reading instruction in the resource room. *Exceptional Children, 64*(2), 211–225. https://doi.org/10.1177/001440299806400205

Vaughn, S., & Schumm, J. (1995). Responsible inclusion for students with learning disabilities. *Journal of Learning Disabilities, 28*(5), 264–270. https://doi.org/10.1177/002221949502800502

von der Embse, N., Ryan, S. V., Gibbs, T., & Mankin, A. (2019). Teacher stress interventions: A systematic review. *Psychology in the Schools, 56*(8), 1328–1343. https://doi.org/10.1002/pits.22279

Watlington, E., Shockley, R., Guglielmino, P., & Felsher, R. (2010). The high cost of leaving: An analysis of the cost of teacher turnover. *Journal of Education Finance, 36*(1), 22–37. https://doi.org/10.1353/jef.0.0028

Watters, A. (2021). *Teaching machines.* The MIT Press.

Weist, M. D., Splett, J. W., Halliday, C. A., Gage, N. A., Seaman, M. A., Perkins, K. A., … Distefano, C. (2022). A randomized controlled trial on the interconnected systems framework for school mental health and PBIS: Focus on proximal variables and school discipline. *Journal of School Psychology, 94*, 49–65. https://doi.org/10.1016/j.jsp.2022.08.002

Wiley, A., Brigham, F., Kauffman, J., & Bogan, J. (2013). Disproportionate poverty, conservatism, and the disproportionate identification of minority students with emotional and behavioral disorders. *Education and Treatment of Children, 36*(4), 29–50. https://doi.org/10.1353/etc.2013.0033

Will, G. F. (2023, April 13). 'I despise, therefore I am' locks in the status quo, editorial. *The Washington Post*, p. A19. https://www.washingtonpost.com/opinions/2023/04/12/republican-democrat-poisonous-partisanship/

Williamson, P., Hoppey, D., McLeskey, J., Bergmann, E., & Moore, H. (2020). Trends in LRE placement rates over the past 25 years. *The Journal of Special Education, 53*(4), 236–244. https://doi.org/10.1177/0022466919855052

Yell, M. (2019). Endrew F. v. Douglas County School District (2017): Implications for educating students with emotional and behavioral disorders. *Behavioral Disorders, 45*(1), 53–62. https://doi.org/10.1177/0198742919865454

Yell, M., Katsiyannis, A., Ennis, R., Losinski, M., & Bateman, D. (2020). Making legally sound placement decisions. *Teaching Exceptional Children, 52*(5), 291–303. https://doi.org/10.1177/0040059920906537

Zaheer, I., Maggin, D., McDaniel, S., McIntosh, K., Rodriguez, B. J., & Fogt, J. B. (2019). Implementation of promising practices that support students with emotional and behavioral disorders. *Behavioral Disorders, 44*(2), 117–128. https://doi.org/10.1177/0198742918821331

Zimmerman, J. (2021, September 19). Why the culture wars in schools are worse than ever before. *Politico.* https://www.politico.com/news/magazine/2021/09/19/history-culture-wars-schools-america-divided-512614

CHAPTER 4

SPECIAL EDUCATION OF STUDENTS WITH INTELLECTUAL DISABILITIES: ADVANCING VALUES

Emily Bouck, Larissa Jakubow and Sarah Reiley

Michigan State University, USA

ABSTRACT

This chapter sought to answer the following questions: (a) what does special education means for students with intellectual disability?, (b) what is being done, and (c) how do we maintain tradition? The answers, while complicated, suggest special education for students with intellectual disability historically and currently involves attention to what, how, and where, with the how being the key elements of special education for students with intellectual disability. This chapter discussed the what, how, and where for students with intellectual disability in a historical and current framework while also providing evidence-based practices for students with intellectual disability to implement to maintain the tradition of high-quality services.

Keywords: Functional curriculum; academic content standards; evidence-based practices; instructional environment; fidelity

STUDENTS WITH INTELLECTUAL DISABILITY

Students with intellectual disability generally involves reference to children and youth identified with lower intellectual functional or intellectual quotient (IQ) as well as adaptive behavior challenges (e.g., social skills, life skills; Schalock et al., 2010). Thus, the focus on students with intellectual disability involves cognitive abilities and cognitive, practical, and social skills (American Association on Intellectual and Developmental Disabilities [AAIDD], n.d.; Greenspan, 2006).

Special Education
Advances in Special Education, Volume 38, 55–68
Copyright © 2024 Emily Bouck, Larissa Jakubow and Sarah Reiley
Published under exclusive licence by Emerald Publishing Limited
ISSN: 0270-4013/doi:10.1108/S0270-401320240000038004

Two main definitions permeate the literature on students with intellectual disability – the American Association on Intellectual and Developmental Disabilities (AAIDD), which focuses on the entire lifespan of individuals with intellectual disability, and the Individuals with Disabilities Education Act (IDEA), which generally focuses on children and youth with intellectual disability from birth to transition age (generally 21 although up to 26 in the state of Michigan). The AAIDD definition of intellectual disability suggests "intellectual disability is characterized by significant limitations both in intellectual functioning and in adaptive behavior as expressed in conceptual, social, and practical adaptive skills. This disability originates during the developmental period, which is defined operationally as before the individual attains age 22" (Schalock et al., 2021a, p. 1). The IDEA definition states, "Intellectual disability means significantly subaverage general intellectual functioning, existing concurrently with deficits in adaptive behavior and manifested during the developmental period, that adversely affects a child's educational performance" (Section 300.8 (c) (6)).

Levels of functioning are often referenced when considering students with intellectual disability. Generally, a student with an intellectual disability is one whose IQ is less than or equal to 70, although some allow for up to 75 (Polloway, Bouck, et al., 2017). A common classification of students with intellectual disability includes mild intellectual disability involving an IQ of 55 to 70, moderate an IQ of 40 to 55, and severe an IQ less than 40 (Grossman, 1983; Polloway et al., 2021; see Table 4.1). Despite the AAIDD dropping this classification system, it still persists within IDEA and typical discussions of individuals with intellectual disability (Luckasson et al., 1992; Polloway et al., 2021). Of course, it is important to remember that IQ is not the only condition that needs to be met for the identification of an individual with an intellectual disability – challenges with adaptive behavior must also be present, and attention must be given to age of onset (Schalock et al., 2021b).

Table 4.1. Intellectual Disability Classifications.

Classification	Description and Information
Mild intellectual disability	• IQ generally between 55 and 70 • Occurs with more prevalence within the population • Diagnosis generally considered more subjective or biased
Moderate intellectual disability	• IQ 40 to 55 • Generally aggregated with students with severe intellectual disability to be considered students with extensive support needs • Typically identified at birth or early in life • Diagnosis generally considered more objective
Severe intellectual disability	• IQ under 40 • Generally aggregated with students with moderate intellectual disability to be considered students with extensive support needs • Typically identified at birth or early in life • Diagnosis generally considered more objective

Notes: Grossman (1983); Polloway et al. (2021); Polloway, Bouck, et al. (2017).

Students with intellectual disability – a heterogenous grouping – display a range of characteristics relative to education and learning, which include challenges related to problem-solving, decision-making, abstract thinking, planning, and judgment (Siperstein & Collins, 2015). Students with intellectual disability can demonstrate challenges associated with attention, such as time on task and maintaining focus. Challenges associated with both short-term and long-term memory can be apparent, as well as motivational obstacles (e.g., learned helplessness). Beyond cognitive developmental challenges, students with intellectual disability can experience issues related to both receptive and expressive language, as well as academic skills (i.e., reading, writing, and mathematics). Students with intellectual disability can also experience challenges involving their social skills, engagement with peers, and social engagement (e.g., suggestibility or gullibility; Patton & Keyes, 2006; Polloway et al., 2021, 2022; Smith et al., 2020).

The prevalence of school-based students with intellectual disability has decreased over the decades since the passage of the law that mandated education for all students, including students with intellectual disability (i.e., PL 94-142 in 1975; Polloway et al., 2021). Recent data suggest less than 1% of school-aged students (i.e., 6–21 years of age) were identified with an intellectual disability (United States Department of Education, 2022). However, researchers have found variation across states in terms of prevalence (Bouck & Satsangi, 2015; Polloway, Auguste, et al., 2017).

Throughout this chapter, we will seek to answer the following questions: (a) what does special education means for students with intellectual disability?, (b) what is being done, and (c) how do we maintain tradition? However, the context of what special education means for students with an intellectual disability is complex and connected to an antiquated classification of intellectual disability that still permeates schooling and educational issues. Likewise, what is being done and what needs to be maintained may also have different answers if considering students with mild intellectual disability as opposed to students with severe disabilities.

WHAT SPECIAL EDUCATION MEANS FOR STUDENTS WITH INTELLECTUAL DISABILITY

Historically, special education for students with intellectual disability meant simply access to school or education (Spaulding & Pratt, 2015). Prior to PARC versus *Commonwealth of Pennsylvania* in 1971 and the Education for All Handicapped Children Act of 1975, students with disabilities – including students with intellectual disability – were excluded from public schools. But court cases and federal law indicated all students had the right to a free appropriate public education (Spaulding & Pratt, 2015). Of course, the origins of special education itself can be traced back prior to these legal aspects (Polloway et al., 2021).

Contemporarily, when one considers special education for students with intellectual disability, one is generally contemplating the *what* and the *where* as well as the *how* (Dymond & Orelove, 2001; Kauffman & Hung, 2009). Special education means providing high-quality content using research-based or evidence-based interventions and instruction for students with intellectual disability in their least restrictive environment. Despite attention to the *where* (e.g., general education setting vs pull-out setting), what truly makes special education special for students with intellectual disability is *what* is taught and more importantly the instructional approach or *how* it is delivered (Cook & Schirmer, 2003).

A HISTORICAL PERSPECTIVE OF SPECIAL EDUCATION

Historically, and currently, the where and what to teach students with intellectual disability are connected (Polloway, Bouck, et al., 2017). Special education is not a place but often students with intellectual disability are in more restrictive educational settings than students without intellectual disability (Polloway et al., 2019). The trend toward more pull-out educational placements for students with intellectual disability is a historical one (Polloway, Bouck, et al., 2017; Polloway et al., 2022). Researchers suggested students in more inclusive placements tended to receive more academic instruction and those in more pull-out placements received more functional curricula, as well as vice versa (i.e., those needing more life skills instruction were taught in pull-out settings and those given more academic curricula educated in more inclusive settings; Bouck, 2009).

Historically, a functional curriculum was a common approach to educating students with intellectual disability (Browder & Cooper-Duffy, 2003; Kolstoe et al., 1970; see Table 4.2 for information on a functional curriculum). In the late

Table 4.2. Functional Curriculum Components.

Functional Skill	Description or Example
Functional academics (e.g., functional literacy and functional mathematics)	Word recognition on signs, warnings, and safety information; signing one's name; purchasing skills (e.g., budgeting as well as money skills); telling time and keeping a calendar
Career and technical education, including vocational education	Exploring careers, job skills support
Financial planning and management	Budgeting, banking, paying via debit or credit card
Community living and participation	Navigating the community and its resources (e.g., shopping at grocery stores and eating at restaurants)
Daily living including personal health and safety and home living	Household skills including laundry, food preparation, cleaning as well as maintaining one's own hygiene
Travel and mobility	Learning to drive a car or navigate public transition
Self-determination	Making one's own decision and learning to problem-solve
Socialization, recreation, and leisure	Engaging in hobbies or recreational activities as well as socializing with others (e.g., making and keeping friends)

Notes: Adapted from Bouck et al. (2015). Curated from Browder and Snell (1993); Cronin and Patton (1993); Dattilo and Hoge (1999); Gajar et al. (1993); Retish et al. (1991); Sands and Doll (1996); Snell and Browder (1987); Storey and Miner (2011); Wehmeyer et al. (2002); Westling and Fox (2009).

1970s and early 1980s, the peak attention toward a functional curriculum occurred, followed by a decline as more attention was given to academic instruction (Billingsley, 1997; Billingsley & Albertson, 1999; Kolstoe et al., 1970; Nietupski et al., 1997). Researchers captured the decline in attention to a functional curriculum through the substantial decrease in articles published in the 1990s regarding a functional curriculum (Billingsley, 1997; Billingsley & Albertson, 1999; Nietupski et al., 1997). As attention to a functional curriculum decreased, discussion and consideration of academic content for students with intellectual disability increased. Researchers and scholars began to question not just the usefulness of skills and concepts to daily living but also the relevance to academic content standards (Browder & Cooper-Duffy, 2003). As such, contention existed regarding what to teach students with intellectual disability – functional life skills or academic content standards-based instruction.

This tension toward *what* to teach students with intellectual disability was best captured in a series of articles in *Education and Training in Autism and Developmental Disabilities* in 2011 and 2012 which explored curricular focus for students with intellectual disability (Ayres et al., 2011, 2012; Courtade et al., 2012). A large question in the debate involved not whether students with intellectual disability could learn standards-based curriculum or academic content – that debate was generally settled given researchers repeatedly demonstrated students with intellectual disability, including those with extensive support needs, can learn academic skills – but whether they should. Ayres et al. (2011) argued teaching students standards-based content decreased teachers' ability to provide functional or life skills to students with intellectual disability, which are important for supporting students' independent living as well as vocational skills for earning a living. In response, Courtade et al. (2012) noted that not only do students with extensive support needs have a right to academic content but that it is relevant and avoids limiting expectations of students.

While the consideration of what to teach occurred, researchers were also answering how to teach. Although evidence-based practice was not yet touted as the goal, researchers focused on identifying effective practices for students with intellectual disability. Ault et al. (1989) reviewed studies comparing instructional approaches for students with intellectual disability to examine their effectiveness. Ault et al. indicated stimulus shaping or stimulus fading was superior to other approaches but less recommended due to time to prepare and the complexity to deliver. They also suggested the efficacy of most-to-least prompting and noted the lack of support for the system of least prompts. Ault et al. also supported the use of constant time delay and progressive time delay. Within the last two decades, the National Secondary Transition Technical Assistance Center (NSTTAC) suggested many of these same instructional approaches are evidence-based relative to secondary transition practices for students with intellectual disability: constant time delay, most-to-least prompting, progressive time delay, among others (e.g., least-to-most prompting, self-monitoring, and simulation) (NSTTAC, 2013; Test et al., 2009).

Self-operated prompting systems became a consistent instructional approach for students with intellectual disability. Researchers and educators focused on self-operated prompting systems, including picture prompts, audio prompts, and video prompting or modeling (Mechling et al., 2010). Self-operated prompting systems started as static picture prompts (e.g., Singh et al., 1995), moved to audio technology, (e.g., Taber-Doughty, 2005) and finally to video (e.g., Graves et al., 2005; Taber-Doughty et al., 2011; Van Laarhoven et al., 2007). The shift in technologies for self-operating prompting systems reflects the field keeping up with modern technologies as well as responding to the increasing need for portable systems (Mechling et al., 2010). In terms of video modeling, the NSTTAC (2013) suggested video modeling as an evidence-based practice for students with intellectual disability for secondary transition.

THE CURRENT STATUS OF SPECIAL EDUCATION

The current state of special education for students with intellectual disability does not differ drastically from the more recent past. From recent data, students with an intellectual disability still continue to be primarily educated in settings outside of the general education setting. Data from the Office of Special Education Programs (OSEP) suggest that 82.1% of students with intellectual disability spend at least 79% of their day outside of general education placements (OSEP, 2022). This percentage is higher than most other disability groups. The current OSEP (2022) data also suggest a continued variation in state placement data. In terms of what to teach, the focus has been less about pitting an academic and functional curriculum or approach against one another and more about a focus on infusing one into the other (Bouck, 2012; Bouck et al., 2015; Collins et al., 2010; Kleinert et al., 2010). As such, considerations of how to integrate content area instruction into functional curriculum and skills as well as embedded functional life skills into academic instruction has been an increased focus (Bouck et al., 2015; Collins et al., 2011).

A strength of the current status of special education for students with intellectual disability is the *how*. Over the past few decades, the field has placed attention in how to determine evidence-based practices for students with disabilities, including intellectual disability (Courtade et al., 2015; West et al., 2013). Multiple quality indicators and standards exist for evaluating special education research, each with different elements and focus (e.g., Cook et al., 2014; Council for Exceptional Children, 2014; Horner et al., 2005; Kratochwill et al., 2013; What Works Clearinghouse, 2020). As such, a determination of evidence-based for a particular intervention, instructional approach, or practice may exist following the application of one framework but not for another. However, such evaluation tools allow researchers and educators to speak more toward what practices are high-quality and should be used for students with intellectual disability.

We have evidence-based practices for teaching students with intellectual disability that make special education special (Cook & Schirmer, 2003; see Table 4.3). For example, historically, video modeling has been suggested as an evidence-based practice (e.g., NSTTAC, 2013). More recently, researchers suggested video

Table 4.3. Evidence-Based Practices for Students With Intellectual Disability.

Evidence-Based Practices	Description or Information
Audio prompting	• Series of steps broken down from a larger skill provided as audio cues or prompts, which students can play and pause as needed (Chen & Yakubova, 2019).
Constant time delay	• A single response prompt that occurs initially after 0 s and then later after a preset time (e.g., 5 s; Horn et al., 2023).
Explicit instruction	• A form of systematic instruction in which the teacher first models – with a verbal think aloud – how to do the task, then guides the student with prompts or cues as they engage in the task, and finally the student engages independently (Doabler & Fien, 2013).
System of least prompts (SLP)	• Providing increasingly intrusive prompts to students, starting with least instruction, to support correct responding (Shepley et al., 2019).
Task analysis	• Breaking down a skill into smaller, more manageable steps that must be performed in a particular sequence (McConomy et al., 2021).
Video modeling/ prompting	• Video modeling involves a task being shown as a series of steps and presented in a video format, which a student watches continuously (Delano, 2007). • Video prompting involves a series of steps broken down and presented as video cues or prompts, which students can play and pause as needed (Chen & Yakubova, 2019).
Virtual manipulatives	• Digital versions of concrete manipulatives to support students with mathematical concepts (Bouck & Long, 2021).

modeling or video prompting continue to be effective interventions for students with intellectual disability across a variety of skills (Park et al., 2019). Park et al. (2019), in a review of video modeling and video prompting for students with intellectual disability, found the interventions to positively support students with intellectual disability across both academic skills as well as independent living skills and job skills. Researchers also found video modeling to support academic skills, such as mathematics (Wright et al., 2020). Wright et al. (2020) noted the value of video modeling given that videos can be played on portable devices; portable devices allow students flexibility to use video models (or video prompting) in a variety of settings (Bouck et al., 2012, 2013).

Aside from the most advanced self-operated prompting systems being evidence-based practices – video modeling and video prompting (Aljehany & Bennett, 2019) – researchers suggest other self-operated prompting systems such as audio prompting systems are also evidence-based practices (Chen & Yakubova, 2019). In an effort to create more flexibility, accessibility, and ease of use within community settings, audio prompting can replace video prompting as supports are faded. Both systems involve audio cues; audio prompting just removes the video scaffold (Chen & Yakubova, 2019).

Task analysis is another evidence-based practice and used often with students with intellectual disability (McConomy et al., 2021; Moyer & Dardig, 1978). Task analysis is a process by which a skill is broken down into smaller, easier-to-manage steps that are to be performed within a particular order (McConomy et al., 2021). Task analysis can be used for academic tasks (e.g., math) as well as independent or daily living skills. Task analysis can be used in both instruction as well as assessment (McConomy et al., 2021). Using task analysis for instruction supports students in learning a chained task while the use of a task analysis in assessment allows educators to determine student independence in completing a task or skill (Wade et al., 2021). A task analysis is used to support a variety of other interventions, including audio prompting and video modeling. Audio and or video prompting systems break the target academic, functional, or vocational task into small manageable steps (i.e., a task analysis), and then provide prompt to complete said step.

Response prompting systems, such as constant time delay, progressive time delay, or the system of least prompts, are considered evidence-based practices (Knight & Sartini, 2015). Constant time delay and progressive time delay both provide a prompt immediately after cuing (i.e., 0 s delay), while the system of least prompts provides increasingly intrusive prompts if a student fails to respond or responds incorrectly (Shepley et al., 2019). While the system of least prompts is a commonly used instructional approach by educators (Fisher et al., 2007), historically researchers suggested it was less effective than constant time delay or progressive time delay (Ault et al., 1989; Schuster et al., 1998; Wolery & Hemmeter, 2011). More recently, Shepley et al. (2019) determined that as a stand-alone intervention, the system of least prompts is an evidence-based practice for secondary students with intellectual disability for particular skills. They did, however, note they could not recommend the system of least prompts for all skills (e.g., discrete academics) based on their review.

For academics, researchers have determined virtual manipulatives to be an evidence-based practice for supporting students with intellectual disability in mathematics (Bouck & Long, 2023; Long et al., 2022). Whereas concrete manipulatives demonstrate mathematical concepts by allowing students to physically move objects, virtual manipulatives achieve the same thing via the use of digital tools (Bouck et al., 2020). Virtual manipulatives can be used as stand-alone tools or as part of a graduated sequence of instruction that begins with a virtual manipulative (Bouck & Long, 2021). Within a virtual manipulative-based instructional sequence, such as the virtual-representational-abstract (VRA) or its variations (e.g., virtual-abstract [VA], virtual-representational [VR]), teachers start by teaching students to solve the problems with a virtual manipulative, then move to the representational or drawings, and finally to the abstract (or numerical strategy phase) that occurs without any tools. In the VR, students do not progress to the abstract and in VA, students skip the representational or drawing phase (Bouck & Long, 2021).

One thing to note about the evidence-based practices for students with intellectual disability is that they are often used together (e.g., Kuntz & Carter, 2019). Often researchers and educators are using intervention packages for students with intellectual disability, rather than just one stand-alone intervention (Knight et al., 2020; Kuntz & Carter, 2019). As such, it can be difficult to parse the precise effects of any single practice. For example, video prompting is also frequently used in conjunction with strategies including error correction and the system of least prompts. Researchers suggest that these packages are more effective than video modeling alone (Knight et al., 2020; Kuntz & Carter, 2019; Park et al., 2019). And instruction with virtual manipulatives typically involves explicit instruction and sometimes the system of least prompts (Bouck & Long, 2023; Long et al., 2022). Explicit instruction, a form of systematic instruction, is a common element of intervention packages for students with intellectual disability across a variety of areas (e.g., Bouck & Long, 2023; Cannella-Malone et al., 2015; Knight et al., 2018).

CONCLUSION – MAINTAINING THE GOOD OF SPECIAL EDUCATION

Despite a history of critics (see a rebuttal from Fuchs & Fuchs, 1995), there is good in special education for all students with disabilities including students with intellectual disability. In keeping the good or the special of special education for students with intellectual disability, a key element is a continual focus on evidence-based instructional practices or interventions. There has been consistency throughout time with regards to effective, high-quality, research-based, or evidence-based practices for students with intellectual disability (e.g., prompting systems, time delay; e.g., Ault et al., 1989; Park et al., 2019). As such, a focus on maintaining good special education services is to attend to the *how* more than the where. Special education for students with intellectual disability is special because special educators provide high-quality, evidence-based practices that support students' ascertainment, maintenance, and generalization of skills, including daily living and academic skills (Shurr et al., 2019). Implementing evidence-based, or at a minimum, research-based practices for educating students with intellectual disability with fidelity should be the goal of all educators (Shurr et al., 2019). Historically, teachers have not implemented research-based practices frequently or with fidelity (Ayres et al., 1994; Locke et al., 2014), if they were even aware of such practices (Agran & Alper, 2000). Despite an increase in attention to and knowledge of evidence-based practices for students with intellectual disability, implementation remains a challenging but desirable goal.

As such, how we maintain high-quality educational experiences for students with intellectual disability while moving forward involves the implementation of evidence-based practices while simultaneously continually to seek out more evidence-based practices. As researchers continue to explore promising practices and determine the evidence-based, it expands the quantity of evidence-based practices that support the education of students with intellectual disability. As such, the field must continue a three-prong approach: (a) continue to engage in high-quality research that results in the ability to determine practices as evidence-based, (b) the implementation with fidelity of evidence-based practices in the education of students with intellectual disability, and (c) prepare preservice and in-service teachers at institutions of higher education to implement evidence-based practices with fidelity.

REFERENCES

Agran, M., & Alper, S. (2000). Curriculum and instruction in general education: Implications for service delivery and personnel preparation. *Journal of the Association for Persons with Severe Handicaps, 25*(3), 167–174. https://doi.org/10.2511/rpsd.25.3.167

Aljehany, M. S., & Bennett, K. D. (2019). Meta-analysis of video prompting to teach daily living skills to individuals with autism spectrum disorder. *Journal of Special Education Technology, 34,* 17–26. https://doi.org/10.1177/0162643418780495

American Association on Intellectual and Developmental Disabilities. (n.d.). *Adaptive behavior.* https://www.aaidd.org/intellectual-disability/definition/adaptive-behavior

Ault, M. J., Wolery, M., Doyle, P. M., & Gast, D. L. (1989). Review of comparative studies in the instruction of students with moderate and severe handicaps. *Exceptional Children, 55*(4), 346–356. https://doi.org/10.1177/001440298905500410

Ayres, K. M., Lowrey, K. A., Douglas, K. H., & Sievers, C. (2011). I can identify Saturn but I can't brush my teeth: What happens when the curricular focus for students with severe disabilities shifts. *Education and Training in Autism and Developmental Disabilities, 46*(1), 11–21.

Ayres, K. M., Lowrey, K. A., Douglas, K. H., & Sievers, C. (2012). The question still remains: What happens when the curricular focus for students with severe disabilities shifts? A reply to Courtade, Spooner, Browder, and Jimenez (2012). *Education and Training in Autism and Developmental Disabilities, 47*(1), 14–22.

Ayres, B. J., Meyer, L. H., Erevelles, N., & Park-Lee, S. (1994). Easy for you to say: Teacher perspectives on implementing most promising practices. *The Journal of the Association for Persons with Severe Handicaps, 19*(2), 84–93.

Billingsley, F. (1997, December). The problem and the place of functional skills in inclusive settings. In G. Singer (Chair.), *The role of functional skills and behavior instructional methods in inclusive education.* The Annual Meeting for Persons with Severe Handicaps. Boston, MA.

Billingsley, F. F., & Albertson, L. R. (1999). Finding a future for functional skills. *The Journal of the Association for Persons with Severe Handicaps, 24*(4), 298–302.

Bouck, E. C. (2009). No child left behind, the individuals with disabilities education act and functional curricula: A conflict of interest? *Education and Training in Developmental Disabilities, 44,* 3–13.

Bouck, E. C. (2012). Secondary curriculum and transition. In P. Wehman (Ed.), *Life beyond the classroom: Transition strategies for young people with disabilities* (5th ed., pp. 215–233). Paul H. Brookes Publishing Co., Inc.

Bouck, E. C., Flanagan, S., Miller, B., & Bassette, L. (2012). Technology in action: Rethinking everyday technology as assistive technology to meet students' IEP goals. *Journal of Special Education Technology, 27*(4), 47–57. https://doi.org/10.1177/016264341202700404

Bouck, E. C., Jasper, A., Bassette, L., Shurr, J., & Miller, B. (2013). Applying TAPE: Rethinking assistive technology for students with physical disabilities, multiple disabilities, and other health impairment. *Physical Disabilities Research & Practice, 32*(1), 31–54.

Bouck, E. C., & Long, H. (2021). Manipulatives and manipulative-based instructional sequences. In E. C. Bouck, J. R. Root, & B. Jimenez (Eds.), *Mathematics education and students with autism, intellectual disability, and other developmental disabilities* (pp. 104–134). Division on Autism and Developmental Disabilities.

Bouck, E. C., & Long, H. (2023). Academic mathematics instruction and intervention for students with mild intellectual disability: An updated review. *Education and Training in Autism and Developmental Disabilities, 58*(2), 144–161.

Bouck, E. C., Mathews, L. A., & Peltier, C. (2020). Virtual manipulatives: A tool to support access and achievement with middle school students with disabilities. *Journal of Special Education Technology, 35*(1), 51–59. https://doi.org/10.1177/0162643419882422

Bouck, E. C., & Satsangi, R. (2015). Is there really a difference? Distinguishing mild intellectual disability from similar disability categories. *Education and Training in Autism and Developmental Disabilities, 50*(2), 186–198.

Bouck, E. C., Taber-Doughty, T., & Savage, M. (2015). *Footsteps toward the future: A real- world focus for students with intellectual disability, autism spectrum disorder, and other developmental disabilities.* Council for Exceptional Children.

Browder, D. M., & Cooper-Duffy, K. (2003). Evidence-based practices for students with severe disabilities and the requirement for accountability in "no child left behind". *The Journal of Special Education, 37*(3), 157–163. https://doi.org/10.1177/00224669030370030501

Browder, D. M., & Snell, M. E. (1993). Functional academics. In M. E. Snell (Ed.), *Instruction of students with severe disabilities* (4th ed., pp. 442–475). Merrill.

Cannella-Malone, H. I., Konrad, M., & Pennington, R. C. (2015). ACCESS! Teaching writing skills to students with intellectual disability. *Teaching Exceptional Children, 47*(5), 272–280. https://doi.org/10.1177/0040059915580032

Chen, B. B., & Yakubova, G. (2019). Promoting independence with vocational audio and video prompting for students with ASD. *Teaching Exceptional Children, 52*(2), 98–106. https://doi.org/10.1177/0040059919874308

Collins, B. C., Hager, K. D., & Galloway, C. C. (2011). The addition of functional content during core content instruction with students with moderate disabilities. *Education and Training in Developmental Disabilities, 46*, 22–39.

Collins, B. C., Karl, J., Riggs, L., Galloway, C. C., & Hager, K. D. (2010). Teaching core content with real-life applications to secondary students with moderate and severe disabilities. *Teaching Exceptional Children, 43*(1), 52–59. https://doi.org/10.1177/004005991004300106

Cook, B. G., Buysse, V., Klingner, J., Landrum, T. J., McWilliam, R. A., Tankersley, M., & Test, D. W. (2014). CEC's standards for classifying the evidence base of practices in special education. *Remedial and Special Education, 36*(4), 220–234. https://doi.org/10.1177/0741932514557271

Cook, B. G., & Schirmer, B. R. (2003). What is special about special education? Overview and analysis. *The Journal of Special Education, 37*(3), 200–205. https://doi.org/10.1177/00224669030370031001

Council for Exceptional Children. (2014). Council for exceptional children: Standards for evidence-based practices in special education. *Teaching Exceptional Children, 46*(6), 206–212. https://doi.org/10.1177/0040059914531389

Courtade, G., Spooner, F., Browder, D., & Jimenez, B. (2012). Seven reasons to promote standards-based instruction for students with severe disabilities: A reply to Ayres, Lowrey, Douglas & Sievers (2011). *Education and Training in Autism and Developmental Disabilities, 47*(1), 3–13.

Courtade, G. R., Test, D. W., & Cook, B. G. (2015). Evidence-based practices for learners with severe intellectual disability. *Research and Practice for Persons with Severe Disabilities, 39*(4), 305–318. https://doi.org/10.1177/1540796914566711

Cronin, M. E., & Patton, J. R. (1993). *Life skills instruction for all students with special needs: A practical guide for integrating real-life content into the curriculum.* Pro-Ed.

Dattilo, J., & Hoge, G. (1999). Effects of a leisure education program on youth with mental retardation. *Education and Training in Mental Retardation and Developmental Disabilities, 34*, 20–34.

Delano, M. E. (2007). Video modeling interventions for individuals with autism. *Remedial and Special Education, 28*(1), 33–42. https://doi.org/10.1177/07419325070280010401

Doabler, C. T., & Fien, H. (2013). Explicit mathematics instruction: What teachers can do for teaching students with mathematics difficulties. *Intervention in School and Clinic, 48*(5), 276–285. https://doi.org/10.1177/1053451212473151

Dymond, S. K., & Orelove, F. P. (2001). What constitutes effective curricula for students with severe disabilities? *Exceptionality, 9*(3), 109–122. https://doi.org/10.1207/S15327035EX0903_2

Fisher, W. W., Kodak, T., & Moore, J. W. (2007). Embedding an identity-matching task within a prompting hierarchy to facilitate acquisition of conditional discriminations in children with autism. *Journal of Applied Behavior Analysis, 40*, 489–499. https://doi.org/10.1901/jaba.2007.40-489

Fuchs, D., & Fuchs, L. S. (1995). What's "special" about special education? *Phi Delta Kappan, 76*, 522–530.

Gajar, A., Goodman, L., & McAfee, J. (1993). *Secondary schools and beyond: Transition of individuals with mild disabilities.* Merrill.

Graves, T. B., Collins, B. C., Schuster, J. W., & Kleinert, H. (2005). Using video prompting to teach cooking skills to secondary students with moderate disabilities. *Education and Training in Developmental Disabilities, 40*, 34–46.

Greenspan, S. (2006). Functional concepts in mental retardation: Finding the natural essence of an artificial category. *Exceptionality, 14*(4), 205–224. https://doi.org/10.1207/s15327035ex1404_3

Grossman, H. J. (1983). *Classification in mental retardation.* American Association on Mental Deficiency.

Horner, R. H., Carr, E. G., Halle, J., McGee, G., Odom, S., & Wolery, M. (2005). The use of single-subject research to identify evidence-based practice in special education. *Exceptional Children, 71*(2), 165–179. https://doi.org/10.1177/001440290507100203

Horn, A. L., Roitsch, J., & Murphy, K. A. (2023). Constant time delay to teach reading to students with intellectual disability and autism: A review. *International Journal of Developmental Disabilities, 69*(2), 123–133. https://doi.org/10.1080/20473869.2021.1907138

Kauffman, J. M., & Hung, Y. L. H. (2009). Special education for intellectual disability: Current trends and perspectives. *Current Opinion in Psychiatry, 22*(5), 452–456. https://doi.org/10.1097/YCO. 0b013e32832eb5c3

Kleinert, H., Collins, B. C., Wickham, D., Riggs, L., & Hager, K. (2010). Embedding life skills, self-determination, social relationships, and other evidence-based practices. In H. Kleinert & J. Kearns (Eds.), *Alternate assessment for students with significant cognitive disabilities: An educator's guide.* Brookes Publishing Company.

Knight, V. F., Creech-Galloway, C. E., Karl, J. M., & Collins, B. C. (2018). Evaluating supported eText to teach science to high school students with moderate intellectual disability. *Focus on Autism and Other Developmental Disabilities, 33*(4), 227–236. https://doi.org/10.1177/1088357617696273

Knight, V. F., & Sartini, E. (2015). A comprehensive literature review of comprehension strategies in core content areas for students with autism spectrum disorder. *Journal of Autism and Developmental Disorders, 45*, 1213–1229. https://doi.org/10.1007/s10803-014-2280-x

Knight, V. F., Wood, L., McKissick, B. R., & Kuntz, E. M. (2020). Teaching science content and practices to students with intellectual disability and autism. *Remedial and Special Education, 41*(6), 327–340. https://doi.org/10.1177/0741932519843998

Kolstoe, O. P. (1970). *Teaching educable mentally retarded children.* Holt, Rinehart, & Winston.

Kratochwill, T. R., Hitchcock, J. H., Horner, R. H., Levin, J. R., Odom, S. L., Rindskopf, D. M., & Shadish, W. R. (2013). Single case intervention research design standards. *Remedial and Special Education, 34*(1), 26–38. https://doi.org/10.1177/0741932512452794

Kuntz, E. M., & Carter, E. W. (2019). Review of interventions supporting secondary students with intellectual disability in general education classrooms. *Research and Practice for Persons with Severe Disabilities, 44*(2), 103–121. https://doi.org/10.1177/1540796919847483

Locke, J., Kratz, H., Reisinger, E., & Mandell, D. (2014). Implementation of evidence-based practices for children with autism spectrum disorders in public schools. In R. Beidas & P. Kendall (Eds.), *Child and adolescent therapy: Dissemination and implementation of empirically supported treatments* (pp. 261–276). Oxford University Press.

Long, H. M., Bouck, E. C., & Kelly, H. (2022). *An evidence-based practice synthesis of virtual manipulatives for students with ASD and IDD.* Focus on Autism and Other Developmental Disabilities. [Advanced Online]. https://doi.org/10.1177/10883576221121654

Luckasson, R., Coulter, D., Polloway, E. A., Reiss, S., Schalock, R. L., Snell, M. E., Spitanik, D., & Stark, J. A. (1992). *Mental retardation: Definition, classification, and systems of supports.* American Association on Mental Retardation.

McConomy, M. A., Root, J., & Wade, T. (2021). Using task analysis to support inclusion and assessment in the classroom. *Teaching Exceptional Children, 54*(6), 414–422. https://doi.org/10.1177/00400599211025565

Mechling, L. C., Gast, D. L., & Seid, N. H. (2010). Evaluation of a personal digital assistant as a self-prompting device for increasing multi-step task completion by students with moderate intellectual disabilities. *Education and Training in Autism and Developmental Disabilities, 45*, 422–439.

Moyer, J. R., & Dardig, J. C. (1978). Practical task analysis for special educators. *Teaching Exceptional Children, 11*(1), 16–18. https://doi.org/10.1177/004005997801100105

National Secondary Transition Technical Assistance Center. (2013). *Evidence-based practices in secondary transition.* www.nsttac.org/content/evidence-base-practices-secondary-transition

Nietupski, H., Hamre-Nietupski, S., Curtin, S., & Shrikanth, K. (1997). A review of curricular research in severe disabilities from 1976 to 1995 in six selected journals. *The Journal of Special Education, 31*, 59–60.

Office of Special Education Programs. (2022). *OSEP fast facts: Educational environments of school aged children with disabilities.* https://sites.ed.gov/idea/osep-fast-facts-educational-environments-school-aged-children-disabilities/?utm_content=&utm_medium=email&utm_name=&utm_source=gov delivery&utm_term

Park, J., Bouck, E. C., & Duenas, A. (2019). The effect of video modeling and video prompting interventions on individuals with intellectual disability: A systematic literature review. *Journal of Special Education Technology, 34*(1), 3–16. https://doi.org/10.1177/0162643418780464

Patton, J. R., & Keyes, D. W. (2006). Death penalty issues following *Atkins. Exceptionality, 14*(4), 237–255.

Polloway, E. A., Auguste, M., Smith, J. D., & Peters, D. (2017). An analysis of state guidelines for intellectual disability. *Education and Training in Autism and Developmental Disabilities, 52*(3), 332–339.

Polloway, E. A., Bouck, E. C., & Everington, C. E. (2021). *Introduction to intellectual disability, autism, and developmental disabilities.* Pro-Ed.

Polloway, E. A., Bouck, E. C., Patton, J. R., & Lubin, J. (2017). Intellectual and developmental disabilities. In D. Hallahan & J. Kauffman (Eds.), *Handbook of special education.*

Polloway, E. A., Bouck, E. C., Patton, J. R., & Lubin, J. (2022). Intellectual and developmental disabilities. In D. Hallahan & J. Kauffman (Eds.), *Handbook of special education* (3rd ed.). (in press).

Polloway, E. A., Bouck, E. C., & Yang, L. (2019). Educational programs for students with intellectual disability: Demographic patterns. *Education and Training in Autism and Developmental Disabilities, 54*, 30–40.

Retish, P., Hitchings, W., Horvath, M., & Schmalle, B. (1991). *Students with mild disabilities in the secondary school.* Longman.

Sands, D. J., & Doll, B. (1996). Fostering self-determination is a developmental task. *Journal of Special Education, 30*(1), 58–76. https://doi.org/10.1177/002246699603000104

Schalock, R. L., Borthwick-Duffy, S. A., Bradley, V. J., Buntinx, W. H. E., Coulter, D. L., Craig, E. M., Gomez, S. C., Lachapelle, Y., Luckasson, R., Reeve, A., Shogren, K. A., Snell, M. E., Spreat, S., Tassé, M. J., Thompson, J. R., Verdugo-Alonso, M. A., Wehmeyer, M. L., & Yeager, M. H. (2010). *Intellectual disability: Definition, classification, and systems of supports* (11th ed.). American Association on Intellectual and Developmental Disabilities.

Schalock, R. L., Luckasson, R., & Tassé, M. (2021a). *Intellectual disability: Definition, classification, and systems of supports* (12th ed.). American Association on Intellectual and Developmental Disabilities.

Schalock, R. L., Luckasson, R., & Tassé, M. J. (2021b, March). *Twenty questions and answers regarding the 12th edition of the AAIDD manual: Intellectual disability: definition, diagnosis, classification, and systems of supports.* American Association on Intellectual and Developmental Disabilities.

Schuster, J. W., Morse, T. E., Ault, M. J., Crawford, M. R., & Wolery, M. (1998). Constant time delay with chained tasks: A review of the literature. *Education & Treatment of Children, 21*(1), 74–106.

Shepley, C., Lane, J. D., & Ault, M. J. (2019). A review and critical examination of the system of least prompts. *Remedial and Special Education, 40*(5), 313–327. https://doi.org/10.1177/0741932517751213

Shurr, J. M., Jimenez, B., & Bouck, E. C. (Eds.). (2019). *Educating students with intellectual disability and autism spectrum disorder. Book 1: Research-based practices and education science.* Council for Exceptional Children.

Singh, N. N., Oswald, D. P., Ellis, C. R., & Singh, S. D. (1995). Community-based instruction for independent meal preparation by adults with profound mental retardation. *Journal of Behavioral Education, 5*(1), 77–91. https://doi.org/10.1007/BF02110215

Siperstein, G., & Collins, M. A. (2015). Intellectual disability. In E. A. Polloway (Ed.), *The death penalty and intellectual disability* (pp. 21–36). American Association on Intellectual and Developmental Disabilities.

Smith, T. E. C., Polloway, E. A., & Doughty, T. (2020). *Teaching students with special needs in inclusive settings* (8th ed.). Pearson.

Snell, M., & Browder, D. (1987). Domestic and community skills. In M. Snell (Ed.), *Systematic instruction of persons with severe handicaps* (pp. 390–434). Charles E. Merrill.

Spaulding, L. C., & Pratt, S. M. (2015). A review and analysis of the history of special education and disability advocacy in the United States. *American Educational History Journal, 42*(1), 91–109.

Storey, K., & Miner, C. (2011). *Systematic instruction of functional skills for students and adults with disabilities*. Charles C Thomas.

Taber-Doughty, T. (2005). Considering student choice when selecting instructional strategies: A comparison of three prompting systems. *Research in Developmental Disabilities, 26*(5), 411–432. https://doi.org/10.1016/j.ridd.2004.07.006

Taber-Doughty, T., Bouck, E. C., Tom, K., Jasper, A. D., Flanagan, S. M., & Bassette, L. A. (2011). Video modeling and prompting: A comparison of two strategies for teaching cooking skills to students with mild intellectual disabilities. *Education and Training in Autism and Developmental Disabilities, 46*, 499–513.

Test, D. W., Fowler, C. H., Richter, S. M., White, J., Mazzotti, V., Walker, A. R., Kohler, P., & Kortering, L. (2009). Evidence-based practices in secondary transition. *Career Development for Exceptional Individuals, 32*(2), 115–128. https://doi.org/10.1177/0885728809336859

United States Department of Education. (2022). *43rd annual report to congress on the implementation of the individuals with disabilities education act*. Author.

Van Laarhoven, T. R., Munk, D. D., Lynch, K., Bosma, J., & Rouse, J. (2007). A model for preparing special and general education preservice teachers for inclusive education. *Journal of Teacher Education, 58*(5), 440–455. https://doi.org/10.1177/0022487107306803

Wade, T., McConomy, A., & Root, J. (2021). Using upside-down task analysis to monitor student progress. *DADD Express, 32*(2). http://www.daddcec.com/uploads/2/5/2/0/2520220/dadd_spring2021_ebp.pdf

Wehmeyer, M. L., Sands, D. J., Knowlton, H. E., & Kozleski, E. B. (2002). *Providing access to the general curriculum: Teaching students with mental retardation*. Paul H. Brookes Publishing Co.

Westling, D. L., & Fox, L. (2009). *Teaching students with severe disabilities* (4th ed.). Pearson Education, Inc.

West, E. A., McCollow, M., Umbarger, G., Kidwell, J., & Cote, D. (2013). Current status of evidence-based practice for students with intellectual disability and autism spectrum disorders. *Education and Training in Autism and Developmental Disabilities, 48*(4), 443–455.

What Works Clearinghouse™. (2020). *Standards handbook. Version 4.1*. https://ies.ed.gov/ncee/wwc/Docs/referenceresources/WWC-Standards-Handbook-v4-1-508.pdf

Wolery, M., & Hemmeter, M. L. (2011). Classroom instruction: Background, assumptions, and challenges. *Journal of Early Intervention, 33*(4), 371–380. https://doi.org/10.1177/1053815111429119

Wright, J. C., Knight, V. F., & Barton, E. E. (2020). A review of video modeling to teach STEM to students with autism and intellectual disability. *Research in Autism Spectrum Disorders, 70*(February), 101476. https://doi.org/10.1016/j.rasd.2019.101476

CHAPTER 5

SPECIAL EDUCATION OF STUDENTS WHO ARE DEAF/HARD OF HEARING: ADVANCING VALUES

Angi Martin and Julie Cox

Western Illinois University, USA

ABSTRACT

The education of deaf and hard of hearing (d/DHH) students is largely dependent on the preferred mode of communication. Historically, the mode of communication for d/DHH students was determined by society rather than by students and families. This resulted in divisiveness between the Deaf culture and proponents of oral communication. The adoption of IDEA allowed family participation in the decision-making process. Advances in technology increased student access to sound, resulting in more educational placement options. Despite the positive changes, the complex nature of hearing loss and the wide variety in cultural considerations have made it difficult to determine the best approach to deaf education. Thus, educators and providers are left in a conundrum of which version of "traditional" deaf education is best for students.

Keywords: Deaf education; educational placement; hearing loss; sign language; oral communication

INTRODUCTION

Change is inevitable. Change allows for growth and increased effectiveness. Deaf education has experienced many dramatic changes throughout history. Many changes are initiated to create positive outcomes; however, change can also result in new hurdles. This is undoubtedly true for deaf education in America. Many of

Special Education

Advances in Special Education, Volume 38, 69–85

Copyright © 2024 Angi Martin and Julie Cox

Published under exclusive licence by Emerald Publishing Limited

ISSN: 0270-4013/doi:10.1108/S0270-401320240000038005

the changes initiated in the early beginnings of deaf education were abrupt and dramatic, resulting in some challenges that we still face today. One of the most prominent challenges is that there are very different, sometimes opposing, personal and professional perceptions of what deaf education should look like.

Advances in technology have impacted all aspects of education, and the advances in technology have had an even greater impact on the education of deaf and hard of hearing (d/DHH) students (Carstens et al., 2021; Rekkedal, 2011). In general, technology has increased student engagement and the ability to personalize education (Major et al., 2021; Mo, 2011). For students with hearing loss (HL), technological advancements have allowed for better access to sound, resulting in more educational opportunities and placement options.

HEARING LOSS

Approximately 1% of all US students aged 6–21 have some degree of HL (National Center for Educational Statistics, 2022). Many of those children enter school with some degree of speech and language delay (Walker et al., 2014), which often impacts academic performance (Catts et al., 2002; Cross et al., 2019). Because children learn language through exposure, the quantity and quality of exposure are critical components of overall language development and literacy skills (Hart & Risley, 1995; Hirsh-Pasek et al., 2015; Humphries et al., 2022). Many factors, such as the type and severity of the HL, access to early intervention, and the type and use of amplification, all impact language exposure and ultimately contribute to the amount of impact on student learning (Halliday et al., 2017; Moeller, 2000). Karchmer and Mitchell (2003) reported that adequate language exposure for many children with HL is less than ideal. For students participating in auditory-oral programs or those learning in general education classrooms, the severity of the HL and access to sound is especially important (Tomblin et al., 2014; Walker et al., 2014).

Type and Degree of HL

The three types of HL are conductive, sensorineural, and mixed. The location of the damage to the hearing system determines the type of HL. Damage to the outer or middle ear results in conductive HL, while damage to the inner ear results in sensorineural HL. Mixed HL is a combination of both types of HL (ASHA, n.d.a.).

The amount of damage to the auditory system determines the degree of HL. A hearing threshold is measured in decibels (dB) and is defined as the quietest sound that can be heard 50% of the time (Martin & Clark, 2006). HL can be slight (16–25 dB), mild (26–40 dB), moderate (41–55 dB), moderately severe (56–70 dB), severe (71–90 dB), or profound (90+ dB) (American Speech Language Hearing Association [ASHA], n.d.). See Table 5.1 for the degrees of HL.

The configuration of HL refers to the shape of the HL or the level of HL across speech frequencies. Most English speech sounds are produced between 20 and 60 dB and at frequencies ranging from 250 to 4000 Hz (ASHA, n.d.a.).

Table 5.1. Degree of Hearing Loss.

Severity of Loss	Threshold
Normal	<15 dBHL
Slight	16–25 dBHL
Mild	26–40 dBHL
Moderate	41–55 dBHL
Moderately severe	56–70 dBHL
Severe	71–90 dBHL
Profound	90+ dBHL

Hearing thresholds are obtained at each frequency and recorded on an audiogram (a graph representing hearing thresholds). The degree of HL at each frequency provides information about an individual's ability to perceive the various speech sounds produced by a communication partner. Some of the more common descriptors used to describe the configuration of HL are high frequency, low frequency, or symmetrical versus asymmetrical (ASHA, n.d.a.).

HISTORY OF DEAF EDUCATION

Deaf education in the United States experienced many changes over the last century, which resulted in a cultural divide. While deaf education in Europe dates as far back as the 1500s, formal education for the d/DHH in the United States was not established until the 1800s. Laurent Clerc and Thomas Gallaudet are credited for establishing the first state-funded residential institution for the hearing impaired in the United States. The American School for the Deaf was founded in Hartford, Connecticut, in 1817. The school utilized a sign-based pedagogy using components of French sign language and manual communication of the students attending the program, ultimately resulting in the establishment of American Sign Language (ASL). The use of ASL proved an effective educational approach for DHH students, many of whom developed literacy skills similar to their hearing peers (Shapiro, 1994; Strong & Prinz, 1997). The success of the American School for the Deaf and the creation of ASL was applauded and served as a model for creating many more residential schools for deaf students across the United States. Moreover, the establishment of ASL led to the creation of deaf organizations and social relations among d/DHH individuals, marking the beginning of Deaf culture (National Association of the Deaf, n.d.a.).

Deaf education was upended during the second half of the nineteenth century when oral theories of deaf education were first introduced. The Clark Institute for the Deaf opened in 1867 and used an oral pedagogy. The use of speech and lip reading to communicate was referred to as oralism. Alexander Graham Bell was among the most notable supporters of an oral approach to deaf education. Bell's mother was deaf and was considered an oral communicator. Bell's father, a teacher for the deaf, developed "visual speech," a system of symbols used to aid deaf students with correct speech production. Alexander Graham Bell became a teacher at the Clark Institute and dedicated much of his time and money to promoting oralism.

As the concept of oralism gained popularity, a division was formed between the proponents of the two approaches. This division was exacerbated in 1880, following the International Convention in Milan, Italy, where delegates world-wide met to determine the "best methods" in deaf education. The delegates, only five of whom were from the United States, voted to adopt oralism as the best practice. Moreover, the delegates voted to prohibit teaching sign language in deaf schools. As the number of oral programs increased, deaf educators who taught sign language were replaced by hearing teachers to facilitate speech and language. Many deaf students were not able to learn language effectively in oral programs; they were not able to achieve their full academic potential. This resulted in lower academic expectations for deaf students (Hill, 2012). The impact of the International Convention stretched far beyond deaf education; to some, it was viewed as an attack on Deaf culture. The divisiveness created between the Deaf and hearing cultures in the latter half of the 19th century is still felt today.

Although the impact of the International Conference in Milan on deaf education was felt well into the 20th century, many Deaf individuals continued to teach and use sign language in secret, preserving both the language and the culture. Nevertheless, some significant developments during the 20th century further altered the course of deaf education. In 1960, William Stoke, a linguist, published his research, which provided evidence of the shared characteristics between sign language and other languages, arguing sign language should be considered a viable method of communication and education for d/DHH individuals (Higgins & Lieberman, 2016). Subsequently, the concept of *total communication* (TC) was introduced by Roy Holcolm in 1967 (Scheetz, 2012). In this communication philosophy, one or several modes of communication (e.g., manual, oral, auditory, and written) were considered and employed based on the child's individual needs. This philosophy allowed teachers to use the most appropriate communication method for any given child in any given situation. The introduction of TC allowed some educational freedom and served as a bridge between proponents of manual communication and oralism (Hawkins & Brawner, 1997).

One of the most significant changes in deaf education resulted from the Education of All Handicapped Children Act-Public Law 94-12 in 1975 and later the Individuals with Disabilities Education Act (IDEA) in 1990. The law ensured a free and appropriate education (FAPE) in the least restrictive environment (LRE) for all children with disabilities. The passing of this law was especially significant for d/DHH students because it allowed them to attend schools within their own communities rather than residential programs. Before 1975, residential programs were considered standard practice in deaf education, with as many as 80% of d/DHH students placed in residential programs (Lane et al., 1996). Although the adoption of IDEA was positive, it did bring about challenges in deaf education. Many school districts were unprepared and lacked an understanding of the unique educational needs and considerations of d/DHH students (U.S. Department of Education-Deaf Student Education Services, 1992; Zimmerman & Thomas, 2017). In addition, there was a shortage of teachers with the training and expertise to work with d/DHH students. Roeser and Downs (2004) stated:

> The solution for many school districts was to place deaf students in special education classrooms where other special needs children were taught. Academic expectations in many of these "self-contained" settings were homogenized and typically set so even the lowest achiever could accomplish them. Further complicated by a system that perpetuated failure for deaf and hard-of-hearing students with normal cognitive abilities, this dynamic set in motion a trend of underachievement that has not been successfully reversed, statistically speaking, even today. (p. 11)

Unfortunately, research suggests that many districts and teachers continue to remain unprepared to provide adequate educational opportunities for d/DHH students (Eriks-Brophy & Whittingham, 2013; Roppolo, 2016).

ADVANCES IN TECHNOLOGY

Technology advancements have played a crucial role in the evolution of education for students with HL. Advances in technology have increased the educational opportunities for many d/DHH students by increasing their access to sound. Hearing aids and cochlear implants (CIs) are the two main types of amplification used by children with HL. Both are considered personal hearing devices that aim to provide an individual with access to sound and increase overall communication. Hearing aids amplify sound and deliver the sound directly to the user's ear. They are most appropriate for children with mild to moderate sensorineural HL (National Institute on Deafness and Other Communication Disorders, 2017). A CI is a medical device for individuals with severe-to-profound HL (National Institute on Deafness and Other Communication Disorders, 2016). CIs are surgically implanted and bypass the auditory system's damaged portion to stimulate the auditory nerve directly. Although hearing aids and CIs do not restore normal hearing, they provide access to sounds they would otherwise be able to hear. Such devices have allowed many d/DHH students to participate in less restrictive educational environments.

In addition to hearing aids and CIs, additional hearing assistive technologies are available to facilitate the needs of d/DHH students in the classroom environment. Remote microphone (RM) technology is the most common assistive technology used in schools today (Johnson & Seaton, 2021). The use of RM technology in classrooms has proven to be beneficial for both normal hearing children and children with any level of HL (Eriks-Brophy et al., 2009; Flagg-Williams et al., 2011; Ryan, 2009; Zanin & Rance, 2016). RM technologies use a microphone to pick up the speaker's voice and transmit the sound to the listener's ear in an amplified manner (Crandell & Smaldino, 2000; Johnson & Seaton, 2021). These technologies are designed to increase accessibility to sound by improving the signal-to-noise ratio (SNR). The SNR is the difference between the noise level and the intensity of the signal (Martin & Clark, 2006). A lower SNR results in a decreased understanding of speech (Hawkins & Yacullo, 1984). Because of the nature of HL and the impact of classroom noise on speech understanding, an optimal SNR is critical to the academic success of students with HL (Crandell & Smaldino, 2000).

Two types of RM systems are used in classrooms and other listening environments. One type of RM system commonly used with d/DHH students is a personal RM system. With a personal RM system, the amplified sound is delivered to the listener's ear through their hearing device (hearing aid or CI) or the use of headphones (Madell et al., 2019). Because the auditory signal is delivered directly to students' ears, they provide the most significant improvements to the SNR and speech understanding abilities (Madell et al., 2019; Schafer & Kleineck, 2009). The other type of RM system is a sound-field system. This system type is often referred to as a classroom amplification system (Cole & Flexer, 2011). This system delivers the auditory signal to speakers placed throughout the classroom or listening environment. Sound-field systems do not provide as much improvement to the SNR as personal RM systems; however, sound-field systems have the potential to benefit all of the students in the listening environment (Cole & Flexer, 2011; Johnson & Seaton, 2021; Madell et al., 2019).

Another advancement in technology that has allowed for increased access to sound is the development of dynamic systems. Dynamic systems are designed to adapt to the acoustic environment by monitoring the noise levels in the environment and adjusting the amount of gain provided (Johnson & Seaton, 2021). Prior to this advancement, fixed-gain systems provided a consistent level of gain and did not adjust for the noise levels within the environment. Research has indicated that dynamic technology results in better speech understanding in noise when compared to fixed-gain systems (Schafer & Kleineck, 2009; Thibodeau, 2010). This type of smart technology that allows a device to assess the listening environment and automatically adjust the auditory signal is also available in hearing aids and CIss. Such advancements have allowed d/DHH students to have better access to speech within the classroom environment.

COMMUNICATION APPROACHES AND EDUCATIONAL PLACEMENT

The educational approach for students with HL often depends upon the communication approach selected by the student and their families. The amount of HL, access to sound, and cultural considerations may dictate which communication approach and the appropriate educational placement for a student. Students who are members of the deaf culture use ASL to communicate, while other d/DHH students may use an oral approach to communicate. The communication approach utilized often dictates educational placement for the d/DHH students. The communication approaches or methods for d/DHH students can be divided into three broad categories: Auditory Methods, Manual Communication, and TC.

COMMUNICATION APPROACHES

Auditory methods. Auditory methods rely on the use of any residual hearing to develop listening and spoken language skills. This approach relies heavily on technology such as hearing aids, CIs, and RM systems to maximize residual hearing to facilitate auditory learning and develop speech. A common auditory method is the auditory-oral communication approach. With this approach, the children rely heavily on the auditory signal but are also encouraged to use any visual cues or methods to facilitate speech understanding (Cole & Flexer, 2011). This includes the use of gestures or facial expressions and speechreading.

Another auditory communication method is the auditory-verbal approach. With this approach, the child is expected to rely solely on the auditory signal to develop listening and spoken language (Rhoades, 2010). Research suggests auditory approaches result in better language development outcomes when compared to other communication approaches (Binos et al., 2021; Dettman et al., 2013). Likewise, Demers and Bergeron (2019) conducted a systematic review of the research to determine the effectiveness of the communication approaches for children with severe-to-profound HL on hearing, speech, and language skills. The results of the review suggested that children that used an auditory approach showed better auditory, speech, and expressive language outcomes. This is important because decreased speech and language abilities often result in academic challenges for students, especially those with some degree of HL (Catts et al., 2002; Cross et al., 2019).

Manual communication. Manual communication refers to the use of visual stimuli to communicate. Although there are various forms of manual communication, the most common manual communication methods are ASL and Signed English. These methods do not require a child to learn to speak or develop speechreading skills. These approaches, specifically the use of ASL, are widely accepted by the deaf community (NAD, n.d.a).

ASL is a complete visual language with unique rules and features (Scheetz, 2012). According to the National Association of the Deaf (NAD), "American Sign Language (ASL) is the backbone of the American Deaf Culture" (NAD, 2023, American Sign Language). Because ASL is a visual language, there is no written form. Consequently, ASL users often learn English and are considered bilingual. Sign bilingualism considers sign language as the child's first language. Once they develop a strong sign language foundation, the second language (e.g., English) is incorporated through speech or writing. Research has documented the academic benefits of a bilingual approach for d/DHH students (Geeslin, 2007; Hrastinski & Wilbur, 2016; Lange et al., 2013). The NAD also supports bilingual language development, citing the benefits and recognizing it as a more inclusive educational approach.

Signed English is a visual model of the English language, mimicking the exact grammar and sequence of the language (Scheetz, 2012). Signed English resulted from concerns regarding lower levels of academic achievement for d/DHH students, specifically with their writing skills (Gustaston, 1990). Signed English incorporates ASL signs, finger spelling, and hand gestures or sign markers to represent grammatical structures, resulting in a visual representation of the English language (Scheetz, 2012). Seeing Essential English (SEE1) and Signed Exact English (SEE2) were developed as more advanced versions of Signed English to include more specific grammatical information, such as more specific pronouns as plurals (Scheetz, 2012). SEE1 is no longer used formally; thus, SEE2 is often referred to as only SEE in the literature (Luetke-Stahlman & Milburn, 1996). Research suggests that the use of SEE, more specifically providing a visual representation of the grammatical structures of the language, results in improved academic outcomes for d/DHH students when compared to other communication approaches (Nielsen et al., 2011, 2016).

Total communication. TC refers to the use of multiple modes of communication depending on the needs of the individual. TC was developed in the 1960s and is referred to as a philosophy rather than a communication approach (Schow & Nerbonne, 2017). TC incorporates manual, oral, auditory, visual, and written modes of communication to facilitate language learning and academic achievement.

EDUCATIONAL PLACEMENT OPTIONS

IDEA mandates that students are educated in the LRE, with the goal often being a regular education classroom setting (IDEA, 2004). Determining the most appropriate placement for d/DHH students can be tricky. Because of the nature of HL and possible communication barriers, special considerations must be factored into determining educational placement and services for d/DHH students. In 1992, the US Department of Education responded to concerns about LRE and the provision of services for d/DHH students brought forth by the Commission on the Education of the Deaf. The additional guidance issued by the US Department of Education recommended the following considerations when determining educational services for students with HL: preferred mode of communication; communication needs, linguistic needs; degree of HL and access to appropriate amplification; academic level; and social, emotional, and cultural needs (U.S. Department of Education-Deaf Student Education Services, 1992). More recently, the US Department of Education reiterated that if an educational setting does not meet the individual needs of a student with HL, it cannot be considered the LRE and does not meet the free and appropriate public education (FAPE) required by IDEA. In such cases, placement options outside of a regular education setting must be considered to ensure students are able to communicate and learn in a language-rich environment.

Because students with HL can be educated in a variety of settings, determining the most appropriate placement may be overwhelming for parents and school personnel. The most recent data suggest that nearly half of d/DHH students spend most of their time in a regular education setting; however, there is no one-size-fits-all approach to deaf education (Gallaudet Research Institute, 2013). Educational placements for d/DHH students can be divided into three broad categories. These include residential schools, self-contained classrooms, and a regular classroom setting with resources.

Residential and day programs. Prior to 1975, residential programs were considered standard practice in deaf education. Residential schools typically require that a student live full time at the school while attending; however, some day programs are available. These programs allow students to attend the program during the day and return home at night. Students who attend these programs are educated with other d/DHH students. The teachers at day programs and residential schools have extensive training in deaf education and the communication philosophy employed by the program (National Association of State Directors of Special Education, 2018). The students are often exposed to ASL and immersed in Deaf culture. Because the communication approach is consistent across students and teachers, residential programs may provide d/DHH students with natural communication opportunities. Seaver and DesGeorges (2004) highlighted the importance of direct instruction and communication between student and teacher in the student's preferred mode of communication rather than through the use of an interpreter. They stated:

> Both student and teacher invest more of themselves in the teaching/learning dynamic and its outcome. Both benefit from a greater understanding of each other's style and expectations. And there is no chance that the teaching is compromised by the intervention of an interpreter who may substitute vocabulary or lack knowledge of the subject and unintentionally misrepresent it to the student. (pp. 19–20)

For some d/DHH students, residential programs may be the most appropriate option to facilitate language, academic, and social development.

Although there are many benefits to residential programs, there are also some drawbacks that should be considered. Currently, there are fewer than 50 residential programs in the United States and even fewer day programs available for d/DHH students (Educational Programs for Deaf Students, 2022). For many families, day programs are not a feasible option because of distance. Moreover, children attending residential programs may be far from their families, resulting in limited family interactions and possible feelings of isolation. Because students in residential programs primarily interact with other d/DHH students, they may not have many opportunities to communicate with their hearing peers. This may make communication outside the school environment more challenging. Parents, teachers, and administrators must determine the hearing and communication needs of the student; however, they must also consider the benefits and drawbacks of a residential placement to ensure the students' social, emotional, and educational needs are being met.

Self-contained classroom. A self-contained classroom setting implies that students spend most of their school day in a special education classroom. The students receive more specialized interventions, and the student-to-teacher ratio is lower than in a regular classroom. This may allow for more individualized learning opportunities and a better listening environment. Placement in a self-contained classroom does not guarantee that the teacher has the appropriate training to work with d/DHH students. Depending on teacher training, students who use sign language may have to rely on an interpreter in the classroom. In some instances, a student's home school may not have an appropriate classroom to meet a student's needs forcing schools to come up with alternative solutions outside the student's home district. The National Association of State Directors of Special Education (2018) wrote:

> Some state education agencies have established a regional network of deaf or hard of hearing programs at select schools. These regional programs allow districts to pool and optimize resources and classroom settings. Teachers and other professionals can collaborate with other specialists. Providing these settings is one way of meeting the LRE provisions and should be encouraged. (p. 35)

Although district networking allows for more specialized programs and teachers, there are also some drawbacks. Students may spend significant time commuting daily and may feel isolated from their hearing siblings, neighborhood friends, and community (Gettemeier, 2023).

Regular education classroom setting. The provision of services in a regular classroom setting is what is traditionally referred to as LRE. This educational placement implies that students with HL are educated in regular education classrooms with their hearing peers. This option also allows students to attend classes in their home school, have access to the general curriculum, and the ability to participate in extracurricular activities with their peers. Mainstreaming provides d/DHH students with real-world experiences and may allow them to develop the skills necessary to interact effectively in a hearing world (Leppert, 2014). On the contrary, some have argued that placing d/DHH students in a regular classroom with hearing peers could result in feelings of isolation due to communication barriers (Roeser & Downs, 2004). Because there are numerous variables related to the nature of HL, the potential benefits and barriers of mainstreaming should be considered on an individual basis.

Although nearly 65% of d/DHH students spend more than 80% of their time in a regular classroom environment, students placed in a regular education classroom often require additional support depending on their individual needs (National Center for Education Statistics, 2022). The amount and types of support services provided depend on the student's individual needs as defined in their Individualized Education Program (IEP). Various support services are available, including sign language interpreters, classroom aids, and notetakers. Students can also receive additional support with speech, language, hearing, and academics. Gallaudet Research Institute (GRI, 2013) reported that 43.9% of students received assistive technology services, 62.2% received audiology services, and 60.6% received speech and language services.

Many students receive specialized services outside of the classroom setting. This allows the student to receive more intensive instruction and additional support in a small group or one-on-one setting. Many d/DHH students work with Itinerant Teachers of the Deaf and Hard of Hearing (ITDHH). They have specialized training and knowledge about HL, hearing technology, and how to maximize student learning. In addition to providing services to d/DHH students, ITDHH works with classroom teachers to modify the curriculum when appropriate and recommend any necessary environmental modifications to ensure students have the best possible listening environment (Scheetz, 2012). This education placement option aims to provide students with the additional support and resources necessary for student learning without excluding them from the regular classroom environment and their hearing peers. The severity of HL, access to hearing technology, and primary communication method may impact the level of additional support needed.

There are many educational placement options available for students with HL. In order to ensure the most appropriate placement, the communication and hearing needs of the student, as well as the knowledge and training of the teachers, should be carefully considered. The IEP team, which includes parents, must also consider the barriers and benefits of each educational placement option for the student. Fiedler (2001) wrote, "The contrasting nature of some of the educational approaches can cause frustrations for many parents trying to determine what is best for their own child and for educators trying to meet the individual needs of students who are deaf and hard of hearing and their families" (p. 56). Regardless of placement, each student should receive a quality education with access to the knowledge and resources to learn and succeed.

VALUE AND TRADITION

The word "value" is a subjective and personally defined term; however, we may find that the level of subjectivity in terms of the value of education is never quite as variable as it is in d/Deaf education. Individuals who are deaf or hard of hearing fall into a unique cultural category. Whereas some individuals strive for "normalcy," in this case, to live in and actively participate in a hearing world, others identify with Deaf culture, which emphasizes the strengths of and heritage of living in a nonhearing world (O'Brien & Placier, 2015). A simple example to highlight the differences between students who are deaf and Deaf students is the difference between the lowercase "d" and the uppercase "D." We often see the text printed as d/DHH referring to an all-encompassing group of "deaf" (as in a medical diagnosis or disability), "Deaf" (as in a cultural representation), and "hard of hearing" individuals (O'Brien & Placier, 2015). However, when the discussion turns to the value of d/Deaf education, it becomes increasingly difficult to pinpoint the differing viewpoints and opinions along the continuum from deaf to Deaf.

As educators, it is imperative to understand how one's personal biases are reflected in the classroom and how one addresses students with different abilities. Our biases are inherently linked to the ethical principles by which we live and work. Professionals on a team for a student who is d/DHH often bring highly different perspectives to the discussion. Those who are primarily healthcare professionals (e.g., physicians and otolaryngologists) often operate under the four widely accepted ethical principles of healthcare: autonomy, beneficence, non-maleficence, and justice (Morrison & Furlong, 2013, p. 61). Educators, on the other hand, are in conflict between the legalities of No Child Left Behind and the

IDEA. IDEA states that teachers and school administrators must provide truly individualized education to students with disabilities, whereas No Child Left Behind promotes inclusion and mainstreaming (Frick et al., 2012). That, in itself, is enough of a battle. Now, layer on top of that the perspective of the parents and the student on whether or not they want to participate in a fully hearing world or if they embrace Deaf culture, preferring to communicate in ways other than the oral modality (Fullwood & Levinson, 2023). Finally, the interprofessional team for d/Deaf students also includes "hybrid" professionals (i.e., speech-language pathologists and audiologists) who are dually trained under a healthcare model but also advocate for best communication practices (Naude & Bornman, 2014).

The bias held by teachers directly affects their perception of the value of deaf education. A qualitative study by Musyoka and Clark (2017) analyzing the importance of various goals on an IEP showed that teachers of d/DHH students have three main priorities. The top three goals for students were: (1) school readiness, (2) improved sign communication, and (3) improved speech communication (Musyoka & Clark, 2017). The second and third goals can be juxtaposed with one another depending on the values of the individual students and their families. Based on this study, teachers prefer both sign and speech (TC approach), which may or may not meet the cultural needs of the students. Of the three most common modes of communication found in that study (i.e., spoken, signed, or sign-supported spoken), it was found that the students who used sign-supported spoken language received the most other special education services compared to students who received only spoken or only signed instruction (Musyoka & Clark, 2017). It was unclear in their study if those students were d/DHH or if they had concomitant disabilities since past research has shown that 40%–50% of students who are deaf also have a co-occurring disability (Guardino, 2015).

The challenge of determining the value of an educational paradigm rests in the priorities of the professionals, families, and, ultimately, students. Research has shown that teachers' perspectives on d/Deaf students are dependent on whether or not the student has other disabilities (e.g., learning disabilities). Morgan (2015) reported that teachers who taught students who were only physically impaired, visually impaired, or deaf were quickly "full members" of the inclusive educational community. Teachers often cited reasons in favor of full membership as the ability to be a part of the greater group and to build social relationships. Special education teachers with more experience with students of varying abilities were less likely to make a blanket statement regarding full membership in the school community because of the need for more individualized education following the principles of IDEA (Morgan, 2015). Guardino (2015) stated that 40%–50% of deaf students also have another disability, meaning that approximately half of all deaf students likely lack full inclusion in their educational setting.

Tradition is defined as "an inherited, established, or customary pattern of thought, action, or behavior" (Merriam-Webster, n.d.a.). What is considered tradition in deaf education? The evolution of deaf education has been erratic. Many of the early changes could be described as abrupt and radical. Historically, communication methods were decided by society as a whole with little or no consideration of individual and family characteristics. Likewise, the education of d/DHH students was highly dependent on the communication approach. Students with HL had little say in communication or education until the adoption of IDEA.

IDEA ensured a FAPE in LRE and allowed students and families to participate in the decision-making process (U.S. Department of Education, 2011, 2015). However, even with the newer provisions to include students and families in the decision-making process, there is still controversy over the best approach to deaf education dating back hundreds of years. Although students have benefitted from each communication approach and educational placement, researchers have yet to identify an approach that is successful for *all* d/DHH students (Fiedler, 2001). Additionally, Seaver and DesGeorges (2004) stated that "Depending on the political climate where you live, the push for a 'full inclusion' model may be strong or weak. In other words, if one part of the law is given more weight than another (LRE over special considerations for deaf or hard of hearing), the placement issue of the student may not be in his or her individual best interests." (p. 20). This suggests that although students and families are protected under IDEA, they may still be at the mercy of others when determining educational placement. Moreover, variability in teacher preparedness and district resources adds to the complexity of determining the best educational approach for d/DHH students.

With the moderate (and growing) number of students who are deaf or deaf with another disability (DWD), deaf educators feel increasingly ill-prepared for the challenges present in their classrooms (Guardino, 2015). Added to the complexity of many d/DHH (or DWD) students is the idea that tradition has shown us that we still do not have a "best practice" for deaf education due to the stark differences in values. Deaf education tends to be a unique challenge because, in some cases, HL is considered a cultural difference rather than a medical or educational issue. The most consistent theme in the history of deaf education is the broad inconsistency of how students are instructed, how those methods are determined, and by whom.

CONCLUSION

The evolution of deaf education could be described as tumultuous and controversial, with much of the early controversy centering on communication modality and cultural identity. Recent advancements in technology and changing perspectives over time have left the field of deaf education in a current state of weighing one's options carefully. Families of children who are d/DHH currently have more options and must consider their own goals for their children. Mode of communication (e.g., verbal, ASL, TC) and access to technology for amplification help to determine the most appropriate educational placement for d/DHH students. Because of the variability in modes of communication and the unique educational needs of d/DHH students, it is difficult to determine the "best" way to provide instruction for students with HL. In addition, providing the appropriate services and accommodations for d/DHH students requires teachers and staff with specialized knowledge and training related to their unique needs (e.g., HL, amplification, communication mode). Despite the fact that the changes in deaf education have been overwhelmingly positive, they resulted in new challenges, leaving school districts and deaf educators to contend with the ever-changing needs of the students.

REFERENCES

American Speech Language Hearing Association. (n.d.). *Hearing loss (ages 5+)*. https://www.asha.org/practice-portal/clinical-topics/hearing-loss/

Binos, P., Nirgianaki, E., & Psillas, G. (2021). How effective is auditory–verbal therapy (AVT) for building language development of children with cochlear implants? A systematic review. *Life, 11*(3), 239. MDPI AG. http://doi.org/10.3390/life11030239

Carstens, K. J., Mallon, J. M., Bataineh, M., & Al-Bataineh, A. (2021). Effects of technology on student learning. *The Turkish Online Journal of Educational Technology, 20*(1), 105–113.

Catts, H. W., Fey, M. E., Tomblin, J. B., & Zhang, X. (2002). A longitudinal investigation of reading outcomes in children with language impairments. *Journal of Speech, Language, and Hearing Research, 45*(6), 1142–1157.

Cole, E., & Flexer, C. (2011). *Children with hearing loss birth to six: Developing listening and talking* (2nd ed.). Plural Publishing.

Crandell, C., & Smaldino, J. (2000). Classroom acoustics for children with normal hearing and with hearing impairment. *Language, Speech, and Hearing Services in Schools, 31*, 362–370. https://doi.org/10.1044/0161-1461.3104.362

Cross, A. M., Joanisse, M. F., & Archibald, L. M. (2019). Mathematical abilities in children with developmental language disorder. *Language, Speech, and Hearing Services in Schools, 50*(1), 150–163.

Demers, D., & Bergeron, F. (2019). Effectiveness of rehabilitation approaches proposed to children with severe-to-profound prelinguistic deafness on the development of auditory, speech, and language skills: A systematic review. *Journal of Speech, Language, and Hearing Research, 62*(11), 4196–4230. https://doi.org/23814764000300140072

Dettman, S., Wall, E., Constantinescu, G., & Dowell, R. (2013). Communication outcomes for groups of children using cochlear implants enrolled in auditory-verbal, aural-oral, and bilingual-bicultural early intervention programs. *Otology & Neurotology, 34*(3), 451–459. https://doi.org/10.1097/MAO.0b013e3182839650

Educational programs for deaf students. (2022). *American Annals of the Deaf, 167*(2), 1–75. https://doi-org.wiulibraries.idm.oclc.org/10.1353/aad.2022.0025

Eriks-Brophy, A., Durieux-Smith, A., Olds, J., Fitzpatrick, A., Duquette, C., & Whittingham, J. (2009). Facilitators and barriers to the inclusion of orally educated children and youth with hearing loss in schools: Promoting partnerships to support inclusion. *Volta Review, 106*(1), 53–88. http://web.b.ebscohost.com.lynx.lib.usm.edu/ehost/pdfviewer/pdfviewer?sid=f3504021-fd45-406c-a16b-69dd52a42e36%40sessionmgr115&vid=1&hid=101

Eriks-Brophy, A., & Whittingham, J. (2013). Teachers' perceptions of the inclusion of children with hearing loss in general education settings. *American Annals of the Deaf, 158*. http://muse.jhu.edu.lynx.lib.usm.edu/journals/american_annals_of_the_deaf/v158/158.1.eriks-brophy.html

Fiedler, B. C. (2001). Considering placement and educational approaches for students who are deaf and hard of hearing. *Teaching Exceptional Children, 34*(2), 54–59. http://www.casenex.com/casenex/cecReadings/consideringPlacement.pdf

Flagg-Williams, J. B., Rubin, R., & Aquino-Russell, C. (2011). Classroom soundscape. *Educational and Child Psychology, 28*, 89–99.

Frick, W. C., Faircloth, S. C., & Little, K. S. (2012). Responding to the collective and individual "best interests of students": Revisiting the tension between administrative practice and ethical imperatives in special education leadership. *Educational Administration Quarterly*, *49*(2), 207–242.

Fullwood, L., & Levinson, M. (2023). Fifty years on- and still no resolution: Deaf education, ideology, policy and the cost of resistance. *Teaching and Teacher Education*, *129*, 104–145.

Gallaudet Research Institute (GRI). (2013). *Regional and national summary report of data from the 2011–2012 annual survey of deaf and hard of hearing children and youth*. Gallaudet Research Institute.

Geeslin, J. D. (2007). *Deaf bilingual education: A comparison of the academic performance of deaf children of deaf parents and deaf children of hearing parents*. Doctoral dissertation, Indiana University. http://gradworks.umi.com/3287372.pdf

Gettemeier, D. (2023). Educational settings. In S. Lenihan (Ed.), *Preparing to teach, committing to learn: An introduction to educating children who are D/HH* (pp. 10-1–10-14). National Center for Hearing Assessment and Management. https://www.infanthearing.org/ebook-educating-children-dhh/

Guardino, C. (2015). Evaluating teachers' preparedness to work with students who are deaf and hard of hearing with disabilities. *American Annals of the Deaf*, *160*(4), 415–426.

Gustaston, G. (1990). Signing exact English. In H. Bornstein (Ed.), *Manual communication: Implications for education* (pp. 108–127). Gallaudet University Press.

Halliday, L. F., Tuomainen, O., & Rosen, S. (2017). Language development and impairment in children with mild to moderate sensorineural hearing loss. *Journal of Speech, Language, and Hearing Research*, *60*, 1551–1567.

Hart, B., & Risley, T. R. (1995). *Meaningful differences in the everyday experience of young American children*. Paul H Brookes.

Hawkins, L., & Brawner, J. (1997). *Educating children who are deaf or hard of hearing: Total communication*. ERIC Digests. #559. https://files.eric.ed.gov/fulltext/ED414677.pdf

Hawkins, D. B., & Yacullo, W. S. (1984). Signal-to-noise ratio advantage of binaural hearing aids and directional microphones under different levels of reverberation. *Journal of Speech and Hearing Disorders*, *49*(3), 278–286. https://doi.org/10.1044/jshd.4903.278

Higgins, M., & Lieberman, A. M. (2016). Deaf students as a linguistic and cultural minority: Shifting perspectives and implications for teaching and learning. *Journal of Education*, *196*(1), 9–18. https://doi.org/10.1177/002205741619600103

Hill, J. C. (2012). *Language attitudes in the American deaf community* (1st ed.). Gallaudet University Press.

Hirsh-Pasek, K., Adamson, L. B., Bakeman, R., Owen, M. T., Golinkoff, R. M., Pace, A., & Suma, K. (2015). The contribution of early communication quality to low-income children's language success. *Psychological Science*, *26*, 1071–1083. https://doi.org/10.1177/0956797615581493

Hrastinski, I., & Wilbur, R. B. (2016). Academic achievement of deaf and hard-of-hearing students in an ASL/English bilingual program. *Journal of Deaf Studies and Deaf Education*, *21*(2), 156–170. https://doi.org/10.1093/deafed/env072

Humphries, T., Mathur, G., Napoli, D. J., Padden, C., & Rathmann, C. (2022). Deaf children need rich language input from the start: Support in advising parents. *Children*, *9*(11), 1609. https://doi.org/10.3390/children9111609

Individuals with Disabilities Education Improvement Act (IDEA 2004). (2023, June). *The individuals with disabilities education improvement act: Public law 108-446: IDEA 2004 [Web Bulletin]*. https://www.wrightslaw.com/idea/law.htm

Johnson, C. D. C., & Seaton, J. B. (2021). *Educational audiology handbook*. Plural Publishing, Inc.

Karchmer, M., & Mitchell, R. (2003). Demographic and achievement characteristics of deaf and hard-of-hearing students. In M. Marschark & P. Spencer (Eds.), *The Oxford handbook of deaf studies, language, and education* (pp. 21–37). Oxford University Press.

Lane, H., Hoffmeister, R., & Bahan, B. J. (1996). *A journey into the deaf-world*. DawnSignPress.

Lange, C. M., Lane-Outlaw, S., Lange, W. E., & Sherwood, D. L. (2013). American Sign Language/English bilingual model: A longitudinal study of academic growth. *Journal of Deaf Studies and Deaf Education*, *18*, 532–544. https://doi.org/10.1093/deafed/ent027

Leppert, Maggie. (2014, August). Mainstream deaf education. *Lifeprint*. https://www.lifeprint.com/asl101/topics/mainstream-deaf-education.htm

Luetke-Stahlman, B., & Milburn, W. O. (1996). A history of seeing essential English (SEE I). *American Annals of the Deaf, 141*(1), 29–33. https://doi.org/10.1353/aad.2012.0001

Madell, J. R., Felxer, C. A., Wolfe, J., & Schafer, E. (2019). *Pediatric audiology: Diagnosis, technology, and management*. Thieme.

Major, L., Francis, G. A., & Tsapali, M. (2021). The effectiveness of technology-supported personalized learning in low- and middle-income countries: A meta-analysis. *British Journal of Educational Technology, 52*, 1935–1964. https://doi.org/10.1111/bjet.13116

Martin, F. N., & Clark, J. G. (2006). *Introduction to audiology* (9th ed.). Pearson/Allyn and Bacon.

Merriam-Webster. (n.d.). *Tradition*. Merriam-Webster.com dictionary. https://www.merriam-webster.com/dictionary/tradition

Mo, S. (2011). Evidence on instructional technology and student engagement in an auditing course. *Academy of Educational Leadership Journal, 15*(4), 149.

Moeller, M. P. (2000). Early intervention and language development in children who are deaf and hard of hearing. *Pediatrics, 106*(3), E43. https://doi.org/10.1542/peds.106.3.e43

Morgan, P. S. (2015). General and special education high school teachers' perspectives of full membership for students with disabilities. *Values and Ethics in Educational Administration, 11*(3), 1–9.

Morrison, E. E., & Furlong, B. (2013). *Health care ethics: Critical issues for the 21st century* (3rd ed.). Jones & Bartlett Learning.

Musyoka, M. M., & Clark, M. D. (2017). Teacher perceptions of individualized education program (IEP) goals and related services. *Journal of Developmental and Physical Disabilities, 29*, 5–23.

National Association of the Deaf. (n.d.a). *American Sign Language*. https://www.nad.org

National Association of State Directors of Special Education (NASDSE). (2018). *Optimizing outcomes for students who are deaf or hard of hearing: Educational service guidelines* (3rd ed.). Author. www.nasdse.org

National Center for Education Statistics. (2022). *Students with disabilities*. https://nces.ed.gov/programs/coe/indicator/cgg/students-with-disabilities

National Institute on Deafness and Other Communication Disorders. (2016, February). *Cochlear implants*. U.S. Department of Health and Human Services. https://www.nidcd.nih.gov/sites/default/files/Documents/cochlear-implants.pdf

National Institute on Deafness and Other Communication Disorders. (2017, March). *Hearing aids*. U.S. Department of Health and Human Services. https://www.nidcd.nih.gov/health/hearing-aids

Naude, A. M., & Bornman, J. (2014). A systematic review of ethics knowledge in audiology (1980–2010). *American Journal of Audiology, 23*, 151–157.

Nielsen, D., Luetke, B., McLean, M., & Stryker, D. (2016). The English language and reading abilities of a cohort of Deaf students speaking and signing standard English: A preliminary study. *American Annals of the Deaf, 162*.

Nielsen, D., Luetke, B., & Stryker, D. (2011). The advantage of signing morphemes when learning to read. *Journal of Deaf Studies and Deaf Education, 16*, 275–288.

O'Brien, C. A., & Placier, P. (2015). Deaf culture and competing discourses in a residential school for the deaf: "Can do" versus "can't do". *Equity & Excellence in Education, 48*(2), 320–338.

Rekkedal, A. M. (2011). Assistive hearing technologies among students with hearing impairment: Factors that promote satisfaction. *Journal of Deaf Studies and Deaf Education, 17*(4), 499–517.

Rhoades, E. A. (2010). Auditory-verbal practice: Toward a family-centered approach. In E. A. Rhoades & J. Duncan (Eds.), *Toward family centered practice* (1st ed., pp. 167–186). Charles C Thomas Publisher.

Roeser, R. J., & Downs, M. P. (2004). *Auditory disorders in school children: The law, identification, remediation* (4th ed.). Thieme Medical Publishers, Inc.

Roppolo, R. L. (2016). *The perceptions of general education teachers on the inclusion of students who are deaf or hard of hearing in the general education classroom*. Honors Theses, University of Southern Mississippi. https://aquila.usm.edu/honors_theses/375

Ryan, S. (2009). The effects of a sound-field amplification system on managerial time in middle school physical education settings. *Language, Speech, and Hearing Services in Schools, 40*(2), 131–137. https://doi.org/10.1044/0161-1461(2008/08-0038

Schafer, E., & Kleineck, M. (2009). Improvements in speech recognition using cochlear implants and three types of FM systems: A meta-analytic approach. *Journal of Educational Audiology, 15,* 4–14.

Scheetz, N. A. (2012). *Deaf education in the 21st century: Topics and trends.* Pearson Education, Inc.

Schow, R. L., & Nerbonne, M. A. (2017). *Introduction to audiologic rehabilitation.* Pearson.

Seaver, L., & DesGeorges, J. (2004). Special education law: A new IDEA for students who are deaf or hard of hearing. In M. Roeser & R. Downs (Eds.), *Auditory disorders in school children* (pp. 9–24). Thieme Medical Publishers. https://www.handsandvoices.org/pdf/SpecEdLaw.pdf

Shapiro, J. P. (1994). *No pity: People with disabilities forging a new civil rights movement.* Random House Publishers.

Strong, M., & Prinz, P. (1997). A study of the relationship between American sign language and English literacy. *Journal of Deaf Studies and Deaf Education, 2*(1), 37–46. https://doi.org/10.1093/oxfordjournals.deafed.a014308

Thibodeau, L. (2010). Benefits of adaptive FM systems on speech recognition in noise for listeners who use hearing aids. *American Journal of Audiology, 19*(1), 36–45. https://doi.org/10.1044/1059-0889(2010/09-0014

Tomblin, J. B., Oleson, J. J., Ambrose, S. E., Walker, E., & Moeller, M. P. (2014). The influence of hearing aids on the speech and language development of children with hearing loss. *JAMA Otolaryngology-Head & Neck Surgery, 140*(5), 403–409. https://doi.org/10.1001/jamaoto.2014.267

U.S. Department of Education. (1992). Deaf students education services: Policy guidance; Notice. *Federal Register, 57*(211), 49274–49276.

U.S. Department of Education. (2011). *Letter to stern.* https://sites.ed.gov/idea/files/idea/policy/speced/guid/idea/letters/2011-3/stern093011lre3q2011.pdf

U.S. Department of Education. (2015). *Free and appropriate public education for students with disabilities: Requirements under Section 504 of The Rehabilitation Act of 1973.* https://www2.ed.gov/about/offices/list/ocr/docs/edlite-FAPE504.html#:~:text=FAPE%20Provisions%20in%20the%20Individuals,ranges%20residing%20in%20the%20state

Walker, E. A., Holte, L., Spratford, M., Oleson, J., Welhaven, A., & Harrison, M. (2014). Timeliness of service delivery for children with later-identified mild-to-severe hearing loss. *American Journal of Audiology, 23*(1), 116–128. https://doi.org/10.1044/1059-0889(2013/13-0031

Zanin, J., & Rance, G. (2016). Functional hearing in the classroom: Assistive listening devices for students with hearing impairment in a mainstream school setting. *International Journal of Audiology, 55*(12), 723–729. https://doi.org/10.1080/14992027.2016.1225991

Zimmerman, H., & Thomas, H. (2017). Origins of deaf education: From alphabets to America. In S. Lenihan (Ed.), *Preparing to teach, committing to learn: An introduction to educating children who are D/HH.* Early Hearing Detection and Intervention. https://www.infanthearing.org/ebook-educating-children-dhh/

CHAPTER 6

SPECIAL EDUCATION OF STUDENTS WITH VISUAL IMPAIRMENTS: ADVANCING VALUES

Molly Pasley and Stacy M. Kelly

Northern Illinois University, USA

ABSTRACT

This chapter discusses what special education means for students with visual impairments (that is, those who are blind or have low vision) including what is being done and how traditions are maintained. More specifically, this chapter explores the importance of advancing values for the diverse population of students with visual impairments, focusing on cultivation of supportive, inclusive, and collaborative educational environments that continue to stand the test of time. This chapter highlights the increasing heterogeneity of this population of students and specific instructional strategies to support the cultural and linguistic diversity of learners with visual impairments in today's classrooms. This chapter also discusses the significance of promoting core concepts that are rooted in a traditional and specialized instructional framework for students who are visually impaired.

Keywords: Blind; collaboration; culture; diversity; family; low vision; visual impairment

INTRODUCTION

Education plays a pivotal role in shaping the minds and futures of young individuals, and providing children with knowledge, skills, and values necessary to thrive in a diverse and an ever-changing world. Within the realm of education, it is imperative to ensure that students with visual impairments (that is, those who are blind or have low vision) are not only equipped with academic knowledge but

Special Education
Advances in Special Education, Volume 38, 87–104
Copyright © 2024 Molly Pasley and Stacy M. Kelly
Published under exclusive licence by Emerald Publishing Limited
ISSN: 0270-4013/doi:10.1108/S0270-401320240000038006

are also empowered with the values and skills that will guide them to lead fulfilling and meaningful lives. Advancing values for students with visual impairments involves recognizing and addressing the unique challenges they encounter in their educational journeys.

While this advancement of values is essential for all students, it holds particular significance for students with visual impairments, who encounter additional obstacles and barriers in schools, communities, and throughout their lives as a result of their limited visual access to a world that is primarily designed for sight. Visual impairments, for example, can make it challenging for students who are blind or have low vision to gather information from visual aids used in the classroom, such as smart boards, charts, diagrams, or slides. In academic subjects such as science, math, or art, students with visual impairments face difficulties when instruction relies heavily on visual demonstrations, modeling of step-by-step procedures, or hands-on activities that primarily cater to visual access. When these barriers and obstacles are effectively addressed by educational teams, students with visual impairments can meaningfully participate in and learn about academic and expanded core content at the same time as their sighted peers. The purpose of this chapter is, therefore, to equip educators, families, and others within these communities with knowledge and strategies that advance values and overall well-being of students with visual impairments in all learning spaces.

Introducing the Expanded Core Curriculum (ECC) Framework for Students With Visual Impairments

The ECC is a widely recognized and used instructional framework in the field of visual impairments that guides best practices. The ECC framework developed in 1996 by Hatlen focuses on teaching and addressing specific skills and knowledge areas that are essential for the educational and functional needs of students with visual impairments. It is designed to complement and enhance the general curriculum taught in schools. The ECC recognizes that students with visual impairments require specialized instruction in areas beyond academic subjects to develop skills for independence, socialization, and overall well-being.

The ECC consists of the following nine core areas (Hatlen, 1996):

(1) Assistive technology: Instruction in the use of assistive technology tools, such as screen readers, magnifiers, braille displays, and accessible software enables students with visual impairments to access information and perform tasks effectively.
(2) Career education: Students with visual impairments receive guidance and instruction to explore career options, develop vocational skills, and plan for postsecondary education or employment opportunities in the area of career education.
(3) Compensatory skills: This area focuses on developing alternative techniques for accessing information, such as braille reading and writing, auditory skills, and adaptive technology for reading and writing.

(4) Independent living skills: Instruction in daily living skills helps students with visual impairments develop self-care abilities, including personal hygiene, household tasks, organization, time management, and money management.
(5) Orientation and mobility (O&M): Instruction in O&M enables students who are blind or have low vision to travel safely and independently, using skills and tools such as a white cane, auditory cues, and spatial awareness.
(6) Recreation and leisure skills: This area focuses on promoting active participation in recreational activities, hobbies, sports, and other leisure pursuits that enhance overall well-being and social engagement.
(7) Sensory efficiency skills: This area emphasizes the development of skills to use remaining senses effectively, including auditory and tactile skills, to gather information and engage with the environment.
(8) Self-determination skills: Students who are visually impaired learn from self-determination skills about the development of self-awareness, goals setting, decision-making, and self-advocacy while promoting their independence, confidence, and sense of personal agency.
(9) Social interaction skills: Students with visual impairments learn social skills, communication strategies, and self-advocacy techniques to interact effectively with peers, teachers, and the broader community as parts of this area of the ECC.

Instruction in the ECC is tailored to meet the individual needs of students with visual impairments, enabling students with visual impairments to develop essential skills in school and life. Each of the nine areas of the ECC should be taken into consideration in educating learners who are blind or have low vision. There is a natural overlap among the nine areas of the ECC. Students who are blind or have low vision and are working on their O&M skills may also at the same time be developing their sensory efficiency skills (for example, while listening for the surge of traffic at a light controlled intersection) and self-determination skills (for example, while soliciting assistance from others when traveling a predetermined route in a business district). Also, notably, the ECC complements the general education curriculum. Table 6.1 provides additional information about each area of the ECC along with examples of instructional strategies to support the diverse population of students with visual impairments in this instructional framework.

Heterogeneity of the Population

When addressing this chapter's topic of advancing the long-standing values that enhance the learning of students with visual impairments, the unique characteristics of this population need to be presented. It is well established in the literature that students who are visually impaired comprise a heterogeneous population (Dote-Kwan et al., 2001; Hatton et al., 2007; Pogrund & Fazzi, 2002). Visual impairment, ranging from partial sight to complete blindness, encompasses a wide range of eye conditions that can be present from birth or acquired at any point in life. Furthermore, it is important to note that each student with a visual

Table 6.1. Overview of the Expanded Core Curriculum (ECC) and ECC-Related Culturally Responsive Teaching (CRT) Activities for Students With Visual Impairments by Grade Level.

ECC Area	Overview of the Area of the ECC (Hatlen, 1996)	ECC-Related Culturally Responsive Teaching Activities by Grade Level (Coleman et al., 2023)		
		Early Elementary Grade Levels	Upper Elementary Grade Levels	Secondary Grade Levels
Assistive technology	Includes no-tech, low-tech, and high-tech adaptive tools that are commercially or custom made for students who are blind or have low vision.	Student uses assistive technology (video magnifier, magnifier, audiobook reader) to read a story in their first language, is relevant to their culture, or has a main character with whom they see themselves or can relate (The Circuit).	Student works collaboratively on a joint assignment where the student with a visual impairment utilizes their assistive technology; student uses assistive technology to create a product that teaches their class or family about what they are using and why.	Student uses their assistive technology of choice to read and analyze news articles and commentaries on current events relevant to their world.
Career education	Includes meaningful exploration of careers as well as job-readiness skills that are learned incidentally by sighted people but may need to be explicitly taught.	Teacher asks families of children with visual impairments to share pictures and/ or descriptions of some of the people in their families and careers they have.	Student researches someone that is more culturally similar to them within a particular content area or field of study.	Student interviews an individual from a similar cultural background who has the job they would like to pursue; collaborate with families and students to learn about their desires for future career when transitioning out of secondary education and how that fits in the context of the family's culture.
Compensatory skills	Includes literary and mathematical braille codes, concept development, tactile graphics, and specialized communication skills.	Teacher cocreates experience books with students and families in their reading medium (Coleman et al., 2023, p. 6); for emergent bilingual children, include the student's first language and	Student conducts surveys of classmates about their likes and dislikes on a variety of topics and creates a graph that depicts the results in media formats accessible to the student who is	Student uses the necessary literary and mathematical braille codes to create a living wage budget for themselves that includes any stipends provided by vocational rehabilitation and Supplemental

Table 6.1. *(Continued)*

ECC Area	Overview of the Area of the ECC (Hatlen, 1996)	ECC-Related Culturally Responsive Teaching Activities by Grade Level (Coleman et al., 2023)		
		Early Elementary Grade Levels	Upper Elementary Grade Levels	Secondary Grade Levels
		English; story boxes.	visually impaired and their peers.	Security Income (SSI) and takes into account their cultural values (e.g., tithing, caring for family members).
Independent living skills	Includes daily routines and tasks (e.g., personal care, food preparation, money management, household tasks) that are often learned incidentally by sighted people but often need to be explicitly taught to students with visual impairments.	Student packs for school (getting book bag ready, zipping up clothes); teacher interviews students and families to learn about chores in the classroom that mimic activities that are completed at home.	Teacher interviews families to learn their expectations and what is relevant in that family's home for the child to do as independently as appropriate (e.g., washing dishes, washing/folding/ hanging clothing).	Student identifies structural causes of food deserts. Student researches and finds out their local legislator's contact information (phone and email) and initiates contact using telephone or email skills to share their concerns.
Orientation and mobility (O&M) skills	Includes methods for safe and efficient travel as well as basic and advanced concept development in the areas of O&M in school, at home, and within communities.	Student problem solves with O&M specialist to travel to rooms within the building. Record video of the child demonstrating their knowledge of routes to share with the family in the family's home language.	Student problem-solves with O&M specialist to travel between community cultural points of interest and home.	Student researches transportation options in their area and assesses their accessibility. Student creates a plan of action to address areas of need in regard to access for available transportation options.
Recreation and leisure skills	Includes development of skills for lifelong physical and leisure activities that are often learned incidentally by sighted people, but are often explicitly taught to students	Teacher asks the student's family about pretend activities they do in the home. Next, teacher asks the student to choose a specific pretend activity and asks the student to determine appropriate	Student selects a physical endurance activity from a culture of their choosing (their own, their school, or another culture they have learned about). The student teaches this activity with	Student learns about community resources recreation and leisure activities that align with his cultural traditions and interests. The student will plan a route to a location he frequents for

(Continued)

Table 6.1. *(Continued)*

ECC Area	Overview of the Area of the ECC (Hatlen, 1996)	ECC-Related Culturally Responsive Teaching Activities by Grade Level (Coleman et al., 2023)		
		Early Elementary Grade Levels	Upper Elementary Grade Levels	Secondary Grade Levels
	with visual impairments.	clothes for the activity.	classmates and they time one another to see how long each participant can maintain the endurance.	recreation and leisure activities.
Self-determination skills	Includes the skills such as decision-making and problem-solving that enhance self-advocacy and well-being in life.	Navigating common fears activity: use a Venn diagram (tactile or large print) and put on one side student fears about school/life and the other side with teacher fears. Work with students to find commonalities in teacher/student fears as a way to establish that it's human nature to have concerns/fears when starting something new. Try to address each student fear to put them at ease.	Student researches and writes a report on their eye condition and reflects on how their culture influences their experience as part of self-determination.	Student creates a short-term goal and an action plan for accomplishing the goal. The student keeps track of the steps they have accomplished and describes obstacles they have encountered. The student evaluates the level of success of the goal and lists changes to the goal, the action plan, or actions that they could take to improve completion of the short-term goal.
Sensory efficiency skills	Includes efficient use of available senses (e.g., visual, tactual, and auditory skills) to maximize learning and participation in school, at home, and within communities.	Go on a "sound scavenger hunt," looking for sounds at school of which they are unfamiliar. Problem-solves to identify sound source, localize sound, and travel to the sound location. Invite families to share unique sounds in their home that can be recreated at school.	Student uses a monocular telescope to read a sign for a cultural location in the community.	Student uses a combination of sensory skills to locate food in a grocery store for a dish they can prepare for their family at home.

Table 6.1. (Continued)

ECC Area	Overview of the Area of the ECC (Hatlen, 1996)	ECC-Related Culturally Responsive Teaching Activities by Grade Level (Coleman et al., 2023)		
		Early Elementary Grade Levels	Upper Elementary Grade Levels	Secondary Grade Levels
Social interaction skills	Includes the verbal and nonverbal social interaction skills that are often learned incidentally by sighted people, but are often explicitly taught to students with visual impairments.	Student shows appreciation and gratitude toward others in their first language and another language of their choosing.	Student identifies and describes the feelings that are being expressed by others by recreating through their own body language and facial expressions.	Student compares and contrasts typical social interaction norms between two or more different cultures.

Sources: Overview of the ECC adapted from Hatlen (1996) as cited in Kelly (2018, 2019, 2021). Examples of CRT Activities adapted from Coleman et al. (2023), BetterLesson (2020), and Allman and Lewis (2014).

impairment who has some degree of residual vision (i.e., remaining vision) uses this residual vision differently from another student with the same eye condition or degree of visual functioning (Corn & Lusk, 2010).

Additionally, students who are visually impaired may or may not have concomitant disabilities. The term "concomitant disability" refers to the presence of multiple disabilities or conditions that occur simultaneously in an individual. This term implies that an individual has more than one disability or impairment, which may have a combined impact on their overall functioning and daily life. These disabilities or conditions can vary in nature and severity, and they may interact or coexist in ways that influence an individual's abilities, needs, and support requirements.

Researchers have consistently noted that the proportion of students with visual impairment who have concomitant disabilities (i.e., other disabilities in addition to their visual impairment) has been steadily increasing for the past half century. Recent demographic data pertaining to learners with visual impairments show that they are more likely to also have an additional disability than they are to have just a visual impairment (Erin, 2017). These additional disabilities include any of the other federal disability categories outlined by the Individuals with Disabilities Education Improvement Act (IDEIA, 2004a, 2004b) in any particular combination with each other (e.g., autism spectrum disorder, emotional disturbance, hearing impairment, and visual impairment) or in conjunction with the visual impairment only (e.g., hearing impairment and visual impairment). Thus, educational programming for students who are visually impaired needs to address the following heterogeneous characteristics of this population outlined by Kelly (2023):

- There are no two students who are visually impaired who see or use their remaining vision in the same way.
- Most students who are visually impaired have some degree of remaining vision.
- Most students who are visually impaired have additional disabilities.
- Students who are visually impaired with additional disabilities can have any combination of additional disabilities (e.g., visual impairment, autism, orthopedic impairment, and speech or language impairment) or a single additional disability (e.g., visual impairment and specific learning disability).
- At the same time, students who are visually impaired (having a unique degree of remaining and usable vision) without any additional disabilities need to be supported as well.
- Also, at the same time, students who are totally blind (have no remaining or usable vision) need to be supported too.

In order to address these overarching characteristics of this heterogeneous population, the educational programming of students with visual impairments involves extensive collaboration and specialized instruction by special education service providers and special education–related service providers specifically trained to support the unique learning needs of students with visual impairments. Furthermore, this diverse population of students with visual impairments also includes children who are multilingual and children who are from racially and ethnically diverse backgrounds as well as other underrepresented groups.

CULTURALLY RESPONSIVE TEACHING (CRT) PRACTICES

As explained by Ortiz (2001), more than 20 years ago in the forward of the seminal book *Diversity and Visual Impairment: The Influence of Race, Gender, Religion, and Ethnicity on the Individual*:

> Despite standards-based reforms, there continues to be a significant gap between outcomes for individuals with special needs (such as students with disabilities, those from low-income backgrounds, students of color, and students for whom English is not their first language) and their middle-class, majority-group peers. A contributing factor is that educators and policymakers have essentially ignored the country's changing demography and the increasing diversity of American society. In too many instances, programs and services address disability-related needs but are inconsistent with the individual's racial, linguistic, cultural, socioeconomic, and other background characteristics. As a result, the very programs designed to improve outcomes for individuals with disabilities become part of the problem, not the solution. (p. ix)

Unfortunately, educators, families, students with disabilities, and the educational system at large are still grappling with these same challenges today in providing adequate support for underrepresented groups within the educational system (U.S. Department of Education, 2022). There is a need to effectively deliver services and education for students with visual impairments, and it is important to recognize that this includes students with visual impairments who are multilingual and students with visual impairments who are from racially and ethnically diverse backgrounds as well as other underrepresented groups.

Also, notably, CRT practices are not new to the educational system or, more specifically, the field of visual impairments. Proponents of multicultural education and CRT practices such as James Banks, Geneva Gay, Zaretta Hammond, and Gloria Ladson-Billings have been researching and implementing frameworks about such practices for multiple decades (Banks, 2019; Gay, 2018; Hammond, 2014; Ladson-Billings, 1995, 2012). The main components of CRT are the following: well-developed cultural diversity knowledge base, implementation of culturally relevant curricula, display of high expectations for all students (not solely those in the majority culture), appreciation for different communication styles, and use of multicultural examples in instructional materials (Gay, 2002). Culturally responsive educators utilize student experience, perspectives, characteristics, and customs for classroom instruction and to create a more inclusive space for learning. Krasnoff (2016) outlines specific strategies for creating a classroom that is more culturally responsive in their work, *Culturally Responsive Teaching: A Guide to Evidence-Based Practices for Teaching All Students Equitably.*

Muñiz (2020) of New America has written *Culturally Responsive Teaching: A Reflection Guide* and in doing so provided a much-needed framework for educators to reflect on their current practices and challenge the status quo of education. Muñiz (2020) shared eight competencies necessary for CRT:

(1) Reflect on one's cultural lens.
(2) Recognize and redress bias in the system.
(3) Draw on students' culture to shape curriculum and instruction.
(4) Bring real-world issues into the classroom.
(5) Model high expectations for all students.
(6) Promote respect for student difference.
(7) Collaborate with families and the local community.
(8) Communicate in linguistically and culturally responsive ways (p. 3).

These eight competencies are also included in many statewide CRT standards.

The extent to which the theory has moved into practice across the United States varies between and within states. To capture the progress of state level integration of CRT standards across individual state level professional teaching standards, Muñiz (2019) published a report of her investigation of teaching standards across all 50 states and their inclusion of CRT in said standards. In this review of standards, Muñiz (2019) indicated that all 50 states include some mixture of the eight competencies in their teaching standards.

CRT and Students With Visual Impairments

As states require university personnel preparation programs to include statewide CRT standards in their teacher preparation programs, the goal is that newly minted educators will enter classrooms more prepared to teach learners from diverse backgrounds. Teachers of students who are visually impaired (TVIs) are taught to teach students who are blind or have low vision based on their unique *needs*. In CRT, TVIs are utilizing unique *strengths* and experiences of their students to connect to what their students are learning and providing them opportunities to demonstrate in unique ways how this learning is taking place. Researchers in the field of visual impairments have built on the seminal work of Banks, Gay, Hammond, and Ladson-Billings to apply these principles to working with students who are culturally and linguistically diverse and who are also visually impaired (Coleman et al., 2023; Conroy, 2005; Gee & Zebehazy, 2020). Recommendations related to working with students with visual impairments and who are also culturally and linguistically diverse include using braille books with culturally diverse characters and culturally conscious content in literacy instruction, constructing story boxes, creating experience books with input from family about home and community, and collaborating with culturally diverse families to support advocacy (Coleman et al., 2023). Conroy (2005) provides examples and descriptions of planning and direct teaching strategies when working with students who are English Language Learners and visually impaired based on strategies used in second language acquisition. A few strategies described by Conroy (2005) include using predictable routines to reduce student anxiety, using concrete objects to build concept knowledge and language, and previewing and reviewing lesson vocabulary and content to give multiple opportunities for student learning.

Also, notably, it was more than a decade ago that researchers investigated TVIs' skills in regard to CRT practices (Correa-Torres & Durando, 2011) and working with English language learners (Topor & Rosenblum, 2013). Subsequently, researchers in the field of visual impairments offered recommendations for teachers who work with students who are visually impaired and from culturally and linguistically diverse backgrounds based on specific information learned from families and the TVIs working with these families (Correa-Torres & Zebehazy, 2014). Correa-Torres and Zebehazy (2014) interviewed Hispanic mothers of children with visual impairments in the United States and, based on these interviews made recommendations that, where appropriate, could be applied to working with families of children with visual impairments from other cultural backgrounds and underrepresented groups:

- Be comfortable asking questions to and of the family, and show interest in them as individuals, and interest in their culture, language, and customs.
- Offer to work directly with families to show techniques and suggestions for working with their child and offer to do home visits.
- Consider the perspective of culture when creating the activity/context for teaching skills.
- Remember to avoid stereotypes. Although a student and their family might identify with a specific ethnic group, in this case Hispanics, remember that not all members of that group have the same needs or experiences.

Individualization when working with different families to address their unique needs is crucial.

• Create a system that works for the family to provide information in their native language.
• Learn how to find and use interpreter services effectively and know what to do when these services are not available.
• Find ways to provide materials in the native language of families and know what to do when they are not available.
• Communicate with families about barriers preventing use of resources and help families problem-solve through those barriers (p. 197).

Table 6.1 in this chapter includes examples of CRT activities for students with visual impairments as they relate to ECC-specific skills. It is important to note that the activities listed in Table 6.1 related to CRT are intended as examples and are not representative or exhaustive of the possibilities for CRT of students with visual impairments. Also, the activities in Table 6.1 do not replace the need to do the internal reflective work required to become a culturally responsive educator. As Ladson-Billings (2012) notes, practicing CRT "is one of the ways of 'being' that will inform ways of 'doing'" (p. 43). These activities shown in Table 6.1 may, therefore, serve as an example for ways in which grade levels, abilities, cultures, and ECC-specific content areas may be incorporated into CRT practices for students with visual impairments.

Overview of Specialized Educators for Students With Visual Impairments

In order to further discuss what is being done in special education for the diverse population of students with visual impairments, it is important to explain some information about the service providers and related services providers who are specifically trained and licensed/certified to teach students with visual impairments. Teachers of students with visual impairments, Certified Orientation and Mobility Specialists (COMS), and Certified Assistive Technology Instructional Specialists for People with Visual Impairment (CATIS) are vision education and rehabilitation professionals trained and certified/licensed to teach students who are blind or have low vision. Other educational team members collaborate with TVIs, COMS, and/or CATIS to support the educational programming of students with visual impairments with and without additional disabilities.

TVIs are special education teachers who provide specialized instruction, adapt the curriculum, and facilitate access to materials and technology that promote learning and independence among students with visual impairments. TVIs collaborate with families, educators, and other professionals to support students with visual impairments in receiving a comprehensive education tailored to their unique needs and abilities. The COMS is a special education–related services provider who provides instruction and guidance to students with visual impairments to develop skills for safe and independent travel and orientation in their environment. The COMS plays a major role in promoting mobility and spatial awareness for students with visual impairments. The COMS works collaboratively with individuals, families, educators, and other professionals to support students with visual impairments in navigating their surroundings and fully participating in their communities. The CATIS is a professional who specializes in assisting people with visual impairments in accessing and effectively using assistive technology devices and software. The CATIS assesses and instructs people with visual impairments in the use of assistive technology to enhance their independence, communication, learning, and overall quality of life. The CATIS collaborates with individuals, families, educators, and other professionals to identify appropriate assistive technology solutions and provide ongoing support and training for students with visual impairments with and without additional disabilities.

Shortage of Specialized Personnel in the Field of Visual Impairments

It is a well-documented fact that there is a severe shortage of qualified TVI, COMS, and CATIS to serve students who are visually impaired. The demand for these special education teachers and related services personnel exceeds the available supply (Boe et al., 2013; Browder et al., 2014; Council of Administrators of Special Education, 2020; Mason-Williams et al., 2020; McLeskey & Brownell, 2015; U.S. Department of Education, 2022). The chronic shortage of personnel qualified to serve students with visual impairments has been recognized for decades (Ambrose-Zaken & Bozeman, 2010; Bozeman & Zebehazy, 2014; Kirchner & Diament, 1999; Mason & Davidson, 2000). For more than a half century, experts in the field have published research detailing the desperate need for trained professionals. This grave situation has long been recognized among the leaders in the field and, unfortunately, exists to this day. Innovative methods for recruiting new personnel in the field of visual impairments are much needed across the United States and throughout the world.

Diverse Service Delivery Models

One of the byproducts of the COVID-19 pandemic exposed long-standing challenges in a multitude of access areas for individuals from marginalized communities, including those with disabilities. As a result, there has been a concerted effort to improve access to reliable internet, quality instructors through technology, gainful employment, and much more in the special education service delivery models for students who are visually impaired (Silverman et al., 2022). Unfortunately, the shortage of special educators who provide services to students with visual impairments (e.g., TVI, COMS, and CATIS) have been exacerbated even further by the COVID-19 pandemic and are at a crisis point nationally (Silverman et al., 2022). While it is clear that the pandemic will have lasting impacts on students, families, and educators, it has also provided important lessons that are guiding the future of education for all students, including students with visual impairments.

The American Foundation for the Blind's (AFB's) *Access and Engagement III* report elaborated on these lessons and the changes among families of children with visual impairments, "the pandemic has led some families to opt for other school placements for their child, often to a placement that provided more individualized attention for the child (Silverman et al., 2022, p. 24)." The diversity of school placements can be leveraged by providing intensive, evidence-based individualized instruction and interventions in person and through distance learning technologies in a variety of early intervention, early childhood, and school settings for students with visual impairments (e.g., natural environments; public schools, including charter schools; private schools; and other nonpublic education settings, including home education). Schools are becoming increasingly more reflective of these unexpected benefits of and changes in technology and infrastructure resulting from the pandemic (Silverman et al., 2022).

Also, at the start of the pandemic, students who are visually impaired and their families needed to master digital learning platforms very quickly. Students who are visually impaired vary widely in the level of exposure to or training with technology they had received prior to the pandemic (Kelly, 2009, 2011, 2021, 2022). For example, students with visual impairments often struggle to access digital learning and require high levels of support from their families and teachers to complete their coursework, or even for basic functions like logging in to a video meeting (Silverman et al., 2022). Notably, families, educators, and consultants have expressed their support for having technology and assistive technology instruction begin at younger ages, and be more intensive and inclusive, for students who are visually impaired (Silverman et al., 2022).

ADVANCING INCLUSION THROUGH NONDRIVER AND LOW VISION DRIVER EDUCATION

In terms of inclusivity, driver education is another important topic area and long-standing challenge that has unique implications for students who are blind or have low vision. The ability to drive in the United States and many other countries worldwide has been considered a rite of passage generation after generation (Sacks & Rosenblum, 2006). Additionally, in many geographic regions of the world, driving is a necessity for gainful employment. Also, although the ability to drive is centered and highly valued in the United States and other countries, it is a privileged status to have the money to afford a car, gas, and car insurance, of which not all people have access. Not all individuals are eligible to engage in this activity, which for students with visual impairment, can be emotionally devastating as they observe their peers going through the steps to obtain a driver's license and often feel "left behind" (Pasley, 2019, 2022). One of the ways educators attempt to mitigate these feelings is by offering nondriver education as a means to include learners with visual impairments in the transportation conversation. Typically, the responsibility of teaching about nondriving options has fallen to the COMS, or in instances where there is not a COMS available, the teacher of students with visual impairments. In 2000, Drs. Anne Corn and Penny Rosenblum authored *Finding Wheels: A Curriculum for*

Nondrivers with Visual Impairments for Gaining Control of Transportation Needs to support educators when preparing adolescents with visual impairments with recognizing and problem-solving for practical difficulties and emotional obstacles when navigating the built environment. The first iteration of this curriculum was designed for the instructor. In 2020, Corn and Rosenblum updated *Finding Wheels* so it was written directly to the adolescent/young adult traveler with a visual impairment as a guidebook with vignettes to illustrate concepts and activities to identify, problem-solve, and plan for current and future transportation needs. The topics covered in *Finding Wheels* (2020) and that are typical of nondriver and low vision driver education are presented in Table 6.2.

In addition to alternative modes of transportation, Corn and Rosenblum (2020) address driving with low vision, specifically with the use of bioptic lenses. Their inclusion of this topic in their curriculum is further evidence of the diversity of visual impairment, not simply those with vision and those without. When broaching the topic of low vision driving, it is important to recognize that not all who qualify to obtain a driver's license feel comfortable and/or the necessity to do so. Access to alternative modes of transportation and age of onset may account for these feelings. As with all decisions regarding a child's education, it is important to first talk with students who are visually impaired and their families to learn the goals of the student with visual impairments and their family members as well as how these goals fit within the context of their culture and future life plans. The importance of this collaboration and family involvement will be discussed next in terms of this chapter's focus on the advancement of values in the education of students who are blind or have low vision.

Table 6.2. Nondriver and Low Vision Driver Education Topics and Descriptions.

Topic	Description
Foundation building	Understanding learner's visual impairment and implications for nondriving
Personal wheels	Modes of transportation including walking, biking, rollerblading, and skateboarding
Public wheels	Modes of transportation including buses, trains, subways, ferries, airplanes, and paratransit
Drivers providing wheels	Modes of transportation include taxis; limousines; rideshare services; carpools; rides with family members, friends, or coworkers; and hiring private drivers
Low vision driving	Driving with bioptics, positive and negative personal feelings about driving with bioptics, and skills needed by low vision drivers
Paying for transportation	Budgeting, funding, exchanging, and reciprocating for accepted rides
Soft skills needed for successful transportation	Social skills, problem-solving, waiting for transportation, and managing frustrating situations

Source: Adapted from Corn and Rosenblum (2020).

COLLABORATION AND FAMILY INVOLVEMENT

Collaboration is of importance in the advancement of values involved in teaching students with visual impairments as it ensures a comprehensive and inclusive educational experience to support some of the challenges experienced by students with visual impairments that have been presented thus far in this chapter. Phillips et al. (1995) reviewed transcripts of collaborative teams of special education and general education teachers who worked together to develop inclusive practices within their schools. The following conclusions were established by this study:

> Collaborative efforts between special and general educators tended to progress through identifiable phases or stages... (a) experiencing anxiety, (b) working out the logistics, (c) determining classroom roles, (d) sharing planning and curriculum development, (e) recognizing and articulating the benefits of collaboration, (f) learning to recognize when a more restrictive setting may be appropriate, and (g) evaluating the overall effort. (p. 265)

The findings of this study are examples of key strategies that can be implemented by educational teams for successful collaboration in the assessment and resulting instruction of learners with visual impairment across educational settings. Thus, by working together in these various ways, teachers, specialists, families, and other professionals can pool their expertise, resources, and perspectives to address the diverse needs of students who are visually impaired in the most effective ways. Collaboration allows for a holistic approach to instruction, where strategies, accommodations, and adaptations can be shared and tailored to the specific needs of each student who is blind or has low vision. It facilitates the exchange of knowledge and best practices, enabling educators to stay informed about the latest advancements in teaching techniques, assistive technology, and accessibility. Moreover, collaboration fosters a supportive network that promotes the social–emotional well-being of students with visual impairments and enhances their sense of belonging within the educational community. By joining forces, these various interest parties can create an inclusive environment where students with visual impairments can thrive academically, socially, and personally.

Family involvement is also paramount in the education of students with visual impairments as families provide a strong foundation for academic and personal development. When families actively participate in their child's education, they become valuable partners in the educational journey. Family members bring essential insights into the unique strengths, needs, and preferences of their child who is visually impaired, enabling educators to individualize instruction and support. Families collaborate with teachers, specialists, and school staff to ensure that appropriate accommodations, adaptations, and resources are in place for students who are blind or have low vision. Additionally, families play a crucial role in reinforcing skills, practicing strategies, and providing emotional support at home that was only exacerbated further during the COVID-19 pandemic (Silverman et al., 2022). Family involvement promotes consistency, continuity, and a holistic approach to learning, supporting students with visual impairments in achieving their full potential and their involvement is an integral part of engaging in CRT practices.

CONCLUSION

Advancing values for students with visual impairments is not only important for their academic and social development but also empowers them to navigate a visual world with resilience and effective strategies for overcoming barriers and obstacles as a result of having limited or no vision. By creating inclusive learning environments, incorporating values into the curriculum, promoting social–emotional development, and leveraging assistive technology, educators, families, and communities foster the well-being of students with visual impairments, including those students with visual impairments from underrepresented groups. Through family involvement, mentorship, and real-world experiences, the diverse population of students with visual impairments gains support and guidance, reinforcing and advancing commitment to such values. With a collective effort, educational teams create an educational system that supports the heterogeneous population of students with visual impairments, enabling them to lead purposeful and fulfilling lives.

REFERENCES

Allman, C. B., & Lewis, S. (Eds.). (2014). *ECC essentials: Teaching the expanded core curriculum to students with visual impairments*. AFB Press.

Ambrose-Zaken, G., & Bozeman, L. (2010). Profile of personnel preparation programs in visual impairment and their faculty. *Journal of Visual Impairment & Blindness, 104*(3), 148–169.

Banks, J. A. (2019). Approaches to multicultural curriculum reform. In J. A. Banks & C. A. M. Banks (Eds.), *Multicultural education: Issues and perspectives* (10th ed., pp. 137–157). John Wiley & Sons.

BetterLesson (2020, October 15). *100+ strategies for culturally responsive teaching and learning co-created with the Kauffman Foundation*. BetterLesson.com. https://betterlesson.com/blog/culturally-responsive-teaching-learning-kauffman

Boe, E. E., deBettencourt, L., Dewey, J. F., Rosenberg, M. S., Sindelar, P. T., & Leko, C. D. (2013). Variability in demand for special education teachers: Indicators, explanations, and impacts. *Exceptionality, 21*(2), 103–125.

Bozeman, L. A., & Zebehazy, K. (2014). Personnel preparation in visual impairment. In E. D. McCray, P. T. Sindelar, M. T. Brownell, & B. Lignugaris-Kraft (Eds.), *Handbook of research in special education teacher preparation* (pp. 353–368). Routledge.

Browder, D. M., Wood, L., Thompson, J., & Ribuffo, C. (2014). *Evidence-based practices for students with severe disabilities* (Document No. IC-3). http://ceedar.education.ufl.edu/tool/innovation-configurations/

Coleman, M., Kan, D., Bruce, S., Miller, K., & Tiggs, S. (2023). An introduction to culturally sustaining pedagogy for students with sensory disabilities. *Teaching Exceptional Children, 55*(5), 366–375. https://doi.org/10.1177/00400599221090867

Conroy, P. W. (2005). English language learners with visual impairments: Strategies to enhance learning. *Review, 37*(3), 101.

Corn, A. L., & Lusk, K. E. (2010). Perspectives on low vision. In A. L. Corn & J. N. Erin (Eds.), *Foundations of low vision: Clinical and functional perspectives* (2nd ed., pp. 3–34). AFB Press.

Corn, A. L., & Rosenblum, L. P. (2000). *Finding wheels: A curriculum for nondrivers with visual impairments for gaining control of transportation needs*. Pro-Ed.

Corn, A. L., & Rosenblum, L. P. (2020). *Finding wheels: Strategies to build independent travel skills for those with visual impairments*. Texas School for the Blind and Visually Impaired.

Correa-Torres, S. M., & Durando, J. (2011). Perceived training needs of teachers of students with visual impairments who work with students from culturally and linguistically diverse backgrounds. *Journal of Visual Impairment & Blindness, 105*(9), 521–532. https://doi.org/10.1177/0145482X1110500904

Correa-Torres, S. M., & Zebehazy, K. T. (2014). Lessons learned from Hispanic mothers in the United States: Recommendations for personnel preparation and research in visual impairment. *British Journal of Visual Impairment, 32*(3), 521–532.

Council of Administrators of Special Education. (2020). *Proceedings of special education legislative summit 2020.* https://exceptionalchildren.org/sites/default/files/2020- 07/AllBriefs_2020.pdf

Dote-Kwan, J., Chen, D., & Hughes, M. (2001). A national survey of service providers who work with young children with visual impairments. *Journal of Visual Impairment & Blindness, 95*(6), 325–337.

Erin, J. (2017). Students with visual impairments and additional disabilities. In M. C. Holbrook, C. Hannan, & T. McCarthy (Eds.), *Foundations of education: Volume II* (3rd ed., pp. 309–349). AFB Press.

Gay, G. (2002). Preparing for culturally responsive teaching. *Journal of Teacher Education, 53*(2), 106–116.

Gay, G. (2018). *Culturally responsive teaching: Theory, research, and practice* (3rd ed.). Teachers College Press.

Gee, S., & Zebehazy, K. T. (2020). Supporting students with visual impairments who are culturally and linguistically diverse: The role of the cultural liaison within educational teams. *Journal of Visual Impairment & Blindness, 114*(4), 249–262.

Hammond, Z. (2014). *Culturally responsive teaching and the brain: Promoting authentic engagement and rigor among culturally and linguistically diverse students.* Corwin Press.

Hatlen, P. (1996). The core curriculum for blind and visually impaired students, including those with additional disabilities. *Review, 28,* 25–32.

Hatton, D. D., Schwietz, E., Boyer, B., & Rychwalksi, P. (2007). Babies count: The national registry for children with visual impairment, birth to 3 years. *Journal of American Association for Pediatric Ophthalmology and Strabismus, 11*(4), 351–355.

Individuals with Disabilities Education Improvement Act (IDEIA), 20 U.S.C. § 614 (2004a).

Individuals with Disabilities Education Improvement Act (IDEIA), 20 U.S.C. § 1400 (2004b).

Kelly, S. M. (2009). Use of assistive technology by students with visual impairments: Findings from a national survey. *Journal of Visual Impairment & Blindness, 103*(8), 470–480.

Kelly, S. M. (2011). Assistive technology use by high school students with visual impairments: A second look at the current problem. *Journal of Visual Impairment & Blindness, 105*(4), 235–239.

Kelly, S. M. (2018). Interventions for students with visual impairments. In F. E. Obiakor & J. P. Bakken (Eds.), *Viewpoints on interventions for learners with disabilities* (Vol. 33, pp. 107–126). Emerald Publishing Limited.

Kelly, S. M. (2019). Special education transition services for students with visual impairments. In J. P. Bakken & F. E. Obiakor (Eds.), *Special education transition services for students with disabilities* (Vol. 35, pp. 83–97). Emerald Publishing Limited.

Kelly, S. M. (2021). Traditional and innovative assessment techniques for students with visual impairments. In F. E. Obiakor & J. P. Bakken (Eds.), *Traditional and innovative assessment techniques for students with disabilities. Advances in special education* (Vol. 36, pp. 89–102). Emerald Group Publishing Limited.

Kelly, S. M. (2022). *Assistive technology for school-age learners with visual impairments.* EBSCO Pathways to Research. https://www.ebsco.com/products/research-databases/pathways-research

Kelly, S. M. (2023). Using technology to enhance learning for students with visual impairments. In J. P. Bakken & F. E. Obiakor (Eds.), *Using technology to enhance special education. Advances in special education* (Vol. 37, pp. 87–104). Emerald Group Publishing Limited.

Kirchner, C., & Diament, S. (1999). Estimates of the number of visually impaired students, their teachers, and orientation and mobility specialists: Part 1. *Journal of Visual Impairment & Blindness, 93*(9), 600–606.

Krasnoff, B. (2016). *Culturally responsive teaching: A guide to evidence-based practices for teaching all students equitably*. Region X Equity Assistance Center at Education Northwest. https://educationnorthwest.org/sites/default/files/resources/culturally-responsive-teaching.pdf

Ladson-Billings, G. (2012). Yes, but how do we do it? Practicing culturally relevant pedagogy. In J. Landsmen & C. W. Lewis (Eds.), *White teachers/diverse classrooms: Creating inclusive schools, building on students' diversity, and providing true educational equity* (2nd ed., pp. 33–46). Stylus Publishing, LLC.

Ladson-Billings, G. (1995). But that's just good teaching! The case for culturally relevant pedagogy. *Theory Into Practice, 34*(3), 159–165.

Mason-Williams, L., Bettini, E., Peyton, D., Harvey, A., Rosenberg, M., & Sindelar, P. T. (2020). Rethinking shortages in special education: Making good on the promise of an equal opportunity for students with disabilities. *Teacher Education and Special Education, 43*(1), 45–62.

Mason, C., & Davidson, R. (2000). *National plan for training personnel to serve children with blindness and low vision*. The Council for Exceptional Children.

McLeskey, J., & Brownell, M. (2015). *High-leverage practices and teacher preparation in special education (Document No. PR-1)*. http://ceedar.education.ufl.edu/wpcontent/uploads/2016/05/High-Leverage-Practices-and-Teacher-Preparation-in-Special-Education.pdf

Muñiz, J. (2019). Culturally responsive teaching: A 50-state survey of teaching standards. *New America*. http://www.newamerica.org/education-policy/reports/culturally-responsive-teaching/

Muñiz, J. (2020). Culturally responsive teaching: A reflection guide. *New America*. https://d1y8sb8igg2f8e.cloudfront.net/documents/Culturally_Responsive_Teaching_A_Reflection_Guide_2021_WAMBwaO.pdf

Ortiz, A. (2001). Forward. In M. Milian & J. Erin (Eds.), *Diversity and visual impairments: The influence of race, gender, religion, and ethnicity on the individual* (pp. ix–xi). AFB Press.

Pasley, M. (2019). *Young adults with visual impairments and driver's education: Journeys of self-efficacy, identity, and transition to adulthood.* (Publication No. 1-30-2018). Doctoral dissertation, Illinois State University. ISU ReD: Research and eData.

Pasley, M. (2022). A study of young adults with visual impairments and driver's education. *Disabilities, 2*(3), 462–473. http://doi.org/10.3390/disabilities2030033

Phillips, L., Sapona, R. H., & Lubic, B. L. (1995). Developing partnerships in inclusive education: One school's approach. *Intervention in School and Clinic, 30*, 262–272.

Pogrund, R., & Fazzi, D. (Eds.). (2002). *Early focus: Working with young blind and visually impaired children and their families* (2nd ed.). AFB Press.

Sacks, S. Z., & Rosenblum, L. P. (2006). Adolescents with low vision: Perceptions of driving and nondriving. *Journal of Visual Impairment & Blindness, 100*(4), 212–222. http://doi.org/10.1177/0145482X0610000404

Silverman, A. M., Munguia Rodriguez, G., Rhoads, C. R., & Bleach, K. (2022). *Access and engagement III: Reflecting on the impacts of the COVID-19 pandemic on the education of children who are blind or have low vision*. American Foundation for the Blind.

Topor, I., & Rosenblum, L. P. (2013). English language learners: Experiences of teachers of students with visual impairments who work with this population. *Journal of Visual Impairment & Blindness, 107*(2), 79–91. https://doi.org/10.1177/0145482X1310700202

U.S. Department of Education. (2022). *School pulse panel (2021–22)*. Institute of Education Sciences, National Center for Education Statistics. https://ies.ed.gov/schoolsurvey/spp/

CHAPTER 7

SPECIAL EDUCATION OF STUDENTS WITH EXTENSIVE SUPPORT NEEDS: ADVANCING VALUES

Jennifer A. Kurth and Alison L. Zagona

The University of Kansas, USA

ABSTRACT

Values have long guided special education services and supports for students with extensive support needs; over the past four decades, those values have been backed by research evidence demonstrating the critical nature of values related to inclusive education, self-determination, and seeking strengths and assets. In this chapter, we investigate these values and their supporting research, documenting strengths and needs in extant research. We emphasize the need to continue to embrace and maintain these values while pursuing research that addresses research gaps while centering the priorities, perspectives, and preferences of people with extensive support needs.

Keywords: Extensive support needs; inclusive education; communication supports; self-determination; behavior supports

INTRODUCTION

Students with extensive support needs are a heterogeneous group of students who have support needs across multiple learning and living domains, including communication, academic, social, behavioral, and/or physical domains. They are the 1% of all students who are eligible to take their state's alternate assessment due to significant cognitive disability (Every Student Succeeds Act, 2017). Most students with extensive support needs have disability labels of autism, intellectual disability, or multiple disabilities.

Special Education
Advances in Special Education, Volume 38, 105–122
Copyright © 2024 Jennifer A. Kurth and Alison L. Zagona
Published under exclusive licence by Emerald Publishing Limited
ISSN: 0270-4013/doi:10.1108/S0270-401320240000038007

All students with disabilities are general education students, some of whom also receive special education and related services. An especially enduring problem facing schools and educational teams has been the issue of placement, or the location where eligible students with disabilities receive their special education and related services. This issue of placement has endured since the beginning of special education in the 1970s, when schools were forced to grapple with how to educate all students with disabilities for the first time (Education for All Handicapped Children Act, PL 94-142, 1975). Decisions needed to be made on issues ranging from teacher preparation to what students with disabilities could learn to how to best teach them. All these decisions were being made in the context of a system in which students with disabilities had historically been separated from nondisabled students in all facets of life, including living in institutions and attending special day centers with the purpose of housing or managing people with disabilities. It is of little surprise, then, that school systems essentially recreated separate systems of educating students with and without disabilities; this siloing has been maintained to this day.

Yet at the same time as federal special education law arose in the 1970s, widespread social justice movements were occurring around the globe, introducing values that continue to guide the field of special education. Racial and ethnic desegregation of schools and communities were well underway, with disability advocates borrowing many of the same values to desegregate people with disabilities, including the National Association for Retarded Children (thearc.org) who immediately recognized the implications of the Brown vs Board of Education (1954) findings as a basis to press for equal educational opportunities for children with disabilities. Federal disability policy has reflected these values, including a commitment to educating students with disabilities in the least restrictive environment (Individuals with Disabilities Education Improvement Act (IDEA), 2004), achieving full integration and inclusion in all aspects of American life (Americans with Disabilities Act, 1990), and asserting that unjustified segregation of people with disabilities is a violation of their civil rights (Olmstead Act, 1999).

WHAT DOES SPECIAL EDUCATION MEAN FOR STUDENTS WITH EXTENSIVE SUPPORT NEEDS?

Despite this obligation to ensure full participation in general education contexts for students with extensive support needs, 93% of all students with extensive support needs are taught outside of general education classrooms for most, if not all, of the school day (Kleinert et al., 2015). This routine segregation has been resistant to change for decades (Kurth et al., 2014; Morningstar et al., 2017), despite clear empirical evidence supporting teaching students with extensive support needs in general education. Specifically, learning in general education has been associated with enhanced rigor of Individualized Education Program (IEP) goals (Kurth & Mastergeorge, 2010), development of more robust social networks (Jameson et al., 2022), improved academic skill development (Mansouri et al., 2022), more progress on individualized learning goals (Gee et al., 2020), development of self-determination skills (Hughes et al., 2013), and acquisition of communication skills (e.g., Kleinert et al., 2015). Yet, as noted, most students with extensive support needs spend most of their school day in special classrooms or schools, removed from the context of general education and limiting their opportunities to learn general education content with their peers. In fact, when students with extensive support needs do gain entry to general education classrooms, it is typically for special activities like recess, art, or physical education, rather than core academic instruction (Kurth et al., 2019; Snider & Dymond, 2023).

Why, given empirical evidence supporting inclusion, are students with extensive support needs overwhelmingly segregated from their nondisabled peers? Researchers have proposed a variety of possibilities (e.g., Agran et al., 2020), including incorrect assumptions that special classrooms are more intensive and individualized than general education settings (Mayton et al., 2014). An overarching rationale for the persistent segregation of students with extensive support needs rests, however, on the miserably low expectations held for these students (Giangreco, 2020). Low expectations refer to an expectation that students with extensive support needs cannot or will not learn or contribute, reducing their education to a watered-down curriculum without a scope or sequence (Bacon et al., 2016), meaningless tasks (Kurth et al., 2016; Zagona et al., 2022), and an overemphasis on personal care (Kurth et al., 2021). Such low expectations reflect the pervasive ableism in schools and communities; people with extensive support needs are seen as deficient or unable, while their ways of thinking and being are pathologized (Dukes & Berlingo, 2020). Ableism similarly compels educators to "fix" the student instead of investing in ways to eliminate barriers and provide supports for all students to succeed in inclusive learning spaces.

The tyranny of low expectations has consequences: teachers' high expectations are correlated to improved student outcomes (de Boer et al., 2018). In the absence of high expectations, students with extensive support needs have not experienced positive outcomes. For example, most students with extensive support needs graduate from school without an effective or reliable means of communicating (Andzik et al., 2018). Similarly, self-determination, critical to achieving education-related goals and positive postschool outcomes (Burke et al., 2018), is imperiled because educators enforce compliance in all facets of student life (Malone et al., 2023) rather than empowering students to direct their own life. When considering postschool outcomes, the status quo of separation and segregation is equally concerning.

The IDEA (2004) specifies schools should prepare students with disabilities for postsecondary education, employment, and independent living. Unfortunately, young adults with extensive support needs experience the poorest postschool outcomes of any disability group (Newman et al., 2011), and students with extensive support needs continue to exit school without the skills they need to be successful. Although people with extensive support needs report preferring to live in apartments with support of their choosing (Ioanna, 2018), nearly 71% lived with a family or caregiver (Braddock et al., 2015).

Employment data offer equally bleak outcomes (Sannicandro et al., 2018), with rates of employment for persons with disabilities remaining static at around 34% (Smith et al., 2017). Eighty-one percent of adults with disabilities received segregated services in day habilitation, clinic, rehabilitation, or other segregated day programs (Braddock et al., 2015). Additionally, earnings of employees in sheltered workshops and other segregated settings are significantly reduced (Kregel & Dean, 2002). Only 19% of adults with extensive support needs work in supported employment arrangements (Braddock et al., 2015), which substantially increases the earnings of workers (Wehman et al., 2018). Furthermore, the jobs available to workers with extensive support needs remains centered on food, flowers, and filth (Kumin & Schoenbrodt, 2016), suggesting limited work opportunities for adults with extensive support needs. Together, these studies demonstrate a systemic failure of the current, segregated school systems in pro-moting positive postschool outcomes for students with extensive supports. Converging evidence, then, suggests new skills should be prioritized and taught to promote positive, enviable outcomes for young adults with extensive support needs.

WHAT IS BEING DONE NOW TO IMPROVE OUTCOMES?

Considering the need to improve outcomes for children and young adults with extensive support needs, school teams and researchers are shifting practices and thinking, including greater adoption of social–ecological models of disability, promoting self-determination, enhancing access and progress in inclusive settings, supporting communication skills, and proactively creating environments and systems to prevent and respond to challenging behavior. We consider each of these next.

Social–Ecological Model of Disability

For most of human history, including when providing special education support and services, professionals have sought to identify and subsequently remediate student deficits. These deficits are central to how professionals describe students, creating malignant narratives about students that are used to create assumptions and set current and future (low) expectations about students (e.g., Ruppar et al., 2022). For example, professionals describe students using phrases such as "Johnny is unable to speak clearly" or "due to her significant cognitive disability, Beth is unable to engage in grade level instruction." Often, along with lowering expectations and focusing on deficits, euphemisms for disability are employed to describe people with disabilities, including "special" or "exceptional needs," ignoring the human needs of people with disabilities and instead positioning them as being somehow fundamentally different or unable (Ruppar et al., 2022). This form of positioning reflects an ableist and medical point of view in which having a need for frequent or intensive support is pathologized. At the same time, the expectations of students are diminished and professional opinion is elevated, with professionals assumed to be more capable of making decisions about what is right or best for students, instead of students themselves making these decisions about their own priorities and interests. Together, the relentless professional pursuit of seeking deficits and relying on euphemisms results in descriptions and beliefs of students with disabilities, particularly those with extensive support needs, as being so different in terms of their needs and priorities that a separate special education is needed, in segregated rooms or schools, where they are taught a special (often watered down) curriculum, by special people.

The social–ecological model of disability is in direct contrast: rather than seeking deficits in the person, this model of disability situates disability as a mismatch between the demands and opportunities of the environment and the strengths and assets of the person. As such, in this model, disability does not exist just in the person; instead, it exists when this mismatch occurs. For example, a person who uses a wheelchair experiences no disability when they have access to ramps, elevators, and curb cuts. However, without these environmental supports, the person will be limited in where they can go and what they can do. Likewise, a learner with a cognitive disability might have no difficulty participating in the general education curriculum when they have access to visuals, speech-to-text software, plain language texts, or other individualized supports. Integral to the social–ecological model of disability is an understanding that all humans have physical and/or mental variation that can become a source of vulnerability or an asset, and that it is the work of professionals and families to seek those assets and strengths when assessing and serving students with disabilities. It is further the responsibility of professionals and families to support people with disabilities to identify, appreciate, develop, and pursue their own strengths and resources (Weick et al., 1989).

All people bring their own unique strengths and assets to every situation. A strengths-based approach focuses on the positive attributes of a person, positioning people as resourceful, and resilient, striving to make positive changes in their own lives. Thus, the responsibility of educators and families is to focus on building strengths and maximizing personal growth and participation through individualized supports (Shogren et al., 2017). In fact, many people with disabilities develop strengths navigating systems and spaces that are not designed for them (Van der Klift & Kunc, 2019); learning more from disabled people about these innovative approaches would serve to position people with disabilities as experts and to remove unnecessary barriers.

Like all people, people with disabilities also possess unique character strengths, such as creativity, honesty, curiosity, self-regulation, and perseverance, among others. Completing a strengths finder assessment, such as the VIA Survey (https://www.viacharacter.org/character-strengths-via) can be one easy and interesting way to identify, and ultimately build on, strengths that help chart a path to student learning and thriving. By designing and providing opportunities, supports, and instruction aligned with strengths and assets, educators facilitate student growth and development (Shogren & Raley, 2022). As schools continue to adopt a more strengths-based and asset seeking approach, including in the development of IEPs (IEPs; Ruppar & Kurth, 2023), we are optimistic that improved student outcomes, including in self-determination (Shogren, Wehmeyer, et al., 2015), will be realized.

Self-Determination

Interventions aimed at promoting self-determination have been effective at increasing skills such as choice-making, decision-making, problem-solving, goal setting, and self-management; educators and other service providers are increasingly adopting these approaches to support students with extensive support needs to experience positive outcomes (Burke et al., 2018; Shogren, Wehmeyer, et al., 2015; Wehmeyer et al., 2013). Self-determined behavior is defined as "volitional actions that enable one to act as the primary causal agent in one's life and to maintain or improve one's quality of life" (Wehmeyer, 2005, p. 17). As educators seek to improve outcomes for students with extensive support needs, a focus on skills associated with self-determination is important because of the need to improve in- and post-school outcomes for this population of students. Interventions focused on self-determination have been associated with positive post-school outcomes in the areas of employment and community access, in addition to other positive outcomes (Shogren, Wehmeyer, et al., 2015).

The Self-Determined Learning Model of Instruction (SDLMI) has been established as an effective intervention for increasing the self-determination of students with disabilities (Burke et al., 2020). The SDLMI is a model for teaching skills associated with self-determination that both special and general educators have learned to implement in their classrooms (Raley et al., 2021; Wehmeyer et al., 2012). Through the use of the SDLMI, students self-select goals and engage in a reflection and problem-solving process to achieve those goals (Shogren et al., 2012). Educators, or facilitators, who implement the SDLMI within their classrooms guide students through a process in which they identify a goal they wish to achieve, develop an action plan to achieve the goal, implement the action plan, and reflect on barriers and successes at specific times, as a way to ensure their success with the process. Students may or may not achieve their goal, but if they do not, then the SDLMI encourages them to reflect on what they would want to achieve the next time they set a goal (Shogren et al., 2019).

The implementation of the SDLMI has been effective at improving outcomes in the areas of self-determination, employment, community access, recreation, independent living, and quality of life (McDougall et al., 2010; Shogren, Wehmeyer, et al., 2015; Wehmeyer et al., 2013). For students with extensive support needs, future areas of focus may include adapting the SDLMI and assessments of self-determination to support teachers and other service providers to implement them when the student has complex communication needs, or other support needs requiring adaptations to the process (Alsaeed et al., 2023). General and special education teachers will benefit from considering ways to integrate self-determination interventions such as the SDLMI into inclusive, general education classrooms in order to contribute to the need to improve access to inclusive settings for students with extensive support needs. This can be accomplished with deliberate co-planning and co-teaching to ensure the needs of students with extensive support needs are met during the implementation of self-determination interventions.

Inclusive Education

When advocates, researchers, and families began advocating for inclusive education, little empirical evidence existed to support their efforts. Instead, claims related to social justice, equity, and civil rights were guiding principles. Today, the field continues to embrace these values, now with ample empirical evidence documenting positive outcomes associated with inclusive education for students with extensive support needs (e.g., Mansouri et al., 2022) along with research-based practices and strategies to enhance effective inclusive education. Further, federal investments in technical assistance centers, such as the SWIFT Education Center (swiftschools.org) and the TIES Center (tiescenter.org), reveal the importance of inclusive education in federal policy as well. Thus, as a field, we are better positioned than ever before to create high-quality inclusive education supports and services.

A range of instructional strategies have been identified to promote learning in inclusive settings. For example, embedded instruction (Jimenez & Kamei, 2015) has been identified as an evidence-based practice that can be implemented by general and special education teachers, paraprofessionals, and peer tutors to provide quality learning opportunities to students. Systematic instruction, including prompting, time delay, and reinforcement systems, are integrated in general education settings to provide research-based instruction (Kuntz & Carter, 2019). Use of accommodations and modifications in conjunction with systematic instruction facilitates access to and progress in the general education classroom, using tools such as ecological assessment to identify support needs (Haney & Cavallaro, 1996) and participation plans to organize the delivery of supports, accommodations, modifications, and systematic instruction (Kurth et al., 2020). Teams further have guidance for aligning instruction, IEP goals, and assessment with state standards (e.g., Quenemoen & Thurlow, 2017), connecting students with extensive support needs to the general education curriculum in ways that support their learning of grade-aligned content. Finally, the use of natural supports, such as peer assisted learning (Kuntz & Carter, 2019) have been identified as strategies that are effective in promoting student learning in inclusive settings.

Beyond classroom-based instructional strategies, researchers have identified systems that enhance inclusive supports and instruction for students with extensive support needs. Administrative leadership for inclusive education, including hiring practices and professional development, are key strategies for initiating and sustaining effective inclusion (Burstein et al., 2004; Salisbury & McGregor, 2002). Such administrative support can promote other effective practices, including creating schedules that support co-planning and co-teaching (e.g., McLeskey et al., 2014; Pratt et al., 2017). Other strategies rely on partnerships with families, including the development of strengths-based IEPs that reflect the lifespan priorities of people with disabilities and their families (Love et al., 2017).

The field is better positioned than ever before to prepare general and special education teachers at the pre- and in-service levels to design and deliver high-quality inclusive instruction. For far too long, special educators have been minimized as only caring or patient workers (Marks, 2011), with little attention to the professional skills utilized to teach and make instructional decisions while enacting social justice for and with their students. To meet these demands, institutes of higher education faculty are identifying key components of course-work and fieldwork to prepare future teachers to meet the needs of students with extensive support needs in inclusive settings, including teaching teacher candidates the technical skills needed for instruction and the interpersonal skills needed for advocacy (Kurth et al., 2021; Miller et al., 2020). Designing inclusive field-work experiences has also become critical, given the dearth of such placements in most areas of the United States (Kurth & Foley, 2014). As such, teacher edu-cators must be part of the advocacy work involved in developing and sustaining inclusive schools to better prepare the next generation of teachers. Finally, a growing acknowledgment of the intersection of race and disability is shaping teacher development practices. Multiple systems of oppression converge to impact the academic, social, and disciplinary inequities facing students of color with extensive support needs, including racism and ableism which is integrated in all aspects of schooling (Annamma et al., 2013). Linguicism can also negatively impact all students with extensive support needs, including a lack of communi-cation supports to promote their learning and participation.

Augmentative and Alternative Communication Supports

Students with extensive support needs may have complex communication needs, meaning they do not rely on oral speech as their primary mode of communica-tion. Students with complex communication needs benefit from a variety of different communication supports, including Augmentative and Alternative Communication (AAC) Supports. AAC refers to an area of research and inter-vention that includes strategies to supplement communication when an individual has support needs in speech or language production and/or comprehension. AAC may involve sign language, gestures, objects, line drawings, photographs, and/or speech-generating devices (American Speech-Language-Hearing Association, n.d.). Communication is an essential aspect of life; we communicate to connect with others, learn in school, share our needs with others, and to indicate enjoy-ment and satisfaction. However, students with extensive support needs have experienced a lack of support to access AAC, due in part to low expectations of service providers on their teams (Johnson et al., 2006; Towles-Reeves et al., 2012).

Recent research has uncovered effective strategies for implementing AAC as a support for students with extensive support needs. Nondisabled peers of students with extensive support needs have used augmented input to successfully provide natural, conversational supports (Biggs et al., 2019). Augmented input is defined as "providing ongoing communication input through the use of aided AAC paired with verbal speech" (Biggs et al., 2019, p. 446). This contrasts with giving prompts, which can promote more of a teacher–student feel to the interaction. In addition to peer supports, the use of high-tech AAC, including speech-generating devices, is an evidence-based practice for supporting students with extensive support needs (e.g., autism and intellectual disability) to increase social-communication skills. Students with extensive support needs have received AAC supports from a variety of different service providers and family members, and have participated in these interventions in both natural and clinical settings. Inclusion of students with extensive support needs in general education class-rooms can support their progress in communication skills (Gee et al., 2020), and can also provide students with greater access to peer models and a stronger sense of belonging in the school community (Biggs & Hacker, 2021).

Future efforts to support students with extensive support needs must occur in inclusive classrooms, given that 80% of school-based research into AAC has occurred in segregated special education classrooms (Iacono et al., 2022). Like-wise, many special educators report not knowing how to use AAC, thus limiting its use in school contexts (Pennington et al., 2021). Future research should, therefore, also focus on effective and efficient teacher training in all aspects of AAC, including how to use it in a natural context and how to update AAC systems. Finally, research and practice in AAC for students with extensive sup-port needs have largely focused on requesting (Brady et al., 2016); thus, there is a clear need to expand the focus of communication interventions to incorporate all aspects of communication, including commenting, requesting, asking questions, and extending and repairing interactions. In doing so, students with extensive support needs are better positioned to live full and enviable lives in inclusive contexts of their choosing, while also avoiding the serious trauma, isolation, and harm associated with lacking efficient and effective means of communicating. One such harm is reliance on challenging behavior, including aggression or self-harm, to meet needs when unable to effectively communicate.

Positive Behavior Interventions and Support

Approximately 80% of people with extensive support needs engage in challenging behavior (Simó-Pinatella et al., 2019) due in large part to a lack of communi-cation supports (Chezan et al., 2017). In other words, when students cannot effectively express their needs and preferences, they may be forced to rely on challenging behaviors to achieve their desired outcomes. A major tenet of positive behavior interventions and supports (PBIS), therefore, is to teach students replacement behaviors, including communication skills, which are more efficient and effective in meeting their needs than challenging behavior. PBIS relies on collaboration, planning, and interdisciplinary interventions (Sugai & Horner, 2010) to achieve its purposes of reducing and eliminating challenging behavior while increasing the fluency and accuracy of using the replacement behavior. PBIS was initially focused on supporting the behavior of students with extensive support needs but extended to a more universal implementation for all students through a multi-tiered system of support.

There are three Tiers of PBIS, and in schools that implement PBIS, this system for support is intended to be used by all teachers, all staff, and all students. The first Tier of PBIS refers to universal supports, including instruction, rewards, and data collection procedures that seek to prevent problem behavior for all students in the school. Tiers 2 and 3 intensify and individualize supports around this instruction, and all three tiers are intended to be cumulative and iterative. Researchers have documented significant positive outcomes associated with the implementation of this tiered approach to supporting positive behavior as well as its intended use for all students (e.g., Zagona et al., 2021). However, too often students with extensive support needs do not receive instruction and support across all three tiers due to their programmatic and physical segregation from general education. To ensure positive behavior outcomes for students with extensive support needs, research and practice must converge to provide accessible Tier 1 instruction and activities while simultaneously guaranteeing students with extensive support needs are physically and programmatically included.

WHAT TRADITIONS DO WE MAINTAIN?

Although the field of special education for students with extensive support needs has made tremendous gains in the past several decades, additional work is critically needed, including a relentless pursuit of socially just and inclusive supports that build upon student strengths and interests and center the student in all decisions. We turn our attention to these next.

The Platinum Rule and Inclusive Research

Many of us grew up learning about the golden rule: do unto others as you would have them do unto you. This rule is a valuable exercise in perspective taking and ensuring professionals, or others in positions of power, act in ways that are the best of interest of those they aim to serve. Advocates in fields as diverse as medicine and disability, however, argue that the golden rule is not sufficient, and in fact, centers the perspectives and priorities of professionals. They argue people will necessarily vary in their values, lived experiences, and sense of what is acceptable. In other words, what one person may want in a given circumstance might be vastly different than what another person would want, in effect highlighting the shortcomings of the golden rule and the need to make decisions that emphasize what the person receiving support or interventions would want. The platinum rule thus extends the golden rule and asserts professionals and supporters should do unto others as they would want done unto themselves (Chochinov, 2022). By relentlessly enacting the platinum rule through seeking strengths, enhancing communication and self-determination skills, and providing opportunities for people with extensive support needs to be the causal agents in their own lives, we can be part of creating a world that truly centers the needs and priorities of students with extensive support needs from their perspectives.

In the field of special education related to students with extensive support needs, efforts to advance inclusive research have been increasing as a means to pursue meaningful topics and to shift the power dynamics typically present in research. Inclusive research is defined as research in which people with disabilities are involved in the research process as "instigators of ideas, research designers, interviewers, data analysts, authors, disseminators, and users" (Walmsley & Johnson, 2003, p. 10). Individuals with extensive support needs have been traditionally excluded from the research process, often viewed only as the participants in the research, or those who are observed or supplying information for the study (Shogren, 2023). However, recent movements toward inclusive research, or research in which individuals with disabilities engage in the research process as equitable partners, contributing to the development, implementation, analysis, and dissemination of research have resulted in a shift toward partnering with individuals with disabilities in the research process (Jivraj et al., 2014; Nicolaidis et al., 2019). Partnering with adults with disabilities, for example, in the development of research questions for a study focused on special education and students with extensive support needs provides the opportunity to integrate their lived experiences in all aspects of research and to focus on the issues relevant and meaningful for the disability community. Further, partnering with individuals with disabilities in the implementation of research and dissemination of the results addresses the common exclusion of the disability community from scientific initiatives.

All research designs can be inclusive, and future work in the area of inclusive research must carefully document the procedures the research team implemented to engage in the process. Recent inclusive research may not be written in a level of detail that is replicable (Frankena et al., 2019), and if it is, the authors may have written about their partners with lived experience with disability in a way that tokenizes them or does not document their equitable participation in the process. Future research in the area of special education and students with extensive support needs must be inclusive, detailed, and it must include individuals with lived experience with disability to ensure equitable opportunities to engage in the scientific process to truly impact change that is desperately needed for people with extensive support needs.

Expanding and Enhancing Inclusive Practices

The future of special education for students with extensive support needs must also continue efforts to expand research in inclusive, general education classrooms, in order to identify the most effective interventions and supports in these contexts. Embedded instruction has been identified as an evidence-based practice (Jimenez & Kamei, 2015), but there is a need to identify additional evidence-based practices to provide educators with additional tools and strategies for supporting students with extensive support needs in inclusive classrooms. Going forward, our field will benefit tremendously from general and special education teachers partnering in the education of students with extensive support needs to co-plan and co-teach in classrooms that include students with extensive support needs in natural proportions. To accomplish this, research is needed to identify practices and strategies for co-planning and co-teaching in efficient ways that make it possible for teachers who support many students to still co-plan with their general education colleagues. Students in co-taught classrooms have expressed highly positive perspectives regarding co-teaching (Shogren, Gross, et al., 2015), and it is important to ensure these same instructional strategies are available for students with extensive support needs.

Future planning for students with extensive support needs receiving special education services must also be person-centered, prioritizing the perspectives of the student and their family (Blaskowitz et al., 2019). Such efforts for person-centered planning may involve the implementation of student-led IEPs, where educators develop a relationship with the student and family, provide the student with opportunities and support to practice skills associated with self-determination by preparing content to share at an IEP meeting, communicating their goals to the team, and debrief with the student family (Cavendish et al., 2017). Additionally, student-led IEPs have frequently been implemented for high school or transition-age students; however, this practice must be expanded across grade levels. A preschool student or elementary age student could certainly attend their IEP meeting and share with the team their strengths, areas of support needs, and desired goals. This level of participation would center the student and their family as the experts in their education, which would be an important and needed direction for the future.

An additional future direction for both research and practice in special education and students with extensive support needs is the implementation of peer supports. Peer supports have been identified as an evidence-based practice, and there is a need to ensure teachers learn about this intervention in their preparation programs as a way to address the research-to-practice gap that commonly exists in special education (Carter et al., 2016). Teachers need practice in planning and implementing peer supports, and utilizing freely available resources (e.g., https://afirm.fpg.unc.edu/node/2) is one step toward meeting this need. The need to increase the implementation of inclusive practices for students with extensive support needs also necessitates the need to continue to advance the implementation of natural supports for students in the general education classroom. Peer supports provide an alternative to the overuse of adults, including paraprofessionals, who might "hover" over the student or create stigmatizing conditions. Considering, researching, and implementing peer supports is a valuable future step toward supporting the advancement of inclusive education as well as naturalistic supports for students with extensive support needs.

CONCLUSIONS

In this chapter, we have considered the educational experiences of students with extensive support needs. Tremendous research and practice gains have been achieved over the past 45 years of special education for students with extensive support needs, including a depth and breadth of research on how to support students in achieving positive outcomes through centering the needs and priorities of students and their families in inclusive contexts. As a field, we have also identified frameworks for supports that facilitate student outcomes, including, for example, communication and behavior supports that enhance lifelong outcomes and self-determination. We advocate that maintaining these values and traditions is essential; new directions to pursue focus on making these successes and supports more universal, efficient, and effective. We further assert there is a need to abandon deficit perspectives of students, particularly those that lead to segregated experiences and diminished in- and post-school outcomes. The field is better positioned than at any time in its history, with people with disabilities leading efforts to achieve these outcomes including through inclusive research and expanding and enhancing inclusive practices.

REFERENCES

Americans with Disabilities Act, Pub. L. No. 101-336, 104 Stat. 328 Cong. Rec. (1990).

American Speech-Language-Hearing Association. (n.d.). Augmentative and Alternative Communication (AAC). https://www.asha.org/practice-portal/professional-issues/augmentative-and-alternative-communication/#:~:text=Augmentative%20and%20alternative%20communication%20(AAC)%20is%20an%20area%20of%20clinical,and%20written%20modes%20of%20communication

Agran, M., Jackson, L., Kurth, J. A., Ryndak, D., Burnette, K., Jameson, M., Zagona, A., Fitzpatrick, H., & Wehmeyer, M. (2020). Why aren't students with severe disabilities being placed in general education classrooms: Examining the relations among classroom placement, learner outcomes, and other factors. *Research and Practice for Persons with Severe Disabilities*, *45*, 4–13. https://doi.org/10.1177/1540796919878134

Alsaeed, A., Mansouri, M. C., Shogren, K. A., Raley, S. K., Kurth, J. A., Leatherman, E. M., & Lockman Turner, E. (2023). A Systematic review of interventions to promote self-determination for students with extensive support needs. *Research and Practice for Persons with Severe Disabilities*, *48*(1), 3–24. https://doi.org/10.1177/15407969231153397

Andzik, N. R., Schaefer, J. M., Nichols, R. T., & Chung, Y. C. (2018). National survey describing and quantifying students with communication needs. *Developmental Neurorehabilitation*, *21*(1), 40–47. https://doi.org/10.1080/17518423.2017.1339133

Annamma, S. A., Connor, D., & Ferri, B. (2013). Dis/ability critical race studies (DisCrit): Theorizing at the intersections of race and dis/ability. *Race Ethnicity and Education*, *16*(1), 1–31. https://doi.org/10.1080/13613324.2012.730511

Bacon, J., Rood, C. E., & Ferri, B. A. (2016). Promoting access through segregation: The emergence of the "prioritized curriculum" class. *Teachers College Record*, *118*(14), 1–22.

Biggs, E. E., Carter, E. W., & Gilson, C. B. (2019). A scoping review of the involvement of children's communication partners in aided augmentative and alternative communication modeling interventions. *American Journal of Speech Language Pathology*, *28*(2), 743–758. https://doi.org/10.1044/2018_AJSLP-18-0024

Biggs, E. E., & Hacker, R. E. (2021). Ecological systems for students who use AAC: Stakeholders' views on factors impacting intervention and outcomes. *Research and Practice for Persons with Severe Disabilities*, *46*(4), 259–277. https://doi.org/10.1177/15407969211052309

Blaskowitz, M., Layer, L., Scalero, S., Gore, A., Castagnino, A., & McNally, K. (2019). Use of a person-centered planning approach to encourage vocational goal setting among adults with intellectual and developmental disabilities. *The American Journal of Occupational Therapy*, *73*(4_Supplement_1), 7311500035p1.

Braddock, D., Hemp, R., Rizzolo, M. C., Tanis, E. S., Haffer, L., & Wu, J. (2015). *The state of the states in intellectual and developmental disabilites: Emerging from the great recession* (10th ed.). The American Association on Intellectual and Developmental Disabilities.

Brady, N. C., Bruce, S., Goldman, A., Erickson, K., Mineo, B., Ogletree, B. T., Paul, D., Romski, M. A., Sevcik, R., Siegel, E., Schoonover, J., Snell, M., Sylvester, L., & Wilkinson, K. (2016). Communication services and supports for individuals with severe disabilities: Guidance for assessment and intervention. *American Journal on Intellectual and Developmental Disabilities, 121*(2), 121–138. https://doi.org/10.1352/1944-7558-121.2.121

Burke, K. M., Raley, S. K., Shogren, K. A., Hagiwara, M., Mumbardó-Adam, C., Uyanik, H., & Behrens, S. (2018). A meta-analysis of interventions to promote self-determination for students with disabilities. *Remedial and Special Education, 41*(3), 176–188. https://doi.org/10.1177/0741932518802274

Burke, K. M., Shogren, K. A., Antosh, A. A., LaPlante, T., & Masterson, L. H. (2020). Implementing the SDLMI with students with significant support needs during transition planning. *Career Development and Transition for Exceptional Individuals, 43*(2), 115–121. https://doi.org/10.1177/2165143419887858

Burstein, N., Sears, S., Wilcoxen, A., Cabello, B., & Spagna, M. (2004). Moving toward inclusive practices. *Remedial & Special Education, 25*(2), 104–116. http://www.proedinc.com/

Carter, E. W., Asmus, J., Moss, C. K., Biggs, E. E., Bolt, D. M., Born, T. L., Brock, M. E., Cattey, G. N., Chen, R., Cooney, M., Fesperman, E., Hochman, J. M., Huber, H. B., Lequia, J. L., Lyons, G., Moyseenko, K. A., Riesch, L. M., Shalev, R. A., Vincent, L. B., & Weir, K. (2016). Randomized evaluation of peer support arrangements to support the inclusion of high school students with severe disabilities. *Exceptional Children, 82*(2), 209–233. https://doi.org/10.1177/0014402915598780

Cavendish, W., Connor, D. J., & Rediker, E. (2017). Engaging students and parents in transition-focused individualized education programs. *Intervention in School and Clinic, 52*(4), 228–235. https://doi.org/10.1177/1053451216659469

Chezan, L. C., Wolfe, K., & Drasgow, E. (2017). A meta-analysis of functional communication training effects on problem behavior and alternative communicative responses. *Focus on Autism and Other Developmental Disabilities, 33*(4), 195–205. https://doi.org/10.1177/1088357617741294

Chochinov, H. M. (2022). Seeing Ellen and the platinum rule. *JAMA Neurology, 79*(11), 1099. https://doi.org/10.1001/jamaneurol.2022.2400

de Boer, H., Timmermans, A. C., & van der Werf, M. P. C. (2018). The effects of teacher expectation interventions on teachers' expectations and student achievement: Narrative review and meta-analysis. *Educational Research and Evaluation, 24*(3–5), 180–200. https://doi.org/10.1080/13803611.2018.1550834

Dukes, C., & Berlingo, L. (2020). Fissuring barriers to inclusive education for students with severe disabilities. *Research and Practice for Persons with Severe Disabilities, 45*, 14–17. https://doi.org/10.1177/1540796919895968

Education for All Handicapped Children Act. PL 94-142 Pub. L. No. 94-142, U.S. Statutes at Large. 899. 777-796. (1975).

Every Student Succeeds Act. (2017). *Every Student Succeds Act under Title 1, Part A & Title 1, Part B: Summary of Final Regulations.* https://www2.ed.gov/policy/elsec/leg/essa/essaassessmentfactsheet1207.pdf

Frankena, T. K., Naaldenberg, J., Cardol, M., Garcia Iriarte, E., Buchner, T., Brooker, K., Schrojenstein Lantman, H. M. J. V., & Leusink, G. (2019). A consensus statement on how to conduct inclusive health research. *Journal of Intellectual Disability Research, 63*(1), 1–11. https://doi.org/10.1111/jir.12486

Gee, K., Gonzalez, M., & Cooper, C. (2020). Outcomes of inclusive versus separate placements: A matched pairs comparison study. *Research and Practice for Persons with Severe Disabilities, 45*(4), 223–240. https://doi.org/10.1177/1540796920943469

Giangreco, M. F. (2020). "How can a student with severe disabilities be in a fifth-grade class when he can't do fifth-grade level work?" Misapplying the least restrictive environment. *Research and Practice for Persons with Severe Disabilities, 45*, 23–27. https://doi.org/10.1177/1540796919892733

Haney, M., & Cavallaro, C. C. (1996). Using ecological assessment in daily program planning for children with disabilities in typical preschool settings. *Topics in Early Childhood Special Education, 16*(1), 66–81. https://doi.org/10.1177/027112149601600107

Hughes, C., Agran, M., Cosgriff, J. C., & Washington, B. H. (2013). Student self-determination: A preliminary investigation of the role of participation in inclusive settings. *Education and Training in Autism and Developmental Disabilities, 48*(1), 3–17.

Iacono, T., Goldbart, J., Douglas, S. N., & Garcia-Melgar, A. (2022). A Scoping Review and Appraisal of AAC Research in Inclusive School Settings. *Journal of Developmental and Physical Disabilities, 34*(6), 963–985. https://doi.org/10.1007/s10882-022-09835-y

Individuals with Disabilities Education Improvement Act, Pub. L. No. P.L. 108-446, H.R. 1350 (2004).

Ioanna, D. (2018). Independent living of individuals with intellectual disability: A combined study of the opinions of parents, educational staff, and individuals with intellectual disability in Greece. *International Journal of Developmental Disabilities, 66*(2), 153–159. https://doi.org/10.1080/20473869.2018.1541560

Jameson, J. M., Hicks, T., Lansey, K., Kurth, J. A., Jackson, L., Zagona, A. L., Burnette, K., Agran, M., Shogren, K., & Pace, J. (2022). Predicting the frequency and significance of social contacts across placements: A Bayesian multilevel model analysis. *Research and Practice for Persons with Severe Disabilities, 47*(4), 229–243. https://doi.org/10.1177/15407969221136538

Jimenez, B. A., & Kamei, A. (2015). Embedded instruction: An evaluation of evidence to inform inclusive practice. *Inclusion, 3*(3), 132–144. https://doi.org/10.1352/2326-6988-3.3.132

Jivraj, J., Sacrey, L. A., Newton, A., Nicholas, D., & Zwaigenbaum, L. (2014). Assessing the influence of researcher–partner involvement on the process and outcomes of participatory research in autism spectrum disorder and neurodevelopmental disorders: A scoping review. *Autism, 18*(7), 782–793. https://doi.org/10.1177/1362361314539858

Johnson, J. M., Inglebret, E., Jones, C., & Ray, J. (2006). Perspectives of speech language pathologists regarding success versus abandonment of AAC. *Augmentative and Alternative Communication, 22*(2), 85–99. https://doi.org/10.1080/07434610500483588

Kleinert, H., Towles-Reeves, E., Quenemoen, R., Thurlow, M., Fluegge, L., Weseman, L., & Kerbel, A. (2015). Where students with the most significant cognitive disabilities are taught. *Exceptional Children, 81*(3), 312–328. https://doi.org/10.1177/0014402914563697

Kregel, J., & Dean, D. H. (2002). Sheltered vs. supported employment: A direct comparison of long-term earnings outcomes for individuals with cognitive disabilities. In *Achievements and Challenges in Employment Services for People with Disabilities: The Longitudinal Impact of Workplace.*

Kumin, L., & Schoenbrodt, L. (2016). Employment in adults with Down Syndrome in the United States: Results from a national survey. *Journal of Applied Research Intellect Disabilities, 29*(4), 330–345. https://doi.org/10.1111/jar.12182

Kuntz, E. M., & Carter, E. W. (2019). Review of Interventions Supporting Secondary Students with Intellectual Disability in General Education Classes. *Research and Practice for Persons with Severe Disabilities, 44*(2), 103–121. https://doi.org/10.1177/1540796919847483

Kurth, J. A., Allcock, H., Walker, V. L., Olson, A., & Taub, D. (2021). Faculty perceptions of expertise for inclusive education for students with significant disabilities. *Teacher Education and Special Education, 44*(2), 117–133. https://doi.org/10.1177/0888406420921582

Kurth, J. A., Born, K., & Love, H. (2016). Ecobehavioral characteristics of self-contained high school classrooms for students with severe cognitive disability. *Research and Practice for Persons with Severe Disabilities, 41*(4), 227–243. https://doi.org/10.1177/1540796916661492

Kurth, J. A., & Foley, J. A. (2014). Reframing teacher preparation: Preparing teachers for inclusive education. *Inclusion, 2*(4), 286–300. https://doi.org/10.1352/2326-6988-2.4.286

Kurth, J. A., & Mastergeorge, A. M. (2010). Individual education plan goals and services for adolescents with autism: Impact of grade and educational setting. *Journal of Special Education, 44*(3), 146–160. https://doi.org/10.1177/0022466908329825

Kurth, J. A., Miller, A. L., & Toews, S. G. (2020). Preparing for and implementing effective inclusive education with participation plans. *Teaching Exceptional Children, 53*(2), 140–149. https://doi.org/10.1177/0040059920927433

Kurth, J. A., Morningstar, M. E., & Kozleski, E. (2014). The persistence of highly restrictive special education placements for students with low-incidence disabilities. *Research and Practice for Persons with Severe Disabilities, 39*(3), 227–239. https://doi.org/10.1177/1540796914555580

Kurth, J. A., Ruppar, A. L., Toews, S. G., McCabe, K. M., McQueston, J. A., & Johnston, R. (2019). Considerations in placement decisions for students with extensive support needs: An analysis of LRE statements. *Research and Practice for Persons with Severe Disabilities, 44*(1), 3–19. https://doi.org/10.1177/1540796918825479

Love, H. R., Zagona, A. L., Kurth, J. A., & Miller, A. L. (2017). Parents' experiences in educational decision making for children and youth with disabilities. *Inclusion, 5*(3), 158–172. https://doi.org/10.1352/2326-6988-5.3.158

Malone, E. J., Kurth, J. A., & Zimmerman, K. N. (2023). Engagement as an alternative to noncompliance measurement: Promoting validity and accuracy. *Beyond Behavior.*

Mansouri, M. C., Kurth, J. A., Lockman Turner, E., Zimmerman, K. N., & Frick, T. A. (2022). Comparison of academic and social outcomes of students with extensive support needs across placements. *Research and Practice for Persons with Severe Disabilities, 47*(2), 111–129. https://doi.org/10.1177/15407969221101792

Marks, S. U. (2011). Special education: More about social justice, less about caring. *Phi Delta Kappan* (September), 80.

Mayton, M. R., Carter, S. L., & Wheeler, J. J. (2014). Intrusiveness of behavioral treatments for adults with intellectual disability. *Research in Developmental Disabilities, 35*(1), 54–61. https://doi.org/10.1016/j.ridd.2013.10.023

McDougall, J., Evans, J., & Baldwin, P. (2010). The importance of self-determination to perceived quality of life for youth and young adults with chronic conditions and disabilities. *Remedial and Special Education, 31*, 252–260. https://doi.org/10.1177/0741932509355989

McLeskey, J., Waldron, N. L., & Redd, L. (2014). A case study of a highly effective, inclusive elementary school. *Journal of Special Education, 48*(1), 59–70.

Miller, A. L., Wilt, C. L., Allcock, H. C., Kurth, J. A., Morningstar, M. E., & Ruppar, A. L. (2020). Teacher agency for inclusive education: An international scoping review. *International Journal of Inclusive Education*, 1–19. https://doi.org/10.1080/13603116.2020.1789766

Morningstar, M. E., Kurth, J. A., & Johnson, P. J. (2017). Examining national trends in educational placements for students with significant disabilities. *Remedial and Special Education, 38*(1), 3–12. https://doi.org/10.1177/0741932516678327

Newman, L., Wagner, M., Knokey, A. M., Marder, C., Nagle, K., Shaver, D., & National Center for Special Education Research. (2011). *The post-high school outcomes of young adults with disabilities up to 8 years after high school: A report from the National Longitudinal Transistion Study-2.* N. C. f. S. E. Reserach.

Nicolaidis, C., Raymaker, D., Kapp, S. K., Baggs, A., Ashkenazy, E., McDonald, K., Weiner, M., Maslak, J., Hunter, M., & Joyce, A. (2019). The AASPIRE practice-based guidelines for the inclusion of autistic adults in research as co-researchers and study participants. *Autism, 23*(8), 2007–2019. https://doi.org/10.1177/1362361319830523

Olmstead v. L. C. (United States Court of Appeals for the Eleventh Circuit 1999).

Pennington, R. C., Walker, V. L., & Tapp, M. C. (2021). Teacher preparation in communication instruction for students with extensive support needs. *Teacher Education and Special Education, 44*(3), 239–254. https://doi.org/10.1177/0888406420978606

Pratt, S. M., Imbody, S. M., Wolf, L. D., & Patterson, A. L. (2017). Co-planning in co-teaching: A practical solution. *Intervention in School and Clinic, 52*(4), 243–249.

Quenemoen, R. F., & Thurlow, M. L. (2017). Standards-based reform and students with disabilities. In J. Kauffman, D. P. Hallahan, & P. C. Pullen (Eds.), *Handbook of special education* (pp. 203–217). Taylor & Francis.

Raley, S. K., Shogren, K. A., Rifenbark, G. G., Lane, K. L., & Pace, J. R. (2021). The impact of the self-determined learning model of instruction on student self-determination in inclusive, secondary classrooms. *Remedial and Special Education, 42*(6), 363–373. https://doi.org/10.1177/0741932520984842

Ruppar, A., Kurth, J., Bubash, S., & Lockman Turner, E. (2022). A framework for preparing to teach students with extensive support needs in the 21st century. *Teacher Education and Special Education*. https://doi.org/10.1177/08884064211059853

Ruppar, A. L., Kurth, J. A., McCabe, K. M., Toews, S. G., McQueston, J. A., & Johnston, R. (2022). Present levels of academic achievement and functional performance: Unravelling the narratives. *Journal of Disability Studies in Education*, 1–25. https://doi.org/10.1163/25888803-bja10016

Ruppar, A. L., & Kurth, J. A. (2023). *Equitable and inclusive IEPs for students with complex support needs: A roadmap*. Brookes Publishing.

Salisbury, C. L., & McGregor, G. (2002). The administrative climate and context of inclusive elementary schools. *Exceptional Children*, 68(2), 259–274. http://www.cec.sped.org

Sannicandro, T., Parish, S. L., Fournier, S., Mitra, M., & Paiewonsky, M. (2018). Employment, income, and SSI effects of postsecondary education for people with intellectual disability. *American Journal on Intellectual and Developmental Disabilities*, 123(5), 412–425. https://doi.org/10.1352/1944-7558-123.5.412

Shogren, K. A. (2023). The right to science: Centering people with intellectual disability in the process and outcomes of science. *Intellectual and Developmental Disabilities*, 61(2), 172–177. https://doi.org/10.1352/1934-9556-61.2.172

Shogren, K. A., Palmer, S. B., Wehmeyer, M. L., Williams-Diehm, K., & Little, T. D. (2012). Effect of intervention with the self-determined learning model of instruction on access and goal attainment. *Remedial and Special Education*, 33(5), 320–330. https://doi.org/10.1177/0741932511410072

Shogren, K., & Raley, S. K. (2022). *Self-determination and causal agency theory: Integrating research into practice*. Springer.

Shogren, K. A., Raley, S. K., Burke, K. M., & Wehmeyer, M. L. (2019). *The self-determined learning model of instruction teacher's guide*. Kansas University Center on Developmental Disabilities.

Shogren, K., Gross, J., Forber-Pratt, A., Francis, G. L., Satter, A., Blue-Banning, M., & Hill, K. (2015). The perspectives of students with and without disabilities on inclusive schools. *Research and Practice for Persons with Severe Disabilities*, 40, 243–260. https://doi.org/10.1177/1540796915583493

Shogren, K., Wehmeyer, M., Palmer, S., Forber-Pratt, A., Little, T. D., & Lopez, S. (2015). Causal agency theory: Reconceptualizing a functional model of self-determination. *Education and Training in Autism and Developmental Disabilities*, 50(3), 251–263. https://www.jstor.org/stable/24827508

Shogren, K., Wehmeyer, M., Schalock, R. L., & Thompson, J. R. (2017). Reframing educational supports for students with intellectual disability through strengths-based approaches. In M. Wehmeyer & K. Shogren (Eds.), *Handbook of research-based practices for educating students with intellectual disability* (pp. 17–30). Routledge.

Simó-Pinatella, D., Mumbardó-Adam, C., Alomar-Kurz, E., Sugai, G., & Simonsen, B. (2019). Prevalence of challenging behaviors exhibited by children with disabilities: Mapping the literature. *Journal of Behavioral Education*, 28(3), 323–343.

Smith, D. L., Atmatzidis, K., Capogreco, M., Lloyd-Randolfi, D., & Seman, V. (2017). Evidence-based interventions for increasing work participation for persons with various disabilities. *OTJR (Thorofare N J)*, 37(2_suppl), 3S–13S. https://doi.org/10.1177/1539449216681276

Snider, J. E., & Dymond, S. K. (2023). Curricular areas in which students with intellectual disability receive instruction. *Journal of Developmental and Physical Disabilities*. https://doi.org/10.1007/s10882-023-09891-y

Sugai, G., & Horner, R. H. (2010). Schoolwide positive behavior supports: Establishing a continuum of evidence-based practices. *Journal of Evidence-Based Practices for Schools*, 11(1), 62–83.

Towles-Reeves, E., Kearns, J., Flowers, C., Hart, L., Kerbel, A., Kleinert, H., Quenemoen, R., & Thurlow, M. (2012). *Learner characteristics inventory project report (A product of the NCSC validity evaluation)*. National Center and State Collaborative. http://www.ncscpartners.org/media/default/pdfs/lci-project-report-08-21-12.pdf

Van der Klift, E., & Kunc, N. (2019). *Being realistic isn't realistic: Collected essays on disability, identity, inclusion and innovation*. Tellwell Talent.

Walmsley, J., & Johnson, K. (2003). *Inclusive research with people with learning disabilities: Past, present and futures.* Jessica Kingsley Publishers.

Wehman, P., Taylor, J., Brooke, V., Avellone, L., Whittenburg, H., Ham, W., Brooke, A. M., & Carr, S. (2018). Toward competitive employment for persons with intellectual and developmental disabilities: What progress have we made and where do we need to go. *Research and Practice for Persons with Severe Disabilities, 43*(3), 131–144. https://doi.org/10.1177/1540796918777730

Wehmeyer, M. L. (2005). Self-determination and individuals with severe disabilities: Re-examining meanings and misinterpretations. *Research and Practice for Persons with Severe Disabilities, 30*(3), 113–120.

Wehmeyer, M. L., Palmer, S. B., Shogren, K., Williams-Diehm, K., & Soukup, J. H. (2013). Establishing a causal relationship between intervention to promote self-determination and enhanced student self-determination. *The Journal of Special Education, 46*(4), 195–210. https://doi.org/10.1177/0022466910392377

Wehmeyer, M. L., Shogren, K. A., Palmer, S. B., Williams-Diehm, K. L., Little, T. D., & Boulton, A. (2012). The impact of the self-determined learning model of instruction on student self-determination. *Exceptional Children, 78*(2), 135–153. https://doi.org/10.1177/001440291207800201

Weick, A., Rapp, C., Sullivan, W. P., & Kisthardt, W. (1989). A strengths perspective for social work practice. *Social work, 34*(4), 350–354.

Zagona, A. L., Kurth, J. A., Lockman Turner, E., Pace, J., Shogren, K., Lansey, K., Jameson, M., Burnette, K., Mansouri, M., Hicks, T., & Gerasimova, D. (2022). Ecobehavioral analysis of the experiences of students with complex support needs in different classroom types. *Research and Practice for Persons with Severe Disabilities, 47*(4), 209–228. https://doi.org/10.1177/15407969221126496

Zagona, A. L., Walker, V. L., Lansey, K. R., & Kurth, J. (2021). Expert perspectives on the inclusion of students with significant disabilities in schoolwide positive behavioral interventions and supports. *Inclusion, 9*(4), 276–289. https://doi.org/10.1352/2326-6988-9.4.276

CHAPTER 8

SPECIAL EDUCATION OF STUDENTS WITH TRAUMATIC BRAIN INJURIES: ADVANCING VALUES

Quentin M. Wherfel and Jeffrey P. Bakken

Bradley University, USA

ABSTRACT

This chapter provides an overview on the traditions and values of teaching students with traumatic brain injury (TBI). First, we discuss the prevalence, identification, and characteristics associated with TBI and how those characteristics affect learning, behavior, and daily life functioning. Next, we focus on instructional and behavioral interventions used in maintaining the traditions in classrooms for working with students with TBI. Findings from a review of the literature conclude that there are no specific academic curriculums designed specifically for teaching students with TBI; however, direct instruction and strategy instruction have been shown to be effective educational interventions. Current research on students with TBI is predominately being conducted in medical centers and clinics focusing on area of impairments (e.g., memory, attention, processing speed) rather than academic achievement and classroom interventions. Finally, we conclude with a list of accommodations and a discussion of recommendations for future work in teaching students with TBI.

Keywords: Traumatic brain injuries; TBIs; direct instruction (DI); strategy instruction (SI); behavioral interventions; accommodations

INTRODUCTION

Traumatic brain injury or TBI is a devastating experience for both the individual and their family. The true impact of a brain injury and its unintended consequences may not manifest until months after the initial trauma (Masel, 2006).

Special Education
Advances in Special Education, Volume 38, 123–142
Copyright © 2024 Quentin M. Wherfel and Jeffrey P. Bakken
Published under exclusive licence by Emerald Publishing Limited
ISSN: 0270-4013/doi:10.1108/S0270-401320240000038008

According to Faul et al. (2010), there are nearly 1.7 million Americans who sustain a TBI annually. In addition, nearly half a million children aged 0–14 visit the emergency room for TBI-related incidences that most commonly occur from a fall (Faul et al., 2010). Yet, children with TBI account for less than 0.5% of all students served under the Individuals with Disabilities Education Act (IDEA) (National Center for Education Statistics, 2022). Further, TBIs are less frequently reported to schools than other disability categories. In many instances, TBIs have been either undiagnosed or unidentified because parents never notified the school of such trauma (Nagele et al., 2019).

Taylor et al. (2017) noted that 18,000 TBI-related hospital admissions each year come from children under 14 years old. Further, in the 2019–2020 school year, there were 24,993 (0.40%) students between 5 and 21 years old that received special education services under TBI. This is vastly contrasted with students receiving services under other disability categories such as specific learning disability (SLD) 2,379,448 (37%), speech language impairment (SLI) 1,090,207 (17%), other health impairment (OHI) 1,079,301 (17%), and emotional disturbance (ED) 345,782 (5%) (US Department of Education, 2021). Interestingly, some of the symptoms and impairments of TBI are consistent across the larger disability categories noted above. Yet, this population of students are less likely to be admitted for special education services under TBI, and instead, may be referred for services under other labels such as SLD, SLI, OHI, or ED that may not fully meet their needs. From the standpoint of eligibility of special education services, TBI would appear to be a low-incidence disability; however, the underreporting and underdiagnosis of TBI may indicate TBI is more common in the schools than perceived (Xun et al., 2023). DePompei and Bedell (2008) reported a large gap between the number of incidence of students with TBI being reported by hospital personnel to the Centers for Disease Control (CDC) than the number of students identified under the TBI category for special education services in K-12 schools. This underrepresentation of actual and expected numbers of students with TBI being served in schools is puzzling (Nagele et al., 2019).

TBI is an extremely complex disability to treat because the brain in and of itself is a highly complex organ. The complexity of postinjury effects depends upon the severity of impact to the skull in the accident, the duration of unconsciousness, and issues related to post-traumatic amnesia (Martinez et al., 2018). The intensity of the trauma to the head, and the longer the student has experienced unconsciousness the more likely for severe brain damage resulting in intensive medical and educational services that could last a lifetime. There are two common types of TBI: open and closed head trauma. Open head traumas are visible wounds that may include scars, stitches, and/or bandages, whereas closed head traumas occur when there is rapid shaking and movement of the brain inside the skull resulting in bruising and tearing of brain tissue (Johns Hopkins Medicine, 2023). Both open and closed head trauma can cause debilitating effects. At times, closed head injuries may be misleading in the severity of the head trauma to parents and teachers because symptoms are not initially present. Once the swelling and bruising subsides, the cognitive, behavior, and emotional impairments become clearer to detect. Closed head trauma may appear less serious than open head injuries because there is no visible scarring, but if closed head traumas are left undetected, the child will not receive the services needed to fully recover and this can be devastating (Jantz & Coulter, 2007).

Faul et al. (2010) commented that TBI is a "silent epidemic" because many students who have experienced a TBI may be denied services because of the hidden complications associated with TBI, and the limited public awareness of TBI. In many instances, students with TBI may appear to act, think, and look similar to their peers making it difficult for school personnel to know whether a trauma to the head occurred in the first place. It may not be until the student begins to demonstrate prolonged academic failure, escalating aggressive behaviors, or acts in a way not characteristic of the student preinjury that the school may then consider eligibility for special education services. Further, students who exhibit scars and display externalized behaviors (e.g., physical aggression, property destruction, or classroom disruptions) are more likely to receive special education services than those without visible scars and internalized behaviors (e.g., social withdrawal, depression, or anxiety) (Lundine et al., 2020). This is disconcerting considering many individuals who sustain a TBI do not have physical scars (Delach, 2018).

Identification

To qualify for TBI under IDEA, individuals must have medical documentation from a neurologist, neuropsychologist, or physician referring to the event that caused the consequential effects of the TBI. The physicians will commonly use the Glasgow Coma Scale which is a standardized scale that measures the person's ability to open their eyes, move their body, and communicate (Jantz & Coulter, 2007). Depending on the severity of the trauma case, CT scans and MRI scans may also be used as direct measures in locating bleeding, bruising, or swelling in the brain resulting from a suspected head trauma (Jantz & Coulter, 2007). Further, educational assessments, usually conducted by a licensed school psychologist, should provide evidence of discrepancies in academic and daily life functions between pre and postinjury (Glang, Todis, et al., 2008). It is imperative that communications between hospital and school are frequently conducted to ensure the student with TBI is receiving a continuum of medical and educational services (Glang, Todis, et al., 2008).

When a student returns to school after experiencing a TBI, the school may put temporary accommodations in place such as limitations on computer screen time, extended deadlines, or more breaks throughout the school day. However, if symptoms continue to adversely affect the learning of the student who experienced a TBI even with those accommodations, then an eligibility meeting would be initiated to determine if either a 504 plan or an Individualized Education Program (IEP) is warranted for more intensive services under the TBI category.

In the first amendment to IDEA in 1990 and later in IDEA (2004), TBI was added as a disability category for students to receive services. IDEA defines TBI as:

> ...an acquired injury to the brain caused by an external physical force, resulting in total or partial functional disability or psychosocial impairment, or both, that adversely affects a child's educational performance. Impairments may result in one or more areas, such as cognition; language; memory; attention; reasoning; abstract thinking; judgment; problem-solving;

sensory, perceptual, and/or motor abilities, psychosocial behavior; physical functions; information processing; and speech [§300.8(c)(12)].

TBIs that are congenital, degenerative, induced by birth trauma during pregnancy or due to substance abuse or seizure disorders are not included in the definition of TBI. Rather, these conditions may be referred under OHI (Jantz & Coulter, 2007).

Symptoms Associated With TBI

Although the scars may not be present, students with TBI may experience one or more different combinations of impairments depending on the severity of the head trauma. Bigler (2007) states that brain injuries occur most often in the frontal and temporal regions of the brain. The frontal lobe controls executive functioning, thinking, planning, organizing, problem-solving, emotional regulation, and personality, and the temporal lobe controls language, memory, and understanding (Dettmer et al., 2018). Clearly, damage to these lobes can cause significant debilitating effects on school performance, behavior, and overall quality of life. In general, there are four categories of impairments with multiple associated symptoms that may be exhibited as a result of the brain injury. The categories are: physical, cognitive, behavioral and emotional, and social impairments (Brain Injury Association, 2023). Physical impairments include symptoms such as vision changes and ringing in the ears where the environment is potentially causing the student to experience these difficulties. Cognitive impairments include symptoms such as difficulty remembering, slower thinking, and unable to process information logically which affects academic performance. Behavioral and emotional impairments include changes in temperament, restlessness, irritability, and displaying externalized and/or internalized behaviors. Social impairments are associated with not getting along with others or social awkwardness that tend to include anti-social behavior and withdrawal from interactions. Table 8.1 provides a list of symptoms associated under each of the four impairment categories which should help teachers understand how particular symptoms affect learning and behavioral performance.

Table 8.1. Impairments Associated With Brain Injury.

Physical Impairments	Cognitive Impairments
Speech articulation problems	Memory deficits
Vision changes	Difficulty sustaining attention
Hearing problems, ringing in the ears	Difficulty concentrating
Poor motor coordination and balance	Slower thinking
Headaches	Difficulty planning
Lethargy and fatigue	Difficulty reading and writing
Confusion	Poor judgment
Difficulty moving body parts, body numbness	Poor information processing
Dizziness	Poor executive functioning

Table 8.1. *(Continued)*

Behavioral and Emotional Impairments	Social Impairments
Frequent mood swings	Social isolation and withdrawal
Reduced self-esteem	Problems with variety of relationships
Depression	Difficulty participating in usual social activities
Anxiety	Social awkwardness
Restlessness	
Irritability	
Difficulty controlling emotions	
Reduced motivation	
Disinhibition	
Aggression	
Sexual acting out	

Source: Adapted from Brain Injury Association of America (2023); Martinez et al. (2018); Nolin et al. (2006); Slifer and Amari (2009); Ylvisaker et al. (2007).

INSTRUCTIONAL INTERVENTIONS FOR STUDENTS WITH TBI

Many neurological problems that are associated with trauma to the brain interfere with learning (Jantz & Coulter, 2007). Teachers need empirical-based instructional programs to meet the needs of students with TBI while addressing the impairments that are preventing them from learning the academic material properly, and behaving in socially appropriate ways. In this section, instructional interventions are not synonymous with accommodations. Instructional interventions are the teaching methods, strategies, and approaches teachers and specialists use to explain, model, and assess learning across content and skills. Whereas, accommodations are academic learning and behavioral supports that are put in place to allow the student greater access to the academic programs, curriculum, and materials. Accommodations will be discussed later in this chapter.

There is a scarcity of well-designed instructional interventions for students with TBI (Catroppa & Anderson, 2009; Glang, Ylvisaker, et al., 2008). Linden et al. (2018) conducted both a systematic review and meta-analysis on instructional interventions for children and adolescents with acquired brain injury to assess the improvement of academic performance. The authors found four studies meeting inclusion criteria where the studies needed to employ a randomized controlled trial to improve learning in an academic area (e.g., reading, math, or spelling). The interventions used in these studies were Captain's Log Cognitive Training software (Bangirana et al., 2009, 2011), Cognitive Remediation program (CRP; Butler et al., 2008), and general academic tutoring and memory and task preparation strategies (King et al., 2007). These authors reported a small effect size suggesting the instructional interventions were not as effective in improving the academic performance of children and adolescents with acquired brain injury. While this synthesis suggests a clear need for further research in evidence-based instructional interventions that meet the needs of students with TBI, teachers must continue to rely on current curriculum and programs that have sufficient evidence for improving the learning performance of students with disabilities. Although these current curriculums do not specifically address working on all the possible impairments and symptoms of students with TBI, there are validated research-based programs aimed to improve the achievement of students with and without disabilities, including students with TBI. These validated programs target areas such as processing speed, attention, concentration, and planning and organization that are necessary in increasing academic achievement in content areas.

Over the years, there has been sufficient research conducted on direct instruction (DI) (Glang et al., 1992; Glang, Ylvisaker, et al., 2008; Sohlberg et al., 2005; Stockard et al., 2018) and strategy instruction (SI) (Galbiati et al., 2009; Glang, Ylvisaker, et al., 2008; Kennedy & Coelho, 2005; Laane & Cook, 2020; Sohlberg et al., 2005) to improve academic, behavioral, and functional life skills for students with disabilities. These systematic instructional approaches focus on teaching material efficiently that allows students to generalize the skill learned to other situations and materials (Watins & Slocum, 2004).

Direct Instruction (DI)

DI was originated by Siegfried Engelmann and colleagues in the 1960s with the goal of improving and accelerating academic performance for at-risk children (National Institute for Direct Instruction, 2023). Research has been conducted on DI for over 40 years (see Stockard et al., 2018). If the DI curriculum is performed with fidelity, students can make two-year gains across one year of instruction (Mason & Otero, 2021). The central philosophy of DI, according to Siegfried Engelmann, is that if the student is not learning then it is the fault of the instruction rather than the student (Stockard et al., 2018).

According to Glang et al. (1992), many of the unique features of DI can be applied to various impairments associated with TBI. To address the difficulty of students concentrating and sustaining attention, the DI program features rapid instructional pacing, breaking tasks into meaningful chunks, not focusing on a single skill for the entire lesson, and creating opportunities of high student responding and success rates. To address the memory deficits students with TBI frequently encounter, the DI program embeds sufficient practice and review so students can achieve mastery before moving onto new or more complex tasks. Students do not move onto new material until they have demonstrated proficiency in previously taught material (Watins & Slocum, 2004). To address organization and planning deficits, the DI program provides logical and systematic steps in solving problems across academic areas.

In addition to the features that specifically address deficit skills for students with TBI, there are four key elements in the organization of the DI program that are helpful for students with disabilities. These features are grouping, instructional time, presentation scripts, and ongoing assessment (Watins & Slocum, 2004). Grouping students based on prerequisite knowledge and skills is important because this reduces potential boredom and acting out, particularly if the material is too easy or the pace is too slow. Further, teaching skills at the student's proper instructional level will ensure sustained concentration and attention because of the momentum of correct responding. The second feature, instructional time, is important because the student is given the appropriate amount of time to engage in various skills throughout a single lesson as well as time to process. The DI curriculum spirals so skills or items missed in previous attempts will be reintroduced in future lessons and in later lessons to build maintenance. This keeps the pace of the lesson moving while keeping the learner focused and engaged. In addition, reinforcement is carefully embedded throughout the program which helps in maintaining focused learning over time. The third feature, presentation scripts, keeps the teacher from having to improvise and design and refine lesson after lesson. The presentation scripts are written in a way that allows the student to engage in well-designed lessons that are worded and explained properly (Watins & Slocum, 2004). Finally, DI programs incorporate ongoing assessment and feedback on lesson objectives where the teacher makes a series of instructional decisions after each lesson. For example, if the student is consistently meeting criterion, the teacher may skip lessons or may change the grouping level. On the other hand, if the student is struggling and not meeting lesson objectives, reassignment of group level, reteaching lessons, or providing additional supplemental activities may be decided (Watins & Slocum, 2004).

Other prominent features of DI programs include general case programming, reteaching, and spiraling of skills for memory retention. Despite the positive findings of the effectiveness related to DI, many teachers have not fully embraced the DI program commenting that they do not want their teaching to be relegated to reading scripts, or they push for more of a constructivist teaching philosophy. Yet, advocates for DI programs insist that students with learning difficulties need curriculum that is structured, clear in presentation, and unambiguous (Stockard et al., 2018). In addition, students need to be monitored with sufficient and adequate feedback so the students learn the material correctly and efficiently. Below are a few of those components that can serve as supplemental or stand-alone strategies used for students with TBI in the classroom. These strategies include: explicit instruction, errorless learning, and task analysis (TA).

Explicit Instruction
Explicit instruction emphasizes "teaching in small steps, providing student practice after each step, guiding students during initial practice, and providing all students with high level of successful practice" (Rosenshine, 1987, p. 34). During explicit instruction, the teacher models new skills and concepts while students ask questions. Then, the teacher and students work on problems together through repetition and error correction. Finally, multiple trials of guided practice are given where the teacher serves as a facilitator providing prompts and hints when needed. The guided practice stage is done until the student is independently proficient. Archer and Hughes (2011) provide guidelines for designing explicit lessons and teaching strategies. The formula for teaching an explicitly designed lesson is *I do it*, where the teacher describes and demonstrates the new skill or

problem while the student observes. *We do it*, where the teacher and student work the problem together in a step-by-step and clear manner. *You do it*, where the student completes the skill or problem with the teacher serving as a facilitator providing prompts and corrective feedback when needed (Archer & Hughes, 2011). Additional components of explicit instruction include, frequent opportunities to respond, carefully delivered praise and corrective feedback, and constant monitoring of progress (Archer & Hughes, 2011).

Errorless Learning

The term "errorless learning" was first introduced by H. S. Terrance (1963) with the study of pigeons discriminating between red and green keys using error and fading procedures. Soon after, similar error prevention procedures were used by Sidman and Stoddard (1967) who worked with individuals with intellectual disabilities to discriminate between circles and ellipses. Scaffolds and prompts were delivered to keep the individuals from making incorrect responses (Wilson et al., 1994). This type of procedure is different from trial-and-error procedures because the student is immediately corrected when errors are made and, in many cases, asked to repeat the correct response. Errorless learning can enhance learning for students with TBI because of the careful attention in helping students retrieve and recall information with confidence through the gradual delivery of scaffolds. Errorless learning is used to eliminate errors done during the acquisition phase of learning in efforts to build motivation, confidence, and overall achievement in the student (Baddeley & Wilson, 1994; Wilson et al., 1994). Repetition to solidify newly learned skills is critical especially with the goal of building automaticity, fluency, and retrieval. Neuroplasticity allows our brain to relearn functions affected by injury. Teachers can boost neuroplasticity through repetitive exercises and consistency (Flint Rehab, 2022).

Task Analysis (TA)

A supplemental element to both DI and explicit instruction is teaching complex skills and strategies into smaller instructional units to complete a variety of skill acquisition tasks (Archer & Hughes, 2011). TA is a helpful instructional strategy for students with TBI because in many instances, the prefrontal cortex, which houses executive function, has been damaged causing problems for the student to initiate and follow through on tasks that require multiple steps (Friedman & Robbins, 2022). TA has been used with individuals with disabilities to teach a variety of academic, domestic, leisure, and community skills (Benson et al., 2021; Randall et al., 2020; Root et al., 2021). TA breaks complex tasks into several manageable steps where the individuals are evaluated on their level of independence across each step with the goal of performing the task independently. Teachers and special education specialists can then teach each step using a level of prompting from least intrusive (i.e., visual or verbal prompt) to more intrusive (i.e., partial or full physical assistance) in providing errorless learning for each step. Although there are numerous studies that have examined TA for individuals with developmental disabilities, there are only a few have investigated TA for individuals with TBI. For example, Velikonja et al. (2017) used TA to teach showering and dressing skills to 24 admitted patients with moderate to severe TBI. Results indicated that over the course of several weeks, the individuals improved in their showering and dressing skills and needed less supervision and prompting. TA can be used in a variety of contexts such as learning how to solve a two-step algebraic problem, or how to sort and organize materials. TA helps students who struggle with planning and completing tasks by ensuring that the students can correctly complete each step with success.

Summary

Currently, there are no educational curriculums or interventions specifically designed for students with TBI. However, DI and explicit instruction contain components such as rapid instructional pacing, high mastery criteria, generalizable strategies, and sufficient practice that benefit the learning characteristics of students with TBI (Archer & Hughes, 2011; Glang et al., 1992; Glang, Ylvisaker, et al., 2008). In an effort to move forward in educating individuals with TBI, educational research should focus on creating programs and interventions to help teachers address the common sequelae associated with students with TBI that hinder academic achievement. For example, these new programs and interventions should elicit new ways to help students with TBI increase in their processing speed, plan for short- and long-term assignments and life events, or build their stamina in concentrating for extended periods of time. Ultimately, addressing these impairments will help overall achievement in academic content areas and adaptive skills.

Strategy Instruction (SI)

According to Montague and Dietz (2009), SI is an evidence-based practice separated by cognitive skills (i.e., how to complete the skill/task), metacognitive skills (i.e., monitor their own learning performance), and problem-solving skills (e.g., plan, execute, and evaluate learning). Students need to be explicitly taught each strategy so it becomes automatic. The goal of SI is for the student to be able to apply the correct strategy and then perform the strategy across different problems, contexts, and settings. SI is important for students with TBI because these strategies offer opportunities to improve their independence through systematically rehearsing and implementing the strategy without having to rely on others. In addition, SI can be used in areas such as organization, social skills, and adaptive living skills. The same lesson plan format used in DI and explicit instruction can also be applied to SI to systematically teach students to apply strategies to various problems without too much cognitive demand. The components in teaching a strategy include: modeling, guided practice, independent practice, and assessment. A unique feature to SI is the importance of the student thinking about their learning. This is done through self-regulation, which is a difficult skill for students with TBI to master (Kennedy & Coelho, 2005).

Self-Regulation

Self-regulation pertains to how an individual processes and adjusts their performance toward behavioral and communication goals (Hunt et al., 2013). Damage to the frontal lobes is where self-regulatory impairments originally manifest (Kennedy & Coelho, 2005). Students with self-regulation impairments will have difficulty in executive functions such as starting tasks, monitoring their performance of a task, and self-control to use a particular strategy. A common self-regulatory strategy taught by teachers is self-monitoring of their own performance.

Self-Monitoring

Self-monitoring is when the student compares actual performance with an expected performance goal (Kennedy & Coelho, 2005). Self-monitoring creates internal feedback (i.e., self-talk) that is used to make decisions about the problem or strategy (Kennedy & Coelho, 2005). Self-monitoring is helpful for students with TBI because it requires them to think, process, and execute using internal and external strategies to compensate for damage to the frontal lobe that affects memory and attention (Rabinowitz & Levin, 2014). Teachers can provide other types of self-monitoring strategies such as teaching students to use a checklist when checking off steps in an activity, or demonstrating how to use positive self-talk to work through a problem.

Generalization

Generalization involves performing the behavior in environments that are different from the original teaching conditions (Lee & Axelrod, 2005). Students with TBI should not be expected to spontaneously generalize new strategies learned on their own in different contexts (Kennedy & Coelho, 2005). After the student is confident in using the new strategy in a specific situation, the teacher should work with the student to use that strategy in other contexts and settings. For example, once the student has successfully learned to gather the most critical information from a science textbook using the SQ3R strategy, the student can then use that same strategy to gather important information from other sources such as journal articles, newsfeeds, or other content textbooks. However, the teacher would need to program for generalization using a variety of generalization techniques to help the student see the similarities and differences in using SQ3R with different texts (see Scheeler et al., 2019; Stokes & Baer, 1977).

Metacognitive Strategies

Executive functioning is an area of concern for students with TBI. Executive functions are a set of cognitive skills necessary to plan, organize, focus attention, self-correct, and engage in goal-directed behaviors (Jantz & Coulter, 2007; Kennedy et al., 2008). Executive function deficits are a common cognitive difficulty experienced by students with TBI. Metacognitive strategies are tools teachers can use to help their students work on executive functioning skills that require the student to think about their actions and recognize their own cognitive processes before initiating in that task (Pezzica et al., 2018). Thinking about one's own thinking can be an extremely challenging task particularly if the student is having difficulty with brain function. One strategy to help with executive functioning deficits is metacognitive strategy instruction (MSI). A systematic review conducted by Coelho et al. (1996) concluded that self-monitoring, self-control procedures, and explicit feedback improved executive functions. Further, a review of 10 intervention studies teaching a step-by-step MSI for young to middle-aged adults with TBI was found to be a promising intervention to improve problem-solving, planning, organization, and multitasking (Kennedy et al., 2008). The step-by-step procedures for MSI include several components: generating goals, self-monitoring, self-recording their performance, deciding which strategy is needed to meet the goal, and self-feedback on performance of the goal (Kennedy et al., 2008).

Mnemonic devices are another type of metacognitive strategy commonly seen in classrooms that are used to facilitate memorization and recall of the strategy steps (Deshler et al., 1996). Although we would most likely have a student with TBI write down information due to memory deficits, mnemonic devices may be helpful to the individual in remembering small bits of information and building memory capacity. For students with TBI, mnemonics can be helpful in beginning to rebuild memory function that occurred from brain trauma. Mnemonic (memory-enhancing) SI helps students make connections to new information from prior knowledge through visual and acoustic cues (Mastropieri et al., 2000). Mnemonic strategies such as keyword method, pegword method, and letter strategy are evidence-based strategies proven to improve the learning of students with disabilities (Scruggs et al., 2010). According to Scruggs et al. (2010), keyword and pegword methods and letter strategy use familiar words to associate with an unfamiliar word through interactive images of pictures, rhymes, and/or acronyms.

Expanding on metacognitive strategies described by Scruggs et al. (2010), Natalia and Agnieszka (2021) tested whether visual metacognitive strategies such as mind maps and sketch-noting helped in strengthening the emotional and motivational self-regulation (number or errors and average reaction time) in children with ADHD. Mind maps is a visual tool that uses keywords, diagrams, and drawings to deepen understanding in a concept, whereas sketch-notes use sketches, pictures, arrows, dots, boxes, and words to convey thoughts particularly in a note-taking format (Natalia & Agnieszka, 2021). The results found that after 3 months, students with ADHD in the intervention group made fewer errors using either mind maps or sketch-notes, than students with ADHD in the control group.

Summary

Students with TBI have consistently demonstrated difficulties in executive function, organization, and problem-solving (Glang, Ylvisaker, et al., 2008). SI that includes self-regulation, self-monitoring, and metacognition can be incorporated in a student's instructional program to work on demonstrated difficulties noted above. In maintaining tradition, a focus must be on instructing students with TBI to work through problems and monitor their progress. SI allows students these opportunities to learn a variety of strategies to not only improve their learning but to improve their quality of life.

BEHAVIORAL INTERVENTIONS FOR STUDENTS WITH TBI

Another common impairment for students with TBI is the tendency for them to exhibit behavioral and emotional challenges. Students with TBI may exhibit challenging behaviors for a variety of reasons. These students may be experiencing physical symptoms such as headaches or lethargy that is causing agitation and frustration because of a task demand or the physical environment. Behavioral problems can range from 35% to 70% after a brain injury (Ylvisaker et al., 2007). Once the special education specialist notice changes in behavior such as increases in the frequency and severity of outbursts and aggression, a first step is to determine the function of the challenging behavior by conducting a functional behavioral assessment (FBA). After the function of behavior is determined, the IEP team designs a behavior intervention plan teaching the student alternative ways that are socially appropriate to either gain attention or escape demands without engaging in challenging behaviors. In addition to executing the FBA, teachers should also be aware of the environmental factors that contribute to challenging behaviors. Teachers should have in place several antecedent-based interventions to curb triggers that lead to challenging behavior by removing and adjusting materials, people, and tasks.

Antecedent-Based Interventions

Antecedent-based interventions involve changing the physical and social environment to prevent the challenging behavior from escalating and thus increasing the probability of future occurrences of desirable behavior (Slifer & Amari, 2009). Examples of antecedent-based interventions include decreasing physical environmental distractors that may accelerate undesirable behavior such as dimming the lights to reduce headaches or reducing the number of people in the room to lower the noise level. Another example may include decreasing the duration of time in therapy and instructional settings to reduce cognitive overload and frustration. Assigning the student to work with a trusted teacher or instructional assistant in a one-on-one or small group setting develops trust and rapport that is necessary for the student to feel comfortable. Another antecedent intervention includes providing daily and weekly schedules for predictability and structure as well as memory journals for the student to refer back to (Slifer & Amari, 2009). These antecedent interventions are intentionally planned by the teacher in anticipation of possible challenging behaviors to occur.

Emotional Wellness

Emotional wellness is the "ability to successfully handle life's stresses and adapt to change and difficult times" (National Institute of Health, 2022). Students with TBI can have great difficulties with adapting to new environments, routines, and people. In addition, frequent life changes can be troubling for students with TBI because of their need for consistency and routine.

Depending on the severity of symptoms, students with TBI may exhibit internal or external behaviors that may offset their emotional wellness. Internal behaviors such as depression and fear are invisible behaviors suppressed within the student and unknown to parents and teachers. Whereas, physical aggression, anger, and agitation are visible behaviors in how the student acts out their frustration that may have resulted from frustration and helplessness (Jantz et al., 2014).

TBI brings about feelings of frustration, agitation, and grief usually due to the inability to perform a task they were once able to do. Other examples that induce frustration include difficulty thinking of a word in a conversation, or remembering names, places, and past experiences, or the inability to express their needs in socially acceptable ways. Teachers should use calming strategies when the student begins exhibiting agitation to reduce the possibility of escalation. Calming strategies may include removing the student from the stressful task or situation, having the student take long deep breaths with pushing the diaphragm out while inhaling through the nose and exhaling through their mouth with eyes closed. Breathing is a natural relaxation strategy where oxygen serves to open mental pathways for focus and clarity (Noble & Hochman, 2019). Another strategy is for the student to use positive affirmations when referring to their strengths and weaknesses. For example, when the student cannot do something instead of them using negative self-talk about what they cannot do, the teacher might encourage the student to use phrases such as "I am still learning this..." or "this will take some time, but I will get the hang of it." Positive affirmations and self-talk energize the mind in a direction toward positive future thinking. Table 8.2 describes different behavioral strategies teachers and special education specialists can implement to increase motivation, attention, inhibition, and the overall classroom environment for students with TBI.

Summary

Students with TBI frequently exhibit challenging behavior. In maintaining tradition, it is important for teachers to be preventative rather than reactive when dealing with challenging behaviors. Teachers must be aware of the neurological factors within the student as well as the environmental factors within the classroom setting that may contribute to the challenging behavior. In moving forward, teachers should continue to focus their attention on antecedent-based strategies to anticipate and remove any behavioral triggers. In addition, teachers should use alternative strategies determined from the FBA to address the function that serves the challenging behavior.

Table 8.2. Behavioral Strategies.

Increase Overall Classroom Environment	Increase Motivation
• Establish clear expectations and classroom routines • Praise correct behavior rather than incorrect behavior • Get to know students as individuals • Anticipate problems and then adjust the learning environment accordingly • Use precorrection with assurance of errorless learning	• Set up a system for scheduling positive reinforcement • Continuously use encouraging, supportive, and positive affirmations • Create daily schedules distinguishing work time from break time • Visually display daily and weekly student goals that are attainable to achieve • Use instructional momentum
Increase Attention and Concentration	**Increase Inhibition**
• Remove distractive objects • Break assignments into manageable sections • Connect previous learned content to new content • Seat the student closer to the teacher • Use "gists" rather than elaborate summaries and provide guided notes	• Provide step-by-step visual directions • Teach student to pause and reflect before acting • Have student perform correct behavior and use modeling scripts • Teach student to use a self-talk strategy • Assist in guided imagery and/or deep breathing techniques

Source: Adapted from Bowen (2005); Dettmer et al. (2018); Ylvisaker et al. (2007).

ACCOMMODATIONS FOR STUDENTS WITH TBI

A strategy is an individual's approach to a task (Deshler et al., 1996), or how the individual attempts to solve a problem. Accommodations do not require the individual to cognitively plan, evaluate, and/or execute a strategy to complete a task. Rather, accommodations are supports applied within the learning environment to increase student access to the materials, tasks, and activities. There are numerous accommodations teachers can implement that may be beneficial for students with TBI in the classroom. Table 8.3 provides a list of accommodations teachers and special education specialists can use in their classrooms to help students with organization, memory, processing, and sensory impairments.

Table 8.3. Accommodations for Students With TBI.

Accommodation	Purpose	Brain Processes
Provide posted daily schedule and task-oriented checklists	• Helps anticipate what will happen during the day and monitors what has been completed and what still needs to be completed	• Organization
Provide two sets of books and other class materials	• Keep one book at home and one book at school to limit the student from forgetting to bring materials to class or home	• Organization • Memory
Use a notetaker	• Allows student to focus on one cognitive task at a time (i.e., thinking) instead of multiple tasks	• Organization • Memory
Record lessons	• Student can review material over again that may have been forgotten	• Memory

Table 8.3. *(Continued)*

Accommodation	Purpose	Brain Processes
Memory notebook	• Writes important information such as telephone numbers, names of people, and medication and appointment times	• Memory
Use visual and verbal prompts with directions and explanations	• Allows the student to process the information more effectively	• Memory • Processing speed
Provide wait time for directions and task explanations	• Allows the student time to process what was said and then think about how to act and proceed from what was said	• Processing speed
Allow extra time to complete assignments and tests	• Allows the student time to process the information from tests and assignments	• Processing speed
Reduce light and sounds	• Bright lights and loud noise may induce headaches or ringing in ears	• Sensory
Provide quiet space	• Student may be lethargic and need time to rest, or a place to concentrate without extraneous noise and distractions	• Sensory

Source: Adapted from Dettmer et al. (2018); Silverberg et al. (2020).

RECOMMENDATIONS

Based on a review of the literature, a few recommendations can be offered. First, although the medical research in TBI is flourishing, the same cannot be said about educational research for students with TBI, particularly as it relates to specific curriculum and teaching materials. We need to expand on the breadth of research on finding instructional strategies and curricula that help students with TBI advance academically, behaviorally, and socially. Further, it is important to devise specific curricula that not only works to increase academic achievement but also works to improve underlying impairments such as executive function, sensory-motor, processing speed, and attention (Dettmer et al., 2018).

Second, teachers and instructional assistants are not receiving the supports and training they need to work effectively with students with TBI (Kahn et al., 2018; Sohlberg et al., 1998). Teachers need professional development in learning how to implement programs such as DI with fidelity. In addition, these professional development opportunities should incorporate ways teachers and teaching assistants understand the etiology behind TBI, how TBI is similar and different from other disabilities as well as specific strategies to work with students with TBI. Professional development will require an investment in resources and financial procurement from the school districts. However, this will be a wise investment considering many students may have sustained a TBI and are sitting in our classrooms without formal acknowledgment of such trauma (Xun et al., 2023). Further, school personnel should be provided professional development in assistive technologies for students with TBI that have been proven successful.

Third, students with TBI may have the intellectual capacity to successfully perform complex academic tasks; however, their struggles with performing simple executive tasks may prohibit them from demonstrating their full potential. For example, tasks such as remembering to bring materials to class, meeting homework and project deadlines, understanding the multiple steps needed to complete short- and long-term projects, and persisting through setbacks during an activity may prevent teachers from understanding what the student actually knows or can do (Sohlberg et al., 1998). There needs to be a coordinated effort across all school professionals including parents to discuss and implement strategies that have been successful for students with TBI.

A final recommendation is for introductory special education courses in higher education institutions to focus more attention on identification, characteristics and specific strategies, and accommodations for students with TBI. Also, discussions in what to look for in a concussion protocol, and how to initiate the process for evaluating a student for special education services for a suspected TBI would be advantageous for the preservice teacher.

CONCLUSION

In the spirit of advancing values, when students with TBI present with a variety of impairments (e.g., attention, memory, behavior deficits), the teacher's primary goal should not be to re-establish impaired functions that resulted from the brain injury. Rather, the goal must be equipping those students to work through those deficit areas with evidence-based curriculum and accommodations that provide meaningful access in achieving those goals written in their IEP. This chapter discussed the characteristics, identification, and academic and behavioral strategies that have been found effective for students with TBI in maintaining tradition. There is still much work needed for students with TBI particularly with finding appropriate curriculum materials that address both the academic achievement and underlying impairments associated with TBI. While TBI research is still ongoing, teachers and special education specialists should continue to invest in instructional programs and practices such as DI and SI that have proven to provide success for students with disabilities.

REFERENCES

Archer, A. L., & Hughes, C. A. (2011). *Explicit instruction: Effective and efficient teaching.* The Guilford Press.

Baddeley, A., & Wilson, B. (1994). When implicit learning fails: Amnesia and the problem of error elimination. *Neuropsychologia, 32,* 53–68. https://doi.org/10.1016/0028-3932(94)90068-X

Bangirana, P., Allebeck, P., Boivin, M. J., John, C. C., Page, C., Ehnvall, A., & Musisi, S. (2011). Cognition, behavior and academic skills after cognitive rehabilitation in Ugandan children surviving severe malaria: A randomised trial. *BMC Neurology, 11*(1), 96. https://doi.org/10.1186/1471-2377-11-96

Bangirana, P., Giordani, B., John, C. C., Page, C., Opoka, R. O., & Boivin, M. J. (2009). Immediate neuropsychological and behavioral benefits of computerized cognitive rehabilitation in Ugandan pediatric cerebral malaria survivors. *Journal of Developmental and Behavioral Pediatrics, 30*(4), 310–318. http://doi.org/10.1097/DBP.0b013e3181b0f01b

Benson, V. K., Wakeman, S. Y., Wood, C. L., & Muharib, R. (2021). Using picture-based task-analytic instruction to teach students with moderate intellectual disability to email peers without disabilities. *Journal of Special Education Apprenticeship*, *10*(1). Article 3. https://scholarworks.lib.csusb.edu/josea/vol10/iss1/3

Bigler, E. D. (2007). Anterior and middle cranial fossa in traumatic brain injury: Relevant neuroanatomy and neuropathology in the study of neuropsychological outcome. *Neuropsychology*, *21*, 515–531. https://doi.org/10.1037/0894-4105.21.5.515

Bowen, J. M. (2005). Classroom interventions for students with traumatic brain injuries. *Preventing School Failure*, *49*(4), 34–41. https://doi.org/10.3200/psfl.49.4.34-41

Brain Injury Association of America. (2023). *Brain injury diagnosis*. https://www.biausa.org/brain-injury/about-brain-injury/diagnosis

Butler, R. W., Copeland, D. R., Fairclough, D. L., Mulhern, R. K., Katz, E. R., Kazak, A. E., Noll, R. B., Patel, S. K., & Sahler, O. J. (2008). A multicenter, randomized clinical trial of a cognitive remediation program for childhood survivors of a pediatric malignancy. *Journal of Consulting and Clinical Psychology*, *76*, 367–378. https://doi.org/10.1037/0022-006X.76.3.367

Catroppa, C., & Anderson, V. (2009). Traumatic brain injury in childhood: Rehabilitation considerations. *Developmental Neurorehabilitation*, *12*, 53–61. https://doi.org/10.1080/17518420802634476

Coelho, C. A., DeRuyter, F., & Stein, M. (1996). Treatment efficacy: Cognitive-communication disorders resulting from traumatic brain injury in adults. *Journal of Speech & Hearing Research*, *39*(5), S5–S17. https://doi.org/10.1044/jshr.3905.s5

Delach, K. (2018). *Addressing the unseen scars of a TBI head on*. https://www.onehealth.upenn.edu/2018/04/02/addressing-unseen-tbi-scars-head-on/

DePompei, R., & Bedell, G. (2008). Making a difference for children and adolescents with traumatic brain injury. *The Journal of Head Trauma Rehabilitation*, *23*(4), 191–196. https://doi.org/10.1097/01.htr.0000327251.16010.3b

Deshler, D. D., Ellis, E. S., & Lenz, B. K. (1996). *Teaching adolescents with learning disabilities: Strategies and methods*. Love Publishing Co.

Dettmer, J., Dise-Lewis, J. E., Colella, P. W., Crawford, N., Hotchkiss, H., McAvoy, K., Thompson, P., & Tyler, J. (2018). *Brain injury in children and youth: A manual for educators*. Colorado Department of Education. http://cde.state.co.us/cdesped/tbi_manual_braininjury. Accessed on May 31, 2023.

Faul, M., Xu, L., Wald, M. M., & Coronado, V. G. (2010). *Traumatic brain injury in the United States: Emergency department visits, hospitalizations and deaths 2002–2006*. Centers for Disease Control and Prevention, National Center for Injury Prevention and Control.

Flint Rehab. (2022). *Can the brain heal itself? Understanding neuroplasticity after brain injury*. https://www.flintrehab.com/how-does-the-brain-repair-itself-after-a-traumatic-injury/#:~:text=The%20brain%20is%20incredibly%20resilient,survivors%20can%20make%20astounding%20recoveries

Friedman, N. P., & Robbins, T. W. (2022). The role of prefrontal cortex in cognitive control and executive function. *Neuropsychopharmacology*, *47*, 72–89. https://doi.org/10.1038/s41386-021-01132-0

Galbiati, S., Recla, M., Pastore, V., Liscio, M., Bardoni, A., Castelli, E., & Strazzer, S. (2009). Attention remediation following traumatic brain injury in childhood and adolescence. *Neuropsychology*, *23*, 40–49. https://doi.org/10.1037/a0013409

Glang, A., Singer, G., Cooley, E., & Tish, N. (1992). Tailoring direct instruction techniques for use with students with brain injury. *The Journal of Head Trauma Rehabilitation*, *7*(4), 93–108. http://doi.org/10.1097/00001199-199212000-00011

Glang, A., Todis, B., Thomas, C. W., Hood, D., Bedell, G., & Cockrell, J. (2008). Return to school following childhood TBI: Who gets services? *NeuroRehabilitation*, *23*, 477–486. https://doi.org/10.3233/nre-2008-23604

Glang, A., Ylvisaker, M., Stein, M., Ehlhardt, L., Todis, B., & Tyler, J. (2008). Validated instructional practices: Application to students with traumatic brain injury. *The Journal of Head Trauma Rehabilitation*, *23*(4), 242–251. https://doi.org/10.1097/01.htr.0000327256.46504.9f

Hunt, A. W., Turner, G. R., Polatajko, H., Bottari, C., & Dawson, D. R. (2013). Executive function, self-regulation and attribution in acquired brain injury: A scoping review. *Neuropsychological Rehabilitation*, *23*, 914–932. https://doi.org/10.1080/09602011.2013.835739

Individuals with Disabilities Education Improvement Act, 20 U.S.C. § 1401 et seq. (2004).

Jantz, P. B., & Coulter, G. A. (2007). Child and adolescent traumatic brain injury: Academic, behavioural, and social consequences in the classroom. *Support for Learning, 22*(2), 84–89. https://doi.org/10.1111/j.1467-9604.2007.00452.x

Jantz, P. B., Davies, S. C., & Bigler, E. D. (2014). *Working with traumatic brain injury in schools: Transition, assessment, and intervention.* Counselor Education and Human Services Faculty Publications. Paper 52. http://ecommons.udayton.edu/edc_fac_pub/52

Johns Hopkins Medicine. (2023, May 30). *Traumatic brain injury.* https://www.hopkinsmedicine.org/health/conditions-and-diseases/traumatic-brain-injury

Kahn, L. G., Linden, M. A., McKinlay, A., Gomez, D., & Glang, A. (2018). An international perspective on educators' perceptions of children with traumatic brain injury. *NeuroRehabilitation, 42*, 299–309. https://doi.org/10.3233/NRE-172380

Kennedy, M. R. T., & Coelho, C. (2005). Self-regulation after traumatic brain injury: A framework for intervention of memory and problem solving. *Seminars in Speech and Language, 26*(4), 242–255. https://doi.org/10.1055/s-2005-922103

Kennedy, M. R. T., Coelho, C., Turkstra, L., Ylvisaker, M., Sohlberg, M. M., Yorkston, K., Chiou, H., & Kan, P. (2008). Intervention for executive functions after traumatic brain injury: A systematic review, meta-analysis and clinical recommendations. *Neuropsychological Rehabilitation, 18*, 257–299. https://doi.org/10.1080/09602010701748644

King, A. A., White, D. A., McKinstry, R. C., Noetzel, M., & DeBaun, M. R. (2007). A pilot randomized education rehabilitation trial is feasible in sickle cell and strokes. *Neurology, 68*, 2008–2011. http://doi.org/10.1212/01.wnl.0000264421.24415.16

Laane, S. A., & Cook, L. G. (2020). Cognitive-communication interventions for youth with traumatic brain injury. *Seminars in Speech and Language, 41*(2), 183–194. https://doi.org/10.1055/s-0040-1701686

Lee, D. L., & Axelrod, S. A. (2005). *Behavior modification: Basic principles* (3rd ed.). PRO-ED.

Linden, M. A., Glang, A. E., & McKinlay, A. (2018). A systematic review and meta-analysis of educational interventions for children and adolescents with acquired brain injury. *NeuroRehabilitation, 42*, 311–323. https://doi.org/10.3233/NRE-172357

Lundine, J. P., Todis, B., Gau, J. M., McCart, M., Wade, S. L., Yeates, K. O., & Glang, A. (2020). Return to school following TBI: Educational services received 1 year after injury. *The Journal of Head Trauma Rehabilitation, 36*(2), E89–E96. https://doi.org/10.1097/HTR.0000000000000591

Martinez, A. P., Scherer, M. J., & Tozser, T. (2018). Traumatic brain injury (TBI) in school-based populations: Common sequelae and assistive technology interventions. *Advances in Neurodevelopmental Disorders, 2*, 310–321. https://doi.org/10.1007/s41252-018-0071-7

Masel, B. (2006). Opening remarks. In *Galveston brain injury conferences, Galveston, TX.*

Mason, L., & Otero, M. (2021). Just how effective is direct instruction? *Perspectives on Behavioral Science, 44*, 225–244. https://doi.org/10.1007/s40614-021-00295-x

Mastropieri, M. A., Sweda, J., & Scruggs, T. E. (2000). Putting mnemonics strategies to work in an inclusive classroom. *Learning Disabilities Research & Practice, 15*(2), 69–74. https://doi.org/10.1207/SLDRP1502_2

Montague, M., & Dietz, S. (2009). Evaluating the evidence base for cognitive strategy instruction and mathematical problem solving. *Exceptional Children, 75*(3), 285–302. https://doi.org/10.1177/001440290907500302

Nagele, D. A., Hooper, S. R., Hildebrant, K., McCart, M., Dettmer, J. L., & Glang, A. (2019). Under-identification of students with long term disability from moderate to severe TBI: Analysis of causes and potential remedies. *Physical Disabilities: Education and Related Services, 38*, 10–25. https://doi.org/10.14434/pders.v38i1.26850

Natalia, K., & Agnieszka, K. (2021). Application of metacognitive strategies in the development of emotional and motivational self-regulation of students with special educational needs: Research in children with ADHD. *Current Problems of Psychiatry, 22*(4), 284–293. https://doi.org/10.2478/cpp-2021-0020

National Center for Education Statistics. (2022). *Students with disabilities. Condition of education.* U.S. Department of Education, Institute of Education Sciences. https://nces.ed.gov/programs/coe/indicator/cgg

National Institute for Direct Instruction. (2023, May 31). *Basic philosophy of direct instruction*. https://www.nifdi.org/15/index.php?option=com_content&view=article&id=52&Itemid=27

National Institute of Health. (2022). *Emotional wellness toolkit*. https://www.nih.gov/health-information/emotional-wellness-toolkit

Noble, D. J., & Hochman, S. (2019). Hypothesis: Pulmonary afferent activity patterns during slow, deep breathing contribute to the neural induction of physiological relaxation. *Frontiers in Physiology*, *10*, 1–17. http://doi.org/10.3389/fphys.2019.01176

Nolin, P., Villemure, R., & Heroux, L. (2006). Determining long-term symptoms following mild traumatic brain injury: Method of interview affects self-report. *Brain Injury*, *20*, 1147–1154. https://doi.org/10.1080/02690500601049247

Pezzica, S., Vezzani, C., & Pinto, G. (2018). Metacognitive knowledge of attention in children with and without ADHD symptoms. *Research in Developmental Disabilities*, *83*, 142–152. https://doi.org/10.1016/j.ridd.2018.08.005

Rabinowitz, A. R., & Levin, H. S. (2014). Cognitive sequelae of traumatic brain injury. *Psychiatric Clinics of North America*, *37*, 1–11. https://doi.org/10.1016/j.psc.2013.11.004

Randall, K. N., Johnson, F., Adams, S. E., Kiss, C. W., & Ryan, J. B. (2020). Use of a iPhone task analysis application to increase employment-related chores for individuals with intellectual disabilities. *Journal of Special Education Technology*, *35*, 26–36. https://doi.org/10.1177/0162643419836410

Root, J. R., Ingelin, B., & Cox, S. K. (2021). Teaching mathematical word problem solving to students with autism spectrum disorder: A best-evidence synthesis. *Education and Training in Autism and Developmental Disabilities*, *56*, 420–436.

Rosenshine, B. (1987). Explicit teaching and teacher training. *Journal of Teacher Education*, *38*(3), 34–36. https://doi.org/10.1177/002248718703800308

Scheeler, M. C., Lee, D. L., & Markelz, A. M. (2019). Teach students to maintain and generalize new learning across time and settings. In J. McLeskey, L. Maheady, B. Billingsley, M. T. Brownell, & T. J. Lewis (Eds.), *Higher leverage practices for inclusive classrooms* (pp. 302–314). Routledge.

Scruggs, T. E., Mastropieri, M. A., Berkeley, S., & Marshak, L. (2010). Mnemonic strategies: Evidence-based practice and practice-based evidence. *Intervention in School and Clinic*, *46*(2), 79–86. https://doi.org/10.1177/1053451210374985

Sidman, M., & Stoddard, L. T. (1967). The effectiveness of fading in programming simultaneous form discrimination for retarded children. *Journal of the Experimental Analysis of Behavior*, *10*, 3–15. https://doi.org/10.1901/jeab.1967.10-3

Silverberg, N. D., Iaccarino, M. A., Panenka, W. J., Iverson, G. L., McCulloch, K. L., Dams-O'Connor, K., Reed, N., & McCrea, M. (2020). Management of concussion and mild traumatic brain injury: A synthesis of practice guidelines. *Archives of Physical Medicine and Rehabilitation*, *101*, 382–393.

Slifer, K. J., & Amari, A. (2009). Behavior management for children and adolescents with acquired brain injury. *Developmental Disabilities Research Review*, *15*(2), 144–151. https://doi.org/10.1002/ddrr.60

Sohlberg, M. M., Ehlhardt, L., & Kennedy, M. (2005). Instructional techniques in cognitive rehabilitation: A preliminary report. *Seminars in Speech and Language*, *26*(4), 268–279. https://doi.org/10.1055/s-2005-922105

Sohlberg, M. M., Todis, B., & Glang, A. (1998). SCEMA: A team-based approach to serving secondary students with executive dysfunction following brain injury. *Aphasiology*, *12*, 1047–1092. https://doi.org/10.1080/02687039808249469

Stockard, J., Wood, T. W., Coughlin, C., & Rasplica Khoury, C. (2018). The effectiveness of direct instruction curricula: A meta-analysis of a half century of research. *Review of Educational Review*, *88*, 479–507. https://doi.org/10.3102/0034654317751919

Stokes, T. E., & Baer, D. M. (1977). An implicit technology for generalization. *Journal of Applied Behavior Analysis*, *10*, 349–367. https://doi.org/10.1901/jaba.1977.10-349

Taylor, C. A., Bell, J. M., Breiding, M. J., & Xu, L. (2017). Traumatic brain injury–related emergency department visits, hospitalizations, and deaths—United States, 2007 and 2013. *MMWR Surveillance Summaries*, *66*, 1–16. https://doi.org/10.15585/mmwr.ss6609a1

Terrance, H. S. (1963). Discrimination learning with and without "errors". *Journal of the Experimental Analysis of Behavior, 6,* 1–27. https://doi.org/10.1901/jeab.1963.6-1

U.S. Department of Education, Office of Special Education Programs. (2021). *OSEP fast facts: School aged children 5 (in Kindergarten) through 21 served under Part B, of the IDEA.* https://sites.ed. gov/idea/osep-fast-facts-school-aged-children-5-21-served-under-idea-part-b-21/

Velikonja, D., Oakes, J., Brum, C., & Sachdeva, M. (2017). Assessing the validity of task analysis as a quantitative tool to measure the efficacy of rehabilitation in brain injury. *Brain Injury, 31*(1), 68–74. https://doi.org/10.1080/02699052.2016.1212090

Watins, C. L., & Slocum, T. A. (2004). In N. E. Marchand-Martella, T. A. Slocum, & R. C. Martella (Eds.), *The components of direct instruction.* Pearson Education, Inc.

Wilson, B. A., Baddeley, A., Evans, J., & Shiel, A. (1994). Errorless learning in the rehabilitation of memory impaired people. *Neuropsychological Rehabilitation, 4,* 301–326. https://doi.org/10. 1080/09602019408401463

Xun, H., Lopez, C. D., Chen, J., Lee, E., Dorafshar, A. H., Manson, P. N., Groves, M., Redett, R. J., & Lopez, J. (2023). Underreporting of traumatic brain injuries in pediatric craniomaxillofacial trauma: A 20-year retrospective cohort study. *Plastic and Reconstructive Surgery, 151,* 105e–114e. https://doi.org/10.1097/PRS.0000000000009783

Ylvisaker, M., Turkstra, L., Coehlo, C., Yorkston, K., Kennedy, M., Sohlberg, M. M., & Avery, J. (2007). Behavioral interventions for children and adults with behavior disorders after TBI: A systematic review of the evidence. *Brain Injury, 21,* 769–805. https://doi.org/10.1080/ 02699050701482470

CHAPTER 9

SPECIAL EDUCATION FOR STUDENTS FROM CULTURALLY AND LINGUISTICALLY DIVERSE BACKGROUNDS: ADVANCING VALUES

Lenwood Gibson

Queens College, City University of New York, USA

ABSTRACT

The number of students from culturally and linguistically diverse (CLD) backgrounds continue to increase in classrooms across the United States. These students have complex needs as they experience more barriers to success when compared to their peers. These barriers are further compounded when CLD students are also identified as having disabilities. To address the barriers and meet the needs of CLD students with disabilities, teaching professionals should move away from the traditional American educational values of individual freedom and self-reliance, equal opportunity and competition, and material wealth and hard work. Conversely, schools and teaching professionals should incorporate the modern values of social justice, diversity, equity, inclusion, accessibility, and belonging when working with students from CLD backgrounds who have disabilities. This chapter presents these values and provides recommendations for teaching professionals and schools.

Keywords: Cultural and linguistic diversity; social justice; diversity; equity; inclusion; belonging

Special Education
Advances in Special Education, Volume 38, 143–158
Copyright © 2024 Lenwood Gibson
Published under exclusive licence by Emerald Publishing Limited
ISSN: 0270-4013/doi:10.1108/S0270-401320240000038009

INTRODUCTION

The United States has long been dubbed a cultural melting pot due to the many different people who come from CLD backgrounds. The history of the United States provides stories of Native American indigenes, enslaved African Americans, and immigrants from all parts of the world. Some of these immigrants came to escape religious persecution, war, or famine, while others came to seek employment and hope for better lives. Regardless of the reasons and means of arrival, the demographics of the US population continue to shift toward a more diverse society. In fact, it is predicted that by the year 2050, more CLD people from CLD backgrounds than people who identify as white will comprise the population of the United States (US Census Bureau, 2017).

Cultural and linguistic diversities in the United States provide many great advantages to our society. The combination of cultures provides enrichment that is unparalleled anywhere else in the world. In any given town or city, one can find a large variety of cultures, languages, arts, and foods. Consider this example, the borough of Queens in New York City is often dubbed the "World's Borough" because of its ethnic, racial, religious, and linguistic diversities (Bank-Munoz et al., 2022). Statistics from the US Census report that over 55.2% of households in Queens, New York, speak a language other than English; this linguistic diversity is only an initial reflection of the people that are represented. People from CLD backgrounds enrich the communities with their food, customs, beliefs, and values. Although Queens, New York, is an extreme example of the diversity in the United States, it is not an outlier. Many cities and towns across the country have populations that vary across racial, ethnic, religious, and/or linguistic lines. While the United States may not be the "melting pot" that it is often described as, it certainly contains flavors and ingredients from many different parts of the world.

Logically, when families from CLD backgrounds emigrate to the United States, many either bring their children or have children after establishing themselves in their new society. Children born here are US citizens and may be one or two generations removed from the people who originally came to the United States. Many grow up and start families of their own and may identify as a specific ethnicity (e.g., Arab or Middle Eastern) or nationality (e.g., Ecuadorian or Nigerian), even though they were born in the United States and are American citizens. These families adapt to the larger cultural norms and values of American society; however, they often still engage in cultural practices of their parents, and grandparents' counties of origin. This may include the language spoken at home, holiday celebrations and customs, and expected values and behaviors. Children of immigrants may adapt and assimilate into American cultures, but they often navigate across their respective cultural boundaries and merge them together. These children also enroll into schools in their communities to take advantage of the public education that is provided by local school districts. As the population of the United States continues to diversify, so does the student body in schools (Billingham & Hunt, 2016; Irizarry & Donaldson, 2012; Turner, 2015).

The impact of the increasing diversity on schools can be subtle or obvious depending on direct efforts of teaching professionals working in individual schools or districts. In some schools, the value of diversity is often emphasized as a strength that is highlighted. Schools with a high number of students from CLD backgrounds provide opportunities to cross cultural learning and enrichment. This is typically reflected in expressions of cultural representation within the school and the classroom. Schools often have students talk about their cultural backgrounds through displays of art, music, or food. For example, schools might host international food day or ask students to dress in traditional clothing from their family's native countries. These overtures are nice attempts to create culturally inclusive school environments; however, they often fall short of true cultural inclusiveness (Kumar et al., 2019; Nganga et al., 2019). This is because most schools in the United States emphasize traditional values of American education that include individual freedom and self-reliance, equal opportunity and competition, and material wealth and hard work. Although these values are based on foundational American ideologies, they are not always in line with the values and traditions of students from CLD families. The questions are: Have schools failed to fulfill their obligations for students with "special needs" who come from CLD backgrounds? If they have made some efforts, have they been consistent in meeting the needs of CLD students, families, and communities? This chapter responds to these questions while prescribing culturally sensitive solutions.

VALUES THAT DOMINATE SCHOOLING

The ideas of American society and culture have long been incorporated into school systems and how students are educated. These ideas are often taught directly by including traditional American values into class discussions, assignments, and assessment practices. They are also present in typical structures and routines of many schools. For example, most schools have students raise and recite the Pledge of Allegiance every morning when school starts. These values are based on the founding principles of the US and Western culture. Moreover, they are designed to teach students from a uniquely American perspective and may be counterintuitive to children from various diverse backgrounds (Martinez-Becerra, 2020; Obiakor, 2001). The founding principles are connected traditional values that have continued to impact general and special education.

Individual Freedom and Self-Reliance

The first traditional value involves the concepts of individual freedom. This value places emphasis on the individual student and choices they (and their family) make in their education. Much of the work that is completed in schools is based on individual assignments as students are assessed on their own work. Moreover, students are taught to value their individualism and choices they make. Although some of this is promoted and taught through the curriculum, assignments, and assessments, others are expressed through choice-making and socialization outside of the classroom. Students are provided with a variety of choice-making opportunities as they progress through the P-12 school systems. These include the classes to take, whether to join certain clubs or a vast variety of extracurricular activities. These choices impact the development and social sphere of individual students. Students who are raised in the mainstream culture are often taught at a young age the value of their individualism. This value is reinforced when children start their school and throughout their school career (Kusserow, 2004; Loose, 2008; Merchant et al., 2012). The second value of self-reliance is closely related to individual freedom and places an emphasis depending on one's self for success. Students are taught self-reliance when completing school work and when testing. This means that they are taught to depend on their own efforts when engaging in academic work. Although group effort and collaboration are part of the school experience, students are mainly evaluated on their individual efforts (Gardner-Neblett et al., 2014). The value of self-reliance is critical to the success of individual students and is an essential marker of American schools. In fact, many report cards include grade indicators for the effort that students put toward their school subjects. In other words, students are evaluated in how self-reliant they are when engaging on their school processes.

For students from CLD backgrounds, their family traditions and values may place more emphasis on collaboration and group dynamics (Obiakor & Yawn, 2014). The values of individual freedom and self-reliance can potentially cause disconnects between students from the mainstream culture (i.e., American) and those from CLD backgrounds. If students from CLD backgrounds grow up in communities that focus on working together, the values of individualism and self-reliance could seem out of place. These students might be suited to work together on assignments that are designed to be completed individually. This could lead to the misperception that these students are not producing their own work. If students from CLD backgrounds are more readily adept at relying on a group dynamic, they may struggle to produce work that requires individual effort. This may be particularly true for children who recently emigrated to the United States and are new to the school system and the expectations of their teachers (McIntyre et al., 2011).

Equal Opportunity and Competition

The value of equal opportunity seems very altruistic on the surface. After all, one of the founding monikers of the United States is the "Land of Opportunity," and everyone has the same chances for success. In schools, this can mean that all students have the same opportunities and chances for success without regard to individual circumstances. Although the idea of equality seems benevolent, not all students enter the classroom with similar levels of support and resources. Students who come from well resources households have more advantages to support their education. For example, if a student is struggling with a specific academic subject but has the resources to obtain a tutor, they will likely perform better than a student who does not have the same resources. The value of equal opportunity only holds true if all students have the same equal resources. Seeing that the United States is the world's leading capitalist society, competition is deemed an essential value to progress. In schools, students learn to be competitive at a very early age, and a continued emphasis is placed on competition as students get older. Placing value on competition is designed to prepare students to enter the workforce and position themselves for success. Competition in schools can start as early as prekindergarten when young children are selected for highly sought-after schools with limited enrollment caps. This competition continues throughout the years of schooling (Shimotsu-Dariol et al., 2012) and into college enrollment. Although competition can be healthy and contribute to success of individual students, it also places students with less resources at a disadvantage. Moreover, competition can put an extraordinary amount of stress on students to outperform each other to be considered successful.

For students from CLD background, values of equal opportunity and competition can be counterproductive and damaging. This is especially true for recently arrived immigrant students and those from disadvantaged socioeconomic backgrounds. These students likely do not have the resources to take advantage of opportunities provided by schools. From example, many schools offer music programs in which students can join the band or orchestra. Although these programs are open to all students, only those with the economic resources to purchase (or rent) musical instruments are able to participate and compete. The same is true to many extracurricular activities and athletics. Those without the resources are not able to take advantage of such programs and therefore miss out on opportunities to explore their untapped potential. This may have a cascading effect on these students since they miss out on ways to build their own portfolio which is typically used to complete future opportunities such as applying for scholarship and college admissions.

Material Wealth and Hard Work

The fifth traditional value focuses on the production of material wealth. The fact that we live in a society that measures success by how much a person makes or where they live places an emphasis on the outcomes of education. Children are taught at a young age to think about "what they want to be when they grow up" and that they can "be anything they put their mind to." The implicit message is that successful employment leads to material wealth. This value is reinforced in schools when students are taught to make decisions about what classes to take or areas of studies to focus on (e.g., STEM). Very early, students are taught that they can accomplish anything if they put their minds to it and work hard enough. The emphasis that is placed on working hard sends an explicit message to students about the effort they are expected to put toward their schooling. If students are serious about being successful in school, they will put forth the hard work needed to master the content. This value places the onus on the student and may not consider other factors that might be impeding the success of students (e.g., lack of resources, underfunded schools, teachers who may not be effective, and the effect of learning problems or disabilities).

Students from CLD backgrounds have situations outside of school that may impede their academic success. These include language or communication barriers for students who are not fluent in English and family obligations that prevent or limit parental involvement or oversight of school work (Bullock et al., 2014). Students who face these situations may want to work hard to be successful in school but can have a hard time overcoming external challenges. These conflicting values cause disruptions and collusions that affect life stabilities.

INTRICACIES OF SPECIAL EDUCATION

When discussing educational attainment in the United States, the role and purpose of special education is often overlooked. Since the passage of Public Law 94-142 in 1975, students with identified disabilities are receiving educational services to help them meet individualized goals. The original law has been amended and reauthorized multiple times over the past 40 plus years (e.g., IDEA of 1994), with the purpose of strengthening the previsions that are designed to improve the education of students with disabilities. These laws have impactful previsions that are now universally accepted and incorporated into special education programs in school districts across the country. These previsions include the placement and planning team (PPT) process, implementation of individualized education plans (IEP), free and appropriate education (FAPE), least restrictive environment (LRE), and due process rights. These previsions have become the values that govern special education services for students with disabilities. The following section discusses these values as they relate to students with disabilities in special education.

Placement and Planning Team

When a student is suspected of having a disability or at the request of a parent/guardian, a special education professional at the student's schools will convene a meeting of the PPT. This team discusses the potential need for special education services and possible assessments. After reviewing all relevant concerns and the student's overall performance, evaluation recommendations are made. Following the completion of all recommended evaluations and assessments, the PPT reconvenes to present and discuss the results. Determinations are made as to whether students have a disability and therefore qualify for special education services. The PPT process has been standardized across many school districts and is essential to identifying students with disabilities and recommending appropriate levels of special education services.

Individualized Education Plan

Following the completion of the assessment process, students who qualify for special education services are provided IEPs. The purpose of the IEP is to outline the services that will be provided by the school professionals. The IEP is a legal document that sets annual goals and objects based on individual needs of each student. It also provides details about services that are to be provided (e.g., speech and language therapy), all modification and accommodations, and transitional needs. The IEP is reviewed and updated annually with parents/guardians of the student.

Free and Appropriate Education

A cornerstone value for special education is to guarantee that all students will be provided a free and appropriate education regardless of their disability and/or level of need. This value is important because students with disabilities may require highly intensive educational services to meet their needs. School districts and educational professionals are obligated under FAPE to provide services that are appropriate to meet the needs of their students. These services are outlined in the IEP and are provided at no cost to students or their families.

Least Restrictive Environment

When students are identified with a disability and provided an IEP, decisions are made about where the services will be delivered. The LRE provision in IDEA mandates that students with disabilities are provided services (i.e., educated) in the LRE possible to ensure progression toward their goals. The goal of the LRE provision is to ensure students with disabilities have access to educational environments that are closely related to those of their nondisabled peer group. Moreover, in order for a school district to move a student to a more restrictive setting, there must be a team meeting that provides documented evidence that supports the need for change. Educating students in the LRE provides them with better access to the general education curriculum and to social opportunities with their nondisabled peers.

Due Process

The function of the IEP team is to work with students and families to ensure their education meets their needs and helps them reach their goals. However, there may be situations in which parents do not agree with the team's recommendations or they question the implementation of their child's IEP. For example, if the IEP recommends a student be placed in a more restrictive setting but the parents disagree, they have the right to due process and an impartial hearing. This means that both school professional and parents (along with any legal representation or advocates) present supporting evidence for or against the proposed change to the IEP. Typically, there will be mediation between the two sides, but if an agreement cannot be reached, the case is heard by an impartial professional to finalize the decision. After the results of the hearing are finalized, both sides come together to continue services for the student.

SHIFTING VALUES IN SPECIAL EDUCATION

Some students from CLD backgrounds may actually be more likely to be identified with a disability. The intersection of CLD and special education converges to place these students at greater risk of poor school outcomes. This is because students from CLD who are also identified as having disabilities experience different life circumstances that need to be addressed from both a culturally responsive perspective and from special education. These are unique challenges faced by special education students and their families, especially those from CLD backgrounds. These challenges include the disproportionate over-representation in specific disability categories (e.g., behavior disorders), underserved communities (e.g., Latinx/Hispanic), lack of diversity in the special education workforce, and lack of familial supports for students from CLD backgrounds.

Disproportionality

The issue of disproportionality has been widely discussed in the field of special education. The majority of these discussions focus on the disproportionate over-representation of African American boys in special education due to their perceived behavior disorders (Allen-Butler, 2019; Gibson, 2022; Obiakor & Gibson, 2015). Scholars from the field of education have debated on whether this over-representation is attributable to uneven disciplinary actions by school professionals (Skiba et al., 2016), misperceptions or over-reaction to the behaviors of African American students (Blanchett, 2006), or misinterpretations of the data (Morgan et al., 2015). Regardless of reasons, outcomes of students who are identified for special education due to a behavioral disorder are grim. These students are more likely to have higher rates of absenteeism, truancy, and school dropout (Keyes, 2022). Furthermore, students who receive special education services for behavior disorders are more likely to get involved with the juvenile justice system and may become incarcerated in adulthood (Mallett, 2016). Needless to say, these outcomes are startling, and the field must continue to propose better solutions for these students.

Although much of the discussion around disproportionality in special education involves African American boys and behavior disorders, there are other students from CLD backgrounds that are affected by disproportionality. For example, children from Latinx/Hispanic communities continue to be under identified with autism spectrum disorder (ASD) and other developmental disabilities (Maenner et al., 2020; Magaña & Vanegas, 2017; Zuckerman et al., 2021). There are several reasons for this under identification. First, in many Spanish speaking communities, there is less awareness and/or acceptance of developmental disabilities (Florindez et al., 2019). Children may not be identified until they reach school age and start interacting with school professionals who may note signs of the disorder. This delay in identification can lead to poorer outcomes for these children because they do not get the services needed in a timely manner (Lopez et al., 2019). The under-representation of Latinx/Hispanic children is an avoidable outcome if medical and social service professionals make more inroads in these communities. More so, in the category of students with gifts and talents, CLD students are under identified because of the presumption that they are not as intelligent. The tools used to assess this category lack reliability and validity (Obiakor, 2001). Gifts and talents must go beyond recital or cultural boundaries (see Obiakor, 2001).

Underserved Communities

Directly related to disproportionality of CLD students in special education is the lack of services that are provided to students from CLD communities. The field of special education frequently emphasizes a multidisciplinary approach to services. Teams often include professionals from various disciplines that are tasked with working collaboratively to provide effective services for students with special needs (Ko et al., 2021). These professionals typically include special educators, school psychologist, social workers, speech/language pathologist, and other auxiliary services. As a team, these professionals are responsible for assessing the needs of students with disabilities and their families.

As indicated above, children from families in the Latinx/Hispanic community are under identified for ASD and other developmental disabilities. This under identification or delayed identification leads to delays in services and poorer treatment outcomes (Lopez et al., 2019). For example, many children with ASD or developmental disabilities are identified at very early ages (e.g., 18 months). Once identified, these children become eligible for Early Intervention (EI) services. These early services are critical to address the needs of young children with emerging disabilities (Vietze & Lax, 2020). Research shows that children who receive EI and other early services are more likely to do better with academic, social, and life skills (Myers et al., 2022; Vietze & Lax, 2020). Under identification of children from CLD communities means that they are not accessing the critical services needed for success. The reasons for under identification and lack of services are multifaceted, and they include cultural discontinuity between the communities and service providers, language barriers, racial politics, stigma associated with disabilities, and sociopolitical concerns (e.g., immigration status) (Burkett et al., 2022; Obiakor, 2001). These barriers must be recognized and removed, so children from CLD communities can reap the full benefit of available services.

Teacher Demographics

As stated previously, the demographics of the student body continue to include more students from CLD backgrounds. However, these shifts are not always paralleled by demographics of the teachers and other professionals. In fact, the majority of school teachers in the United States are white, middle-class females. These teachers have good intensions and want to be effective and compassionate. They pride themselves in being approachable for their students and the families they work with. However, they also come to their classrooms with their world view and learning history, and they likely developed implicit biases about students who are from different cultural and/or social backgrounds (DeCuir-Gunby

& Bindra, 2022). These biases inadvertently influence the way they interact with CLD students and their families (Chin et al., 2020). If implicit biases affect the way teachers perceive students from CLD backgrounds, this can lead to cultural discontinuity. When teachers do not have a sound understanding of cultural practices of their students, they may inadvertently dismiss things that are important for learning (Taggart, 2017). Furthermore, they may misinterpret behaviors or practices that are considered normal for people for certain cultures. They may see those behaviors are inappropriate, disruptive, or detrimental to the learning environment. All of this results in classroom culture that is not accepting or inclusive (Gibson, 2022; Obiakor, 2001). This has a downhill impact on the relationships developed between teachers, students, and their families. When students from CLD backgrounds also have special needs, it is critical that teachers and families communicate well. If cultural discontinuity leads to mis-interpretations or misunderstandings, communications may be negatively impacted (Lovelace & Wheeler, 2006).

To truly address issues of implicit bias and cultural discontinuity, teachers and schools must continually assess their own practices and approaches (Cartledge & Kourea, 2008; Obiakor, 2012). They can do this by engaging in self-reflection and flexibility and by the willingness to assess their own biases as they learn about cultural norms and practices of their CLD students. Schools can help by developing and offering professional development opportunities that address the roll of culture in the classroom and by encouraging open dialogues between teachers and families. Moreover, when situations of cultural discontinuity occur, teachers should work hard to learn from the experience and make appropriate amends.

Family Supports

Students with disabilities from CLD backgrounds face different challenges when compared to other students. This is because many of these students live in communities that are isolated from the mainstream and may need higher levels of supports. For example, many families from CLD backgrounds live in multi-generational households. Parents, grandparents, and other family members are all participants in the education of the school-aged children. When students have disabilities, their familial care is even more meaningful. Schools may be faced with situations that require providing supports to the different family members, as needed. The need for family support cannot be understated when working with children from CLD backgrounds. School professionals may need to create plans for wraparound services. This means that services are connected across the school and educational environment (Espinoza & Taylor, 2021; Gerzel-Short et al., 2019). For example, some students with disabilities may have difficulties with expressive and receptive language and receive services from speech–language pathologist (SLP). Typically, these services take place in school during individual or small group sessions. However, when students speak a different language at home, the SLP may need to create programs, in the student's first language, that can be implemented at home. The purpose of wraparound programs is to help with continuity of services across all learning environments. When done correctly, these plans help support students and families from CLD backgrounds. Another area of family supports for these students involves how to deal with sensitive topics that may not be directly related to the education of their children. This can include things like food and housing insecurity or immigration status. These situations are more likely to be faced by recent immigrants. Recently, as larger cities in the United States are impacted by high numbers of immigrants, they are relying on local schools to support children in school-based settings. Therefore, schools become the de facto center of support for students and their families.

MAINTAINING VALUES FOR THE FUTURE

As the demographics of the population continue to change, so will the composition of classrooms. Students from CLD backgrounds need continued supports to be successful in school and their communities. These supports are even more vital when students are identified as having disabilities (Gerzel-Short et al., 2019). The traditional school values can be in conflict with the values and practices of CLD students and their families. As schools move toward more inclusive practices, they should include modern values that better support the need of these students and their families. These values must place a focus on social justice, diversity, equity, inclusion, acceptance, and belonging.

Social Justice

The first value is social justice, and it encompasses all the other modern values combined. To ensure school environments are socially just, teaching professionals must incorporate the values of diversity, equity, inclusion, accessibility, and belonging. Social justice for special education students from CLD backgrounds promises that they will not be disregarded due to their differences. Rather, by focusing on modern values, teaching professionals can create socially just classroom environments that provide spaces for students to thrive and reach their goals. For students with disabilities, socially just classrooms recognize their strengths and provide opportunities for them to engage across all school environments.

Diversity, Equity, and Inclusion (DEI)

Over the past decade, there has been increasing awareness on the values of DEI. These values are often discussed together as one, but each has its own inherent value when it comes to the educational environment for students from CLD backgrounds. These values are especially important for students with disabilities because they hit right at the heart of how to support these students. Diversity places value on differences among people and emphasizes the benefit of those differences. Traditionally, when discussing diversity, people focus on differences in race, ethnicity, nationality, and/or gender. The acceptance of people from all walks of life is something that is taken for granted but does not always happen in our society. For example, there needs to be a conscious effort in hiring practices or college enrollment strategies to ensure diversity and representation. The implication for students from CLD backgrounds is that many are not automatically accepted in all environments in which they show up. Sadly, there are situations when the diversity they bring is not valued and is actually seen as a detriment. This implication is even more impactful when CLD students also have disabilities. These students bring their unique presence to the classroom and should be celebrated for their accomplishments. When teaching professionals place high value on diversity, they ensure that all students are respected and afforded dignity and create environments that demonstrate the importance of diversity. The second value of DEI is equity. Equity is sometimes mistaken for the more traditional value of equality; however, there are some very important differences that need to be considered. Equality traditionally means that everyone is treated the same or have the same opportunities for success, whereas equity means that each person gets the supports and resources needed to be successful. Some students need more supports and some need less. It is important for teaching professionals to identify and provide the support needed by each student. For special needs students from CLD backgrounds, the value of equity cannot be understated. Many of these students face challenges that other students do not experience, and challenges are compounded because of their cultural/ linguistic backgrounds and their disabilities. Often, these students need additional resources (e.g., wraparound plans) to make progress in the school setting. Educational professionals need to recognize the complex needs of special education students from CLD backgrounds and effectively provide individualized supports. Finally, the third modern value is inclusion. This value focuses on the importance of creating inclusive environments that are welcoming to all students. The value of inclusion is etched into the fabric of special education philosophy. One of the main previsions of IDEA mandates that students with disabilities be educated in the least restrictive environment possible. As important as this tenet of inclusion is, there are times that teaching professionals fall short of being inclusive. Students with significant disabilities are more likely to be placed in restrictive environments without much access to their grade/age level peers (Kurth et al., 2019). Students who are also from CLD backgrounds may be even further isolated if they do not have teaching professionals who have a strong belief in inclusion.

Accessibility and Belonging

Although the values of DEI are well known, they do not provide the full scope of values needed to address social and educational inequities for CLD students with special needs. In recent years, several more values have been identified and added to DEI as being important to help with the success of marginalized people. Two of these added values are accessibility and belonging. The fourth value is accessibility, and it advances equity by ensuring that students are able to access resources needed for success. Although it is important to recognize the need for equity and to identify the services needed to achieve success; however, if those resources and/or services are inaccessible, students will inevitably not progress in their goals. When teaching professionals place value on accessibility, they not only identify the resources and services needed but ensure that students have full access to them. For special education students from CLD backgrounds, accessibility can be challenging. These students are more likely to come from marginalized communities and face additional barriers to success. When teaching professionals recognize accessibility barriers, they can advocate for resources to remove those barriers. The fifth value of belonging advances inclusion and places an emphasis that ensures that CLD students belong in all educational environments. Including students in classrooms or schools is important, but it is equally important to ensure that they belong. For students from CLD backgrounds, the need to create environments that are welcoming goes beyond simple inclusion. Many of these students experience situations that make them feel isolated in mainstream school settings. To promote belonging, school professionals should encourage students from CLD backgrounds to express their home culture and give them space to engage in cultural practices. By creating settings of belonging, all students can feel comfortable to express themselves and successfully thrive in the classroom.

CONCLUSION

Students from CLD backgrounds who have disabilities experience many barriers to succeed in school. These students must learn how to navigate across cultural, linguistic, and social norms while dealing with the challenges of their disabilities. Many of these students come to school from marginalized communities or from home environments that require higher levels of support for success. When these factors are combined, students with disabilities from CLD backgrounds are more prone to struggling academically and socially in school. For these reasons, teaching professionals should place less emphasis on traditional values of mainstream American education. Conversely, the focus should be on creating classroom environments that incorporate values that promote social justice and human valuing.

Clearly, many schools in the United States are not prepared to provide fair and equitable education to students with disabilities who come from CLD backgrounds. In part, this is because as the population of students becomes increasingly diverse, the demographics of teaching professionals remain the same. In order for these teachers and school professionals to move toward realistic modern values, they must put forth conscientious efforts to understand the needs of their students. Moreover, they must understand and agree with the realistic modern values that are connected to the principles of social justice, diversity, equity, inclusion, accessibility, and belonging. The collaborative efforts of teaching professionals and related service providers can improve the lives and outcomes for students with disabilities who also come from CLD backgrounds.

REFERENCES

Allen-Butler, T. (2019). *A comparative case study analysis of the teachers' perceptions causing the overrepresentation of African American males in special education.* ProQuest Dissertation Publishing.

Bank-Munoz, C., Lewis, P., & Molina, E. T. (2022). *Queens* (1st ed., p. 179). University of California Press. https://10.2307/j.ctv2j6xfj4.7

Billingham, C. M., & Hunt, M. O. (2016). School racial composition and parental choice: New evidence on the preferences of white parents in the United States. *Sociology of Education, 89*(2), 99–117. https://10.1177/0038040716635718

Blanchett, W. J. (2006). Disproportionate representation of African American students in special education: Acknowledging the role of white privilege and racism. *Educational Researcher, 35*(6), 24–28. https://10.3102/0013189X035006024

Bullock, L. M., Gable, R. A., Carrero, K., Lewis, C., Collins, E., Zolkowski, S., & Lusk, M. (2014). Facing the challenges of today and the future: Ensuring successful outcomes for students from culturally and linguistically diverse backgrounds. *Multicultural Learning and Teaching, 9*(1), 103–113. https://10.1515/mlt-2012-0005

Burkett, K., Kamimura-Nishimura, K., Suarez-Cano, G., Ferreira-Corso, L., Jacquez, F., & Vaughn, L. M. (2022). Latino-to-Latino: Promotores' beliefs on engaging Latino participants in autism research. *Journal of Racial and Ethnic Health Disparities, 9*(4), 1125–1134. https://10.1007/s40615-021-01053-0

Cartledge, G., & Kourea, L. (2008). Culturally responsive classrooms for culturally diverse students with and at risk for disabilities. *Exceptional Children, 74*(3), 351–371.

Chin, M. J., Quinn, D. M., Dhaliwal, T. K., & Lovison, V. S. (2020). Bias in the air: A nationwide exploration of teachers' implicit racial attitudes, aggregate bias, and student outcomes. *Educational Researcher, 49*(8), 566–578. https://10.3102/0013189X20937240

DeCuir-Gunby, J., & Bindra, V. G. (2022). How does teacher bias influence students?: An introduction to the special issue on teachers' implicit attitudes, instructional practices, and student outcomes. *Learning and Instruction, 78*, 101523.

Espinoza, P. S., & Taylor, K. A. (2021). Latinx teachers advocating and providing support to culturally and linguistically diverse students and their families. *Educational Considerations, 47*(1). https://10.4148/0146-9282.2256

Florindez, L., Como, D., Florindez, D., Cermak, S., & Duker, L. (2019). Perceptions of autism spectrum disorder (ASD) diagnosis among Latino parents and caregivers. *American Journal of Occupational Therapy, 73*(4), NA.

Gardner-Neblett, N., DeCoster, J., & Hamre, B. K. (2014). Linking preschool language and sustained attention with adolescent achievement through classroom self-reliance. *Journal of Applied Developmental Psychology, 35*(6), 457–467. https://10.1016/j.appdev.2014.09.003

Gerzel-Short, L., Kiru, E. W., Hsiao, Y., Hovey, K. A., Wei, Y., & Miller, R. D. (2019). Engaging culturally and linguistically diverse families of children with disabilities. *Intervention in School and Clinic, 55*(2), 120–126.

Gibson, L. (2022). Over represented – Under represented: The juxtaposition of Black males in special education programs. *Multicultural Learning and Teaching, 17*(2), 159–172.

Irizarry, J., & Donaldson, M. L. (2012). Teach for América: The Latinization of U.S. schools and the critical shortage of Latina/o teachers. *American Educational Research Journal, 49*(1), 155–194. https://10.3102/0002831211434764

Keyes, S. E. (2022). Addressing educational inequity of Black students by demolishing the school-to-prison pipeline. *Multicultural Learning and Teaching, 17*(2), 123–141.

Ko, D., Mawene, D., Roberts, K., & Hong, J. J. (2021). A systematic review of boundary-crossing partnerships in designing equity-oriented special education services for culturally and linguistically diverse students with disabilities. *Remedial and Special Education, 42*(6), 412–425. https://10.1177/0741932520983474

Kumar, R., Karabenick, S. A., Warnke, J. H., Hany, S., & Seay, N. (2019). Culturally inclusive and responsive curricular learning environments (CIRCLEs): An exploratory sequential mixed-methods approach. *Contemporary Educational Psychology, 57*, 87–105.

Kurth, J. A., Ruppar, A. L., Toews, S. G., McCabe, K. M., McQueston, J. A., & Johnston, R. (2019). Considerations in placement decisions for students with extensive support needs: An analysis of LRE statements. *Research and Practice for Persons with Severe Disabilities, 44*(1), 3–19. https:// 10.1177/1540796918825479

Kusserow, A. (2004). *American individualisms: Child rearing and social class in three neighborhoods.* Palgrave Macmillan.

Loose, F. (2008). Individualism: Valued differently by parents and teachers of primary, junior high and high school students. *Social Psychology of Education, 11*(2), 117–131.

Lopez, K., Reed, J., & Magaña, S. (2019). Associations among family burden, optimism, services received and unmet need within families of children with ASD. *Children and Youth Services Review, 98*, 105–112. https://10.1016/j.childyouth.2018.12.027

Lovelace, S., & Wheeler, T. R. (2006). Cultural discontinuity between home and school language socialization patterns: Implications for teachers. *Education, 127*(2), 303.

Maenner, M. J., Shaw, K. A., Baio, J., Washington, A., Patrick, M., DiRienzo, M., Christensen, D. L., Wiggins, L. D., Pettygrove, S., Andrews, J. G., Lopez, M., Hudson, A., Baroud, T., Schwenk, Y., White, T., Rosenberg, C. R., Lee, L., Harrington, R. A., Huston, M., . . . Dietz, P. M. (2020). Prevalence of autism spectrum disorder among children aged 8 years – Autism and developmental disabilities monitoring network, 11 sites, United States, 2016. *Surveillance Summaries, 69*(4), 1–12. https://10.15585/mmwr.ss6904a1

Magaña, S., & Vanegas, S. B. (2017). Diagnostic utility of the ADI-R and DSM-5 in the assessment of Latino children and adolescents. *Journal of Autism and Developmental Disorders, 47*(5), 1278–1287. https://10.1007/s10803-017-3043-2

Mallett, C. A. (2016). *The school-to-prison pipeline: A comprehensive assessment.* Springer Publishing Company.

Martinez-Beccera, A. (2020). Introduction to the implication of microaggressions in schools: Its origin and nature, United States historical context, and the impact and toxicity that limits the path of culturally and linguistically diverse student populations. *Journal of Educational Thought, 53*(2), 211–238. https://10.11575/jet.v53i2.71721

McIntyre, T., Barowsky, E. I., & Tong, V. (2011). The psychological, behavioral, and educational impact of immigration: Helping recent immigrant students to succeed in North American schools. *Journal of the American Academy of Special Education Professionals*, 4–21.

Merchant, B., Arlestig, H., Garza, E., Johansson, O., Murakami-Ramalho, E., & Tornsren, M. (2012). Successful school leadership in Sweden and the US: Contexts of social responsibility and individualism. *International Journal of Educational Management, 26*(5), 428–441.

Morgan, P. L., Farkas, G., Hillemeier, M. M., Mattison, R., Maczuga, S., Li, H., & Cook, M. (2015). Minorities are disproportionately underrepresented in special education: Longitudinal evidence across five disability conditions. *Educational Researcher, 44*(5), 278–292.

Myers, A. J., Cleveland, E., Whitby, P. J. S., Boykin, A. A., Burnette, K., Holmes, R., & Ezike, N. (2022). Analysis of a statewide early intervention program for young children with ASD. *Journal of Autism and Developmental Disorders, 52*(11), 4994–5006.

Nganga, L., Kambutu, J., & Han, K. T. (2019). Caring schools and educators a solution to disparities in academic performance: Learners of colors speak. *Sage Open, 9*(2). 215824401984192. https:// 10.1177/2158244019841923

Obiakor, F. E. (2001). *It even happens in good schools: Responding to cultural diversity in today's classrooms.* Corwin Press.

Obiakor, F. E. (2012). Culturally responsive teaching and special education. In J. A. Banks (Ed.), *Encyclopedia of diversity in education* (pp.552–556). SAGE.

Obiakor, F. E., & Gibson, L. (2015). Reversing the use of Hobson's choice: Culturally relevant assessment and treatment practices for culturally and linguistically diverse learners with problem behaviors. *The Journal of the International Association of Special Education, 16*(1), 77.

Obiakor, F. E., & Yawn, C. D. (2014). Reducing achievement gaps and increasing the school success of culturally and linguistically diverse students using the comprehensive support model. In C. M. Wilson & S. D. Horsford (Eds.), *Advancing equity and achievement in America's diverse schools* (pp. 159–170). Routledge.

Shimotsu-Dariol, S., Mansson, D. H., & Myers, S. A. (2012). Students' academic competitiveness and their involvement in the learning process. *Communication Research Reports*, *29*(4), 310–319. https://10.1080/08824096.2012.723643

Skiba, R. J., Artiles, A. J., Kozleski, E. B., Losen, D. J., & Harry, E. G. (2016). Risks and consequences of oversimplifying educational inequities: A response to Morgan et al. (2015). *Educational Researcher*, *45*(3), 221–225. https://10.3102/0013189X16644606

Taggart, A. (2017). The role of cultural discontinuity in the academic outcomes of Latina/o High school students. *Education and Urban Society*, *49*(8), 731–761. https://10.1177/0013124516658522

Turner, E. O. (2015). Districts' responses to demographic change: Making sense of race, class, and immigration in political and organizational context. *American Educational Research Journal*, *52*(1), 4–39. https://10.3102/0002831214561469

Vietze, P., & Lax, L. E. (2020). Early intervention ABA for toddlers with ASD: Effect of age and amount. *Current Psychology*, *39*(4), 1234–1244. https://10.1007/s12144-018-9812-z

Zuckerman, K. E., Chavez, A. E., Wilson, L., Unger, K., Reuland, C., Ramsey, K., King, M., Scholz, J., & Fombonne, E. (2021). Improving autism and developmental screening and referral in US primary care practices serving Latinos. *Autism: The International Journal of Research and Practice; Autism*, *25*(1), 288–299. https://10.1177/1362361320957461

CHAPTER 10

SPECIAL EDUCATION OF STUDENTS WITH PHYSICAL AND OTHER HEALTH IMPAIRMENTS: ADVANCING VALUES

Eugene F. Asola[a] and Festus E. Obiakor[b]

[a]Valdosta State University, USA
[b]Sunny Consulting, USA

ABSTRACT

All over the world, different types of disabilities affect people and their quality of life. And schools, families, and federal and state agencies are obligated to play very important roles in advancing special education values for students with physical and other health impairments. To maintain and advance these values, the needs of students must be met to the greatest extent possible. Advancing values comes with recognizing the strengths, preferences, interests, related services, community experiences, development of employment, other postschool adult living objectives, and the acquisition of daily living skills. The question is, are these values consistently met, especially for students with physical and other health impairments? This chapter answers this question by discussing how these values can be met and advanced for students with physical and other health impairments.

Keywords: Special education; services; students with disabilities; physical disabilities and other health impairments; advancing values

INTRODUCTION

Legally, in accordance with statutes §§300.304 through 300.311 of the 1990 Individuals with Disabilities Education Act (IDEA), persons with physical and

Special Education
Advances in Special Education, Volume 38, 159–166
Copyright © 2024 Eugene F. Asola and Festus E. Obiakor
Published under exclusive licence by Emerald Publishing Limited
ISSN: 0270-4013/doi:10.1108/S0270-401320240000038010

other health impairments have the right to appropriate education and services in least restrictive environments that are nondiscriminating and that respect procedural safeguards. Other values established by the law include the provision of individualized educational programs (IEPS), parental involvement, due process rights, and multidisciplinary team efforts. But they continue to face challenges that are sometimes unnecessary. How can these challenges be reversed to maintain and advance special education values? This chapter answers this question by discussing how these values can be met and advanced for students with physical and other health impairments.

IDEOLOGICAL PERSPECTIVES

Two ideological perspectives dominate services for students with physical disabilities and other health impairments. Relatedly, these perspectives have medical and social model orientations (e.g., Haegele & Hodge, 2016; Okoro et al., 2018; Spencer et al., 2020). In comparing the medical and social models of disability, Haegele and Hodge (2016) described the medical model as "an individual or medical phenomenon that results from impairments in body functions or structures; a deficiency or abnormality" and the social model "describes impairments from the society's perspective" (p. 194). Clearly, it does not matter whether a student's disability or impairment is congenital or acquired so long as the society values and respects the student as a member of the society.

In real life, learning can be affected by students' physical disabilities and/or health impairments. Additionally, the types of services and support these students receive at different levels can go a long way to positively or negatively affect their educational experiences. Even though many students with disabilities receive some types of supports and services, some students still fall through the cracks before or after high school. The National Center for Education Statistics-NCES (2023) reported that there were 435,000 students ages 14–21 served under IDEA who exited school during the school year 2020/2021. Of these students, 75% graduated with a regular high school diploma, 14% *dropped out*, 10% received an alternative certificate, 1% reached the maximum age of 17 to receive special education and/or related services, and less than one-half of 1% died (see NCES, 2023). The report prompts the question: what types of services did these students receive during the academic year leading to this *high dropout rate*? Arguably, in a wealthy country like the United States, 14%, which represents 60,900 students out of the 435,000 is a staggering number of students with disabilities that should be allowed to drop out in one academic year.

It is important to acknowledge that the school year 2020/2021 was particularly troubling during the height of the COVID-19 pandemic, and there is no way to know what proportion of the 14% *dropout* rate was a function of the pandemic. Certainly, there are problems that need to be addressed, given that students with disabilities and other health impairments face many more challenges in their physical, mental, social, and academic lives when compared to nondisabled students. Another critical question is, how do we advance values for the most marginalized populations, even among the poor and less educated, disabled individuals and students with physical disabilities and other health impairments (Okoro et al., 2018)? Whatever the case, it is important to note that, irrespective of the high dropout numbers recorded in the year 2020–2021, notably, at the height of the pandemic, there has been progress worldwide in regard to providing educational services for students with disabilities in general. Even though progress has been slow over the years, there have been lifetime achievements by notable professionals with physical disabilities and other health impairments in the United States and around the world.

RESPECTING THE LAWS TO ADVANCE VALUES

Generally, any student with a disability needs special education and related services (National Archives and Records Administration: Electronic Code of Federal Regulations, 2023). This is particularly important for those with other health impairments such as a child having limited strength, vitality, or alertness, including a heightened alertness to environmental stimuli, that results in limited alertness with respect to the educational environment, due to chronic or acute health problems such as asthma, attention deficit disorder, or attention deficit hyperactivity disorder, diabetes, epilepsy, a heart condition, hemophilia, lead poisoning, leukemia, nephritis, rheumatic fever, sickle cell anemia, and Tourette syndrome. Logically, these problems adversely affect a child's educational performance, which requires special education and related services (National Archives and Records Administration: Electronic Code of Federal Regulations, 2023). Obviously, to assist students with physical disabilities and other health impairments, we must recognize the strengths, preferences, and interests for the purpose of instruction, related services, community experiences, developments of employment, other postschool adult living objectives, and the acquisition of daily living skills (see Asola & Hodge, 2019b).

Students with physical disabilities and other health impairments must be valued and supported. As a matter of need and educational support, the Congress enacted laws (e.g., PL 94–142) which required all public schools that accept federal funds to provide equal access for these students. To ensure the provision of diverse educational services to them, Congress reauthorized the Act in 1990 and 2004. The enactment of various legislation over the years has provided an impetus for valuing and respecting students with disabilities and other health impairments. In 2004, for example, Congress amended the law and further clarified its intended purpose, that is, to provide free appropriate public education for all students aged 3–21, including students with physical disabilities and other health impairments (Asola & Obiakor, 2016). The improvement of this law also increased the awareness and value for students with disabilities in general.

The National Center for Education NCES (2023) reported that in 2021–2022, the number of students ages 3–21 who received special education and/or related services under the IDEA (2004) was 7.3 million, or the equivalent of 15% of all public school students. However, recent data show that during the coronavirus pandemic, the number of students receiving IDEA services dropped by 1% between 2019–2020 and 2020–2021, from 7.3 to 7.2 million students, marking the first time this number had decreased since 2011–2012. Interestingly, from 2021 to 2022, IDEA enrollment largely rebounded to its 2019–2020 prepandemic level, representing 7.3 million students (National Center for Education Statistics, 2023). Unfortunately, the total public school enrollment dropped by 3% from fall 2019 to fall 2020 and remained the same in fall 2021. Therefore, the percentage of public school students who were served under IDEA continued to increase each year during the pandemic and was higher from 2021 to 2022 (15%) than from 2019 to 2020 (14%) (National Center for Education Statistics, 2023). Seemingly, the increase in numbers as the report indicates calls for more professionals working together to provide various services in advancing values for students with physical disabilities and other health impairments.

CHERISHING OUR VALUES

It is common knowledge that not all students with disabilities and other health impairments are valued. For example, one world-famous motivational speaker, Australian Nick Vujicic, recounted his experiences as a quadriplegic with physical, mental, and social challenges. Nick was born with a rare disorder called phocomelia, a disorder characterized by the absence of limbs. He struggled with his disability but still managed to graduate from university at the age of 21. In relation to Nick's contribution to society in general, he is well known for his indomitable fighting spirit. He is the founder of *Attitude is Altitude (AIA)* and the brain behind the *Social Emotional Learning (SEL) Curriculum*, which currently impacts so many students' lives in advancing values. This is a remarkable lifetime achievement considering the physical, mental, and social challenges he had to endure in life. Nick's AIA organization created a curriculum that in many ways advances values because it inspires and challenges students to love themselves and others (Attitude is Altitude [AIA], 2023).

Though providing educational services and support for students with physical disabilities and other health impairments is challenging, some lifetime achievements have been remarkable (see Table 10.1, *Wecappable.com*). For example, one of the world's renowned physicists, Professor Stephen William Hawking, defied a rare early onset progressing form of motor neuron disease (MND) also known as amyotrophic lateral sclerosis (ALS, or Lou Gehrig's disease) to be exemplarily successful worldwide. This neurodegenerative disease gradually paralyzed Hawking over decades as the medical diagnosis came very late at the age of 21 (Ferguson, 2011; Hawking, 2013, 2020). Consequently, when he lost the ability to write, he developed compensatory visual methods, including seeing equations with regard to geometry. Hawking was a fiercely independent individual, unwilling to accept help or make concessions for his disabilities because he valued himself as a "normal" human being with the same desires, drives, dreams, and ambitions as the next person (White & John, 2002). This is why we must advance values for students with physical disabilities and other health impairments.

Table 10.1. Famous People With Physical Disabilities/Health Impairments in the World.

Name	Country	Disability	Specialty	Achievements
Stephen Hawking	British	Amyotrophic lateral sclerosis (ALS)	Theoretical physicist	A scientist that has influenced individuals worldwide.
Franklin D. Roosevelt	American	Polio, wheelchair user	Politician	He served as the 32nd President of the United States.
Christopher Reeve	American	Quadriplegia	Actor	An actor who portrayed the superhero Superman in the original movie (1978) and its three sequels.
Nick Vujicic	Australian American	Born with tetra-amelia syndrome (doesn't have arms and legs)	Motivational speaker, writer	Considered a global icon of the disability movement.
Esther Vergeer	Dutch	Paralysis in legs	Tennis player	An outstanding tennis player known throughout the world.
Peter Dinklage	American	Dwarfism	Actor	Known for being the character of Tyrison Lannister in the Game of Thrones series on HBO.
John Nash	American	Acute Paranoid Schizophrenia	Mathematician	Winner of the Economics Nobel Prize.
Frida Kahlo	Mexican	Polio	Painter	A cultural icon and world famous painter.
Michael J. Fox	Canadian-American	Parkinson's disease	Actor, comedian, author	Created the Michael J. Fox Foundation.
Lewis Carroll	British	Autism	Author	Authored the story of *Alice in the Wonderland*, which was known worldwide.

Source: Kumar (2020, November 23). Adapted From wecapable.com (2023).

While we might not be perfect, special education has done some good. In addition, societies have responded by creating and giving opportunities to people with physical and other health impairments. In response, these individuals have taken advantage of available resources and opportunities. Table 10.1 contains information about Professor Hawking and other notable and famous people with physical and other health impairments who have enhanced our societal values.

The accomplishments of these professionals listed in Table 10.1 attest to the fact that the dignity and value of people with disabilities must not be underestimated or undervalued in any way. Government and state agencies as well as service providers must, therefore, be compelled through education and legislation to play various roles in providing diverse services to people with disabilities and other health impairments. Oliver (2013) called for reinvigorating the social model perspective to guide future policies and disability issues. Making an important distinction between disability (a disadvantage created by society) and impairments (a condition or illness) is useful for diagnostic purposes. However, the goal here is to pursue disability justice and make social, political, and economic changes to create accessibility and acceptance in society. While the social model rejects cultural narratives that stigmatize disability as an individual problem or personal tragedy, it values disability identity and culture. When we pay attention, we make a difference. Advancing values for students with disabilities and other health impairments, therefore, requires a shift from current perceptions to understanding that it is a social justice and equity issue.

A LOOK AT THE FUTURE

It has become clear that persons with physical and other health impairments can live productive lives. Certainly, self-determination, social justice, and inclusion can affect the dignity of students with disabilities and other health impairments. It is critical that all professionals and service providers treat all students the way they expect to be treated, irrespective of their physical or health impairment. That is why in recognizing the dignity of all human beings worldwide, *The Universal Declaration of Human Rights* (UDHR) was drafted in 1948. This document is considered a milestone in the history of human rights. It was drafted by representatives of different legal and cultural backgrounds from all regions of the world and proclaimed by the *United Nations General Assembly* in Paris on December 10, 1948 (General Assembly resolution 217 A), to buttress achievements of all persons and all nations (United Nations: Universal Declaration of Human Rights-UDHR, 2023). Fortunately, "the UDHR is widely recognized as having inspired and paved the way for, the adoption of more than 70 human rights treaties, applied today on a permanent basis at global and regional levels" (UDHR, 2023, para. 1). Article I of the Declaration states that, "All human beings are born free and equal in dignity and rights" and also asserts that everyone is entitled to the rights and freedoms set forth in the document, without distinction of any kind. As it stands, the UDHR has far-reaching implications.

In 2006, the United Nations came up with the *Convention on the Rights of Persons with Disabilities* (CRPD), an international human rights treaty. The convention was put in place to protect the *rights and dignity* of persons with disabilities and therefore underscores their rights to be valued in communities with equal choices and full participation. It represents the universal recognition that basic rights and fundamental freedoms are inherent to all human beings, inalienable and equally applicable to everyone, and that every human being is born free and equal in dignity and rights, and must be valued as such. We must continue to encourage advocacies that foster international human rights laws that advance obligations that all nations are bound to respect. Through the ratification of international human rights treaties, various countries and government agencies strive to put into place domestic measures and legislations compatible with their treaty obligations and duties. This means that, domestic legal systems of various countries must provide the principal legal protection of human rights guaranteed under international law (United Nations: The Foundation of International Human Rights Law, 2023). Clearly, these efforts are important in advancing values for students with disabilities and other health impairments in various societies.

Currently, federal legislation within the United States protects all students with disabilities to have the right to quality education in the least restrictive environment. The Federal laws protect the rights and outline the types of support that must be provided to disabled students (Asola et al., 2023). Public Law 93-112 (Section 504 of the Vocational Rehabilitation Act of 1973, IDEA of 2004, and PL 114-95 (*Every Student Succeeds Act [ESSA]*) are efforts to advance free, appropriate public education and related services to meet current and future learners with physical and other health impairments. In the future, we must continue to advocate for such measurable efforts to foster the quality of life for all people. As Asola et al. (2023) indicated, new technology and innovative teaching strategies are currently available for educators to provide equitable learning opportunities for students with physical disabilities and other health impairments. Emerging technologies such as generative artificial intelligence (AI) offer promising trends in diagnosis that will provide appropriate services to students with disabilities. Truly, the advancement in science, education, health, and transportation services will enable many special education service providers to improve services to these students. More importantly, current technology and advances in science have enabled professionals to perform early diagnosis of students with physical disabilities and other health impairments (Asola & Hodge, 2019a; Hodge & Asola, 2019).

CONCLUSION

Students with physical and other health impairments are "normal" human beings who require special approaches to providing services such as health care, accommodations, education, and transitional services (Asola & Hodge, 2021; Asola & Obiakor, 2016). They must be valued and recognized for their contributions to society in general. This chapter emphasized that we must advocate for them and take advantage of laws that are already in the books. Right now, many of them have made great achievements and contributions to society, and we can use them as great role models in the end; we must advance our values as professionals by making sure that people with physical disabilities and other health impairments maximize their potential.

REFERENCES

Asola, E., & Hodge, S. R. (2019a). Special education for young learners with physical disabilities. In F. E. Obiakor & J. P. Bakken (Eds.), *Advances in special education: Special education for young learners with disabilities* (Vol. 34, pp. 173–185). Emerald Publishing Limited.

Asola, E. F., & Hodge, S. R. (2019b). Transitioning students with physical disabilities and other health impairments. In F. E. Obiakor & J. P. Bakken (Eds.), *Special education transition services for students with disabilities: Advances in special education* (Vol. 35, pp. 167–183). Emerald Publishing Limited.

Asola, E. F., & Hodge, S. R. (2021). Traditional and innovative assessment techniques for students with physical disabilities and other health impairments. In F. E. Obiakor & J. P. Bakken (Eds.), *Advances in special education* (Vol. 36, pp. 181–196). Emerald Publishing Limited.

Asola, E. F., Hodge, S. R., & Grant, M. (2023). Using technology to enhance learning for students with physical disabilities and other health impairments. In F. E. Obiakor & J. P. Bakken (Eds.), *Using technology to enhance special education: Advances in special education* (Vol. 37, pp. 215–231). Emerald Publishing Limited.

Asola, E. F., & Obiakor, F. E. (2016). Inclusion of students with physical disabilities and other health impairments. In J. P. Bakken & F. E. Obiakor (Eds.), *General and special education inclusion in an age of change: Impact on students with disabilities* (Vol. 31, pp. 119–212). Emerald Publishing Limited.

Attitude is Altitude-AIA. (2023). https://www.aiacurriculum.org/

Ferguson, K. (2011). *Stephen Hawking: His life and work*. Transworld.

Haegele, J., & Hodge, S. R. (2016). Disability discourse: Overview and critiques of the medical and social models. *Quest, 68*(2), 193–206.

Hawking, S. W. (2013). *My brief history*. ISBN-13: 978-0345535283. Bantam Books.

Hawking, S. W. (2020). Stephen Hawking. http://www.hawking.org.uk

Hodge, S. R., & Asola, E. (2019). Special education for young learners with other health impairments. In F. E. Obiakor & J. P. Bakken (Eds.), *Advances in special education: Special education for young learners with disabilities* (Vol. 34, pp. 187–207). Emerald Publishing Limited.

Individuals with Disabilities Education Improvement Act of 2004, H.R. 1350, 108th Cong. (IDEA). (2004). http://idea.ed.gov/download/statute.html

Kumar, S. L. (2020, November 23). *Infographic on world famous people with disabilities*. wecapable. com. https://wecapable.com/famous-disabled-people-world/. Accessed on August 23, 2023.

National Archives and Records Administration: Electronic Code of Federal Regulations. (2023). *Title 34: Education §300.34: Child with a disability*. Government Publishing Office. https://www.ecfr. gov/current/title-34/part-300

National Center for Education Statistics. (2023). *Students with disabilities: Condition of education*. U.S. Department of Education, Institute of Education Sciences. https://nces.ed.gov/programs/coe/ indicator/cgg

Okoro, C. A., Hollis, N. D., Cyrus, A. C., & Griffin-Blake, S. (2018). Prevalence of disabilities and health care access by disability status and type among adults – United States, 2016. *MMWR. Morbidity and Mortality Weekly Report, 67*(32), 882–887. https://doi.org/10.15585/mmwr. mm6732a3

Oliver, M. (2013). The social model of disability: Thirty years on. *Disability & Society, 28*(7), 1024–1026. https://doi.org/10.1080/09687599.2013.818773

Spencer, N. L. I., Peers, D., & Eales, L. (2020). Disability language in adapted physical education: What is the story? In J. A. Haegele, S. R. Hodge, & D. R. Shapiro (Eds.), *Routledge handbook of adapted physical education* (pp. 131–143). Routledge.

United Nations: The Foundation of International Human Rights Law. (2023). https://www.un.org/en/ about-us/udhr/foundation-of-international-human-rights-law

United Nations: Universal Declaration of Human Rights. (2023). https://www.un.org/en/about-us/ universal-declaration-of-human-rights

Wecapable.com. (2003). 17 Famous People with Disabilities in the World. https://wecapable.com/ famous-disabled-people-world/

White, M., & John, G. (2002). *Stephen Hawking: A life in science* (2nd ed.). Joseph Henry Press.

CHAPTER 11

WORKING WITH PARENTS OF STUDENTS WITH SPECIAL EDUCATIONAL NEEDS: ADVANCING VALUES

Kristina Rios[a] and Paul Luelmo[b]

[a]California State University of Fresno, USA
[b]San Diego State University, USA

ABSTRACT

Family–school partnerships are an essential component of the special education process for children with disabilities. Notably, recent legislative reauthorizations of IDEA (2004) have focused on increasing parent involvement. For many parents, participation occurs primarily through the individualized education program (IEP) meetings. Parent involvement often includes parent advocating for their children. However, many parents face barriers when advocating to obtain appropriate special education services for their children with disabilities. Culturally and linguistically diverse families face greater systemic barriers (e.g., language and cultural differences) to access services for their own children with disabilities. School professionals can foster opportunities to help families be active members of the IEP process. For example, school professionals should connect families with resources to learn about their special education rights. Specifically, school personnel can encourage families to reach out to their local Parent Training and Information (PTI) Center to be educated and empowered to advocate for services. In addition, parents can be encouraged to attend parent advocacy programs to help increase knowledge, advocacy, and empowerment to access and advocate for services for their own children. Advancing the values of working with parents of students with special education needs is discussed.

Special Education
Advances in Special Education, Volume 38, 167–183
Copyright © 2024 Kristina Rios and Paul Luelmo
Published under exclusive licence by Emerald Publishing Limited
ISSN: 0270-4013/doi:10.1108/S0270-401320240000038011

Keywords: Culturally and linguistically diverse practices; advocacy; family engagement; parent–professional partnerships; parents of students with disabilities

INTRODUCTION

The student population in the United States today is comprised of mainly students of color (NCES, 2021). Hence, this culturally and ethnically diverse student population needs teachers who are culturally responsive (CR). Notably, culturally responsiveness refers to a teacher's ability to recognize their own identity within the context of the school community, recognize potential bias, identify and appreciate cultural and linguistic differences from one's own. This is important because if the teaching force perceives minoritized students from a deficit perspective, it creates the tangible inequities we see today in special education. One of these inequalities is the overrepresentation of students of color in certain special education programs (NCES, 2021). On the other hand, having a CR, asset, and strengths-based approach can help alleviate some of the inequities we see in schools today for students of color.

Effective partnerships between teachers and parents of children with disabilities, including those from culturally and linguistically diverse (CLD) backgrounds, are crucial for promoting positive educational outcomes. Research provides valuable insights into the knowledge and practices that support these partnerships. Firstly, cultural competence is key to building effective partnerships. Teachers who demonstrate an understanding of and respect for the cultural values, beliefs, and practices of CLD parents can establish trust and create an inclusive environment (Harry, 2008). By recognizing and valuing diverse backgrounds, teachers can bridge cultural gaps and foster collaboration with parents. Secondly, communication and collaboration play a vital role in effective partnerships. Ongoing and meaningful communication between teachers and parents is associated with positive outcomes for students with disabilities (Epstein & Dauber, 1991). Teachers can utilize various communication strategies such as home–school notebooks, email, phone calls, and in-person and/or virtual meetings to establish regular dialogue and foster collaboration.

Empowering parents as partners is another essential aspect. When parents feel valued and involved in decision-making processes, they are more likely to be engaged in their child's education (Hill, 2022). Teachers can empower parents by soliciting their input, respecting their perspectives, and actively involving them in educational planning, such as setting goals for their child as parents play a vital role in the individualized education program (IEP) process and they are legal partners in the development of the document. Furthermore, building trust and rapport is fundamental for effective partnerships. Parents who perceive teachers as trustworthy and respectful are more likely to engage collaboratively (Denson, 2021). Teachers can establish trust by maintaining transparency, respecting confidentiality, and demonstrating empathy and understanding toward parents' concerns and perspectives. For example, the Sunshine Model (Haines et al., 2017) is built on the foundation of general and special education policy and aims toward collective empowerment in which "families and professionals agree to build on each other's expertise and resources for the purpose of making and implementing decisions that will directly benefit students and indirectly benefit other family members and professionals" (Turnbull et al., 2015, p. 161). The Sunshine Model seeks to enhance the bond between families and professionals, comparable to the power and nurturing aspects associated with the sun. This model strives to promote collective strength, trust, and mutual support by encouraging creative and collaborative decision-making. It encompasses a proactive approach that encompasses the typical activities and principles involved in family–professional partnerships, while remaining adaptable to the unique needs of individual families who may benefit from diverse educational approaches. The Sunshine Model empowers schools to establish proactive systems that prioritize strong family–professional partnerships for all families, regardless of their children's age or specific needs. Aligned with both general and special education policies, this approach aims to build the capacity of educators and families to

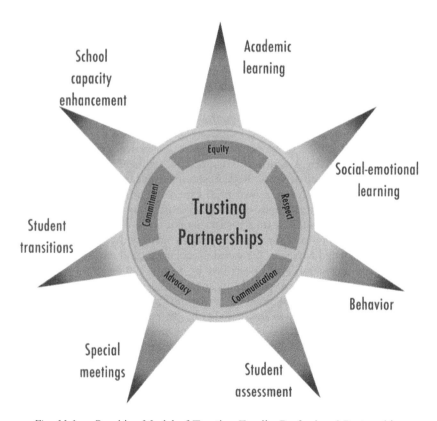

Fig. 11.1.   Sunshine Model of Trusting Family–Professional Partnerships
(Haines et al., 2017).

form reciprocal partnerships that yield positive outcomes for all parties involved. See Fig. 11.1 for the Sunshine Model.

CLD PRACTICES

CR practices are crucial when working with CLD parents. Adapting teaching strategies, materials, and communication styles to align with families' cultural and linguistic preferences enhances partnership effectiveness (Crosnoe & Fuligni, 2012). By incorporating CR practices, teachers can create an inclusive and welcoming environment that supports meaningful parent engagement. Providing teachers with professional development and training is essential. Research suggests that training on working with parents of children with disabilities, particularly CLD parents, enhances teachers' competence in engaging and collaborating with diverse families (Epstein & Van Voorhis, 2012). Professional development programs can address cultural competence, effective communication strategies, and ways to overcome language barriers, equipping teachers with the necessary knowledge and skills for building effective partnerships.

Research highlights the importance of teachers' knowledge and practices in working with parents of children with disabilities, especially those from CLD backgrounds. Cultural competence, effective communication, empowering parents, building trust, employing CR practices, and providing professional development opportunities are all essential elements of effective partnerships. By incorporating these strategies, teachers can establish collaborative relationships that support the educational success and well-being of students with disabilities and their families.

Jenny Muñiz (2019) developed a program associated with the Education Policy program at New America who mapped out eight specific competencies for CR teachers. One competency is "Reflect on one's own cultural lens" which refers to the ability to identify one's own lived experience within the context of the school community. For example, one of the authors of this chapter grew up in the US–Mexico border, within a transborder community (*transfronterizo*); this dual identity of Mexican–American is a very specific identity that filters the way the author perceives and navigates the world. Recognizing and redressing bias in the system is another competency described by Muñiz (2019). For instance, the *transfronterizo* author was a special education teacher co-teaching with a general education teacher in a middle school serving mostly immigrant families. Within this context, one student was reprimanded by the general education teacher for speaking Spanish in the classroom. This could mean that the student is being silenced from their first language by an educator in the classroom. The *transfronterizo* special education teacher was able to identify this as a deficit orientation in part of the teacher, and advocated for the student's cultural and linguistic barriers by addressing the teacher directly and explaining to her that speaking another language is a strength, not a deficit. Nonetheless, the same special education teacher had to wrestle with the idea that a Black parent did not trust him or the school system. The teacher then tried to listen to the parent to understand where the mistrust came from. The teacher quickly learned that a history of abuses and racism by the school system had led some Black parents to a consistent mistrust of the special education school system. The teacher understood and worked to redress biases by listening to the parent and communicating back in a CR way. This collaboration with families, respect for student differences, and CR communication (i.e., listening and learning from families) are three more of the CR competencies that Muñiz describes.

Muñiz (2019) describes three more CR competencies related to instruction: (a) draw on student's culture to shape curriculum and instruction, (b) bring real-world issues into the classroom, and (c) model high expectations for all students. These three competencies draw on the same principle of respect and learning about our student population. For instance, assignments must include names, places, and languages with which the students are familiar, issues that the community might be facing (e.g., police brutality), and having the belief that all students can achieve and master the content. Students with disabilities might need

Table 11.1. Teacher Competencies That Promote Culturally Responsive (CR) Teaching (Muñiz, 2019).

Eight Competencies	Example of the Competency
Reflection on One's Cultural Lens	Culturally responsive (CR) educators regularly ponder their own life experiences and affiliations with different identify groups, such as race, ethnicity, socioeconomic states, sexual orientation, and gender. They aim to avoid stereotypes and unconscious biases in their interactions with students, families, and colleagues, working toward developing cultural competency.
Recognize and Redress Bias in the System	CR educators discern personal bias (e.g., racist speech) from intuitional bias, considering how identity markers like race, ethnicity, ability, socioeconomic status, sexual orientation, and gender affect students' educational opportunities. Accessible resources and professional learning opportunities help teachers understand institutional racism and systemic biases, acknowledging unequal rewards for student efforts.
Draw on Students' Culture to Share Curriculum and Instruction	CR teaching relies on students' culture and knowledge to facilitate new learning. Teachers use cultural scaffolding to connect academic concepts with students' experiences. They involve students in shaping assignments, projects, and assessments. While formal curricula are set by school leaders, CR teachers evaluate instructional resources to avoid perpetuating stereotypes and to include diverse identities.
Bring Real-World Issues Into the Classroom	CR educators tackle the "so what?" aspect of teaching by demonstrating to students the practical value of the knowledge and skills they acquire in school, connecting it to their lives, families, and communities. They prompt students with questions like, "How does this material relate to your daily life?" "Does this knowledge address issues you are about?" and "How can you apply this information to make a difference?"

(Continued)

Table 11.1. *(Continued)*

Eight Competencies	Example of the Competency
Model High Expectations for All Students	CR educators believe all students can achieve high levels of success. The educators understand that Black, Indigenous, students of color, and other marginalized groups are vulnerable to negative stereotypes about their intelligence, academic ability, and behavior. They understand that these stereotypes can inadvertently influence their pedagogical choices and expectations of students, which in turn influence students' perceptions about their own abilities.
Promote Respect for Students Differences	CR educators cultivate learning environments that promote respect, inclusivity, and affirmation. They actively demonstrate how to engage with diverse perspectives and exemplify respect for all forms of diversity. They instill in students a deep appreciation for their own culture and that of others, fostering a sense of responsibility to confront prejudice and mistreatment when encountered.
Collaborate With Families and the Local Community	CR educators operate under the assumption that parents are eager to participate in their children's education and takes steps to facilitate family engagement by removing any barriers that may exist. For instance, they make themselves available for meetings at convenient times and locations, being considerate of any past traumas that families may have experienced in their interactions with the school.
Communicate in Linguistically and CR Ways	CR teachers make an effort to comprehend how culture influences communication, encompassing verbal aspects like tone of voice, rhythm, and vocabulary, as well as nonverbal elements such as spatial distance, eye contact, body movements, and gestures. They allow students to utilize their natural communication styles in the classroom, valuing and accommodating diverse linguistic backgrounds, including advocating for translation services and resources in multiple languages for multilingual students and families.

additional support and scaffolding from the teachers. This is where collaboration with parents in the IEP with a CR lens can help teachers teach students with disabilities more effectively. Refer to Table 11.1 for the eight teacher competencies that promote CR teaching (Muñiz, 2019).

THE ADVOCACY EXPECTATION

Parent advocacy is critical to improving educational access to education and achieving better outcomes for students with disabilities. In 1975, parents were written into the Education for all Handicapped Children Act (EHA) as equal partners in educational decision-making for their children with disabilities. The IDEA (2004) provides many rights for parents of children with disabilities to be involved in the special education process to be able to advocate for services for their own children including: providing consent for evaluations and initial receipt of services and having safeguards for conflict resolution. Advocacy can help families access needed services for their children with disabilities (Burke, Goldman, et al., 2016; Cohen, 2013). Parent advocacy can be characterized in many ways but ultimately the purpose of advocacy is to yield a desired outcome for the individual one is advocating for (Turnbull et al., 2021). Thus, advocacy is critical to access special education services.

The requirement for parent participation under IDEA may have influenced the advocacy expectation (Kalyanpur et al., 2000). The expectation of advocacy may also result from schools' propensity to prioritize IDEA compliance over offering each student an education program tailored to their needs (Phillips, 2008). As a result, parents must advocate for the programs that are in their children's best interests. The financing for IDEA also contributes to the requirement for parent advocacy. While congress mandated that the federal government would cover up to 40% of the additional costs associated with educating children with disabilities, federal funding has not gone above 15% (Congressional Research Service, 2019). Studies indicate that simply having federal mandates in place is not enough to guarantee successful policies in schools. The effectiveness of these policies relies heavily on the values and abilities of local leaders, including families, community members, and school officials. Notable instances of long-term, widespread family involvement have emphasized the significance of fostering strong school cultures through collaborations with families and communities. This involves ongoing efforts to enhance trust and communication between schools and families, as well as implementing two-way support systems that encourage the implementation of effective strategies for promoting high-quality family engagement and involvement (Boberiene, 2013; Kelty & Wakabayashi, 2020).

FAMILY ENGAGEMENT

Family engagement in the IEP can be difficult for teachers who might not be familiar with the family's culture. For instance, special educators might be hesitant to contact parents who do not speak English. Furthermore, they might make incorrect assumptions about families. For example, a Spanish speaking, immigrant family might be quiet during an IEP meeting out of respect for the professionals in the room. However, this behavior can be misinterpreted as a lack of interest or disengagement of the parents. This is an example of how cultural differences can impact the collaboration and partnership between parents and teachers that is so critical to student success. Hence, going back to the CR approach and strengths-based approach is critical for every teacher working with CLD families. For example, school professionals should connect CLD families with resources to learn their special education rights. As parents are better informed about their special education rights, they may be active participating during the IEP process (Rios et al., 2020).

CHALLENGES AND OPPORTUNITIES FOR CLD PARENT PARTICIPATION IN IEPS

While advocacy is often an expectation for parents of children with disabilities, parents often struggle to advocate for their children (Hughes et al., 2008; Rios et al., 2021). Specifically, parents face systemic barriers when advocating for services for their children. Such barriers include: power differential between the parent and the school (Leiter & Wyngaarden Krauss, 2004), and procedural safeguards are written, on average, at a 16th grade reading level (Mandic et al., 2012). CLD (versus white) families of children with disabilities are more predisposed to facing systemic obstacles in advocacy. For example, because of the jargon in IDEA, often times, interpreters do not accurately communicate information stated during IEP meetings (Hughes et al., 2008; Mueller et al., 2009; Rueda et al., 2005). In addition, CLD (versus white) families are more likely to lack information about special education services, and therefore, may advocate less (Burke, Rios, et al., 2018; Shapiro et al., 2004).

There may be several ways to assist families, including CLD families, in overcoming systemic barriers and accessing services for their children with disabilities. For example, providing families with educational materials regarding special education may enable parents to access needed school services for their children. According to school professionals, when families are knowledgeable about special education services, they are more likely to access needed services for their children (Burke, Meadan-Kaplansky, 2018). Further, knowledge about special education is noted as one of the primary advocacy strategies among families of children with disabilities (Burke & Hodapp, 2016; Trainor, 2010).

PARENT ROLE IN THE IEP PROCESS

Recent legislative reauthorizations of IDEA (2004) have focused on increasing parent involvement. For many parents, participation occurs primarily through the IEP meetings. This meeting brings together the parent or guardian and educational professionals on the IEP team to discuss and consider appropriate services that meet the educational needs of eligible children with disabilities (IDEA, 2004). IDEA also requires parents of students with disabilities to: (a) be involved in planning IEP meetings to ensure a mutually agreed upon meeting time and place, (b) provide prior written notice so that parents can attend, (c) provide an invitation to the meeting detailing the time, place, purpose, and list of attendees of the meeting, (d) if a parent is unable to attend the IEP meeting, provide other forms of communication (e.g., teleconference) to ensure attendance at the IEP, (e) provide an interpreter if requested by a parent or legal guardian. During the IEP meeting, parents and school personnel must agree upon the various components of the IEP document (e.g., academic goals and placement decisions) before it can be implemented as a service delivery tool for the student (IDEA, 2004). Thus, parent involvement is a crucial role that is embedded within the entire IEP process.

PARENT–PROFESSIONAL PARTNERSHIPS

Parent–professional relationships are an essential component of the IEP for children with disabilities (IDEA, 2004). Advocacy is also critical to access special education services. It is globally recognized that advocacy can help families access needed services for their children with disabilities (Burke, Goldman, et al., 2016; Cohen, 2013). Because advocacy is an expectation of IDEA (2004) and often results in improved outcomes for families and students with disabilities (e.g., Burke, Meadan-Kaplansky, 2018; Fish, 2008), knowledge about special education is noted as one of the primary advocacy strategies among families of children with disabilities (Burke & Hodapp, 2014; Trainor, 2010). There is a wealth of research suggesting that increased empowerment, advocacy, and knowledge of special education facilitate access to services (Casagrande & Ingersoll, 2017). In a study of correlates of parent advocacy, Burke, Magaña, et al. (2016) found that positive correlates of advocacy included: greater empowerment and special education knowledge. Their findings suggest that parents require better education and training to increase their ability to advocate for their own children. Efforts to address this need for parent education have been reflected in a few parent advocacy programs such as the Families Included in Receiving Better Special Education Services (FIRME; Rios et al., 2021), the Latino Parent Leadership Support Project (LPLSP; Burke, Magaña, et al., 2016), and IEP Advocacy Intervention (Luelmo et al., 2021).

INFORMATION AND RESOURCES FOR ALL PARENTS

Parents and caregivers might come from all walks of life. Some are highly educated and well-versed in the special education system. This might be advantageous for these families, who are able to pull resources from the system and demand better services and support for their children with disabilities. However, other parents might need additional support and information of the IEP as well as the services and support available to them. As educators, we have the duty to fully inform the parents and families we serve. Importantly, this becomes critical in order to build trusting and working relationships with families.

The support and information that educators provide regarding the IEP must be in the parent's native language. Additionally, the information needs to be easy to understand for any parents regardless of level of education. Special education has a plethora of technical language and technical concepts that need to be broken down into easy to understand language. This information needs to be accessible for parents of any race/ethnicity, language, education, or socioeconomic status.

PARENT TRAINING AND INFORMATION CENTERS (PTIS)

Congress established PTIs across the country to assist parents in obtaining services for their children through information and training, education about their rights, and resources. The purpose for these centers is to help families of children from birth to age 26 who have a disability. The main goal of PTIs is to give parents or guardians support and free information on how to receive needed school services. Such supports include information about specific disabilities and issues, parental and child rights under IDEA, support groups, legal assistants, and other local, state, and national resources (IDEA, 2004). Annually, the PTIs serve more than 1.4 million families of children with disabilities (National Parent Technical Assistance Center, 2016). It is vital that parents of children with disabilities be connected with resources such as their local PTI centers to be educated and empowered to advocate for services.

ADVOCACY TRAINING PROGRAMS

To enable parents to participate in educational decision-making, parent advocacy programs are becoming more common (e.g., advocacy programs; Burke, 2013). Rios and Burke (2020) conducted a literature review to better understand parent advocacy interventions to support families of children with disabilities in improving special education knowledge, advocacy, empowerment, and access to services. Altogether, 21 studies were identified across the United States. Of the 21 studies, there were 12 unique interventions conducted. The authors found that parent advocacy programs may yield positive effects on knowledge, advocacy, and empowerment for parents who completed these programs. Specifically, eight studies examined parent advocacy (Burke et al., 2019; Burke, Goldman, et al., 2016; Burke & Goldman, 2017, 2018; Burke, Rios, et al., 2018; Burke & Sandman, 2017; Goldman & Burke, 2017; Taylor et al., 2017). All studies reported that the intervention was successful in improving advocacy. For example, Taylor et al. (2017) investigated the extent to which parents felt comfortable and competent in advocating for young adults with autism spectrum disorder. After participating in the intervention, intervention participants scored higher (compared to the control group), indicating greater ability and comfort in advocating. Advocacy programs may enable families, including CLD families, to effectively collaborate with the school and advocate for their own children with disabilities to receive appropriate services (Luelmo et al., 2021; Rios et al., 2021).

It is crucial to understand and acknowledge the effects of advocacy on health and well-being among parents of children with disabilities. Literature demonstrates an association between the quality of special education experiences and parental health and well-being (i.e., stress) (Burke & Hodapp, 2016; Rios & Burke, 2020). For example, Burke and Hodapp (2016) conducted a descriptive cross-sectional study of over 1,000 families with children with disabilities. They found a negative correlation between parental advocacy and family–school partnership quality. In other words, partnerships with schools weakened as families became more involved in school services. In a qualitative study of 16 Latina mothers of children with autism spectrum disorder (ASD; Rios et al., 2020), participants reported being stressed before, during, and after IEP meetings. Notably, all parents had clinically high levels of stress related to the IEP process. In addition, participants reported that having more special education knowledge would help decrease their stress. Given that some studies (e.g., Burke & Hodapp; Rios et al., 2020) suggest that advocacy may have negative outcomes for parents, it is important that such advocacy programs incorporate mindfulness-based strategies to help alleviate parental stress (Neece et al., 2019; Rios et al., 2021).

CULTURE, LANGUAGE, AND RACIAL/ETHNIC IDENTITY

The ecological validity framework recognizes the importance of considering the contextual factors that influence individuals' experiences and development. When applied to racial/ethnic identity for students with disabilities, the framework highlights the significance of understanding the intersecting dynamics between race/ethnicity and disability within various ecological systems, such as families, schools, communities, and broader societal contexts.

Racial/ethnic identity development is a complex process influenced by a multitude of factors, including cultural values, social interactions, and experiences within specific environments. For students with disabilities, their racial/ethnic identity development is further shaped by the interaction between their disability status and their racial/ethnic background.

Within the ecological validity framework, the family system plays a crucial role in shaping racial/ethnic identity for students with disabilities. Families provide the primary context where cultural values, traditions, and beliefs are transmitted. Students with disabilities may navigate the intersections of disability and race/ethnicity within their families, where cultural practices and attitudes toward disability may vary. For example, some racial/ethnic communities may hold specific beliefs about disability that can influence students' self-perception and their understanding of how their disability intersects with their racial/ethnic identity. Notably, some cultures may have spiritual etiological interpretations and explanations for their child's condition. Parents have a nuanced intimate knowledge of their children, and therefore, information they offer can provide teachers and schools valuable insights.

Schools also play a significant role in the racial/ethnic identity development of students with disabilities. The attitudes, behaviors, and practices of teachers and peers can shape students' experiences and perceptions of their racial/ethnic identity. Schools that promote a CR and inclusive environment can support the positive development of racial/ethnic identity for students with disabilities. Conversely, schools that lack cultural competence or have limited understanding of the intersectionality of race/ethnicity and disability may inadvertently perpetuate disparities and marginalization.

The community and broader societal contexts further influence the racial/ethnic identity development of students with disabilities. Community resources, services, and cultural institutions can provide opportunities for students to engage with their racial/ethnic heritage and develop a positive sense of identity. However, discrimination, stereotypes, and systemic barriers may also exist within these contexts, affecting students' self-perception and shaping their experiences of being both racially/ethnically diverse and having a disability.

Applying the ecological validity framework to racial/ethnic identity for students with disabilities underscores the importance of recognizing and addressing the multifaceted ecological systems that influence their development. It calls for an understanding of the complex interactions between race/ethnicity and disability within various contexts and the need for inclusive practices and policies that promote positive racial/ethnic identity development. By considering the ecological systems that students with disabilities navigate, educators, policymakers, and researchers can work toward creating environments that support the holistic development and well-being of these students, considering their unique experiences at the intersection of race/ethnicity and disability.

Ecological validity in family engagement then refers to incorporating cultural components into parent-involved interventions and programs (Martinez-Torres et al., 2021). There are many elements that may play a role in the ecological validity of parental involvement programs and interventions. Benefits abound when considering parental involvement ecological validity, for example, parent knowledge, acceptance of services, and decreases in parental stress (Agazzi et al., 2010; Bauermeister, 2016). Refer to Table 11.2 for strategies to incorporate the Ecological Validity Framework.

Elements of ecological validity in parental involvement include teachers and staff knowledge of the local culture. For example, Latinx families in a school community might all have a similar background (language, or State of origin in Mexico or Latin America). Then incorporating the nuances in culture becomes critical. For example, a school community with a large immigrant population from the State of Jalisco in Central Mexico might benefit from engaging families with events that highlight some

Table 11.2. Ecological Validity Framework Implementation Example.

Dimension	Example of the Dimension
Language – The language in which information is developed, available, and delivered.	• Trainings/programs that target CLD families. • Trainings/programs that include curricular materials in parent's primary language.
Persons – The instructor and target population characteristics and the dynamic between them.	• Trainings/programs that allow for peer-led activities and/or peer-led interventions.
Metaphors – Symbols and concepts shared by the target population.	• Trainings/programs that incorporate common CLD sayings "e.g., *dichos*" as well as storytelling.
Content and Concepts – Cultural knowledge including values, customs, and traditions.	• Trainings/programs incorporate a curriculum that includes cultural values such as *personalismo* (a focus on relationships) and *familismo* (needs of the family comes before the individual) to develop the content.
Goals – The treatment goals are culturally appropriate and developed jointly with the instructor and target population.	• Trainings/programs implement goals specific to the parents and their children with disabilities.
Methods – The procedures for achieving treatment goals.	• Trainings/programs: Include an instructor, be flexible, foster relationship building, and include the family throughout the program.
Context – The impact of context on participants and context throughout the program (i.e., social context).	• Training/program allows for the delivery format to meet the needs of the families.

Source: Rios and Burke (2021).

of the contributions of immigrants from Jalisco in Mexico's society (e.g., Mariachi). Thus, it is essential to maintain and understanding and appreciation of the diverse cultures, languages, and experiences that students bring to the classroom. By recognizing and valuing these differences, educators can create inclusive and CR learning environments.

MAINTAINING TRADITION

The disparities that exist in schools for diverse families are well-documented in empirical research, highlighting the need for change within school systems. In order to address these disparities effectively, it is crucial for schools to engage in greater cultural introspection and understanding of the families they serve. This can be achieved through implementing inclusive policies, fostering cultural competency among educators, and establishing partnerships with families and communities.

Numerous studies have demonstrated the existence of disparities in educational outcomes and experiences for diverse families. For example, research conducted by the National Center for Education Statistics (NCES) in the United States has consistently shown that students from minority backgrounds, including racial and ethnic minorities, often face lower academic achievement, higher dropout rates, and limited access to advanced courses compared to their white counterparts (NCES, 2021).

In addition to racial and ethnic disparities, disparities in educational outcomes also emerge based on factors such as socioeconomic status, language proficiency, and disability status. A study by Reardon et al. (2019) analyzed national data from the United States and found substantial achievement gaps based on socioeconomic status, with children from low-income families trailing behind their wealthier peers. Similarly, research by Gottfried and Plasman (2018) indicated that English language learners face educational disparities, including lower test scores and graduation rates, when compared to English-proficient students.

To address these disparities, school systems need to engage in cultural introspection to gain a deeper understanding of the families they serve. One crucial aspect of this introspection is the implementation of inclusive policies and practices. By adopting policies that promote equity and inclusion, schools can create a more welcoming environment for diverse families. For instance, policies that support bilingual education or provide targeted support for students with disabilities can help bridge educational gaps (Crosnoe & Fuligni, 2012).

Furthermore, fostering cultural competency among educators is vital to creating an inclusive and supportive learning environment. Research suggests that teachers who possess cultural competency skills are better equipped to meet the diverse needs of their students and establish positive relationships with families (Denson, 2021). Cultural competency training programs and professional development opportunities can help educators develop the knowledge, skills, and attitudes necessary to engage effectively with diverse families (Harry, 2008).

Additionally, establishing partnerships between schools, families, and communities is essential for addressing disparities and promoting student success. Research by Hill (2022) demonstrated that family-school-community partnerships have a positive impact on students' academic achievement, social–emotional development, and overall well-being. Engaging families as active participants in the education process, seeking their input, and involving them in decision-making can lead to more CR and inclusive practices within schools.

CONCLUSION

In conclusion, the existing disparities in schools for diverse families underscore the urgent need for change within school systems. Engaging in cultural introspection by implementing inclusive policies, fostering cultural competency among educators, and establishing partnerships with families and communities are vital steps toward addressing these disparities. By taking these actions, schools can create a more equitable and inclusive educational environment where all students can thrive.

REFERENCES

Agazzi, H., Salinas, A., Williams, J., Chiriboga, D., Ortiz, C., & Armstrong, K. (2010). Adaptation of a behavioral parent-training curriculum for Hispanic caregivers: HOT DOCS Español. *Infant Mental Health Journal: Official Publication of the World Association for Infant Mental Health*, *31*(2), 182–200. https://doi.org/10.1002/imhj.20251

Bauermeister, J. J. (2016). Parental behavior training and Latino/Hispanic children with ADHD and/or disruptive behaviors. *The ADHD Report*, *24*(8), 9–14. https://doi.org/10.1521/adhd.2016.24.8.9

Boberiene, L. V. (2013). Can policy facilitate human capital development? The critical role of student and family engagement in schools. *American Journal of Orthopsychiatry*, *83*(2–3), 346–351. https://doi.org/10.1111/ajop.12041

Burke, M. M. (2013). Improving parental involvement: Training special education advocates. *Journal of Disability Policy Studies*, *23*, 225–234.

Burke, M. M., Buren, M. K., Rios, K., Garcia, M., & Magaña, S. (2019). Examining the short-term follow-up advocacy activities among Latino families of children with autism spectrum disorder. *Research and Practice in Intellectual and Developmental Disabilities*, *6*(1), 76–85. https://doi.org/10.1080/23297018.2018.1439767

Burke, M. M., & Goldman, S. E. (2017). Documenting the experiences of special education advocates. *The Journal of Special Education*, *51*, 3–13. https://doi.org/10.1177/0022466916643714

Burke, M. M., & Goldman, S. E. (2018). Special education advocacy among culturally and linguistically diverse families. *Journal of Research in Special Educational Needs*, *18*, 3–14. https://doi.org/10.1111/1471-3802.12413

Burke, M. M., Goldman, S. E., Hart, M. S., & Hodapp, R. M. (2016). Evaluating the efficacy of a special education advocacy training program. *Journal of Policy and Practice in Intellectual Disabilities*, *13*(4), 269–276. https://doi.org/10.1111/jppi.12183

Burke, M. M., & Hodapp, R. M. (2014). Relating stress of mothers of children with developmental disabilities to family-school partnerships. *Intellectual and Developmental Disabilities*, *52*, 13–23. https://doi.org/10.1352/1934-9556-52.1.13

Burke, M. M., & Hodapp, R. M. (2016). The nature, correlates, and conditions of parental advocacy in special education. *Exceptionality*, *24*(3), 137–150. https://doi.org/10.1080/09362835.2015.1064412

Burke, M. M., Magaña, S., Garcia, M., & Mello, M. P. (2016). Brief report: The feasibility and effectiveness of an advocacy program for Latino families of children with autism spectrum disorder. *Journal of Autism and Developmental Disorders*, *46*, 2532–2538. https://doi.org/10.1007/s10803-016-2765-x

Burke, M. M., Meadan-Kaplansky, H., Patton, K. A., Pearson, J. N., Cummings, K. P., & Lee, C. (2018). Advocacy for children with social-communication needs: Perspectives from parents and school professionals. *The Journal of Special Education*, *51*(4), 191–200. https://doi.org/10.1177/0022466917716898

Burke, M. M., Rios, K., & Lee, C. E. (2018). Exploring the special education advocacy process according to families and advocates. *The Journal of Special Education*, *53*(3), 131–141.

Burke, M. M., & Sandman, L. (2017). The effectiveness of a parent legislative advocacy program. *Journal of Policy and Practice in Intellectual Disabilities*, *14*(2), 138–145. https://doi.org/10.1111/jppi.12173

Casagrande, K. A., & Ingersoll, B. R. (2017). Service delivery out-comes in ASD: Role of parent education, empowerment, and professional partnerships. *Journal of Child and Family Studies*, *26*(9), 2386–2395. https://doi.org/10.1007/s10826-017-0759-8

Cohen, S. R. (2013). Advocacy for the "Abandonados": Harnessing cultural beliefs for Latino families and their children with intellectual disabilities. *Journal of Policy and Practice in Intellectual Disabilities*, *10*(1), 71–78. https://doi.org/10.1111/jppi.12021

Congressional Research Service. (2019). *The Individuals with Disabilities Education Act (IDEA), part B: Key statutory and regulatory provisions.* https://crsreports.congress.gov/product/pdf/R/R41833

Crosnoe, R., & Fuligni, A. J. (2012). Children from immigrant families: Introduction to the special section. *Child Development*, *83*, 1471–1476. https://doi.org/10.1111/j.14678624.2012.01785.x

Denson, C. (2021). A causal-comparative study of teacher perceptions of school culture at Georgia elementary schools. Doctoral dissertation, Northcentral University.

Epstein, J. L., & Dauber, S. L. (1991). School programs and teacher practices of parent involvement in inner-city elementary and middle schools. *The Elementary School Journal*, *91*(3), 289–305. https://doi.org/10.1086/461656

Epstein, J. L., & Van Voorhis, F. L. (2012). The changing debate: From assigning homework to designing homework. In *Contemporary debates in childhood education and development* (pp. 277–288). Routledge.

Fish, W. W. (2008). The IEP meeting: Perceptions of parents of students who receive special education services. *Preventing School Failure: Alternative Education for Children and Youth*, *53*(1), 8–14. https://doi.org/10.3200/psfl.53.1.8-14

Goldman, S. E., & Burke, M. M. (2017). The effectiveness of interventions to increase parent involvement in special education: A systematic literature review and meta-analysis. *Exceptionality*, *25*(2), 97–115. https://doi.org/10.1080/09362835.2016.1196444

Gottfried, M. A., & Plasman, J. S. (2018). From secondary to postsecondary: Charting an engineering career and technical education pathway. *Journal of Engineering Education*, *107*(4), 531–555. https://doi.org/10.1002/jee.20236

Haines, S. J., Francis, G. L., Mueller, T. G., Chiu, C. Y., Burke, M. M., Kyzar, K., Shepherd, K. G., Holdren, N., Aldersey, H. M., & Turnbull, A. P. (2017). Reconceptualizing family-professional partnership for inclusive schools: A call to action. *Inclusion*, *5*(4), 234–247. https://doi.org/10.1352/2326-6988-5.4.234

Harry, B. (2008). Collaboration with culturally and linguistically diverse families: Ideal vs. reality. *Exceptional Children*, *74*(3), 372–388. https://doi.org/10.1177/001440290807400306

Hill, N. E. (2022). Parental involvement in education: Toward a more inclusive understanding of parents' role construction. *Educational Psychologist*, *57*(4), 309–314. https://doi.org/10.1080/00461520.2022.2129652

Hughes, M., Valle-Riestra, D., & Arguelles, M. (2008). The voices of Latino families raising children with special needs. *Journal of Latinos and Education*, *7*(3), 241–257. https://doi.org/10.1080/15348430802100337

Individuals With Disabilities Education Act. (2004). Individuals with disabilities education act, 20 U.S.C. 1400 et seq.

Kalyanpur, M., Harry, B., & Skrtic, T. (2000). Equity and advocacy expectations of culturally diverse families' participation in special education. *International Journal of Disability, Development and Education, 47*(2), 119–136. https://doi.org/10.1080/713671106

Kelty, N. E., & Wakabayashi, T. (2020). Family engagement in schools: Parent, educator, and community perspectives. *Sage Open, 10*(4). https://doi.org/10.1177/2158244020973024

Leiter, V., & Wyngaarden Krauss, M. (2004). Claims, barriers, and satisfaction: Parents' requests for additional special education services. *Journal of Disability Policy Studies, 15*(3), 135–146. https://doi.org/10.1177/10442073040150030201

Luelmo, P., Kasari, C., & Fiesta Educativa, Inc. (2021). Randomized pilot study of a special education advocacy program for Latinx/minority parents of children with autism spectrum disorder. *Autism, 25*(6), 1809–1815. https://doi.org/10.1177/1362361321998561

Mandic, C. G., Rudd, R., Hehir, T., & Acevedo-Garcia, D. (2012). Readability of special education procedural safeguards. *The Journal of Special Education, 45*(4), 195–203. https://doi.org/10.1177/0022466910362774

Martinez-Torres, K., Boorom, O., Peredo, T. N., Camarata, S., & Lense, M. D. (2021). Using the ecological validity model to adapt parent-involved interventions for children with Autism Spectrum Disorder in the Latinx community: A conceptual review. *Research in Developmental Disabilities, 116*, 104012. https://doi.org/10.1016/j.ridd.2021.104012

Mueller, T. G., Milian, M., & Lopez, M. I. (2009). Latina mothers' views of a parent-to-parent support group in the special education system. *Research and Practice for Persons With Severe Disabilities, 34*(3–4), 113–122. https://doi.org/10.2511/rpsd.34.3-4.113

Muñiz, J. (2019). *Culturally responsive teaching: A 50-state survey of teaching standards.* Education Policy. https://www.newamerica.org/education-policy/reports/culturally-responsive-teaching/

National Center for Education Statistics (NCES). (2021). Report on the condition of education 2021. NCES 2021-144. https://nces.ed.gov/pubs2021/2021144.pdf. Accessed on July 27, 2023.

National Parent Technical Assistance Center. (2016). *Parent centers helping families.* Self-Publication.

Neece, C. L., Chan, N., Klein, K., Roberts, L., & Fenning, R. M. (2019). Mindfulness-based stress reduction for parents of children with developmental delays: Understanding the experiences of Latino families. *Mindfulness, 10*(6), 1017–1030. https://doi.org/10.1007/s12671-081-1011-3

Phillips, E. (2008). When parents aren't enough: External advocacy in special education. *The Yale Law Journal*, 1802–1853. https://doi.org/10.2307/20454695

Reardon, C. L., Hainline, B., Aron, C. M., Baron, D., Baum, A. L., Bindra, A., ..., & Engebretsen, L. (2019). Mental health in elite athletes: International Olympic Committee consensus statement (2019). *British Journal of Sports Medicine, 53*(11), 667–699. https://doi.org/10.1136/bjsports-2019-100715

Rios, K., Aleman-Tovar, J., & Burke, M. M. (2020). Special education experiences and stress among Latina mothers of children with autism spectrum disorder (ASD). *Research in Autism Spectrum Disorders, 73*, 101534. https://doi.org/10.1016/j.rasd.2020.101534

Rios, K., & Burke, M. M. (2020). The effectiveness of special education training programs for parents of children with disabilities: A systematic literature review. *Exceptionality*, 1–17. https://doi.org/10.1080/09362835.2020.1850455

Rios, K., & Burke, M. M. (2021). Facilitators and barriers to positive special education experiences and health among Latino families of children with disabilities: Two systematic literature reviews. *Review Journal of Autism and Developmental Disorders, 8*, 299–311. https://doi.org/10.1007/s40489-020-00220-z

Rios, K., Burke, M. M., & Aleman-Tovar, J. (2021). A study of the families included in receiving better special education services (FIRME) project for Latinx families of children with autism and developmental disabilities. *Journal of Autism and Developmental Disorders*, 1–15. https://doi.org/10.1007/s10803-020-04827-3

Rueda, R., Monzó, L., Shapiro, J., Gomez, J., & Blacher, J. (2005). Cultural models of transition: Latina mothers of young adults with developmental disabilities. *Exceptional Children, 71*, 401–414. https://doi.org/10.1177/001440290507100402

Shapiro, J., Monzo, L. D., Rueda, R., Gomez, J. A., & Blacher, J. (2004). Alienated advocacy: Perspectives of Latina mothers of young adults with developmental disabilities on service systems.

Mental Retardation: A Journal of Practices, Policy and Perspectives, 42(1), 37–54. https://doi.org/10.1352/0047-6765(2004)42%3c37:aapolm%3e2.0.co;2

Taylor, J. L., Hodapp, R. M., Burke, M. M., Waitz-Kudla, S. N., & Rabideau, C. (2017). Training parents of youth with autism spectrum disorder to advocate for adult disability services: Results from a pilot randomized controlled trial. *Journal of Autism and Developmental Disorders, 47*, 846–857. https://doi.org/10.1007/s10803-016-2994-z

Trainor, A. A. (2010). Diverse approaches to parent advocacy during special education home-school interactions: Identification and use of cultural and social capital. *Remedial and Special Education, 31*(1), 34–47. https://doi.org/10.1177/0741932508324401

Turnbull, A. P., Turnbull, H. R., Erwin, E. J., Soodak, L. C., & Shogren, K. A. (2015). *Families, professionals, and exceptionality: Positive outcomes through partnerships and trust.* Pearson.

Turnbull, A., Turnbull, H. R., Francis, G., Burke, M. M., Kyzar, K., Haines, S., Gershwin, T., Shepherd, K., Holdren, N., & Singer, G. (2021). Families and professionals: Trusting partnerships in general and special education. https://doi.org/10.1007/978-3-030-81277-5_3

CHAPTER 12

GENERAL EDUCATION TEACHERS AND THE SPECIAL EDUCATION PROCESS: ADVANCING VALUES

Sarah C. Urbanc[a] and Lucinda Dollman[b]

[a]Bradley University, USA
[b]Cindy Dollman Consulting LLC, USA

ABSTRACT

What does special education mean for general education teachers of students with disabilities? In this chapter, we share our approach to advancing values in the classroom placement of special education students in the general education setting. We will take the reader on a journey through time with "Jessie," a special education student, as we examine the historical exclusion of students with disabilities to their inclusion in general education schools, environments and finally, general education classrooms. In doing so, we will examine the evolution of the general education teacher's role and how the historical perspective impacts current practices. Then, we will elucidate the benefits of inclusion, not only for the special education student but for the nondisabled peers as well. We will recommend values that should be maintained and practices that should be examined. This chapter will conclude with a connection between the values and recommendations of best practices for inclusive instruction.

Keywords: Inclusion; general education; special education; best practices; classroom instruction; historical perspectives

INTRODUCING "JESSIE"

Jessie is a young girl residing in "middle America" with an IQ of 60, indicating a mild to moderate intellectual disability (Lee et al., 2022). Not only is she performing below her grade-level peers in reading, writing, and math, Jessie displays

Special Education
Advances in Special Education, Volume 38, 185–205
Copyright © 2024 Sarah C. Urbanc and Lucinda Dollman
Published under exclusive licence by Emerald Publishing Limited
ISSN: 0270-4013/doi:10.1108/S0270-401320240000038012

difficulties with time management, social skills, and personal care. She responds well to explicit instruction with modeling and repetition; however, she still struggles to keep up with grade-level, whole-group instruction. Jessie has consistently performed below grade level since Kindergarten. For the purposes of our journey through time, Jessie is a white, middle-class student, thus eliminating other factors that could contribute to where, when, and how Jessie is educated.

SPECIAL EDUCATION SETTINGS: A HISTORICAL PERSPECTIVE

A discussion of the current state of inclusion in the United States would not be complete without an examination of the past. Therefore, in this section, we will review the many catalysts that have contributed to the current state of inclusion in the general education setting. Fig. 12.1 highlights the acts, mandates, and laws that have influenced both general and special education settings and played pivotal roles in current inclusive practices.

Our journey begins at the very origins of the public school system. The Common School Movement, which is often considered to be the years between 1820 and 1860, was a time period when schools started replacing the church as the carrier of culture in the United States (Fraser, 2019). For the first time, tax monies were utilized to establish a "common" system of schooling, which is what we now refer to as the "public school system" (Fraser, 2019). The movement, led by Horace Mann, was in response to increased industrialization and urbanization occurring in the late 19th century (Urban et al., 2019).

Curriculum during the Common School Movement included reading, writing, math, history, self-discipline, and morality (Urban et al., 2019). In addition to a common curriculum, it also outlined laws requiring compulsory school

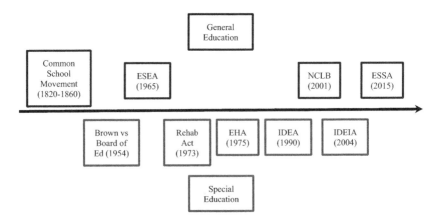

Fig. 12.1.   General and Special Education Laws. *Source:* Common School Movement (1820–1860).

attendance (Fraser, 2019). However, the question becomes, was it compulsory for *all*? For example, during this movement, Jessie would have been excluded from the public school system. Differentiation did not come to the forefront in education until educators, such as John Dewey, proposed a child-centered approach and sought to aid *all* children in reaching their full potential (Ye & Shih, 2021).

Programs for a few select students with special needs did exist in some capacity in the 19th century; however, they were more specifically intended for blind and/or deaf children and proved to be predominantly residential in nature (Sayers, 2020). Another notable detail is that schools such as these housed children with sensory deficits, not cognitive differences. For those with cognitive disabilities, like Jessie, special education programs simply were not available during this time. In the 19th century, the general education teacher would not have been aware of Jessie and would not have had any involvement in the development of her skills. It was not until the 20th century, when legislation was passed in the United States, that Jessie would find some degree of support in the public school system through special education initiatives (Itkonen, 2007).

Brown v. Board of Education (1954)

Brown v. Board of Education (1954) was a landmark decision because little progress had been made in inclusionary practices in the public school system in the past 100 years. *Brown v. Board of Education* (1954) was the first ruling regarding the segregation of schools in the United States based on race (Bowman, 2014). However, after the 1954 ruling, parents of students with disabilities also began filing lawsuits regarding segregation based on disabilities. This led to the enactment of the *Elementary and Secondary Education Act (ESEA) of 1965*.

1965 Elementary and Secondary Education Act

The *Elementary and Secondary Education Act* (1965) addressed some of the inequities students faced in the public school system. Unfortunately for Jessie, *ESEA* mostly focused on including "underprivileged" youth in the public school system rather than those with learning differences due to disability (ESEA, 1965). This means the general education teacher of the 1950s was working on the inclusion of students of different races, but not the inclusion of students like Jessie who had a disability. In 1966, the ESEA (1965) was amended and grant money was targeted to improve the education for handicapped children.

The initial *Elementary and Secondary Act* set specific guidelines by which children in America should be educated in grades Kindergarten through the 12th grade (ESEA, 1965). This means it was then required by law for Jessie to attend school. However, without special funding intended for students with special needs, schools without current programming at the time may not have had the means to establish the framework for including students with special needs into the general public school building (Winzer, 2000). Congress did add an amendment to ESEA (1965) just one year after it was ratified. This amendment included specific funding for new and existing programs for students with disabilities. This was the first time in the course of the American education system specific funding for students with special needs was designated. This became a gateway for local public schools to design and execute the compulsory attendance mandate for all K-12 students. At this time, some students with disabilities were invited into the public school, but unfortunately for some, there was still no place for them to attend (Winzer, 2000).

Under these changes, the general education teacher became more aware of the special needs population as they were invited into the public school building. However, the general education teacher's responsibilities for these students did not change (Winzer, 2000). Their focus was still centralized within their own classroom which was full of students without identified disabilities. For the general education teacher, *ESEA* simply mandated that local school systems incur some method of teaching children in Kindergarten all the way through 12th grade.

1970 Education of the Handicapped Act (PL 91-230)

In 1970, the *Education of the Handicapped Act (PL 91-230)* was ratified in a direct effort to develop programming for students with disabilities (EHA, 1970). It was estimated, at the time, that approximately eight million students enrolled in the public school system were diagnosed with a disability (Winzer, 2000). However, during that same time period, an additional one million students were excluded entirely from public education (Winzer, 2000).

Other cases, such as the *Pennsylvania Association for Retarded Children (PARC) v. Commonwealth of Pennsylvania* (1971) was the country's first "right to education" lawsuit (Itkonen, 2007). This case became a catalyst for change and led to the eventual passing of the *PL 94-142* in 1975. *PL 94-142* established accountability with local educational agencies, requiring them to evaluate students with disabilities and create an Individualized Education Plan (IEP) for each disabled student (Weintraub et al., 1976).

1975 The Education for All Handicapped Children Act (PL 94-142)

With the passage of *PL 94-142*, public schools were finally required to offer a seat in the building for Jessie and students like her (Itkonen, 2007). The purpose of *The Education for all Handicapped Children Act (EAHC) (1975)* was to bring about:

- a free and appropriate education;
- procedural safeguards to students and parents;
- assistance and support to states and local educational agencies for the education of all students; and
- evaluation of the effectiveness of the education provided to children with disabilities (Itkonen, 2007).

Parents in the 1970s were fighting for an education that looked similar to that of typically developing children. But in reality, while students like Jessie were taught in the local public schools, special classes were created within those schools to house those with intellectual disabilities (Winzer, 2000). The details and specificity of "free and appropriate" were not clearly defined under *PL 94-142 (1975)*. So, while Jessie was able to attend public school and had a special classroom designated for her, the setting, instructional design, assessment integrity, and other aspects of equity were markedly different from the students in the general education classroom settings, indicating the role of the general education teacher was still isolated from "the Jessies" of the world. Social policy advocates stressed the importance of access to the "building," before later attending to the quality of education provided to those with special needs in the 1990s (Itkonen, 2007). The provisions set forth in *PL 94-142 (1975)* were in effect from 1975 to 1990.

1990 Americans with Disabilities Act (ADA)

The *Americans with Disabilities Act (ADA)* expanded freedoms gained though the *Civil Rights Act of 1964* by prohibiting discrimination based on the presence of a disability (ADA, 1990). It required that reasonable accommodations be put in place for individuals with disabilities, as well as mandating all public accommodations be accessible to all individuals. With the passage of the ADA (1990), the list of what constitutes a disability widened to include health concerns such as attention deficit disorder (ADD) and epilepsy, as well mental health issues such as depression, obsessive compulsive disorder (OCD), and post-traumatic stress disorder (PTSD) (ADA, 1990).

This now means that Jessie's class has the potential for students with a wider range of exceptionalities. It also means that Jessie's school is required to create accessible means for those with physical impairments, leading to curb cutouts in the parking lot, ramps to enter the school building, and elevators to travel between school floors (ADA, 1990). Other requirements stemming from the passage of the ADA (1990) include service animals, interpreters, and qualified readers (ADA, 1990).

The ADA (1990) finally caught the attention of general education teachers as they were now required to attend IEP meetings. Although their role still did not significantly change in regards to the education of students with special needs, the general education setting was definitely adapting with the building accessibility features being added (Krent et al., 1993). Since the definition of disability expanded under ADA (1990), it is highly probable that general education teachers experienced students leaving their classrooms for the special education setting (Krent et al., 1993). Therefore, except passing by each other in the hallway, Jessie and the general education teachers had little to no interaction (Krent et al., 1993).

1990 Individuals with Disabilities Education Act (IDEA)

The *Education for All Handicapped Children of 1975* was reauthorized in 1990 as the IDEA. This reauthorization brought about numerous changes that affected the ways in which schools identified students with learning disabilities (LD). This shift focused on swift and accurate identification of children with disabilities in order to ensure students were partnered with research-based interventions and/or instruction that aided in the child's academic achievement (IDEA, 1990).

This reauthorization of *PL 94-142 (1975)* provided additional regulations to public schools for students with disabilities. Politicians intentionally chose to change the name of the law from EAHC (1975) to IDEA (1990) to emphasize that the education provided to students with disabilities would focus on the individual (Voulgarides, 2018). The intent was to create equality in the education provided to students with disabilities in order to match that provided to their typically developing peers (Voulgarides, 2018). The organization and language of the law provided specificity of how students with disabilities would be educated, while also expanding services to students with disabilities at both the school and federal levels (Voulgarides, 2018). This was done by designating four distinct parts as indicated in Table 12.1.

The *IDEA* (1990) expanded the four essential purposes of *EAHC* (1975) to include appropriate evaluations and parent and teacher participation. *IDEA* (1990) placed strategic requirements regarding student transition services, discipline to students with disabilities, as well as confidentiality of special education information. The intent was to prepare students for life after high school in terms of employment and independent living.

The *IDEA* (1990) was reauthorized under the same name in 1997. This reauthorization was a catalyst for significant role changes for general education teachers (Patterson, 2005). The 1997 *IDEA* required IEPs for all students receiving special education services between the ages of three and 21 (Patterson, 2005). These IEPs were to be developed with an IEP team composed of the special education teacher, special services personnel, and no less than one general education teacher (Patterson, 2005). The goal of this was to ensure the general education teacher became fully aware of the child's present level of performance, needs, and the child's instructional goals and objectives. A crucial component of the IEP specifies the extent to which the child would spend in the general education setting versus the special education setting. According to Patterson (2005), "IDEA '97 mandates that students with disabilities be educated with children without disabilities to the maximum extent appropriate, and that students with

Table 12.1. Individuals with Disabilities Education Act.

IDEA, Part A	General provisions of the law
IDEA, Part B	Assistance for the education of all children
IDEA, Part C	Inclusion of special education services to children birth to three years of age
IDEA, Part D	Federal level support programs that improve special education services

disabilities be removed to separate classes or schools only when the nature or severity of their disabilities is such that they cannot receive an appropriate education in a general education classroom with supplementary aides and services" (p. 65). This means that Jessie not only has a foot in the door but an equitable seat in the general education classroom.

No Child Left Behind (2002)

The Elementary and Secondary Education Act of 1965 was reauthorized and ratified in 2002 as the *No Child Left Behind Act (NCLB)*. This revision focused on providing fair, equal, and significant opportunities for all students to obtain a high quality of education (NCLB, 2002). *NCLB* sought to ensure that *all* students, regardless of disability or family income status, be provided with the education they need in order to achieve academic success (Darling-Hammond, 2004). *NCLB* (2002) set a precedent that all students, general education and special education alike, should reach at least minimum proficiency on state academic and achievement tests (Darling-Hammond, 2004). In order to ensure this level of academic success was achieved, the law stipulated that all general education teachers must be highly qualified in the area for which they were teaching (NCLB, 2002). The highly qualified requirement came down to an issue of appropriate licensure for general education teachers, while also placing caps on class size (NCLB, 2002).

Under *NCLB*, special education teachers would exude an increased awareness of Jessie, students similar to her, and their needs. During this time period, schools and teachers emphasized closing the achievement gap between special education and nondisabled peers (Darling-Hammond, 2004). While strides to equality had occurred under previous laws and policies, there was a commonly talked about, but perhaps not spoken about, understanding that students with disabilities performed lower and behind their typically developing peers (Darling-Hammond, 2004). More so, it was believed that this state of "behindness" was not temporary, but rather, would be the fate of students with disabilities for the entirety of their life (Cole, 2006). When discussing grade-level expectations, general education teachers may have excused Jessie and her cognitively impaired peers from not only meeting expectations but also from engaging in like-classroom activities, instructional strategies, and assessment methods. At the time, this type of thinking was not considered disparaging, but well-meaning and informed (Cole, 2006). Many general education teachers were unaware and unprepared to engage best practices for adapting and supporting students like Jessie (Cole, 2006).

2004 Individuals with Disabilities Improvement Act (IDEIA)

In 2004, the *IDEA of 1990* was reauthorized and renamed the *Individuals with Disabilities Improvement Act (IDEIA)*. Under *IDEIA* (2004), a student with an IEP must have both academic and functional goals that are aligned with the outcomes of their age-appropriate peers without disabilities. *IDEIA* (2004) also set the standard for reporting on the progress of students with disabilities in the standardized testing provided to nondisabled peers.

In order to align with *NCLB* (2002), *IDEIA* (2004) placed an emphasis on the requirement of "highly qualified" special education staff as it did with general education teachers under *NCLB* (2002) (IDEIA, 2004). For Jessie and her peers, this is the first time we see the mention of the "highly qualified" designation for staff specifically designated to educate students with special needs and oversee the execution of their IEPs (IDEIA, 2004). In addition, the 2004 reauthorization required an emphasis on reading and early intervention with support from a response to intervention process (IDEIA, 2004).

The push for better alignment of services opened the door to a deeper exploration of a free and appropriate education in the least restrictive environment (IDEIA, 2004). To accommodate the need to lessen the educational restrictiveness of separate classrooms for general and special education students, inclusion practices at the time widely presented as entire special education classes traveling to a general education class for some part of the day, typically associated with a particular content area, such as reading. Therefore, Jessie and her classmates would begin their day in their designated special education classroom then move to their general education classroom of the same grade where they would participate in grade-level instruction and activities based on grade-level curriculum and end of grade-level expectations (Yell et al., 2006). This reduced the number of special education minutes for Jessie, increased her access to the general education setting, and ensured her exposure to grade-level instruction. It did not, however, ensure access to the general education curriculum. Co-teaching practices were just beginning and it was rare to find much difference in the general education instruction even though there was a difference in the students sitting in the class (Scruggs et al., 2007).

2015 Every Student Succeeds Act (ESSA)

The most recent reauthorization of the *Elementary and Secondary Education Act* (1965) was named the *Every Student Succeeds Act (ESSA)* and was passed in 2015. *ESSA* (2015) put forth requirements for college and career readiness. This meant that all students, but especially high needs and disadvantaged students, should leave the public school system prepared for work in the "real-world." In 2020, the United States Department of Education found that almost half of the states were not in compliance with federal special education law (United States Department of Education, 2020).

The passage of *ESSA* (2015) did not make significant changes for Jessie. She is still able to attend general education classes with special education support as appropriate for her individual needs. Jessie must still participate in state testing; however *ESSA* (2015) did include alternative assessment methods for special education students, but limited its usage to 1% or less of each state's special education population (ESSA, 2015).

BENEFITS OF INCLUSIVE PRACTICES

Now that we have examined the evolution of the general education setting through a historical perspective, it is time to shift our focus to the benefits of current day inclusive practices. A classroom of true inclusive educational practices does not merely "pull-out" students with disabilities to work on alternative curricular goals and materials, but rather has students with diverse needs, experiences, and backgrounds learning the same or similar content side-by-side their nondisabled peers (Cross et al., 2004). This type of inclusive environment is not only beneficial for the students with diverse needs but for the general education students as well. In fact, the benefits of inclusive education have been well-documented in the literature for almost three decades (Cologon, 2019; Hehir et al., 2016; Lipsky & Gartner, 1995).

Helmstetter et al. (1998) posited that the general education classroom provided more direct and one-on-one instruction than separate, pull-out classrooms. In addition, the general education teacher covered more content utilizing tailored supports. Veritably, McDonnell et al. (2000) found that students with disabilities in the inclusive setting were 23 times more likely to receive one-on-one instruction than their peers in self-contained classrooms.

Another benefit of inclusive education is related to the progress made in the content areas by those with disabilities in the general education setting. Waldron et al. (2001) found that 34% of students with LD in a self-contained, special education setting made progress in math, while 41.7% of students in the general education classes showed growth. Similarly, in a study of 70,000 K-12 students with disabilities, Kurth and Mastergeorge (2010) found that students that were part of an inclusive classroom performed better on language and math skill assessments than those in self-contained classrooms only. Then in 2021, Cole et al. reaffirmed the positive correlation between inclusive education classrooms and student achievement in math and reading. Researchers attributed the greater gains to a higher degree of access to the core curriculum often found in inclusive classrooms (Agran et al., 2020; Soukup et al., 2007; Waldron et al., 2001).

In addition to benefits in math and reading, other researchers noted positive social and emotional connections. Hughes et al. (2013) identified that students with disabilities that were in inclusive settings exhibited improved communication skills and social interactions, such as increased self-determination. Shogren et al. (2015) indicated students of inclusion exude an increased sense of overall belonging. More so, in a longitudinal study of over 11,000 students, Wagner et al. (2006) revealed a positive correlation between students in an inclusive setting and fewer absences, disruptions for "bad" behavior, better financial outcomes post high school, and an increased ability to live independently.

Likewise, researchers have also documented a number of benefits to typically developing peers as well. Opportunities for friendships with those that are different from oneself arise in an inclusive setting and children are able to learn about their differences and how to accept and embrace them (Shogren et al., 2015). However, some parents of nondisabled students expressed concern that time would be taken away from their child in an inclusive classroom.

Dessemontet and Bless (2013) found no significant difference in academic achievement for typically developing students in a traditional general education versus inclusive setting.

The benefits listed above are not an exhaustive list but they do shine a spotlight on the positive outcomes that could manifest in regards to inclusive practices in the general education setting. This leaves one to wonder what is the current reality of inclusion in the general education setting and the role the general education teacher plays? Will an examination of classrooms reflect best practices or rather will instances of exclusion, masked under the title of inclusion present themselves?

DISCREPANCY BETWEEN THEORY AND PRACTICE

In an ideal educational world, Jessie's special and general education teacher(s) would receive training on best practices in co-teaching, which would include how to share responsibility for the needs and growth of Jessie's skills (Jorgensen et al., 2012). Co-planning time would be built into teachers' daily schedules in order to allow for planning of grade-appropriate content lessons that incorporate accessibility, or entry points, in order to accommodate Jessie's below grade-level skill level (Scruggs et al., 2007). Skill practice that correlates with the goals and objectives listed on Jessie's IEP would be interwoven into the instructional plans designed for all students (Jorgensren et al., 2012). Instruction and practice of explicit skills may also benefit other students in the general education setting who either also have IEPs with similar goals or other students in the general education setting that have aligning skill deficits (Jorgensen et al., 2012).

The instructional plans would include opportunities for both teaching professionals to support whole group, small group, and individual one-on-one teaching. Adapted assessments, both formative and summative, would create equity and accessibility for Jessie (Lovett & Lewandowski, 2015). Special testing adaptations such as increased time, small group settings, and tests read aloud would be upheld and monitored by Jessie's special education teacher (Lovett & Lewandowski, 2015). If and when assessment modification needs to occur, the special and general education teachers would work with administration to determine the appropriate method of indicating the change in student expectations within the grade book and all other grade reporting mechanisms in alignment with the protocols set forth in Jessie's IEP (Lovett & Lewandowski, 2015). On the chance that Jessie's special education teacher is unable to physically co-teach in one of Jessie's general education settings, co-planning with the general education teacher would still occur.

Co-responsibility for adaptations to the curriculum, instruction, and assessment would be discussed and implemented. All general education teachers would feel fully informed, supported, and skilled at differentiated classroom activities that not only work toward the goals and objectives listed in Jessie's IEP but also maintain integrity to the grade-level materials and the other students in the class.

Jessie's inclusion in the general education setting would lead to greater academic achievement than she could have attained without the grade-level exposure to the content and peer modeling she receives (Cologon, 2019). Appropriately supported inclusion in the general education setting has lifted limiting expectations that those with special needs inadvertently received under the previous self-contained model of special education services. Maximizing inclusion in the general education setting has also broadened Jessie's access to other children her age. This leads to greater developmentally appropriate social–emotional exposure and growth, allowing the school system to uphold the ideal of addressing the "whole-child (Trifone, 2021)."

Most educators have come to understand that theory and practice are not always in alignment. Therefore, a more probable scenario in today's "least restrictive environment" for Jessie would look different than those set forth in the synopsis above. According to Levenson (2020), "Kids are in the general education classroom, but still not primarily the responsibility of the general education teacher" (p. 18). The lack of shared ownership of Jessie's goals is not an uncommon scenario, as oftentimes general education teachers know students have particular learning needs, but may not know how to blend below grade-level needs into grade-level, whole-group instruction (Choi et al., 2020).

It is likely that in today's classroom, Jessie would spend the majority of her day in the general education classroom, seeing her special education teacher at limited points throughout the day (Choi et al., 2020). Her special education teacher would, of course, manage and monitor progress on her IEP goals and objectives, however most direct instruction and scaffolding for those goals would occur only with her special education teacher during the designated special education minutes listed in the IEP (Agran et al., 2020).

Due to scheduling limitations and teacher shortages, Jessie's general education and special education teachers may not have the opportunity to co-teach (Scruggs et al., 2007). In addition, more often than not, co-planning time would also not occur. This leaves the general education teacher with a limited understanding of how to implement appropriate accommodations for the grade-level curriculum that would provide accessibility to Jessie and her learning needs (Scruggs et al., 2007). Not only does this limit Jessie's participation in instruction and learning opportunities, it can also reflect limited membership in the general education setting (Soukup et al., 2007). Without the opportunity to meet and co-plan during the designated work day, support or guidance on how to adapt or create authentic assessment opportunities would also likely not occur (Soukup et al., 2007). Even if co-teaching opportunities were present, the likelihood of training and professional development on how to appropriately execute it may be limited or nonexistent for staff (Jorgensen et al., 2012).

Under *IDEIA* (2004), schools developed tiered instructional supports that increased the rate of learning in students who were not performing at grade-level. Therefore, Jessie should receive differentiated instruction in the general education classroom with both Tier Two and Tier Three academic and/or social–emotional interventions in place. However, with overcrowding at the top of the Multi-Tiered System of Support (MTSS) pyramid in most school systems, Jessie's learning needs are assumed taken care of with the special education services she is receiving (Scruggs et al., 2007).

This discrepancy between theory and practice brings to light the incredibly concerning predicament of who ultimately bears responsibility for Jessie's adequate yearly growth. Issues of accessibility, membership, and equity surface and we have to question whether the least restrictive environment is actually the most supportive environment for Jessie and students like her.

VALUES AND RECOMMENDATIONS

It has been well established that inclusive education reflects current best practices and totes a plethora of benefits to all students in the classroom (Cologon, 2019; Hehir et al., 2016; Lipsky & Gartner, 1995). However, separateness within schools relative to special and general education still exists and at times it appears that schools are operating as two worlds running parallel to each other instead of fusing together as one cohesive, inclusive environment (Kauffmann & Hornby, 2020). It is time to reframe inclusion and combine it with a "Can Do" approach in order to highlight high expectations for all. Therefore, in the section below Table 12.2, we will outline our values and recommendations for inclusive classroom practices for general education teachers.

Table 12.2. Values and Recommendations.

We Value:	So, We Recommend:
High Expectations for All Students	• A "can do" attitude • Growth mindset
Inclusive General Education Context	• Equal membership in general education classrooms • Full participation in instruction and learning activities
Differentiated Instruction and Support	• Exposure to grade-level curriculum • Meeting student needs at child's current level of performance • Access to the full spectrum of MTSS • Collaborative peer learning • Effective curricular supports

Authentic Assessment	• Ongoing assessment and evaluation of learning
	• Balanced assessment practices
	  – Performance-based assessments
	  – Formative and summative assessments
	  – Frequent progress monitoring
	  – Self-assessment
	• Short-term goal-setting

Social and Emotional Inclusion	• Friendships and social relationships • Support in navigating equitable social relationships • Augmentative and alternative communication supports and/or devices • Inclusive settings beyond the classroom (extracurricular activities)

Table 12.2. *(Continued)*

We Value:	So, We Recommend:
Advocacy	• Assist students in developing and exercising self-advocacy skills • Assume responsibility for identifying potential student needs • Advocate for and access needed resources • Corroborate with administration to acquire resources

Staff Collaboration	• Network of trained individuals
	  – General education teacher(s)
	  – Special education teacher(s)
	  – Parent(s)
	  – Related services provider(s)

Ongoing Professional Development	• Inclusion and inclusive practices • Co-teaching best practices • Communication enhancements • Collaboration • Strategies to support learning • Addressing the needs of the whole child
Future Planning	• Instill the concept of personal growth • Sustain engagement in school through graduation • Foster curiosity for life experiences after PK-12 (Birth-21) • Drive long-term goals with achievable steps toward their culmination • Use of community partnerships for employment opportunities • Build student self-determination skills

APPLICATION IN THE CLASSROOM

The values listed above are based upon best practices for those with disabilities in the general education setting as rooted in the literature. We then outlined corresponding recommendations based on those values. In this section, we will elaborate upon the recommendations and their application by teachers in a general education setting.

According to the National Center for Inclusive Education, there are 12 areas that school systems should address in order to establish and maintain a high-quality inclusive environment that supports all students in reaching their highest potential (Jorgensen et al., 2012). Many of those areas will be addressed and expanded upon below.

High Expectations for All Students

The first value is high expectations for all students, regardless of their disability status. It has been documented in the literature by researchers such as Quenemoen and Thurlow (2019) that there is a history of lower expectations for students with disabilities. In their 2019 brief, the National Center for Educational Outcomes published the reaffirming statement that "Disability does NOT mean inability" (p. 2). In fact, for students with disabilities, overcoming low expectations can sometimes be half the battle (Woodcock & Nicoll, 2022). Therefore, it is recommended that educators approach their teaching practices with a "can do" attitude and growth mindset, reflecting that ALL students can learn rigorous academic content when provided with the accurate amount and consistent level of support (Jorgensen et al., 2012).

A "can do" approach to teaching means that the focus is on what students *can* do instead of what they *cannot* do (Willner & Monroe, 2016). This, coupled with a growth mindset that focuses on guiding students to see that their hard work *can* and *will* help to improve their overall achievements, leads students to feel empowered and take a more active role in their own learning (Willner & Monroe, 2016). In order to foster a growth mindset, general education teachers first need to ensure that the classroom environment is warm and welcoming, in addition to being conducive to taking risks and learning from mistakes (Rhew et al., 2018). Students need a "safe" space to try new ideas and to learn that growth can come from failure.

Inclusive General Education Context

As previously stated, inclusion benefits more than just the students with disabilities, and the benefits extend beyond the classroom. When inclusion is executed as recommended, it provides opportunities for students of all cognitive abilities to connect, collaborate, share, and learn from each other (Cross et al., 2004). These types of opportunities simply would not exist if students with disabilities were placed in self-contained, special education classrooms (Meyer, 2001). Therefore, it is recommended that not only are students with disabilities placed in the general education setting but also be with their nondisabled peers for other activities throughout the day, such as physical education classes, extracurricular activities, recess, lunch, and study hall in order to present the necessary time for a friendship to grow (Jorgensen et al., 2012).

The general education teacher plays an integral role in creating a culture and climate of inclusion and acceptance, as well as advocating for students to be part of the general education environment as much as possible (Gnadinger, 2008). First, students with disabilities should be attending the same school they would attend if they did not have a disability (Cross et al., 2004). This is in addition to being an equal member and participant in the age-appropriate, general education classroom (Cross et al., 2004). Teachers need to ensure that all students can fully participate in instruction and learning activities by providing the appropriate level of scaffolds, supports, and accommodations/modifications needed to ensure equal access to the curriculum. In addition to the curriculum, schools and classrooms should be accessible to those with physical disabilities; therefore, it is imperative to arrange the classroom in a manner that is conducive to the mobility needs of all students (ADA, 1990). Finally, classroom teachers can advocate for those with disabilities to receive necessary related services during the school day through an MTSS and learning (Choi et al., 2020).

Differentiated Instruction and Support

As referenced above, all students deserve the right to equal access to the core curriculum. Even students with disabilities require exposure to grade-level curriculum. It becomes the duty of the general education teacher to utilize effective curricular strategies to help meet students with disabilities at their current level of functioning (Choi et al., 2020). Learning to successfully differentiate instructional delivery, curriculum, and supports is key to providing students with the necessary exposure to grade-level curriculum (Cross et al., 2004). In addition, it is also important for the general education teacher to access the full spectrum of MTSS. Within the classroom, the general educator can also incorporate collaborative peer learning. Researchers recommend using a method of support, such as peer-mediated instruction (PMI) (Gnadinger, 2008). PMI is the use of a tutor/tutee system where a student with a disability is paired with a nondisabled student to work on advancement of basic academic and social skills (Sailor, 2002). PMI is often cited as an effective strategy in inclusive education classrooms at both the primary and secondary levels (Scruggs et al., 2012). When incorporated with fidelity, its use resulted in advancements in academics *and* social skills for both the student with the disability and the paired nondisabled student (McMaster et al., 2007).

Authentic Assessment

The next recommendation is regarding ongoing authentic assessment and evaluation of learning. Traditional paper and pencil style of assessments do not always allow the learner to demonstrate the full range of their understanding of the content (Ysseldyke et al., 2023). Therefore, it is recommended that inclusive assessment practices be incorporated by the general education teacher in the form of balanced assessment practices (Ysseldyke et al., 2023). These practices include the use of authentic assessments such as performance-based assessments and self-assessments that promote student participation in the demonstration of their own learning and an awareness of what direction their learning should go (Ysseldyke et al., 2023). Assessment, afterall, should be more than just grading student work; it should be a checkpoint toward mastery of content objectives and standards as documented through both formative and summative assessments by the classroom teacher (Sackstein, 2020). It is through these checkpoints that interventions can be identified in order to keep student learning on track. Under a balanced assessment system, the classroom teacher should also utilize the data from a variety of formative, summative, formal, informal, local, state/national, and other measures of assessment in order to accurately gauge a student's overall performance (Sackstein, 2020). Therefore, general education teachers also play a pivotal role in data collection and analysis through ongoing progress monitoring and short-term goal setting.

Social and Emotional Inclusion

Teachers' work with students should not strictly be tied to academics. Instead, researchers recommend a whole child approach that encompasses the full scope of a child's developmental needs (Trifone, 2021). This means that in addition to *curricular* inclusion, students with disabilities also warrant *social and emotional* inclusion as well. One obvious way that a classroom teacher can help to achieve this is by establishing an inclusive setting that nurtures friendships and social relationships. General education teachers should dispel myths regarding disabilities, in addition to addressing any challenges that students may face in the classroom, all while ensuring that the overall classroom environment is a welcoming and safe environment. Depending on the disability that a student possesses, he/she may require support in navigating equitable social relationships (Mahoney et al., 2021). Therefore, the classroom teacher can utilize social stories and bring awareness to the topic of disabilities in an open and controlled forum (Mahoney et al., 2021). This will allow all students to understand their role in the friendship.

Students with disabilities may also need to incorporate augmentative and alternative communication devices into the general education setting. These should be supported and reinforced by the general education teacher (Jorgensen et al., 2012). This contributes to students' full participation in all social aspects of the schooling process as well as full access to the curriculum; however, student choice regarding usage and implementation into the classroom setting should be honored (Kent-Walsh & Light, 2003). Teachers need to help guide students in the device's use, as well as help students to navigate any social exclusion or lack of equity in relationships with nondisabled peers attributed to the device. Therefore, training for general education staff is also recommended.

Establishing an inclusive setting within the classroom is imperative; however, it should not stop there. Schools need to ensure that inclusive settings extend beyond the classroom walls into the larger school environment and community as well. Students with disabilities deserve the right to be included in extracurricular activities and participate in community functions in order to achieve full and equitable levels of participation.

Advocacy

A similar role for general education teachers is one that urges students in special education programs to be self-advocates and exercise self-determination. Wehmeyer et al. (2010) stated that components of self-advocacy include, "choice-making, decision-making, and problem solving skills; goal setting and attainment skills, self-management skills; and self-advocacy and leadership skills, as well as perceptions of control and efficacy and self-awareness and knowledge" (p. 477). In order to accomplish this, teachers can work with students to help them recognize when they are in need of assistance and ways to ask for help. This process can be made visible by teachers modeling their thinking out loud through the process of oral metacognition. Another way the general education teacher can assist students in navigating this process is to ensure they have the necessary resources available to aid them in reaching their full potential (Wehmeyer et al., 2010). This may include corroborating with administration in order to acquire the necessary resources. When students know what options are available to them, they are more likely to utilize their resources and make informed decisions. Finally, modeling a growth mindset, as discussed earlier, further aids students with disabilities in understanding that it is ok to not have the answer to every problem. Operating under a growth mindset, students come to realize that advocacy assists in the learning process (Rhew et al., 2018).

Staff Collaboration

Collaboration is also a key component to any successful inclusive setting. Therefore, general education teachers should work together with administrators, special educators, parents, and related service providers in order to have a network of trained individuals working together for the interest of *all* students (Scruggs et al., 2007). When a collaborative, inclusive approach is taken toward education, it often results in increased academic achievement and engagement, as well as a more robust interaction between peers and student-initiated interactions (Hunt et al., 2003). It is important that all members of the IEP or MTSS team understand their role in supporting students' academic, emotional, and behavioral growth as well as be provided ample and ongoing time to meet and discuss student progress and planning for instruction and interventions (Scruggs et al., 2007). In addition, many students with disabilities are provided services by organizations external to the local school district. There are numerous organizations that are able to provide a wealth of in-depth knowledge, expertise, and services in supporting students with disabilities. Therefore, partnerships with both families and community organizations are recommended in order to fully support the needs of diverse learners (Schifter, 2015).

Ongoing Professional Development

Once collaborative roles have been established, teachers should receive ongoing professional development regarding how to effectively lead an inclusive classroom that addresses the needs of the whole child (Jorgensen et al., 2012). This should encompass training on how to incorporate a curriculum that is based on the same standards for all students, including instructional practices that embody differentiation based on the needs of the learners. Teachers also need guidance as to which academic and behavioral supports to utilize while supporting all learners (Jorgensen et al., 2012). In addition to general inclusive practices, general educators need to also receive ongoing support in the field of co-teaching. In order to have a seamless transition between and among the classroom teacher and special educator, both parties need ongoing training in reference to co-planning, instructing, and assessment in order to maximize the potential of the arrangement for both students and staff alike. Researchers such as Gersten et al. (2006) recommend the use of supports that have an overall beneficial curricular outcome. This includes communication enhancements and curricular supports such as graphic/advanced organizers, mnemonics, as well as content enhancement routines, strategy instruction, supplementing grade-level textbooks with other materials, and an inquiry approach to science (Gersten et al., 2006). These types of approaches have proven to be effective with *all* learners.

Future Planning

Finally, inclusive programs should include the student with a disability with future planning and goal setting. While this may not always be the role of the general education teacher, it is important that at all ages and grades the classroom teacher is instilling a love of learning, fostering curiosity for life experiences, and self-determination skills in order for all students to reap the rewards and benefits of sustained engagement in school through graduation and beyond. One study found that students that take part in a quality inclusive program are five times more likely to graduate from high school and twice as likely to go on to higher education (Schifter, 2015). School systems that are fully inclusive and have connections and partnerships with the community can help students obtain employment once they are out of the school system. In fact, students that were part of inclusive styles of education make more money and are more likely to live independently than those whose schools did not guide them through the transition period (Hehir et al., 2016).

CONCLUSION

Jessie's journey throughout the ages has moved from that of full exclusion of the public educational system to one where she is fully immersed in the general education setting. During the start of the public education system in the United States, there was no place for Jessie to receive any type of formal educational or vocational training. With the passage and reauthorization of numerous laws, a more equitable public education became available to all students.

Although it has taken almost 200 years of advocacy and law-making for Jessie to be able to spend a significant portion of her day in a general education classroom, new opportunities exist. Today, these opportunities encompass full support by both the general and special education staff, as well as scaffolded instruction that meets her unique needs. The role of the general education teacher has changed over time and Jessie's teachers now incorporate instructional strategies that are intentionally embedded to help close the achievement gap between her and her typically developing peers. Jessie is now able to achieve at a higher level which will help her to close the achievement gap that exists between her and her peers. She also has a variety of opportunities beyond 12th grade, including future educational settings. In today's schools, Jessie has a higher chance of receiving the same diploma as her typical developing peers due to the advocacy and support roles played by her classroom teachers. Her parents are able to be important members in the educational decision-making team, alongside the general education and special education teachers. Jessie has truly become a student of the school where all teachers consider her "their student." In order to actualize the equity available to Jessie, the values and recommendations advised are fostered and embedded within the general education teacher's classroom and are reflected across the entire public system at-large. This is what the special education process now means for general education teachers and how to truly advance values that support the diverse needs and lived experiences of each and every student.

REFERENCES

Agran, M., Jackson, L., Kurth, J. A., Ryndak, D., Burnette, K., Jameson, M., Zagona, A., Fitzpatrick, H., & Wehmeyer, M. (2020). Why aren't students with severe disabilities being placed in general education classrooms: Examining the relations among classroom placement, learner outcomes, and other factors. *Research and Practice for Persons With Severe Disabilities*, *45*(1), 4–13.

Americans with Disabilities Act of 1990, 42 U.S. 12101 (1990).

Bowman, K. (2014). *The pursuit of racial and ethnic equality in American public schools: Mendez, Brown, and beyond.* Michigan State University Press.

Brown v. Board of Education, 347 U.S. 483 (1954).

Choi, J. H., McCart, A. B., & Sailor, W. (2020). Reshaping educational systems to realize the promise of inclusive education. *Forum for International Research in Education*, *6*(1), 8–23.

Cole, C. (2006). Closing the achievement gap series, part III: What is the impact of NCLB on the inclusion of students with disabilities? *Center for Evaluation and Education Policy Brief*, *4*(1–2).

Cole, S. M., Murphy, H. R., Frisby, M. B., Grossi, T. A., & Bolte, H. R. (2021). The relationship of special education placement and student academic outcomes. *The Journal of Special Education*, *54*(4), 217–227.

Cologon, K. (2019). *Towards inclusive education: A necessary process of transformation.* Children and Young People with Disability Australia.

Cross, F. A., Traub, E. K., Hutter-Pishgahi, L., & Shelton, G. (2004). Elements of successful inclusion for children with significant disabilities. *Topics in Early Childhood Special Education*, *24*(3), 169–183.

Darling-Hammond, L. (2004). From "Separate but Equal" to "No Child Left Behind": The collision of new standards and old inequalities. In D. Meier & G. Wood (Eds.), *How the no child left behind act is damaging our children and our schools: Many children left behind* (pp. 3–32). Beacon Press.

Dessemontet, S. R., & Bless, G. (2013). The impact of including children with intellectual disability in general education classrooms on the academic achievement of their low-, average-, and high-achieving peers. *Journal of Intellectual & Developmental Disabilities*, *38*(1), 23–30.

EAHC. (1975). No. 94-142, 89 Stat. 773 (codified as amended at 20 U.S.C. § 1400-61 (1982)).

Education of the Handicapped Act of 1970, 91-230 U.S. 1926 (1970).

Elementary and Secondary Education Act of 1965, 89-10 U.S. 2632 (1965).

Every Student Succeeds Act, 20 U.S.C. § 6301 (2015). https://www.congress.gov/114/plaws/publ95/PLAW-114publ95.pdf

Fraser, J. W. (2019). *The school in the United States: A documentary history* (4th ed.). Routledge.

Gersten, R., Baker, S. K., Smith-Johnson, J., Domino, J., & Peterson, A. (2006). Eyes on the prize: Teaching complex historical content to middle school students with learning disabilities. *Council for Exceptional Children*, *72*(3), 264–280.

Gnadinger, C. (2008). Peer-mediated instruction: Assisted performance in the primary classroom. *Teachers and Teaching*, *14*, 129–142.

Hehir, T., Grindal, T., Freeman, B., Lamoreau, R., Borquaye, Y., & Burke, S. (2016). *A summary of evidence on inclusive education.* ABT Associates.

Helmstetter, E., Curry, C. A., Brennan, M., & Sampson-Saul, M. (1998). Comparison of general and special education classrooms of students with severe disabilities. *Education and Training in Mental Retardation and Developmental Disabilities*, *33*(3), 216–227.

Hughes, C., Cosgriff, J. C., Agran, M., & Washington, B. H. (2013). Student self-determination: A preliminary investigation of the role of participation in inclusive settings. *Education and Training in Autism and Developmental Disabilities, 48*(1), 3–17.

Hunt, P., Soto, G., Maier, J., & Doering, K. (2003). Collaborative teaming to support students at risk and students with severe disabilities in general education classrooms. *Exceptional Children, 69*(3), 315–332.

Individuals with Disability Education Act, 91-230 U.S. 601 (1990).

Individuals with Disabilities Education Improvement Act, 108-446 U.S. 1440 (2004).

Itkonen, T. (2007). PL 94-142: Policy, evolution, and landscape shift. *Issues in Teacher Education, 16*(2), 7–17.

Jorgensen, C. M., McSheehan, M., Schuh, M., & Sonnenmeier, R. (2012). *Essential best practices in inclusive schools.* University of New Hampshire, Institute on Disability. https://scholars.unh.edu/cgi/viewcontent.cgi?article=1069&context=iod

Kauffmann, J. M., & Hornby, G. (2020). Inclusive vision versus special education reality. *Education Sciences, 10,* 1–13.

Kent-Walsh, J., & Light, J. (2003). General education teachers' experiences with inclusion of students who use augmentative and alternative communication. *Augmentative and Alternative Communication, 19*(2), 104–124.

Krent, N. F., Cairns, S. S., & Dodge, J. A. (1993). *Americans with Disabilities Act: Its impact on public schools.* National School Boards Association. Council of School Attorneys. https://files.eric.ed.gov/fulltext/ED435137.pdf

Kurth, J. A., & Mastergeorge, A. M. (2010). Academic and cognitive profiles of students with autism: Implications for classroom practice and placement. *International Journal of Special Education, 25*(2), 8–14.

Lee, K., Cascella, M., & Marwaha, R. (2022). *Intellectual disability.* Stat Pearls Publishing. https://www.ncbi.nlm.nih.gov/books/NBK547654/

Levenson, N. (2020). *Six shifts to improve special education and other interventions: A commonsense approach for school leaders.* Harvard Education Press.

Lipsky, D., & Gartner, A. (1995). The evaluation of inclusive education programs. *NCERI Bulletin, 2*(2), 2–8.

Lovett, B. J., & Lewandowski, L. J. (2015). *Testing accommodations for students with disabilities: Research-based practice.* American Psychological Association.

Mahoney, J. L., Weissberg, R. P., Greenberg, M. T., Dusenbury, L., Jagers, R. J., Niemi, K., Schlinger, M., Schlund, J., Shriver, T. P., VanAusdal, K., & Yoder, N. (2021). Systemic social and emotional learning: Promoting educational success for all preschool to high school students. *American Psychologist, 76*(7), 1128–1142.

McDonnell, J., Thorson, N., & McQuivey, C. (2000). Comparison of the instructional contexts of students with severe disabilities and their peers in general education classes. *The Journal of the Association for Persons with Severe Handicaps, 25,* 54–58.

McMaster, K. L., Fuchs, D., & Fuchs, L. S. (2007). Promises and limitations of peer-assisted learning strategies in reading. *Learning Disabilities: A Contemporary Journal, 5*(2), 97–112.

Meyer, L. H. (2001). The impact of inclusion on children's lives: Multiple outcomes, and friendship in particular. *International Journal of Disability. Development and Education, 48,* 9–31.

No Child Left Behind Act of 2001, 107-110 U.S. 115, Stat. 1425 (2002).

Patterson, K. (2005). What classroom teachers need to know about IDEA'97. *Kappa Delta Pi Record, 41*(2), 62–67.

Quenemoen, R. F., & Thurlow, M. L. (2019). *Students with disabilities in educational policy, practice, and professional judgment: What should we expect (NCEO Report 413).* University of Minnesota, National Center on Educational Outcomes.

Rhew, E., Piro, J. S., Goolkasian, P., Cosentino, P., & Palikara, O. (2018). The effects of a growth mindset on self-efficacy and motivation. *Cogent Education, 5*(1), 1–16.

Sackstein, S. (2020). Shifting the grading mindset. In S. Blum (Ed.), *Upgrading: Why rating students undermines learning (and what to do instead)* (pp. 74–81). West Virginia University Press.

Sailor, W. (2002). *President's Commission on Excellence in Special Education: Research Agenda Task Force*; Nashville, TN.

Sayers, E. E. (2020). White nation, black deportation, deaf education: The agenda of the founders of sign language education in the United States. *American Annals of the Deaf*, *165*(2), 135–156.

Schifter, L. A. (2015). Using survival analysis to understand graduation of students with disabilities. *Exceptional Children*, *82*(4), 479–496.

Scruggs, T. E., Mastropieri, M. A., & Marshak, L. (2012). Peer-mediated instruction in inclusive secondary social studies learning: Direct and indirect learning effects. *Learning Disabilities Research & Practice*, *27*(1), 12–20.

Scruggs, T. E., Mastropieri, M., & McDuffie, K. A. (2007). Co-teaching in inclusive classrooms: A metasynthesis of qualitative research. *Exceptional Children*, *73*(4), 392–416.

Shogren, K., Gross, J., Forber-Pratt, A., Francis, G., Satter, A., Blue-Banning, M., & Hill, C. (2015). The perspectives of students with and without disabilities on inclusive schools. *Research and Practice for Persons with Severe Disabilities*, *40*(4), 1–39.

Soukup, H., Wehmeyer, M., Bashinski, S., & Bovaird, J. (2007). Classroom variables and access to the general curriculum for students with disabilities. *Exceptional Children*, *74*, 101–120.

Trifone, J. D. (2021). *Whole-child teaching: A framework for meeting the needs of today's students*. Rowman & Littlefield Publishing Group, Inc.

United States Department of Education. (2020, November). *Determination letters on state implementation of IDEA*. https://www2.ed.gov/fund/data/report/idea/ideafactsheet-determinations2020.pdf

Urban, W. J., Wagoner, J. L., & Gaither, M. (2019). *American education: A history* (6th ed.). Routledge.

Voulgarides, C. (2018). *Does compliance matter in special education? IDEA and the hidden inequities of practice*. Teachers College Press.

Wagner, M., Newman, L., Cameto, R., & Lavine, P. (2006). The academic achievement and functional performance of youth with disabilities. *A Report from the National Longitudinal Transition Study-2cite (NLTS2). NCSER 2006-3000*. Online Submission.

Waldron, N., Cole, C., & Majd, M. (2001). *The academic progress of students across inclusive and traditional settings: A two-year study*. Indiana Institute on Disability and Community.

Wehmeyer, M. L., Shogren, K. A., Zager, D., Smith, T. E. C., & Simpson, R. (2010). Research-based principles and practices for educating students with autism: Self-determination and social interactions. *Education and Training in Autism and Developmental Disabilities*, *45*, 475–486.

Weintraub, F. J., Abeson, A., Ballard, J., & LaVor, M. (1976). *Public policy and the education of exceptional children*. The Council for Exceptional Children.

Willner, L. S., & Monroe, M. (2016). *Using a "can do" approach to ensure differentiated instruction intentionally supports the needs of language learners*. Colorin Colorado. https://www.colorincolorado.org/article/using-can-do-approach-ensure-differentiated instruction-intention-ally-supports-needs#:~:text=The%20%22Can%20Do%22%20Approach&text=By%20ensuring%20the%20approach%20to,areas%20of%20weakness%20or%20struggle

Winzer, M. A. (2000). The inclusion movement: Review and reflections on reform in special education. In M. Winzer & K. Mazurek (Eds.), *Special education in the 21st century* (pp. 5–26). Gallaudet University Press.

Woodcock, S., & Nicoll, S. (2022). "It isn't you": Teachers' beliefs about inclusive education and their responses toward specific learning disabilities. *Psychology in the Schools*, *59*(1), 765–783.

Ye, Y., & Shih, Y. (2021). Development of John Dewey's educational philosophy and its implications for children's education. *Policy Futures in Education*, *19*, 877–890.

Yell, M. L., Shriner, J. G., & Katsiyannis, A. (2006). Individuals with Disabilities Education Improvement Act of 2004 and IDEA regulations of 2006: Implications for educators, administrators, and teacher trainers. *Focus on Exceptional Children*, *39*(1), 1–24.

Ysseldyke, J. E., Chaparro, E. A., & VanDerHeyen, A. (2023). *Assessment in special and inclusive education* (14th ed.). PRO-ED Publishing, Inc.

CHAPTER 13

SCHOOL LEADERS AND ADMINISTRATORS AND THE SPECIAL EDUCATION PROCESS: ADVANCING VALUES

Floyd D. Beachum and Yalitza Corcino-Davis

Lehigh University, USA

ABSTRACT

The evolution and trends of special education and educational leadership are evident, especially in recent years. The former has strived to provide equitable educational opportunities to students with disabilities. The latter has dealt with how people in positions of authority in K-12 schools create policy, use resources, and influence other people to achieve educational goals. Together, these notions constitute an idea that school leaders and administrators can provide insight, oversight, assistance, and guidance toward creating educational environments for students with and without disabilities. This chapter examines the current state of special education and educational leadership by exploring the evolution of special education, relevant legal cases, and the enactment of inclusive education. Furthermore, this chapter addresses contemporary issues for leaders, such as the influence of the COVID-19 pandemic, while dealing with special education and the increasing pressure from families for equity for students with disabilities.

Keywords: Special education; changes; students; families; school; leaders

INTRODUCTION – CONTEXT REALLY MATTERS

Much of the modern context for special education and the ensuing controversies stem from duality and competing interests. The situation is steeped in paradox. For

Special Education
Advances in Special Education, Volume 38, 207–223
Copyright © 2024 Floyd D. Beachum and Yalitza Corcino-Davis
Published under exclusive licence by Emerald Publishing Limited
ISSN: 0270-4013/doi:10.1108/S0270-401320240000038013

instance, K-12 schools must try to educate large numbers of students while at the same time addressing the specific concerns of students with special needs. School leaders must make utilitarian decisions daily (decisions that will result in the greatest good for the greatest number); at the same time, they must also seek to protect the rights of numerical minorities, such as students with special needs (Starratt, 1991; Theoharis, 2009). These leaders must deal with pressures, mandates, and vague policies from state education departments while also dealing with the particular demands and concerns of students with disabilities and their families at the school level. These realities can cause confusion, anxiety, and disagreement and may also lead to situations of competing interests. In these circumstances, school leaders and administrators primarily shape their opinions of what is best for the school at the expense of individual students, like students with special needs. They come from a mental space where they believe they are acting in the best interest of the school or district, even if it means going against the family of a student with a disability who may be asking for additional resources, modifications, and instructional aides, to mention a few (McCray et al., 2021). These difficult decisions may render administrators noncollaborative, disagreeable, unsupportive, or negative.

The above perspective does not have to be reality. No social arrangement has to be a constant (Starratt, 1991). In other words, things do not have to be a certain way. Many situations are open to change depending on the will of the people involved. "In integrated, socially just schools and districts, leaders create integrated structures, ensure their schools are safe and that all students feel valued and feel a sense of belonging, and make the high achievement of every single student in the school their highest priority" (Capper & Frattura, 2009, p. xvii). In this case, school leaders should come from a mental space of greater collaboration, humility, and understanding (McCray et al., 2021; Scanlan, 2023). Exploring the historical and legal foundations of special education in the United States is necessary to understand contemporary challenges. The question continues to be, what values have been kept, appreciated, or devalued? This chapter responds to this question.

SPECIAL EDUCATION IN THE UNITED STATES: REVISITED

Throughout history, social perceptions of and commitment to educating people with disabilities waxed and waned depending on public attitudes. According to Winzer (1993), "a society's treatment of those who are weak and dependent is one critical indicator of its social progress. Social attitudes concerning the education and care of exceptional individuals reflect general cultural attitudes concerning the obligations of a society to its individual citizens" (p. 3). Prior to the 1700s, people with disabilities were considered outliers in society and were predominantly (a) treated with contempt, (b) abused, (c) disregarded, and (d) hidden from the public. Persons with disabilities were not considered people with human rights, and "legal mandates denied them basic civil rights and theological cannons excluded them from church membership; philosophy pronounced them incapable of mental or moral improvement" (Winzer, 1993, p. 4). Nevertheless, by the end of the 18th century, social attitudes toward people with disabilities shifted and special education became an established area of education (Winzer, 1993). The change in public perception, treatment, and education of people with disabilities resulted from the philosophical movement started in Europe known as the Enlightenment. The Enlightenment movement sought to create a just and fair society by abolishing social classes and granting each person full human rights and liberties. During this time, many philanthropic organizations and charities served people with disabilities to help improve the lives of children, women, and the poor (Winzer, 1993).

Religious and philanthropic organizations initiated the first schools serving the needs of children with disabilities in the United States (Winzer, 1993). The American School for the Deaf (then called the Connecticut Asylum for the Education and Instruction of Deaf and Dumb Persons), the first school dedicated to serving children with disabilities, was founded in Connecticut by Thomas Gallaudet in 1817 (American School for the Deaf, n.d.; Temple University, 2022; Winzer, 1993). Throughout the 1800s, schools were created for deaf and blind students and those with mental and intellectual disabilities in various states. Additionally, reformatories were created to house neglected children and juvenile prisons for those considered delinquent. However, "a large number of those who were crippled, emotionally disturbed, multiply handicapped, or suffering from a range of undetected or low incidence conditions were simply excluded from special institutions" (Winzer, 1993, p. 83). While the Enlightenment movement helped to increase educational opportunities for some children with disabilities, the overall gains were small. Most children at the time, whether disabled or not, did not attend school. Additionally, public attitudes toward people with disabilities would shift toward the late 1800s and early 1900s. As philanthropic interest in special education waned, the responsibility of schools for children with disabilities shifted from private charitable organizations to the state (Winzer, 1993).

The first special education classroom in a public school system in the United States was taught by Elizabeth E. Farrell in New York City at the turn of the 19th century (Duchan, 2023; Kode, 2002). Her class consisted of 19 children, ages 8–16. The children were labeled misfits because they had behavioral, physical, and mental health or intellectual challenges that impeded them from making academic progress in the general classroom (Filiaci, 2017; Kode, 2002). Through her work with the children in her classroom, Farrell created the first framework for working with children with disabilities, and some of her methods are best practices in the field of education today. Her special education model recommended that lessons be individualized according to the child's ability (Kode, 2002). She explained that:

> every teacher will know what the ability of the child is and the child's burden as it is represented by the course of study he undertakes. That burden will be trimmed to his ability. It will not be the same burden for every child but will be a burden for every child commensurate with his ability to bear. (Farrell via Kode, 2002, p. 26)

Farrell also believed traditional teaching methods at the time prioritized the "study of books," which did not encourage her students to want to learn. Instead, she sought nontraditional or modified methods of teaching the curriculum to increase students' interest in school and their understanding of the subject. For example, instead of memorizing "arithmetic and multiplication tables, they had wood and tools, and things with which to build and make" (Farrell via Kode, 2002, p. 27). Farrell's teaching methods proved effective, and she became the director of special education programs in New York City in 1906 (Duchan, 2023). From 1899 to 1911, special education classrooms in New York City grew from one classroom to 131 due to her success and methodology. Eventually, she would teach special education courses at the university level (Duchan, 2023). Some of her influences in the field of special education include (a) housing special education classrooms within public schools instead of special schools, (b) cautioning on the overreliance on test scores to measure ability, (c) placing students according to their education needs instead of their test scores, (d) integrating special education children into regular classrooms instead of maintaining them in separate classrooms, (e) educating all children in schools regardless of their ability, and (f) identifying the individual special education needs and related services necessary for each child with a disability to learn (Duchan, 2023).

ISSUES OF STERILIZATION, NEGLECT, AND EXCLUSION OF INDIVIDUALS WITH DISABILITIES

During the late 1800s and early 1900s, societal attitudes and perceptions of people with disabilities retrogressed. While Farrell and other early special education proponents made great strides in serving children with disabilities in public schools, another movement simultaneously took place in the United States. "The role of institutions shifted from protecting those who are 'different' from the public to protecting the public from those who are 'different'" (Kode, 2002, p. 8). Influential research published during this time associated people with disabilities with criminal activity, evil, disease, and poverty (Kode, 2002). Researchers argued that people with mental, intellectual, and physical disabilities inherit their conditions from their parents and could pass down the condition from one generation to another (Indiana Historical Bureau, n.d.; Kode, 2002).

The idea of associating disability with genetics was born from Francis Galton's theory of Eugenics (N.H.G.R.I., n.d.). Eugenics means "relating to or fitted for the production of good offspring" (Merriam-Webster, n.d.a). The theory proposes that genetics could improve humanity through the selective breeding of specific populations (Merriam-Webster, n.d.b). Those labeled genetically "unfit" included "ethnic and religious minorities, people with disabilities, the urban poor, and L.G.B.T.Q. individuals" (N.H.R.I., n.d., para. 2). To control the reproduction of those considered "unfit," many states passed sterilization laws. For example, in 1907, the state of Indiana passed the first eugenic sterilization law that mandated the sterilization of "criminals, idiots, rapists, and imbeciles" in the custody of the state (Indiana History Bureau, n.d., para. 13). The law was deemed unconstitutional because it violated the due process clause of the 14th Amendment that declares that a state shall not "deprive any person of life, liberty, or property, without due process of law" (US Const. Amend. XIV). However, the Court of Appeals overturned the lower court's decision, and the sterilization law remained in effect until 1974 (Indiana History Bureau, n.d.). Additionally, 24 other states passed sterilization laws during this time (Temple University, 2022). Over 30,000 people with disabilities were estimated to be sterilized by the early 1960s (Kode, 2002).

DISABILITY RIGHTS MOVEMENT IN EDUCATION

In the first half of the 20th century, the idea of teaching special needs students in public schools gained momentum. "The movement of disabled students from institutionalization to public school – from isolation to segregation – may be dated from about 1910 with the formation of permanent segregated classes in public schools" (Winzer, 1993, p. 367). During this time, people with disabilities, parents, and educators created disability advocacy organizations. For example, one of the most prominent disability advocacy organizations today, the Association for Retarded Citizens, now known as A.R.C., was started in 1950 by parents of children with disabilities (Temple University, n.d.). However, it was not until the ruling in *Brown v. Board of Education of Topeka* (1954) that inclusive education became possible for all children with disabilities. In the *Brown* case, the US Supreme Court ruled that the doctrine of "separate but equal" (*Plessy v. Ferguson*, 1896), which permitted segregation in US public schools, violated the equal protection clause of the 14th Amendment of the Constitution (US Const. Amend. XIV). The court reasoned that segregation based on race in public schools deprived Black children of equal educational opportunities and benefits afforded to white children. Chief Justice Warren wrote, "In the field of public education, the doctrine of 'separate but equal' has no place. Separate educational facilities are inherently unequal" (*Brown v Board of Education of Topeka*, 1954, para. 21).

While *Brown* did not immediately alter the segregation of children with disabilities in public schools, *Brown* laid the groundwork and established the precedent for two critical federal cases in the disabilities rights movement almost two decades later (Disability Justice, 2023). The first was the *Pennsylvania Association of Retarded Children (P.A.R.C.) v. Commonwealth of Pennsylvania* (1972). *P.A.R.C.* filed a class action suit against Pennsylvania for denying 14 children with disabilities access to public education. State laws at the time allowed the exclusion of children identified as mentally younger than five years of age. The plaintiffs claimed the law violated their equal protection and due process rights under the 14th Amendment (Disability Justice, 2023). The court agreed that people with intellectual disabilities are "capable of benefiting from a program of education and training" (*P.A.R.C. v. Commonwealth*, 1972). The court mandated

Pennsylvania to provide a free, public education appropriate to the child's ability and also noted a preference for placement in public schools versus special schools or other programs (Disability Justice, 2023; P.A.R.C. v Commonwealth, 1972). In the second case, *Mills v. Board of Education* (1972), the court found that the District of Columbia (D.C.) could not bar children with intellectual, physical, mental, and behavioral disabilities from public education, and it also indicated that school districts could not deny a child with a disability a public education due to a lack of financial resources. The court noted:

> If sufficient funds are not available to finance all of the services and programs that are needed and desirable in the system, then the available funds must be expended equitably in such a manner that no child is entirely excluded from a publicly supported education consistent with his needs and ability to benefit therefrom. (*Mills v Board of Education*, 1972)

The *P.A.R.C.* and *Mills* cases and 27 other federal court cases that followed led to the passage of the federal law, the Education for All Handicapped Children (EAHC) Act of 1975 (Disability Justice, 2023; USDOE, 2023). EAHC was reauthorized and amended as the Individuals with Disabilities Education Improvement Act (IDEIA) (2004). IDEIA requires that all public schools ensure a free and appropriate public education (FAPE) for students with disabilities "designed to meet their unique needs and prepare them for further education, employment, and independent living" (USDOE, 2019b). To ensure FAPE, teachers, administrators, and parents collaborate on an Individualized Education Program (IEP) designed to meet the specific child's academic, behavioral, and social–emotional needs. In addition, to combat the segregation of students with disabilities, IDEIA also requires local education agencies to ensure that students are educated in the least restrictive environment (LRE) with their nondisabled peers unless education cannot be satisfactorily achieved with the assistance of supplementary aids and services (USDOE, 2019a). While the laws provide general guidelines on the meaning of FAPE, local education agencies and parents have disagreed on what FAPE should look like, and litigation ensued. The first Supreme Court case to define FAPE was the *Hendrick Hudson Central School District Board of Education v. Amy Rowley* (1982). In this case, the school district declined to provide Amy, a deaf student, with a sign-language interpreter, which her parents believed would help her understand more in class and maximize her learning and education. The school district refused to provide the interpreter because after conducting an evaluation, they believed Amy was making academic progress without an interpreter. The court ruled against the parents, reasoning that Amy was receiving FAPE because her education was specially tailored to allow her "to benefit" from her instruction. The court noted that the law's intent was not to guarantee a particular level of education but to grant access to an appropriate education.

In *Rowley*, the Supreme Court "declined to create a single standard for determining when children with disabilities are receiving sufficient educational benefits to satisfy IDEA requirements" (Disability Justice, 2023). As a result, lower courts interpreted education benefits as anything from meaningful improvement to "merely more than de minimis" (Britannica, 2023; *Endrew F. v. Douglas County School*

District, 2017). However, in 2017, the Supreme Court clarified the meaning of education benefit in *Endrew F. v. Douglas County School District* (2017) and rejected some lower courts' minimum education benefit interpretation. The court stated that the "child's educational program must be appropriately ambitious in light of his [her] circumstances, just as advancement from grade to grade is appropriately ambitious for most children in the regular classroom. The goals may differ, but every child should have the chance to meet challenging objectives" (Endrew F. v Douglas County School District, 2017, p. 3).

CONTEMPORARY SPECIAL EDUCATION CHALLENGES: COVID-19 AND BEYOND

The end of the COVID-19 pandemic brought both new opportunities and challenges in American special education. On the one hand, K-12 students were allowed back into most school buildings full-time, and face-to-face related services resumed. There was also a sense of optimism and hopefulness as a new educational era began. On the other hand, the learning loss due to the pandemic is yet to be determined, and many districts are dealing with teacher shortages and the problem of dealing with rapid technological and social changes (Kuhfeld et al., 2022; Nguyen et al., 2022). The COVID-19 pandemic impacted American special education by exacerbating pre-existing problems and unearthing new challenges. Before the pandemic, specific challenges in special education included disproportionate discipline, mis-assessment, misidentification, miscategorization, inadequate teacher and leadership preparation, and scarce transition support for students with disabilities (McCray et al., 2021; Obiakor et al., 2012). The pandemic has amplified past problems and introduced new ones. The abrupt switch to remote learning was a significant challenge across the United States (USDOE, 2021). A study exploring the challenges of remote learning during the pandemic for students with disabilities and their families found two significant challenges (Averett, 2021). First, the closure of schools caused significant disruption concerning teaching/learning and processes for students with special needs. These students frequently rely on routines, structures, and social environments schools provide. However, once in the home environment, the education needs of students with disabilities shifted, meaning that the accommodations that were effective in the school environment were no longer adequate because of home distractions, disrupted routines, and challenges related to online instruction and learning challenges. Additionally, schools struggled to provide students with the individualized support and accommodations mandated by their IEPs. Related services like speech therapy, occupational therapy, physical therapy, and counseling were all interrupted (Averett, 2021). Twenty of the 31 parents in the study reported some form of disruption to services. The second challenge identified in the study was the lack of appropriate technology access. Many students with disabilities struggled to participate in online instruction because of a lack of access to needed technology (Porter et al., 2021; UNESCO Institute for Information Technologies in Education, 2021). In addition, the abrupt change from an active social experience to overnight isolation caused by the pandemic was problematic for the mental health and academic development of many students with disabilities (Porter et al., 2021).

Typically, IEP reports on students' educational levels, provides measurable goals, recommends specially designed instruction (SDI), and provides guidance for delivering academic instruction and related supports and services. These processes were altered, changed, or sometimes suspended because of the pandemic. As a result, many students with disabilities did not receive the same level and amount of individualized education they were entitled to according to their IEPs. Additionally, they "experienced higher rates of absenteeism, incomplete assignments, and course failures compared to their typical peers" (Morando-Rhim & Ekin, 2021, p. 6). The pandemic shutdown created significant interruptions and loss of IEP services and supports (Morando-Rhim & Ekin, 2021).

The COVID-19 pandemic changed the landscape of K-12 education in a short amount of time. The society is still experiencing the lingering effects of this disruption to educational processes, structures, and services, especially concerning students with disabilities. As we enter the postpandemic educational context, educational leaders should look to more strategic, forward-thinking, and culturally appropriate approaches while also exploring some guiding principles borrowed from what is known as "Disciplined Strategic Planning" (Stevenson & Weiner, 2021).

REAFFIRMING VALUES: A GUIDING FRAMEWORK FOR CHANGE

Disciplined Strategic Planning emerged from a fundamental flaw in the broader strategic planning process. Many educational leaders often engage in the laborious and time-consuming process of strategic planning. "A strategic plan is the physical manifestation of the understanding that has been reached of what needs to happen for the organization to meet its goals. . .strategy without a plan is just a dream, and a plan without strategy is pointless" (Stevenson & Weiner, 2021, p. 21). To implement an effective initiative that maintains change, organizations must engage in strategic planning that includes both a plan and a strategy. To a large measure, strategic planning involves an organizational collaboration, usually in the form of a group, coming together in some collective format to review, develop, and adopt values, goals, standards, a mission statement, and/or some set of group standards to improve outcomes or try new initiatives. The result of strategic planning should be for the newly developed plan to guide all organizational practices.

Planning results in creating a brand-new folder or binder that usually gets stored away on some bookshelf or desk and rarely gets used to guide the organization's daily work (K-12 schools, in this case). Stevenson and Weiner (2021) noted that

> plans themselves infrequently included deep discussion about equity or changing practice – the primary process for producing results in schools. Moreover, these plans rarely created the impression that teachers were supposed to teach differently or reflect on how they thought about and understood their relationship to their students. (p. 10)

Thus, educational leaders and those overseeing strategic planning should adhere to four guiding principles: equity, logic, capacity, and coherence. By using the guiding principles in the service of students with disabilities, inclusive education will be encouraged.

EQUITY

Stevenson and Weiner (2021) posited when schools engage in strategic planning to improve student outcomes, they often use a vague, catch-all term such as "all students" to imply equity. A clear equity statement provides a pathway for school leaders to address the specific needs of students with disabilities. Putman-Wakerly and Russell (2016) conducted in-depth interviews with 30 staff members at 15 foundations known for their leadership in the area of equity. Even in these organizations, whose focus was equity-related work, the ideas of diversity and inclusion were conflated with equity. They suggested that organizations understand what equity means for their specific circumstances. "Indeed, foundations that had a clear definition of the term – however unique to that institution – seemed to have more evolved theories of change, frameworks, and plans around equity than foundations that didn't" (Putman-Wakerly & Russell, 2016, para. 5). While foundations may have more freedom to formulate their ideas of equity, school districts are bound by laws, regulations, and policies, such as IDEIA, FAPE, and LRE, that provide a vague framework for equitable practices in public schools. Since Brown v Board of Education (1954) through Endrew F. (2017) and beyond, the results of many legal cases show a positive movement toward equity for students with disabilities. However, in addition to the equity measures mandated by laws, policies, and regulations, school leaders can work with their stakeholders to develop a school-wide or district-wide meaning of equity and, in the process, foster a culture of equity and inclusion. By "centering on equity, we facilitate our ability to identify and address the system- and school-related mechanisms that cause these outcomes, including bias and unequal access to resources" (Stevenson & Weiner, 2021, p. 114). Equity can provide a paradigm to address special education issues, especially pandemic-related issues such as technology access, pandemic learning loss, lapses in services, and strained relationships between all stakeholders. For example, technology access for students with disabilities, including internet, hardware, and software, was a critical equity issue during the pandemic shutdown, which had a negative snowball effect on students' ability to receive FAPE. Since school districts are now more aware of technological challenges that students with disabilities experience outside of school building, school leaders should proactively address this issue from an equity perspective to ensure all students have technology access for their education and FAPE (Sayman & Cornell, 2021). Another example is addressing learning loss and lapses in services by proactively convening IEP meetings and creating revised IEPs which include continuous monitoring to ensure students close their education gaps and meet their educational goals (Yell & Bateman, 2022). School leaders should also tackle equity issues related to curriculum access by collaborating with teachers to implement inclusive practices and innovative teaching methods. Activities might include professional development or participation in learning communities for all teachers, not just special education teachers, on implementing inclusive methods into their curriculum, co-teaching strategies, instructional technologies, and research-based practices for effective online teaching (Aron & Loprest, 2012; Pugach & Warger, 2001; Sayman & Cornell, 2021).

LOGIC

The principle of logic or logic model "seeks to make transparent the relationship between a strategy and its ultimate outcome to determine if the actions performed in service of the strategy accomplish what they were intended to accomplish" (Stevenson & Weiner, 2021, p. 12). The logic model is a map to achieve the goal, including knowledge of available resources and needs, implementation of activities, and a straightforward method of measuring results. For students with disabilities, this means that the decisions and actions taken by school leaders, faculty, and staff align with the overall goals of Individuals with Disabilities Education Act (IDEA) and other disability laws. Unfortunately, sometimes there is a discrepancy between what the law states and how school districts interpret those laws. Without a logic map, school leaders can make value judgements that can harm students with disabilities' ability to learn and gain an education. For example, in *Mills v. Board of Education of the District of Columbia* (1972), the school district argued for denying FAPE because of financial challenges. In this case, school leaders made value judgments, preferring to utilize funds for general education students to the detriment of students with disabilities. More recently, some school districts have contended with lawsuits from parents claiming FAPE and LRE violations. During the COVID-19 pandemic, providing FAPE in LRE was a pressing challenge for most school districts. However, the U.S. Department of Education (USDOE) declined to provide districts IDEA or Section 504 provisions waivers and reinforced providing education for all students, including those with disabilities. The USDOE reiterated that the student's needs should be at the forefront of any decision-making, not the school's circumstances (DeVos, 2020). Nevertheless, in 2022, The Office of Civil Rights (OCR) found that the L.A. Unified School District (LAUSD.) violated FAPE for students with disabilities within the district and mandated the district to take remedial action and provide compensatory services (Yell & Bateman, 2022). The OCR found that LAUSD did not implement a plan to remedy pandemic FAPE violations and failed to satisfactorily track services provided to students with disabilities (USDOE, 2022). If LAUSD had implemented a logic model, including goals, benchmarks, and activities, the result of the OCR might have been different. When designing programs and interventions for students with disabilities, school leaders can minimize potential lawsuits by implementing comprehensive logic mapping. A robust logic map can guide in assessing effectiveness, progress, and goal attainment. Additionally, the logic map provides a systematic way of addressing challenges and creates an accountability system that "facilitates opportunities to consider the effectiveness of an intervention at different points along its implementation" (Stevenson & Weiner, 2021, p. 115).

CAPACITY

Broadly, capacity means the greatest amount or number that can be contained or withstood. In K-12 education, capacity is usually associated with capacity-building, which involves how individuals and groups collectively learn, develop, and strive toward positive student educational outcomes (Bolman & Deal, 2003; Cox, 2001; Fullan, 2004). To be more specific, capacity has to do with "the degree to which districts and schools have the structures, culture, and time and the human, financial, and physical resources (that is, the infrastructure) to enable those on the ground to make each and every element of the intervention work" (Stevenson & Weiner, 2021, p. 15). Capacity plays a prominent role in the work of school leaders who promote inclusive schools.

Capacity is related to the inclusivity of a program. Inclusive education seeks to equalize educational opportunities for students with disabilities. Genuine inclusive education has common indicators such as natural proportions, team teaching, community building, differentiation, engaging instruction, and students not having to leave the room (with their general education peers) in order to learn (Causton & Theoharis, 2014). According to Causton and Theoharis (2014),

> Since the 1990s, we have seen more schools create school-wide systems to provide inclusive services to all students with disabilities in general education...We also know inclusive schools are not possible without leadership. IDEA 2004 ensures that all students with disabilities have access to F.A.P.E. (free appropriate public education) in the L.R.E. (least restrictive environment). (p. 30)

Making inclusivity an educational reality for students is difficult because systems and structures in K-12 schools are built upon years of exclusion, half-hearted attempts at implementation, and years of struggle between reform-minded families and districts, leading to strained relationships. School leaders must take a close look at their school's capacity in order to maximize the potential for inclusive education.

Capacity-building is a significant component of enabling school leaders to produce better educational outcomes for students with disabilities. A culturally relevant leadership framework can enhance theoretical and practical approaches to inclusive education for better assessment and capacity-building. Culturally relevant leadership is a strategy that advocates increased knowledge of diversity, the skills to utilize that knowledge, and the ability to make change and bring diversity to life through leadership actions through liberatory consciousness, pluralistic insight, and reflexive practice. The culturally relevant leadership framework encourages the self-development of school leaders and has been advanced by several scholars in educational leadership (Beachum, 2011; Ezzani & Brooks, 2019; Fraise & Brooks, 2015; McCray et al., 2021). To a large measure, culturally relevant leadership initially intended to address school leaders and their need for more consciousness and capability in racial and ethnic diversity (Beachum, 2011). More recently, it has been applied to other groups like Muslim school leaders (Ezzani & Brooks, 2019). In this case, we advocate for the use of culturally relevant leadership for capacity-building school leaders involved with inclusive education.

As indicated, the first step of culturally relevant leadership is liberatory consciousness, which seeks to raise awareness levels and increase knowledge about inclusive education. School leaders should learn about inclusive education's history, meanings, and challenges. One of the significant issues in special education leadership is a need for more common knowledge concerning inclusion (Yawn & Obiakor, 2013). How can schools and families have a common goal without a common understanding? Educational leaders should read inclusion-related texts, attend conferences, form reading groups, create task forces, and invite speakers/experts to address this topic with staff. This step is an effort to enhance the capacity of self to better serve students with disabilities as well as culturally and linguistically diverse (CLD) learners (Obiakor, 2021).

The second area of culturally relevant leadership is pluralistic insight which has to do with attitude. This concept leans toward an affirming and positive notion of students with disabilities, their uniqueness, experiences, and humanity. These students are often treated as second-class citizens compared to their peers in general education (Capper & Frattura, 2009). This disparate treatment requires educational leaders to interrogate themselves to identify their biases and negative perceptions vigorously. Negative feelings toward students with disabilities are ongoing, and these feelings can come from students or even teachers who do not want to engage in true inclusion. Some teachers may feel that they need more training in the area or that inclusion will require extraordinary effort (Capper & Frattura, 2009; Frattura & Topinka, 2006). The culturally relevant school leader should provide support and training for teachers and directly address any negative comments or biased behaviors. This step begins to move the capacity-building process from self to others in an effort to engage broader groups in inclusive endeavors.

The last component of culturally relevant leadership is reflexive practice that asserts educational leaders engage in ongoing praxis (reflection and action) (Freire, 1970). In this case, school leaders should view themselves as change agents who utilize and promote inclusive practices for increased student success. These leaders should encourage team teaching, build community, promote engaging instruction and differentiation, and believe students with disabilities do not have to be separated from their general education classmates to learn (Causton & Theoharis, 2014). This last step seeks to maximize capacity externally by taking an honest look at resources, personnel, and practices. To a large extent, capacity should help school leaders be inclusive and manage pressure, politics, professionalism, and procedures (Theoharis, 2009). These individual capacity-building goals are also organizational and aspirational. To achieve these aims, these leaders should utilize a culturally relevant leadership framework to increase their knowledge of inclusion, develop an affirming perspective, and engage in practices that produce more inclusive environments.

COHERENCE

The final principle of disciplined strategic planning is coherence or "the extent to which the various parts of an organization are connected and aligned to facilitate the work of the district in reaching its vision" (Stevenson & Weiner, 2021, p. 27). Fullan (2004) stated that "making coherence includes aligning policies and coordinating strategies for changing directions, assessment, professional development, and so on" (p. 166). Both descriptions support organizational alignment, connectivity, and coordination for change to reach the vision. Fullan (2004) underscored the importance of coherence-making in the modern era when he wrote:

> The pace of change will not slow down. Believing the status quo is okay is unrealistic; assuming that change and complexity are constants is realistic. Change is a leader's friend, but its nonlinear messiness causes trouble. Experiencing this messiness is necessary in order to discover the hidden benefits; creative ideas and solutions are often generated when the status quo is disrupted. (p. 159)

As Fullan (2004) indicated the role of leaders is critical in a culture of change. Earlier, Pascale et al. (2000) proposed that organizations are akin to "living systems" and these systems follow certain principles.

> These principles postulate that (1) equilibrium is a precursor to death; (2) in the face of threat, living things move toward the edge of chaos, where higher levels of mutation and experimentation and fresh new solutions are likely to be found; (3) living systems self-organize, and new forms and repertoires emerge from the turmoil; (4) living systems cannot be directed along a linear path...The challenge is to disturb them in a manner that approximates the desired outcome. (Pascale et al., 2000, p. 6)

School leaders need coherence-making for inclusion to navigate this process. According to the "living systems" theory, schools and districts as organizations cannot rest in a constant state of equilibrium or the status quo. Schools that do the same things each year illustrate this concept, especially by ignoring or downplaying the concerns of families of students with disabilities, avoiding innovative teaching methods, giving lip service to differentiation, and/or maintaining separate special education classrooms and facilities (Capper & Frattura, 2009; McCray et al., 2021). The living systems theory indicates that this is not sustainable over time.

In all situations, school leaders should try to move the school toward a direction of change, which could lead to chaos. While chaos seems like an undesirable outcome, moving the organization toward chaos or the unknown is also where one can find experimentation and creativity. School leaders should then foster classrooms that engage in team teaching, differentiation, and innovative lessons for all students. Making coherence means that school leaders stabilize chaos by providing direction, support, encouragement, feedback, and enthusiasm (Fullan, 2004). As Scanlan (2023) concluded, "your fundamental responsibility as an educational leader is to strengthen the organizational culture in manners that nurture inclusivity" (Scanlan, 2023, p. 21). As this process occurs, leaders should remember that it does not happen along a linear path. Unforeseen things happen in the day-to-day operations of K-12 schools, and school leaders need greater flexibility during times of great complexity. Fullan (2004) also identified three additional coherence-making features: *lateral accountability, sorting, and shared commitment*. With lateral accountability, similarly positioned people in organizations usually hold each other accountable. Thus, in schools, leaders work to create cultures where accountability is not only hierarchical but lateral. "In hierarchical systems, it is easy to get away with superficial compliance or subtle sabotage. In an interactive system, it is impossible to get away with not being noticed" (Fullan, 2004, p. 168). In these environments, staff share the goals of inclusive education, and peer pressure and peer support combine to create more supportive school environments.

The notion of sorting helps to establish the criteria for keeping specific ideas (Fullan, 2001). Under this notion, ideas are scrutinized according to questions such as: (1) does it work? and (2) does it feed into our overall purpose? These questions should promote and sustain a knowledge-creation and knowledge-sharing process aimed at enhancing inclusive education. "Knowledge sharing creates a continual, coherence-making sorting device for the organization" (Fullan, 2004, p. 169). Clearly, shared commitment is a deeper understanding and internalization of educational purpose. "People stimulate, inspire, and motivate one another to contribute and implement best ideas, and best ideas mean greater overall coherence" (Fullan, 2004, p. 169). School leaders should understand that shared commitment and greater coherence may only develop after some time and may only come through persistence. "Unsettling processes provide the best route to greater all-around coherence. In other words, the most powerful coherence is a result of having worked through the ambiguities and complexities of hard-to-solve problems" (Fullan, 2004, p. 169). Therefore, shared commitment comes over time as people work together to solve complex problems for greater coherence.

CONCLUSION

There has been a protracted struggle for educational and human rights for students with disabilities. These battles have occurred in classrooms, schools, and courtrooms across the United States. Several influential court cases and federal laws have helped to change the disability landscape in America. School leaders have a unique role in furthering students' rights and creating inclusive educational environments. As such, these leaders can be either oppressors or emancipators, bureaucrats or change agents, liberators or segregators (Beachum & McCray, 2011; Obiakor, 2021; Theoharis & Theoharis-Causton, 2008; Villegas & Lucas, 2002). The four guiding principles of equity, logic, capacity, and coherence can be instructive as school leaders develop more inclusive plans, processes, strategies, and instructional practices. All of these have culminated in critical special education values that school leadership must honor and respect. But some have failed. In Fullan's (2004) change model called "A Framework for Leadership," he suggested that leaders need energy, enthusiasm, and hope. We agree, but of these three, hope is complicated. As West (2008) wrote, "Real hope is grounded in a particularly messy struggle, and it can be betrayed by naive projections of a better future that ignore the necessity of doing the real work" (p. 6). We hope that school leaders engage the "messy struggle," which is the daily grind of working with students, staff, service providers, and communities. This is the real work that should enrich the values of special education and school leaders who cherish its importance.

REFERENCES

American School for the Deaf. (n.d.). *About: History and Cogswell Heritage House*. https://www.asd-1817.org/about/history-cogswell-heritage-house

Aron, L., & Loprest, P. (2012). Disability and the education system. *Future Child, 22*(1), 97–122. https://doi.org/10.1353/foc.2012.0007

Averett, K. H. (2021). Remote learning, COVID-19, and children with disabilities. *A.E.R.A. Open, 7*. https://doi.org/10.1177/23328584211058471

Beachum, F. D. (2011). Culturally relevant leadership for complex 21st century school contexts. In F. W. English (Ed.), *Sage encyclopedia of educational leadership and administration* (2nd ed.) (pp. 27–35). SAGE.

Beachum, F. D., & McCray, C. R. (2011). *Cultural collision and collusion: Reflections on hip-hop culture, values, and schools*. Peter Lang.

Board of Education of Hendrick Hudson Central School District v Amy Rowley, 458 U.S. 176. (1982). https://supreme.justia.com/cases/federal/us/458/176/

Bolman, L. G., & Deal, T. E. (2003). *Reframing organizations: Artistry, choice, and leadership* (4nd ed.). Jossey-Bass.

Britannica, T., & Editors of Encyclopedia. (2023, June 21). *Board of Education of the Hendrick Hudson Central School District v. Rowley*. Encyclopedia Britannica. https://www.britannica.com/topic/Board-of-Education-of-the-Hendrick-Hudson-Central-School-District-v-Rowley

Brown v. Board of Education of Topeka, 347 U.S. 483. (1954). https://supreme.justia.com/cases/federal/us/347/483/

Capper, C. A., & Frattura, E. M. (2009). *Meeting the needs of students of all abilities: How leaders go beyond inclusion*. Corwin Press.

Causton, J., & Theoharis, G. (2014). *The principal's handbook for leading inclusive schools*. Paul H. Brookes.

Cox, T., Jr. (2001). *Creating the multicultural organization: A strategy for capturing the power of diversity*. Jossey-Bass.

DeVos, B. (2020). *Report to Congress of U.S. Secretary of Education Betsy DeVos*. United States Department of Education. https://www2.ed.gov/documents/coronavirus/cares-waiver-report.pdf

Disability Justice. (2023). *The right to education*. https://disabilityjustice.org/right-to-education/

Duchan, J. F. (2023, May 29). *History of Speech-Language Pathology Nineteenth Century: Elizabeth E. Farrell 1870–1932*. http://www.acsu.buffalo.edu/~duchan/new_history/hist19c/subpages/farrell.html

Endrew F. v. Douglas County School District RE-1, 580 U.S. ___. (2017). https://www.supremecourt.gov/opinions/16pdf/15-827_0pm1.pdf

Ezzani, M., & Brooks, M. (2019). Culturally relevant leadership: Advancing critical consciousness in American Muslim students. *Educational Administration Quarterly, 55*(5), 781–811. https://doi.org/10.1177/0013161x18821358

Filiaci, A. M. (2017). Public health progressive: Elizabeth Farrell and special education section II. Lillian Wald. https://www.lillianwald.com/?page_id=1027

Fraise, N., & Brooks, J. (2015). Toward a theory of culturally relevant leadership for school-community culture. *International Journal of Multicultural Education, 17*(1), 6–21. https://doi.org/10.18251/ijme.v17i1.983

Frattura, E. M., & Topinka, C. (2006). Theoretical underpinnings of separate educational programs: The social justice challenge continues. *Education and Urban Society*, *38*(3), 327–344. https://doi. org/10.1177/0013124506287032

Freire, P. (1970). *Pedagogy of the oppressed*. Bloomsbury.

Fullan, M. (2001). *Leading in a culture of change*. Jossey-Bass.

Fullan, M. (2004). *Leading in a culture of change: Personal action guide and workbook*. Jossey-Bass.

Indiana Historical Bureau. (n.d.). *Indiana eugenics law*. Indiana State Government. https://www.in. gov/history/state-historical-markers/find-a-marker/1907-indiana-eugenics-law/#: ~:text=Governor%20Hanly%20approved%20the%20first,and%20imbeciles%20in%20state% 20custody

Individuals with Disabilities Act of 2004, 20 U.S.C. § 1400 et seq. (2004). https://sites.ed.gov/idea/ statute-chapter-33

Kode, K. (2002). *Elizabeth Farrell and the history of Special Education*. Council for Exceptional Children. https://files.eric.ed.gov/fulltext/ED474364.pdf

Kuhfeld, M., Soland, J., & Lewis, K. (2022). *Test Score Patterns Across Three COVID-19-impacted School Years*. (EdWorkingPaper: 22–521). Brown University, Annenberg Institute. https://doi. org/10.26300/ga82-6v47

McCray, C. R., Beachum, F. D., & Reggio, P. (2021). *School leadership in a diverse society: Helping schools prepare all students for success* (2nd ed.). Information Age.

Merriam-Webster. (n.d.a). Eugenic. In the Merriam-Webster.com dictionary. https://www.merriam-webster.com/dictionary/eugenic. Accessed on June 9, 2023.

Merriam-Webster. (n.d.b). Eugenics. In the Merriam-Webster.com dictionary. https://www.merriam-webster.com/dictionary/eugenics. Accessed on June 9, 2023.

Mills v. Board of Education, 348 F. Supp. 866. (D.D.C., 1972). https://law.justia.com/cases/federal/ district-courts/FSupp/348/866/2010674/

Morando-Rhim, L., & Ekin, S. (2021). *How has the pandemic affected students with disabilities? A review of the evidence to date*. Center on Reinventing Public Education. https://crpe.org/wp-content/uploads/final_swd_report_2021.pdf

National Human Genome Research Institute (N.H.G.R.I.). (n.d.). *Eugenics: Its origin and development (1883 – present)*. Genome.gov. https://www.genome.gov/about-genomics/educational-resources/timelines/eugenics

Nguyen, T. D., Lam, C. B., & Bruno, P. (2022). *Is there a national teacher shortage? A systematic examination of reports of teacher shortages in the United States*. EdWorkingPaper: 22–631. Brown University, Annenberg Institute. https://doi.org/10.26300/76eq-hj32

Obiakor, F. E. (2021). *Multiculturalism still matters in education and society: Responding to changing times*. Information Age.

Obiakor, F. E., Harris, M., Mutua, K., Rotatori, A., & Algozzine, B. (2012). Making inclusion work in general education classrooms. *Education & Treatment of Children*, *35*, 477–490. https://doi.org/ 10.1353/etc.2012.0020

Pascale, R., Millemann, M., & Gioja, L. (2000). *Surfing the edge of chaos*. Crown.

Pennsylvania Association of Retarded Children v. Commonwealth of Pennsylvania, 334 F. Supp. 279. (E.D. Pa. 1972). https://law.justia.com/cases/federal/district-courts/FSupp/343/279/1691591/

Plessy v. Ferguson, 163 U.S. 537. (1896). https://supreme.justia.com/cases/federal/us/163/537/

Porter, S. G., Greene, K., & Esposito, M. C. K. (2021). Access and inclusion of students with disabilities in virtual learning environments: Implications for post-pandemic teaching. *International Journal of Multicultural Education*, *23*(3), 43–61. https://doi.org/10.18251/ijme. v23i3.3011

Pugach, M. C., & Warger, C. L. (2001). Curriculum matters: Raising expectations for students with disabilities. *Remedial and Special Education*, *22*(4), 194–213. https://doi.org/10.1177/ 074193250102200401

Putman-Wakerly, K., & Russell, E. (2016). What the heck does "equity" mean? *Stanford Social Innovation Review*. https://doi.org/10.48558/YFPD-DE31

Sayman, D., & Cornell, H. (2021). "Building the plane while trying to fly:" Exploring special education teacher narratives during the COVID-19 Pandemic. *Planning and Changing*, *50*(3/4), 191–207. https://education.illinoisstate.edu/downloads/planning/Planning-Changing%2050-3-4_article% 205_Donna%20Sayman.pdf

Scanlan, M. (2023). *Navigating social justice: A schema for educational leadership.* Harvard Education Press.

Starratt, R. J. (1991). Building an ethical school: A theory for practice in educational leadership. *Educational Administration Quarterly, 27*(2), 185–202. https://doi.org/10.1177/0013161 x91027002005

Stevenson, I., & Weiner, J. M. (2021). *The strategy playbook for educational leaders: Principles and processes.* Routledge.

Temple University. (2022, February 15). *Disability rights timeline.* College of Education and Human Development, Institute on Disabilities. https://disabilities.temple.edu/resources/disability-rights-timeline

Theoharis, G. (2009). *The school leaders our children deserve: Seven keys to equity, social justice, and school reform.* Teachers College Press.

Theoharis, G., & Causton-Theoharis, J. N. (2008). Oppressors or emancipators: Critical dispositions for preparing inclusive school leaders. *Equity & Excellence in Education, 41*(2), 230–246. https://doi.org/10.1080/10665680801973714

UNESCO Institute for Information Technologies in Education. (2021). *Understanding the impact of COVID-19 on the education of persons with disabilities: Challenges and opportunities of distance education: Policy brief.* United Nations Educational, Scientific, and Cultural Organization (UNESCO). https://unesdoc.unesco.org/ark:/48223/pf0000378404

U.S. Const. amend. XIV.

U.S. Department of Education. (2019a, November 7). *Section 1412.* Individuals with Disabilities Education Act. https://sites.ed.gov/idea/statute-chapter-33/subchapter-ii/1412

U.S. Department of Education. (2019b, November 7). *Subchapter I.* Individuals with Disabilities Education Act. https://sites.ed.gov/idea/statute-chapter-33/subchapter-i

U.S. Department of Education. (2021, June 9). *Education in a pandemic: The disparate impacts of COVID-19 on America's students.* U.S. Department of Education, Office for Civil Rights. https://www2.ed.gov/about/offices/list/ocr/docs/20210608-impacts-of-covid19.pdf

U.S. Department of Education. (2022). *Archived information: Office of civil rights reaches resolution agreement with nation's second largest school district, Los Angeles Unified, to meet needs of students with disabilities during COVID-19 pandemic.* https://www.ed.gov/news/press-releases/office-civil-rights-reaches-resolution-agreement-nations-second-largest-school-district-los-angeles-unified-meet-needs-students-disabilities-during

U.S. Department of Education. (2023, January 11). *A history of the Individuals with Disabilities Education Act.* Individuals with Disabilities Education Act. https://sites.ed.gov/idea/IDEA-History#Pre-EHA-IDEA

Villegas, A. M., & Lucas, T. (2002). *Educating culturally responsive teachers: A coherent approach.* State University of New York Press.

West, C. (2008). *Hope on a tightrope: Words and wisdom.* Smiley Books.

Winzer, M. A. (1993). *The history of special education: From isolation to integration.* Gallaudet University Press.

Yawn, C. D., & Obiakor, F. E. (2013). *Urban special education: The New York experience.* Kendall Hunt.

Yell, M., & Bateman, D. (2022). Paying for Compensatory Education or Proactively Addressing Student Learning Loss: Denials of F.A.P.E. During the COVID-19 Pandemic. *Journal of Disability Law and Policy in Education.* https://jdlpe.scholasticahq.com/article/36350-paying-for-compensatory-education-or-proactively-addressing-student-learning-loss-denials-of-fape-during-the-covid-19-pandemic

CHAPTER 14

SPECIAL EDUCATION AND THE FUTURE: ADVANCING VALUES

Festus E. Obiakor[a], Sunday O. Obi[b], Gina C. Obiakor[c], Innocent J. Aluka[d], Emmanuel Mbagwu[e], Stephanie Obi[f], Nkechi Amadife[b] and Phillip Clay[b]

[a]*Sunny Consulting, USA*
[b]*Kentucky State University, USA*
[c]*Unify Public, USA*
[d]*Prairie A & M University, USA*
[e]*Liberty University, USA*
[f]*Fayette County Public Schools, USA*

ABSTRACT

It has become increasingly apparent that one's perception of issues depends largely on his or her personal history. Human beings, professionals, and stakeholders vary in their perspectives, strategies, and solutions. Rather than arbitrarily selecting issues or seeking consensus among interdisciplinary but disparate groups, it is critical to examine the broader array of values and issues that impact learners with exceptionalities and the future of special education. In addition, it is important to conceptualize effective techniques to reverse traditional problems or difficulties while considering the "cycles" of change in general and special education. These cycles are based on the view that educational perspectives have their time since they come and go. When they are innovative, they become the status quo and become finally obsolete as the next group of methods, beliefs, and educational initiatives takes hold. In special education, we have fundamental values that must be respected and followed to deliver services to learners with exceptionalities. These values are sometimes not valued by ill prepared and unprepared professionals, especially

Special Education
Advances in Special Education, Volume 38, 225–235
ISSN: 0270-4013/doi:10.1108/S0270-401320240000038014

since good professionals believe in change. This chapter focuses on how these values can be respected to protect and advance special education and education as a whole.

Keywords: Special education; learners with exceptionalities; old and new values; advancements; future changes

INTRODUCTION

Special education has been compared to a pendulum (Hewett & Forness, 1977) where beliefs and perspectives swing from the right to the left and back again. There is evidence that these historical movements have values that help educators to do their jobs and make predictions based upon the trends of the past. These movements also demonstrate that change is rarely linear, and that modifications and adaptations do not necessarily go in the same direction as the immediate past. As it stands, the special education pendulum is a reminder that the tide will flow in the opposite direction after it has taken a complete swing. The difficulties of future predictions are predicting whether things will change and what will result if they change (Siegel, 1993). Schools are faced with perpetual issues, including who should be served, and how and where they should be served. These issues might be historical; however, they are not beyond resolutions. The major question is, how do we currently and futuristically respect our values and educate all learners with special needs so that they can maximize their potential as human beings? This chapter responds to this critical question.

CONTEXTUAL FRAMEWORKS

There are as many issues and trends in special education as there are in regular education. In fact, there is a growing belief that special education is becoming less and less a separate field of interest. One thing is clear – special education has always been concerned with students' individual needs. This philosophy is slowly becoming similar to the goal of general education. With the practices of integration and inclusion, the line between special education and regular education is becoming increasingly blurry (Siegel, 1993). In the early days of the United States, education was a right of a select and privileged few, typically white males. Not until the mid-19th century did universal education become a reality for most children and youth in this country. Today, all children in the United States have the right to attend school, and it is their legal obligation to attend school until they reach age 16. Side by side, girls and boys, all races and ethnic groups, children of all skill levels and abilities arrive at school every morning hoping to be educated. Such student diversity demands skilled teachers and professionals who are adept at meeting challenges and who eagerly meet students and pledge to help and guide the process of education (Obiakor, 2018). To a large measure, the current state of affairs in special education is marked by significant triumphs and challenges.

Years ago, children with special needs were frequently and systematically isolated, ignored, and institutionalized (Cappper & Frattura, 2009), and K-12 schools relegated them into interior classrooms that segregated them from their peers. Parents were left to fight against massive bureaucracy of institutions, a glut of misinformation, and a pervasive attitude among professionals, educators, and society that their children were not worth to be educated (Beachum, 2017). Children with disabilities in the United States now have access to public schools and right to education, and they are put into categories which include cognitive/ intellectual disability, learning disabilities, speech or language impairment, physical disabilities, and other low incidence disabilities (e.g., autism, deafness, blindness, and traumatic brain injury). Because of the very special challenges that learners from culturally, linguistically, and vulnerable backgrounds (e.g., African American children) confront, many of them are at greater risk of being identified as having a disability. The Education of All Handicapped Children's Act (PL 94-142; 1975) was passed to guarantee that all children with disabilities have a free and appropriate public education (FAPE) in a least restrictive environment (LRE). This law has been reauthorized several times (e.g., the Individual with Disabilities Education Act – IDEA of 1990) to enhance services for all learners with exceptionalities.

As it appears, the history of special education reflects many political changes, medical advances, improved teaching techniques, and changes in societal attitudes and values toward people with disabilities. Advocates, social crusaders, religious leaders, physicians, researchers, parents, educators, and people with disabilities have all contributed to the historical roots of the field and have shaped what special education is today. Clearly, special education has come a long way since it was introduced into American public education over a century ago. It has become an expected part of the US public education system rather than an exception or an experiment. Now, parents and their children have legal rights to FAPE, and they are no more powerless in the face of school administrators who do not want to provide appropriate education and related services. As the field of special education evolves, issues continue to challenge researchers and educators. For example, issues such as changing demographics, transition to adulthood, the alarming dropout rate, classification and labeling, drug exposed mothers and infants, and misplacement have been critical in understanding the roles of general and special education. The resolution of these issues will continue to have a significant impact on what the future of both general and special education should be all about.

VALUES OF SPECIAL EDUCATION

Special education, like other fields, has fundamental values, and these values are enveloped in the knowledge that all human beings are valuable and deserve equitable rights to function in whatever they do. Intertwined in this premise is the fact that there are demographic, economic, and sociopolitical differences among students, school districts, and communities. These differences create multidimensional issues in general and special education that include (a) how to plan for the education of learners with disabilities and (b) paradigm shifts that are needed to advance special education. Before congress passed PL 94-142, more than one million children with disabilities were excluded from school. This law and its reauthorizations (e.g., Public Law 99-457 of 1986, an amendment that addresses special education concerns of children from birth to five years of age and the 1990 Individuals with Disabilities Education Act PL 101-476 that responds to the incessant needs of exceptional individuals) have generally focused on ensuring that learners had access to an equitable education and created more avenues for advocacies, litigations, and legislations. With these efforts, the word "handicap" has become a taboo, and there is now a real understanding that individuals can be disabled or impaired and not be handicapped. Though traditional categories of exceptionalities and fundamental concepts are embedded in the laws, there are clearer knowledge about "who," "when," "why," and "how" to admit exceptional individuals into school programs. For instance, there is more clarity on the intricate values of (a) referral and identification, (b) nondiscriminatory assessment, (c) parental consent, (d) procedural safeguards, (e) placement in the LRE, and (f) individualized education programming. These value-oriented concepts have impacted not only special education programs but all aspects of professional training, including related services.

When Congress reauthorized IDEA in 1997, accountability and improved outcomes were emphasized while maintaining the goals of access and due process. In other words, the 1997 amendment included (a) annual goals and benchmarks or objectives on the Individualized Education Program (IEP), (b) expansion of the IEP team to include a general education teacher, (c) inclusion of students with disabilities in state and school-district assessment of achievement – this decision-making process became part of the IEP, and (d) specific discipline procedures to protect the rights of students with disabilities and to maintain safety and security in schools. In fact, the IDEA (1997) clearly stipulated that school officials may remove students with disabilities who violate school rules to appropriate interim alternative settings, or other settings, or can suspend them for up to 10 school days. In addition, educators could implement such measures only to the extent that they used similar punishments when disciplining students who are not disabled. Students may be removed to interim alternative educational setting for up to 45 days under specified circumstances, without regard to whether their misbehavior was a manifestation of their disabilities. Under the IDEA (1997), school officials were required to conduct functional behavior assessments and implement behavioral intervention plans for any students placed in interim alternative settings. Similarly, some of these provisions simply codified existing case law, some clarified some of the gray areas, and some even settled disagreements that had existed between and among the courts. In other words, these laws cemented the values of special education and advanced the well-being of exceptional children.

Special education has been governed by state statutes as well as the federal laws in order to provide opportunities or access to millions of individuals with disabilities. One of those laws is the No Child Left Behind (NCLB) Act that was enacted in 2001. The NCLB, an extension of the original Elementary and Secondary Education Act of 1965, has impacted the delivery of special education services (Zirkel, 2004). The key elements in NCLB are to (a) improve the academic achievement of students who are economically disadvantaged; (b) assist in preparing, training, and recruiting highly qualified teachers (and principals); (c) provide language instruction for children of limited English proficiency; (d) make school systems rely on teaching methods that are research based and that have been proven effective; and (e) afford parents better choices while creating innovative educational programs, especially where local school systems are unresponsive to parents' needs (Wenkart, 2003). As part of the process of complying with the revised IDEA and the NCLB, school officials must take measurable steps to recruit, hire, train, and retain highly qualified school personnel to provide special education and related services to students with disabilities.

To buttress more stability in the field of special education, Congress passed the Individuals with Disabilities Education Improvement Act (IDEIA) of 2004 which requires schools to use "proven methods of teaching and learning" based on "replicable research." This law, IDEIA 2004, ensures that all children and youth with disabilities have the right to a free, appropriate, public education and defines special education as specially designed instruction that meets the unusual needs of an exceptional student (Huefner, 2006) and which might require special materials, teaching techniques, equipment, and/or facilities. For instance, students with visual impairments might require reading materials in large print or Braille, students with hearing impairments might require hearing aids and/or instruction in sign language, those with physical disabilities might need special equipment, those with emotional or behavioral disorders might need smaller and more highly structured classes, and students with special gifts or talents might require access to working with professionals. Related services (e.g., special transportation, psychological assessment, physical and occupational therapy, medical treatment, and counseling) might be necessary if special education is to be effective. The single most important goal of special education is human valuing of all people, despite their disabilities or vulnerabilities.

NURTURING SPECIAL EDUCATION VALUES

With all the values that are entrenched in or intertwined with special education, one will think that all problems associated with education will be solved. This is far from the truth! It is no surprise that some questions are continuing to emerge. For example, have we truly nurtured special education values? Has special education done what it is supposed to do? It is important to note that the best general education cannot replace special education. Special education is more precisely controlled by intensity, relentlessness, structure, reinforcement, teacher–pupil ratio, curriculum, and monitoring or assessment (Kauffman & Hallahan, 2005; Kauffman & Landrum, 2007). It has been proven that students with exceptionalities benefit greatly from special education and the multicultural method of teaching. A student, for instance, who speaks Spanish as primary language and has a learning disability, may benefit from bilingual instruction to overcome their disability. We must also realize that since the demographics of our schools are shifting at a rapid pace, our educational approaches must strive to catch up with this change. Teaching students who are not succeeding academically and those whose cultural backgrounds differ from those of the teacher requires changing instructional patterns in classroom procedures to facilitate academic success. That is what special education must be all about! Teachers who are sensitive to the diverse nature of the classrooms must always infuse multicultural education in their teaching principles. Multicultural education, like the multiple intelligence principle, is an ethical practice, and good teachers must diversify their instruction to meet the needs of all our children and youth. We should not wait for laws to tell us what, when, how, and where to teach our children. Unfortunately, our general and special education professionals have continued to struggle with this value of equitable teaching and caring.

Schools are still faced with perpetual issues of who should be served and how and where they should be served. Many, or most, of the issues of today have been issues for well over half a century. Clearly, our approaches to these issues may be somewhat more sophisticated today; however, we clearly do not yet have the wisdom or the technical knowledge to put these problems behind us. Multicultural education has been an issue and will continue to be an issue until all teachers and professionals become sensitive to the diverse nature of classrooms and nation. This means that they must begin to infuse such education into their teaching principles. Furthermore, since students with exceptionalities benefit greatly from multicultural methods of teaching, it is important to diversify instruction to ensure that every child or youth is reached. Simply put, the world is constantly changing and becoming more and more diverse, and different people from different cultural backgrounds are sending their children to school in order to become educated. To a large measure, teachers and related professionals must continue to learn about themselves in their own cultures so that cultural bridges can be built.

It is common knowledge that most teachers encounter students with different characteristics in their interactions. For example, students may be unable to read the material that the teacher is using and may speak a language or dialect foreign to them (Grant & Sleeter, 1998). This does not make either the teacher or the student unintelligent – this means that there is a cultural or linguistic situation that must be resolved to enhance learning in the classroom. That is why teachers and professionals must be careful about labeling students derogatorily. A recurring issue about culturally diverse students is whether they are disproportionately represented or identified as "special" learners because traditional Eurocentric curriculum or strategies do not work in their favor. This issue is sometimes trivialized even though representation has been found to be the result of reprehensible practices that reflect bias or discrimination in general and special education. As a consequence, these practices must be corrected to address the issue of equity (Hallahan & Kauffman, 1997). Many scholars and educators (e.g., Obiakor, 2018; Obiakor & Utley, 1997) have argued that learners from culturally and linguistically diverse (CLD) backgrounds have been frequently misidentified, misassessed, miscategorized, misplaced, and misinstructed by poorly prepared teachers who are rigid, insensitive to the demographic changes, and the many differences among children. These practices place these students in at-risk positions and perpetuate already magnified stereotypes. As Obiakor and Utley (1997) pointed out, teachers should rethink their practices, revamp their strategies, and shift their paradigms as they provide services for all.

There is no doubt that family configurations have continued to change. Many or even most students do not go home each afternoon to the traditional two-parent family. Students live with one parent, grandparents, or aunts and uncles – they live in group homes or foster homes. And, some live on the streets and in homeless shelters. Our nation is changing and our student populations are changing – logically, our schools must change to meet the unique needs of our students. By making this marginal shift in our thinking, we are demonstrating in measurable ways that poverty should not be associated with "poor" intelligence, "poor" self-concept, and "poor" ability to succeed in school (Obiakor, 2018). In the end, to nurture our general and special education values, we must modify and adapt instructions to meet the unique needs of students despite their racial, cultural, socioeconomic backgrounds and vulnerabilities.

ADVANCING VALUES TO BOOST THE FUTURE OF SPECIAL EDUCATION

How do we advance our values in special education? Can we advance these values without understanding demographic shifts in power and paradigm? It is time we came to the realization that culturally diverse populations entering public schools are rapidly growing, and with that growth comes increasing numbers of students with exceptionalities. This dramatic change will have profound implications for educational and social institutions that interface with families. One implication is that human service providers will be faced with an ever-increasing number of families who may hold values, beliefs, and preferences different from their own. Given the overrepresentation of CLD students in special education, it is particularly important that personnel working with individuals with disabilities and their families be capable of delivering services in ways that are intensive and focused (Ford, 1992; Harry et al., 1995). Surely, revitalization and reform are needed in special education to meet the complex needs of students. General and special educators must understand how to provide an education that gives equal opportunity to students regardless of gender, socioeconomic status, ethnic group, disability, or other cultural identity. In doing so, the underrepresentation or overrepresentation of some ethnic minorities in certain special education categories will be eliminated (Heward, 1996). Working toward an ideal society demands a multicultural perspective, understanding and accepting one another's cultures, and seeing diversity as strength rather than a fatal flaw. Diversity should not be seen as a disability or a façade that will soon be over. Right now, we need qualified educators and professionals who have knowledge of what to do in general and special education programs.

Our educator preparation programs must help us to reinstitute our values and go beyond well-written mission, vision, goals, and objectives. They must better prepare students in order to meet the needs of variations of all children. A good teacher is a teacher who accepts variation and can use variation as a resource. Changes such as an increase in diverse family and living situations, nontraditional employment, the resulting need for extended hours of special care, and increasing economic inequality among families require innovative solutions and preparations. Many special education teachers in the field are inadequately prepared and receive minimal support (Kauffman, 1999, 2000). According to Kauffman (2000), what has happened in the preparation of teachers and leadership personnel should shock us into unhappiness. This is especially disheartening, given that we have many instructional practices validated by research. Steps must be taken to address inadequate teacher preparation, perpetual teacher shortage, and widespread teacher attrition. Reducing the demand for special education teachers by including more students in general education setting is not a good strategy for addressing the special education shortage. Few would argue against full inclusion if the educational needs of all students with disabilities could be met appropriately in general education settings (Kauffman & Hallahan, 2005). Unfortunately, for so many CLD students with disabilities, opportunities for academic and social success do not exist in general education settings.

In the future, it is critical that educator preparation programs assume the larger share of the burden of imparting cultural information. Future teachers must study and learn new ways of thinking and doing – they must be guided in its use in practicum settings. Before they can impart information regarding cultural characteristics, instructional modifications, and culturally sensitive behavior management practices, they must first educate themselves in this area (McIntyre, 1992). Armstrong (1991) noted some years ago that schools can promote cultural understanding in a number of ways ranging from conducting in-service sessions with national level consultants or local civic leaders of particular cultures, to hiring individuals from CLD groups who are able to communicate information across cultures. To stabilize special education values, school districts must consider projects that focus on recruiting and retraining students and personnel. They must be sensitive to educational practices and hiring procedures to ensure that these procedures address the unique needs of all students with disabilities, as part of their IEPs. Assessment instruments and procedures must be evaluated and modified to eliminate discrimination at all educational and service levels. In the future, authentic assessment will be more useful to address special education issues. In fact, the future must be marked by a strong focus on creating inclusive learning environments with individualized support systems. By implementing inclusive education practices, students with special needs will have the opportunity to learn alongside their peers in general classrooms – these will help to promote social integration and reduce stigma. The increasing use of IEPs and assistive technologies allows for more personalized learning experiences and enables students with special needs to reach their full potential. Furthermore, the incorporation of multisensory learning strategies, universal design for learning (UDL), and cultural competency in the classroom will provide more accessible and engaging learning opportunities for all students, regardless of their abilities or backgrounds. All of these are intertwined with values that must be strengthened in special education and its related fields.

The emphasis on early intervention and an interdisciplinary team approach is paramount in addressing the specific needs of children with special needs. It also highlights the importance of collaboration among educators, therapists, support staff, and parents. This collaborative and data-driven decision-making process will contribute to better informed and targeted educational supports for students with special needs. As remote and online learning opportunities continue to expand, children with special needs will have even more opportunities for personalized and flexible learning experiences. Additionally, transition planning is critical to ensuring that children with special needs are well prepared for postsecondary education, employment, and independent living. This planning process acknowledges the importance of teaching social–emotional skills and mental health practices, as well as fostering parental involvement in the education process. Lastly, the ongoing professional development and training of educators in special education will help maintain and enhance their skills and knowledge, ultimately leading to better outcomes for children with special needs. Overall, these trends are great values that signify a brighter future for special education. In the end, we need special education that has values, that is, the special education where all students are given the opportunity to thrive and succeed.

CONCLUSION

This conclusive chapter has acknowledged that special education has fundamental values that must be protected to provide an education that gives equal opportunities to students regardless of gender, socioeconomic status, ethnic group, disability, or identity. While special education's identity has weakened in some places, special education has continued to create opportunities for those with special needs. The good news is that in the past decade, and especially in the years since the introduction of IDEIA of 2004 and Every Student Succeeds Act (ESSA) of 2015, major shifts are taking place in the education of students with disabilities. We believe special education will continue to apply more powerful versions of assessment and instruction for all atypical learners. As a result, change appears inevitable if the quality of education for these students is to be improved. More specifically, our future could be made brighter by focusing on instruction, demanding and following scientific evidence, preparing manuals and checklists for teachers based on scientific evidence, making students' sustained success our primary objective, and thinking and talking more carefully about what special education is and does.

We agree that threats external to special education certainly exist, but internal threats are most likely to injure or kill the field. Special education has sometimes unwittingly gouged itself and has even threatened to take its own life Kauffman (2014). Yet, special education is an educational phenomenon that follows a human flow. As we value humanity, we value special education, and vice versa.

As a result, it is imperative to modify general and special education, as needed. Special education is neither a label nor a life sentence – it is interwoven with threads of remediation that are divorced from discrimination, misidentification, misassessment, mislabeling/miscategorization, misplacement, and misinstruction (Obiakor, 1999, 2007, 2018; Obiakor et al., 2017). Simply put, we need general and special education that works. Frankly, we must be forward-looking and optimistic as we employ techniques that are available to us and engage each other collaboratively, consultatively, and cooperatively con consistent bases.

REFERENCES

Armstrong, L. (1991, March 20). Census confirms remarkable shifts in ethnic makeup. *Education Week*, pp. 1, 16.

Beachum, F. (2017). Future perspectives of Leadership in special education. In F. E. Obiakor, T. Banks, & C. Utley (Eds.), *Leadership matters in the education of students with special needs in the 21st century* (pp. 203–209). Information Age.

Cappper, C., & Frattura, E. M. (2009). *Meeting the needs of students of all abilities: How leaders go beyond inclusion*. Corwin.

Ford, B. A. (1992). Multicultural training for special educators working with African American youth. *Exceptional Children, 59*, 107–114.

Grant, C. A., & Sleeter, C. E. (1998). *Turning on learning: Five approaches for multicultural teaching plans for races, class, gender, and disability* (2nd ed.). Merrill/Prentice Hall.

Hallahan, D. P., & Kauffman, J. M. (1997). *Exceptional learners: Introduction to special education* (7th ed.). Allyn & Bacon.

Harry, B., Allen, N., & Mclaughlin, M. (1995). Communication versus compliance: African-American parents' involvement in special education. *Exceptional Children, 61*, 364–377.

Heward, W. L. (1996). *Exceptional children: An introduction to special education* (5th ed.). Merrill/Prentice Hall.

Hewett, F., & Forness, S. (1977). *Education of exceptional learners*. Allyn & Bacon.

Huefner, D. S. (2006). *Getting comfortable with special education law: A framework for working with children with disabilities* (2nd ed.). Christopher Gordon.

Kauffman, J. M. (1999). Commentary: Today's special education and its messages for tomorrow. *The Journal of Special Education, 32*, 244–254.

Kauffman, J. M. (2000). The special education story: Obituary, accident report, conversion experience, reincarnation, or none of the above. *Exceptionality, 8*, 61–71.

Kauffman, J. M. (2014). Past, present, and future in EBD and special education. In B. G. Cook, M. Tankersley, & T. J. Landrum (Eds.), *Advances in learning and behavioral disabilities: Special Education, past, present, and future: Perspectives from the field* (pp. 63–87). Emerald Publishing Limited.

Kauffman, J. M., & Hallahan, D. P. (2005). *Special education: What it is and why we need it*. Allyn & Bacon.

Kauffman, J. M., & Landrum, T. J. (2007). Educational service interventions and reforms. In J. W. Jacobson, J. A. Mulick, & J. Rojahn (Eds.), *Handbook of intellectual and developmental disabilities* (pp. 173–188). Springer.

McIntyre, T. (1992). A primer on cultural diversity for educators. *Multicultural Forum, 1,6,13*.

Obiakor, F. E. (1999). Teacher expectations of minority exceptional learners: Impact on "accuracy" of self-concepts. *Exceptional Children, 66*(1), 39–53.

Obiakor, F. E. (2007). Multicultural special education: Effective intervention for today's schools. *Intervention in School and Clinic, 42*(3), 148–155.

Obiakor, F. E. (2018). *Powerful multicultural essays for innovational educators and leaders: Optimizing "hearty" conversations*. Information Age.

Obiakor, F. E., Banks, T., Rotatori, A. F., & Utley, C. (2017). *Leadership matters in the education of students with special needs in the 21st century*. Information Age.

Obiakor, F. E., & Utley, C. A. (1997). Rethinking preservice preparation for teachers in the learning disabilities field: Workable multicultural strategies. *Learning Disabilities Research & Practice*, *12*, 100–106.

Siegel, J. (1993). *Special education issues, trends and future predictions*. ERIC Document Reproduction Service. (EC302415).

Wenkart, R. D. (2003). The No Child Left Behind Act and congress' power to regulate under the spending clause. *Education Law Reporter*, *174*, 589–597.

Zirkel, P. A. (2004). NCLB: What does it mean for students with disabilities? *Education Law Reporter*, *185*, 805–818.

Printed and bound by CPI Group (UK) Ltd, Croydon, CR0 4YY

10/04/2024

14481855-0001